D0537106

5—

To ~~Burdick Kids~~ DANeeN MARie
From ~~Mom & Dad~~ GRANDMA & GRANDPA
Date ~~Christmas 1987~~
September 1999

THE BIBLE FOR CHILDREN

by Walter Wangerin, Jr.

CHECKERBOARD PRESS
New York

Illustrator Credits

Robert Baxter: pages 14–32, 35–39, 234–235, 410–416; **Lee Brubaker:** pages 40, 74, 86, 114, 144, 190, 214, 236, 256, 320, 362, 380; **David Cunningham:** pages 12–13, 34, 57, 78 (left), 81, 120, 123, 202, 209 (top), 230–232; **Bert Dodson:** pages 192–200, 203–213; **Tom Dunnington:** pages 94–95, 116–119, 121, 122, 124–143, 146–189, 271, 281, 390–391; **Monroe Eisenberg:** pages 217–229; **Gwen Green:** pages 364–379, 382–388, 393–408; **Arthur Kirchhoff:** pages 259–268, 272–279, 282–319; **Robert Korta:** pages 1, 2, 42–56, 58–72, 90–91, 323, 332–339, 342–347, 350, 354–361; **Dick Wahl:** pages 238–255; **Jack White:** pages 77–80, 83–85, 88, 92, 97–112, 325, 326, 328, 340, 348–349, 352.

Library of Congress Cataloging-in-Publication Data

Wangerin, Walter.
The Bible for children.

Reprint. Originally published: The Bible. Chicago : Rand McNally, ©1981.
Summary: An illustrated version with simplified text of the Old and New Testaments.
1. Bible stories, English. [1. Bible stories]
I. Title.
BS551.2.W24 1986 220.9'505 86-26430
ISBN 0-02-689000-3
Previously published as The Bible: its story for children.

Printed in U.S.A.

Contents

One Story

THROUGH AND THROUGH the many books of the Bible there weaves a single, living thread. Neither complete nor whole in any one book, this thread is the story of the acts of God among and for his people—Israel first, and then, by Jesus, for all the world.

Stories of events which have actually happened are called histories. They are true. But this thread, this story woven from Moses and the Prophets through the Evangelists and the Apostles—this history—is different from all others because it remembers the deeds whereby God showed the people who he is. This reveals the Truth. And what is so marvelous is that by these same deeds he saved his people alive. These deeds and the doer are our Truth, and the beginning of being for us.

Therefore, we cannot call this thread merely a history, a fine, enchanting story which had the good fortune actually to have happened. No, we call it the Holy History, the History of our Salvation.

It is the Holy History—not the Bible whole, but this single thread—which now you hold in your hands, entitled *The Bible: Its Story for Children.*

So it is not many little stories from which a reader might pick and choose favorites; it is one extended story from the first to the last pages of it. Each individual part is beholden to all the previous parts and supports the parts to come. A wise way to read this story, then, would be that you begin at the beginning; that you wonder and grow throughout, as the story speaks wonders and grows branch from vine and blossom from branch; and that you neglect no part of it.

Since our purpose in this book has been to ravel from the Bible the thread of Holy History and to present it lean, clean, sequential, and alive, certain portions of Scripture shall not be found here.

Neither do we pretend to have made a translation of the Bible.

Nor, if one significant event is told several times over in Scripture, do we repeat that event more than once. Rather, we've gathered the variations of its tellings into a single scene. And in order to preserve the rising rhythm of the story, we have sometimes gathered several events into one.

Details we've added, here and there, to liven the narrative as narrative. We meant in reverence to produce a work of art, a song acceptable to God. Like any artist, then, we fleshed spare bones with the common skin of experience that children might recognize and respond to the life inherent in the History. These details have been derived from the geography and the times in which the Bible stories occurred and have been written in harmony with the holiness of Scripture.

All of this is to say that our small offering does not propose to be the Bible in your homes or in your hearts. Rather, like the stained-glass windows of a cathedral, it is happy to reflect in color, light, and simple art, in joy and faithful worship, the Holy History recorded in the Bible.

Read it aloud, that the song might sing.

To these words, to all the words and work within this book, I add my honest prayer: To God alone be the glory!

Walter Wangerin

Walter Wangerin, Jr.
Pentecost, 1981

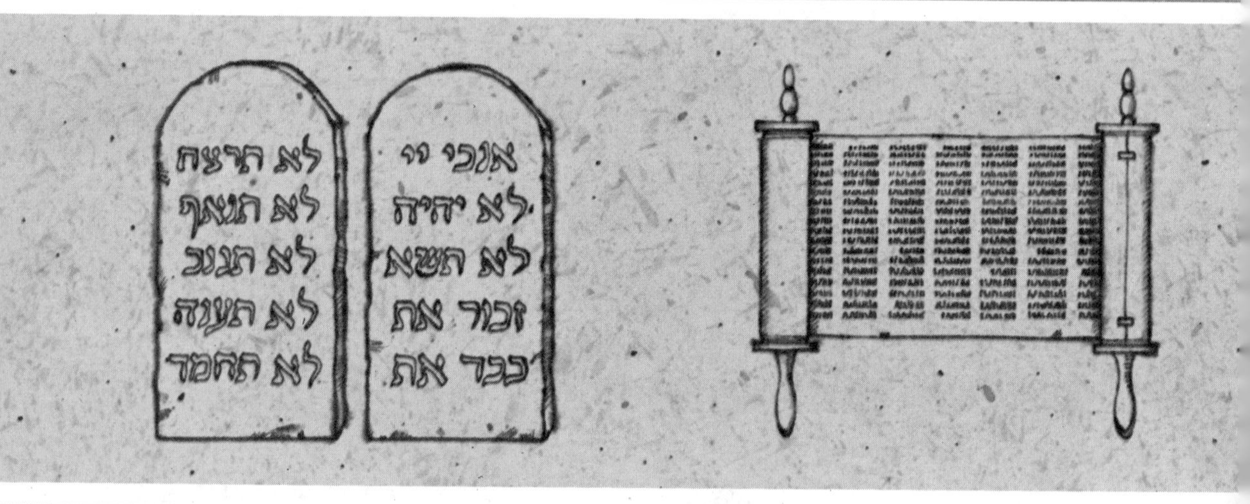
אנכי יי
לא יהיה
לא תשא
זכור את
כבד את
לא תרצח
לא תנאף
לא תגנב
לא תענה
לא תחמד

The Old Testament

THE FIRST OF EVERYTHING

GOD CREATES THE WORLD

IN THE *beginning God created the heavens and the earth. The earth had no shape; there was only emptiness, darkness, and the terrible deep. And God's Spirit was moving over the waters. . . .*

God spoke. He said, "Let there be light!" And there was light; and it was good. He separated the light from the darkness so that there was day and night. That was the first day.

Again God spoke, "Let there be a vast roof in the middle of the waters, to separate the waters below from the waters above!" And it was just as God had said. He called this roof heaven. That was the second day.

God said, "Let the waters under the heavens come together in a single place! Let the dry land appear!" And it was so. He called the dry land earth; he called the gathered waters seas. "Let the earth grow things," he said, "plants, trees, and seeds in each that more and more might grow!" It happened just as God said; so it was good. That was the third day.

God said, "Let there be lights in the heavens to separate day from night! They will be for telling time and for giving light to the earth!" So God made a great light over the day, a little light over the night, and stars. That was the fourth day.

God said, "Let the waters swarm with living creatures! Let birds fly in the sky!" And the waters did teem with life, and the skies were filled with feathers, wings, song—birds! "Good!" said God. "Now bear your young till the whole earth and all of its seas do burst with life!" That was the fifth day.

On the sixth day God made the beasts, the four-footed and the furry and those covered with scales and those with skin, the cattle and all that crawl.

Then on that same sixth day of creation the Lord God did something with a most particular care: He made man.

The dust of the earth the Lord God molded until its shape was the shape of a man. Then he took it, then he himself breathed the breath of life into it. Through its nostrils he breathed the breath of life—and man became a living being!

Mankind, in the image of God!

Unto his man the Lord God spoke. "Behold," he said. "Every living thing that I have made I give to you: everything, that you might rule over it; everything, that you might care for it. Everything."

Then he planted a pleasant garden in Eden, in the east. There were trees and fruit and rivers in wonderful abundance; and in the center of the garden was the tree of the knowledge of good and evil.

This garden, too, was for mankind.

"You will keep it," the Lord God said as he put the man there. "You will till my garden and rejoice in it. But

of the tree that is in the center of it, of the tree of the knowledge of good and evil—of that tree you shall not eat lest you die."

Then God gazed at the one in the garden; and he thought to himself, "No. Man is alone, and he should not be. I will make a helper perfectly fit for him."

So he brought animals to the man, and one by one the man named them; but among the animals none was perfect for him.

So God said "Hush" to the man and put him to

sleep. He took a rib out of the man and made that rib into a woman; the woman he brought to the man, and the woman was perfectly right!

"At last!" said the man. "Bone of my bones and flesh of my flesh! Did she come from man? Then I will call her woman."

And all the while these two lived in Eden. They were naked, but they were never ashamed.

So everything that the Lord God had made was very good; and on the seventh day he rested.

MANKIND DISOBEYS GOD

More than any other creature that God had made, the snake was sly, the snake was clever.

He talked with the woman, Eve, when she was alone. "Did God really say," he said, "that you should not eat of any tree in Eden?"

"Oh, no," she said. "We can eat of all the trees—except for the one in the middle. If we so much as touch that tree, we die."

"Die?" said the snake. "Did God say 'die'? You won't die. Why, God knows that if you eat of it you will become like him, knowing good and evil together. Oh, not death, woman, but wisdom is in the eating!"

Eve looked at the tree. It was a lovely tree. And its fruit looked sweet. And eating, mere eating, might make her wise. . . .

She plucked a piece of fruit. She ate it. She gave some to her husband, and he ate. They stared at each other.

They stared, and suddenly they grew hot with shame—because suddenly their nakedness seemed a vile, shameful thing.

Quickly, quickly they snatched leaves, sewed them together, and covered themselves. But this was not enough; by evening the two of them were terrified. They heard the footsteps of the Lord God, the Almighty Creator, as he came walking through his garden—so they covered themselves from foot to forehead in the brush. They hid from him, and they shook.

"Adam! Where are you?" the Lord God called.

"Hiding," said Adam, his face in the dust.

God said, "Why are you hiding?"

"I am frightened," said Adam.

"And why," said the Lord, "are you frightened?"

"I—I am," the poor man whimpered, "I am naked."

"So!" The Lord God spoke low and slow to the man he had made. "Then who told you that you were naked? Adam, Adam, you ate of the tree!"

But Adam leaped to defend himself. "The woman!" he cried. "The woman gave the fruit to me!"

"Eve?" said the Lord. "You?"

"Me?" she cried. And she, too, made an excuse. "No! The snake! Find the snake and you'll find the one who tricked me into eating!"

The man, the woman, the snake—and the Lord

God had made all three. Now this is what he said to them:

"SNAKE, get down on your belly, low, low down till the end of time. Get down and crawl! Such is my curse on you for what you have done. And your children and the children of this woman shall be enemies; but hers shall crush you dead. WOMAN, when you bear those children, the labor and the bearing shall be difficult for you; yet you will want them of your husband nonetheless, and he shall rule over you.

"ADAM, ADAM, because you have disobeyed my word, this very dirt is cursed. Weeds, thorns, briars, the dirt shall bring forth a tangled patch—and you shall suffer sweat to work it. But you shall work the dirt until the day you go back into it. Dust you are, Adam, and to dust you shall return."

Then the Lord God sent them out of the Garden of

Eden. He set guards on the east side of the garden—and therewith a flaming sword, flashing like lightning to bar the way.

CAIN AND ABEL: BROTHERS AND A SIN

The woman's name was Eve, because she was the mother of all living. Outside of the garden Eve had a son whom she named Cain. When he grew up, he worked the dirt—a farmer. She had a second son who, when he was a man, kept sheep. His name was Abel.

One day each of the brothers brought an offering to the Lord from the produce of his labors: Cain the grain of the earth, and Abel a sheep. God favored Abel's offering, but Cain's he did not. Cain's face twisted with anger, and it was a foul glance he gave his brother.

"Cain," the Lord called to him, "why are you so angry? Do well now and the doing will be accepted; do not, and you are dangerously close to sin. Be careful!"

But Cain's eyes were angry and his ears were plugged. In time he said to his brother, "Why don't you and I go out to the field together?" They did—together. And when they were there, Cain rose up and killed his brother Abel.

Then the Lord God asked, "Cain, where is your brother?"

And Cain mumbled sullen words, "I don't know. Am I my brother's keeper?"

"O Cain, what have you done?" said the Lord. "Abel's blood, which you spilled, cries out from the ground, cries bitterly to me! And you! Now you shall go alone, a stranger wherever you travel!"

Cain heard the word of the Lord, and his anger turned to fear. "Do not do this to me!" he cried. "I shall die! If I am everywhere a stranger, then anyone can kill me and I shall die!"

But the Lord said, "No one will kill you, Cain." He put a mark on the man to protect him against murder.

And so Cain lived, but nevermore did he live before the Lord. Into the land of Nod, east of Eden, he went, the man and his mark. And there he made his home.

THE FLOOD: GOD ANGRY, GOD MERCIFUL

Ages and ages went by. Men and women had children, and then there were families. People spread out on the earth.

But they were a wicked lot, these people. Wherever the Lord God looked he saw, to his sorrow, their violence. Sin sat in the souls of men, sin flashed in their eyes, and in their hands sin was a dagger! God grew sorry that ever he had made a man, and he said, "I shall rid the earth of their kind. I shall be done with them."

But there was one good man among the many. There was Noah, righteous and upright. To Noah alone the Lord spoke, "I have determined to destroy this cruel population, and all life with it, because it has made the whole earth sick. But you, Noah—you. Listen to what I will say to you. Build an ark. Build it as I shall describe it. Get animals, two and two, seven and seven. . . ."

And Noah listened, and Noah obeyed.

Out of gopherwood he built his boat with three decks and a roof: a big boat 450 feet long, 75 feet wide, and 45 feet high. He waterproofed the whole with tar, all as the Lord described.

Then, when God commanded it, he drove into his ark the animals, every kind of beast there was, a male and female at least of every kind. Finally he sent his sons Shem, Ham, and Japheth, and their wives and his own wife into the ark; and he himself entered. And God shut the door.

Seven days they waited inside the ark, eight people and all these animals, some with wings and some with legs and some that only crawled.

Suddenly the storm hit. The windows of heaven opened up, and the rain came down hard, hard and heavy. The ground cracked, and the waters from the deep spouted up in shooting fountains. Water covered the whole face of the earth. The ark began to float. More and more the mighty water swelled, till the valleys were filled, and the hills disappeared, and the mountains themselves sank out of sight. Forty days and forty nights the hard rain came—and everything and everyone that lived on dry land, every thing that needed breath in its nostrils to live, died. Only Noah was left, and those who were safe inside the ark.

The rain stopped, but the vast water lasted on the earth a hundred and fifty days.

In the driving storm, in the lasting flood, God did not forget Noah. He remembered the ark, a chip on the surface of the seas. He caused a wind to blow, and the wind began to dry the earth.

The water went down. Mountains rose like noses from the ocean, and some of them caught the ark. It came to rest on the peaks of the mountains of Ararat. But still Noah could not go out; his mountaintop was naught but a tiny island.

The water went down. After forty days Noah freed a dove into the skies. She flew in search of a place to perch, but she found only water. She came back. Seven days later he let her fly again. Again she returned to him, but this time she bore in her beak an olive twig!

The water went down and down. It was one week later that Noah released his dove for the final time. She flew away and she never came back again. The land was ready for life once more.

"Go forth, Noah—you, your family, and all the creatures with you," the Lord God said unto him. "Go forth, people the earth, stock it, fill it with the living, and hear me: I am done with such destruction. Hear my promise and believe it: I will do this thing no more. Never again shall water be so dangerous to life that it covers the whole of the earth. No more. If, when it rains again, you are afraid that the rain shall become a flood like this one, then look up. I shall place in the sky a rainbow, and that shall be a sign of my promise. See that rainbow, and know that this is the last of such terrible floods. Go forth to the land, Noah. Go forth and live."

THE TOWER OF BABEL

Over the ages people went forth on the earth again. Noah's son Shem had children, and they had children, and those had other children. It was the same with Ham, and with Japheth the same, until the few became many once more.

They were many, yet they were all one because they all spoke one language.

And as they grew in numbers, so they moved—westward, westward for space in which to live. At last they reached the land of Shinar, and there they made a sad mistake.

"Let us," they said in their one language (and everyone understood the plan that was spoken), "let us make bricks."

And bricks they made.

"Now," they said to one another, "let us cement the bricks to build a city." And they began their city.

"Let us," they said while building, "build a tower in the middle—so very mighty, huge, and high that the top touches heaven. We will make a name for ourselves, and we will never be scattered thither and yon on the earth!" So, brick by brick with mortar between, the tower began to grow.

But then the Lord God came down to see what they were doing.

"No!" he cried. "No! This grand, self-glorious thing, this tower cannot be! They are one people. They speak one language. And this is only the beginning. Soon nothing will be impossible for them!"

With a simple stroke, then, the Lord God stopped

The "mighty, huge, and high" Tower of Babel was a *ziggurat,* or "staged tower." Said to have been as tall as a ten-story building, the Tower of Babel was built in seven stages—each smaller than the one below it.

Made of sun- and kiln-dried brick, the *ziggurat* towered above the buildings of Babylon like a mountain rising from the surrounding plain. Archaeologists think the original Tower of Babel was destroyed by weather and warfare and, almost 2,000 years later, was rebuilt by Nebuchadnezzar. The rebuilt *ziggurat* is believed to have been nearly 300 feet tall. To reach the top, priests climbed stairways to the second story and then walked up a ramp.

The best-preserved example of a *ziggurat* is the tower at Ur in southern Iraq where people can still climb the 100 steps of the outer stairway.

them. He made them all speak different languages. Someone said "No," and someone else thought he meant "Yes." One shouted "Here," but another heard "There." "Kiss" was "Kill," and "Love" was "Hate." Nobody understood anybody any more, so each left the other alone, and they scattered thither and yon on the earth after all.

The name of their city was Babel. It is a name that means "confusion." The people never finished building their city.

Israel: God's Chosen, Holy Family

NOW BEGINS the long, wonderful story of a family. Abraham was the father; and he, and his son Isaac, and *his* son Jacob, and Jacob's twelve sons were the great-great-grandfathers of this family—the Patriarchs. After them came many generations and thousands of people. Yet, always, no matter how many people were born to them, *they remained one family:* Israel.

It was a most special *family,* and, for one particular reason, a holy nation. The reason: God himself chose these people to be his own.

For there would come the time when this family lived as slaves in Egypt, when they would be nothing at all—a sad, stumbling family of

nobodies. But the Lord God—as this story will show—would set them free and make them a nation.

"Has any god ever attempted to go and take a family for himself from the midst of another nation—by trials, by signs, by wonders, and by war, by a mighty hand and an outstretched arm, and by terrors, according to all the Lord your God did for you? And because he loved your ancestors and chose their descendants after them, know that the Lord is God in heaven and on earth; there is no other!"

The wonders and the terrors are in this story of Israel: Read it with awe. The taking of a land in which to live, the conquest, is in this story too; read it with excitement. The kingdoms which this family created in the land, the wars they fought and the defeats they suffered at the hands of other nations, and the exile they endured, and the homecoming they enjoyed—it is all here that you might read with reverence. But always and everywhere, watch: This story shall show in every part of it the love which God had for his people, the special care with which he directed his own, his chosen people, Israel.

It is all one story. It is God's story. It is the story of the Family Israel. And it is so much of the Scriptures.

Israel's Great-Great-Grandfathers

THE FAMILY STARTS WITH ABRAHAM

THE MAN'S NAME was Abram, but God would change that. For much of his life he lived with his family, first in the city of Ur and after that in Haran. His wife's name was Sarai, but God would change that, too.

Together Abram and Sarai lived in Haran until he was seventy-five years old—an elderly couple and sad for the lack of a child. She was past the age of childbearing, so they thought they would never rejoice in a son, nor ever rear a family. But they were wrong. That, too, God would see fit to change.

God Calls Abram

It all began with a command from God and with a promise from God to Abram.

"Abram, rise up," the Lord God said unto him. "This is your country. Leave it. These are your relatives and this your father's house. Leave them. Go to a land which you know not yet, but which I will show you." That was the command. And the promise was as much a surprise.

"Abram, I shall make you a father, a grandfather, and a great-grandfather. Your children shall multiply until they are a family in the thousands. I shall bless you so that you shall *be* a blessing. Those that bless you, I will bless; and I will curse the one who curses you. In you, Abram, shall all of the families of the earth be blessed!"

Abram heard the words of God. Quietly he gathered together his possessions. He told Sarai that he knew not where they were going, but yet they must be gone. He invited his nephew Lot to come along; and then they left.

To the south and the west they traveled hundreds of miles, stopping, moving, stopping and moving again—until they came to the land of Canaan and to a place called Shechem.

Here the Lord God made Abram another spectacular promise.

"Look west, Abram," he said, "as far as you can see. Look east. And to the north and to the south, look! One day all of this land shall belong to the children of your children. I will give it them!"

So Abram built an altar in that place in Canaan and worshiped the Lord his God.

Then, in the following years, Abram traveled much in Canaan, always finding what green grass he could for his flocks and his cattle to eat.

Lot Picks a Place to Live

Flocks and cattle had the old man Abram, so that they covered the hills wherever he sat. But his nephew, too, had great flocks and herds of cattle. And when they all tried to drink from a single well, when they all tried to graze the selfsame hill, their shepherds and herdsmen fought one another. "Let Lot's go first!" they cried, or else, "No, Abram's sheep have the right! Let Abram's sheep go first!"

Finally Abram said to his nephew, "I think we should separate, you and I, or we will have fighting forever. There is land enough for both of us and for all of our flocks. You choose, Lot, whichever way you will, and I will take the other."

Whichever way you will: For Lot that meant *the best, the sweetest land.*

Lot lifted up his eyes to the Jordan valley where the land was watered, where green was the color because good was the growing and rich was the soil. It was as sweet as Eden, that land, and it had two cities in which Lot might live. This way looked the best to him; therefore, this is the way that he went.

But evil is invisible. Lot did not see that the two cities were filled with men and women most wicked. He settled down on his good land, in a house in the city named Sodom. And the other city was called Gomorrah.

Abram went the other way, as he said he would. He did not settle down, but traveled continually over the bare, brown hills of Canaan. And that was the difference between the two men. Ages and ages hence Abram's children would remember this thing about their great-great-grandfather, and they would repeat with reverence, "A wandering Aramaean was my father. . . ."

God's Promises to Abram

Abram was seventy-five years old when he left Haran to wander through the strange land of Canaan. Soon he was eighty-five, and then ninety, and then an old, old man of a hundred heavy years. In all that time his wife, herself grown ninety years old, did not bear him a son.

But God had promised him a son and a family numbering in the thousands, and God kept *repeating* that promise so that Abram could not forget it.

"Abram, can you count the dust of the earth?" God asked. Abram said, "No." And

Lot and Abram went their separate ways. Lot chose the green lands of the Jordan valley and the cities of Sodom and Gomorrah. Abram, with his family and flocks, turned toward the brown hills of Canaan.

God said, "Even so many shall your children and your children's children be.

"Abram," God asked, "can you count the stars in the heavens?" Abram said, "No." And God said, "Even so many shall your children and your children's children be.

"Abram," God said, "one day your great family shall fill this land. I brought you here to give this land to you.

"Abram," said the Lord God, "I will bless your wife so that she shall bear a son for you—a son, and by him children and children uncountable. She shall be the mother of a nation, and kings shall come from her...."

Finally the old man shook his head and closed his eyes and chuckled softly to himself, wondering at this incredible promise of his God, and yet believing.

"How?" Abram whispered. "How is this dragged and ancient body to produce even the first son? I am one hundred years old. My wife is ninety, long, long past the time when women have their children. Then how can I father such a family? Oh, ho-ho," he chuckled. "How is this to be?"

Now the Lord God did more than merely *speak* his promise to Abram. He insured it. He signed and sealed it, as it were. He made it real for the old man: He entered into a covenant with him.

"Abram, bring me a heifer," he commanded, "a goat, and a ram, each three years old. Bring me a turtledove and a pigeon."

When Abram had brought these animals, he took a strong knife and cut them—the heifer, the goat, and the ram—into two pieces, then laid the pieces on the ground across from each other.

Throughout that afternoon the smell of the blood drew wild, carrion-eating birds, but when they flew down to claw the carcasses, Abram drove them away.

Then came the night, the black darkness.

The Lord God promised aged Abram a son. When Abram doubted, God directed him to sacrifice animals. Abram did so, and he drove away the wild birds that came to eat of the meat.

Abram slept and God spoke to him. "Abram you are no longer, but Abraham," said the Lord God. Glowing symbols of God's presence lighted the darkness as a sign of God's promise that Abraham would have a son.

Abram fell into a deep sleep. The darkness grew even more heavy, and the old man, asleep though he was, was terrified.

The Lord God began to speak to Abram as never he had spoken before.

He told him the history of the family that was to be—sorrow and suffering, sadness and slavery, joy and freedom and victory.

He said, "Is your name Abram? It shall be Abram no more, but *Abraham,* for you shall be the father of many nations. And no more shall your wife's name be Sarai but *Sarah:* 'princess' of a people.

"Abraham, I am making my covenant with you. Hereafter, you and all the sons of your family shall bear the mark of my covenant in your own bodies. Hereafter forever you shall cut around the foreskin of every male. From this time forward and forever you shall circumcise them."

Suddenly there appeared out of the dreadful darkness a smoking firepot, a flaming torch. These glowing symbols of the presence of the mighty God came and passed between the animals that Abraham had cut in two. In this way God assured Abraham that the promise would most certainly be kept.

And when the covenant had thus been made, and when the fateful night was done, Abraham believed the Lord. He and every man with him were circumcised.

Sarah Hears the Promise and Laughs

The days grew frightfully hot in Canaan. At noon Abraham would sit in the shade of his tent and sleep, or else gaze across the land. He was an old man with much of the past,

Abraham offered food to three strangers. One of the men spoke of a wonderful thing which would soon come to pass: Sarah would give birth to a son.

and even more of the future, upon his soul.

One day as he sat this way Abraham suddenly noticed three strangers coming toward him. He was by habit a very good host, so he ran through the heat to greet the men.

"Sirs, will you stay with me awhile?" he asked, and they nodded. "Will you honor me by sharing food with me?" he asked, and they nodded. "Good!" The old man smiled. Then he rushed to prepare a dinner for the strangers.

Abraham had no idea who they were. That they were hungry and hot was enough to know. And that he had food and shade was enough to make them welcome. Abraham was an excellent host: Any traveler in need would be his guest.

While they sat eating, one of the men asked Abraham a question. "Where is your wife? Where is Sarah?"

Abraham glanced toward the tent. "Not far away," he said. "She is just inside."

"One year from now," the stranger said with a piercing look of knowledge, "we will pass this way again. By then she shall have borne a son."

The walls of Abraham's tent were the thin

Sarah overheard the promise. She looked down at her aged body and shook with laughter. Surely the stranger was joking! No one as old as she could have a child!

skins of goats. They kept out the rain and the sunshine, but they could not stop sound. Sarah heard the stranger's words. She looked down at her wrinkled, withering body and began to shake her head. A son? Oh, no, this body was dry; this body was old; this body would bear no children any more. She covered her mouth and laughed silently at the stranger's peculiar joke.

But the stranger's voice came into the tent a second time. "Sarah," he said, "why are you laughing?"

"No!" Sarah said aloud. "I didn't laugh."

"Yes, you did," said the stranger.

Sarah said no more. She was afraid.

Abraham sat, astonished to hear this conversation.

And the stranger, without so much as lifting his eyes, continued to speak to Sarah. "You suppose that you are too old, Sarah," he said. "Is anything too hard for the Lord?"

The Lord!

Suddenly Abraham knew the divine authority of his guest. And just as suddenly, his guest, the spokesman of the Lord, spoke of other things.

"Abraham, it is time that we go, now. We had only this moment to stay with you and to say what needed to be said. But there is another reason, a sadder reason for our coming." He stood up, and the two companions stood with him.

"Such an anguished outcry has arisen against the two cities of Sodom and Gomorrah," said the Lord, "such ugly sinning happens in those places, that I have chosen to destroy them."

Abraham leaped to his feet. "My nephew," he cried. "My nephew Lot lives in Sodom!"

"He does," said the Lord.

"And you are going to destroy that city?"

"I am," said the Lord.

"O Lord," said Abraham, "I know I am but dust and ashes. I know I have no right to ask even one thing of you, but there are righteous people there! Surely they should not perish with the wicked. I will ask you this: Will you remember my nephew Lot?"

The men had turned to go, their faces already set to the east and to Sodom, and they were walking. Abraham stood behind them, wringing his hands.

"I will," said the Lord.

The Destruction of Sodom

"Such sinning in Sodom. . . ."

Near evening the two angels of the Lord entered Sodom and asked for Lot's house. As they walked the streets, the men of Sodom whispered to one another that foreigners had arrived.

Less than an hour after Lot had welcomed the strangers inside, every man and every boy of the city had surrounded his house. They began to drum on the doors and the walls, shouting.

"Send them out! Lot, send them out," they roared, "or else we're coming in to take them!"

Lot slipped outside and shut the door behind him. "What is the matter with you?" he hissed. "These men are my guests!"

"Don't tell us what to do," someone challenged him. "You, too, are no more than a foreigner here, fellow!"

"Out of the way," all the men screamed. "Open the door, or we will break it down!" They pressed so hard against Lot that the door did begin to crack.

Suddenly the angels let the door fly open. Lot fell inside, and they slammed it again. Then, before the men of Sodom could break in, the angels struck them blind, and they became confused. The men of Sodom groped and whimpered in the street, and finally they stumbled away.

"Is that enough for you?" the angels asked Lot. "Have you seen enough of the sin in this city?" And then they said plainly, "Lot, leave this place!"

But Lot was not quickly convinced. "Perhaps I will leave," he said, "but not now. You are asking a man to give up his house and all he owns. A man has to think about such a decision."

The men of Sodom surrounded Lot's house. "Open the door," they roared, "or we will break it down."

While the angels of the Lord waited inside his house, Lot stepped outside. "These strangers are my guests," he said. "No harm must come to them."

With a clap of thunder, God began to rain a horrible fire down upon Sodom and Gomorrah. For such sinning was there that nothing could be left alive. Only four—Lot and his family—escaped the flames.

"You don't understand," said the angels. "There is no time to think! Tomorrow the Lord God shall utterly destroy both Sodom and Gomorrah. Only because he is merciful does he give you this warning."

"Tomorrow?" Lot asked. "Then I have tonight to think about it," he said, and he went to bed.

But by morning Lot was still thinking, still lingering. So the angels grabbed him and dragged him to the city gate. They brought his wife and his daughters, and they pleaded with him to run.

"Run to the hills," they cried.

Still Lot hesitated. "Who can live in the hills when he's used to the city?" he said. "Perhaps I could run to the town of Zoar—"

"Stop asking! Stop thinking!" the angels ordered him. "Run! And for the love of God, do not look back to this place again!"

The tiny family of four left Sodom just in time.

With a clap of thunder, God began to rain a horrible fire down on the city. Sulphur streamed through the streets. Every building burst into flames. Screams were swallowed up in the roaring heat, and a fat column of black smoke went up to heaven. Every breathing thing, and every green thing, died.

When Lot came to Zoar, he saw that his daughters were with him, but he could not find his wife.

In spite of the angels' warning, she had turned to look at her city in flames. It was the last look she took forever, for she was turned into a pillar of salt.

A Son for Abraham—Isaac

Within a year the Lord God kept his promise to Abraham.

To a man one hundred years old, and to his wife, ninety, he gave a miracle. To Abraham and Sarah he gave a son.

They remembered that Sarah had laughed in the tent while the Lord sat outside. So they named the boy Isaac.

Isaac means "laughter."

Though Abraham and Sarah were long past the age of bearing children, God kept his promise. To this old and wrinkled couple he gave a son.

God tested Abraham. He commanded him to offer up his son as a sacrifice. Just as Abraham was about to slay Isaac, God called out to him, saying, "Do not touch the boy, hand or knife. Now I know that you fear God."

God Tests Abraham

The boy Isaac grew into a comely youth. He was his father's son, his father's best possession, and Abraham loved him deeply.

But one day the Lord said, "Abraham," and the old man answered, "Here I am."

"Take your son," said the Lord, "your son Isaac, and go to a mount in Moriah. There offer him to me as a burnt sacrifice."

Early in the morning the old man Abraham rose up. He cut wood for the sacrifice. He saddled his donkey. He called two of his servants, and they left for Moriah. Isaac was with them.

For three days they traveled. Then Abraham lifted his old eyes and saw the place. "Wait here," he said to his men. "The boy and I will go ahead and worship the Lord God, and then return to you."

He laid the wood on Isaac, his son. In his own left hand he carried fire; in his right, the knife. They went ahead together.

Isaac looked at the wood and at Abraham's hands. "Father?" he whispered.

"My son?" said Abraham.

"Here are the fire and the wood," said Isaac. "But where is the lamb for sacrifice?"

"Ah," Abraham sighed. "God will provide it, my son," he said.

When they came to the place, the old man bent and built an altar. On the altar he carefully laid the wood. He took his son, tied him up, and on the wood he laid Isaac.

Then he took the knife and stretched forth his hand to slay the boy.

"Abraham! Abraham!" God called him suddenly.

"Here I am!" Abraham cried.

"Enough!" said the Lord. "Do not touch the boy, hand or knife! Now I know that you fear God, for you have not withheld your only son from me!"

A rustling behind him made the old man turn around. There, caught by its horns in the thicket, was a ram. Abraham seized this ram, slew it, and sacrificed it instead of his son Isaac.

Together the boy and his father returned to the waiting men, and they all went home again.

The Last Days of Abraham

Sarah, Abraham's wife, lived one hundred and twenty-seven years, and then she died. Abraham mourned her death. He bought a field east of Hebron and buried her in a cave at that place.

When the time came that his son should marry, the old man sent back to the city he had left so long ago, to Haran. From among his relatives he found a wife for Isaac. Her name was Rebekah. A dear and faithful woman she was, and she was quick to come to Canaan.

Then Abraham followed Sarah. In the hundred and seventy-fifth year of his age he breathed his last and died. An old man and full of years, Abraham was gathered to his people.

JACOB, THE GRABBER

His name was Jacob, but God would change that in time. He was the son of Isaac.

He was not, however, Isaac's *eldest* son. Esau was. Therefore, Esau should have received their father's best blessing, and this story should, by rights, have been about Esau. But Jacob cheated his brother out of the blessing: Jacob sinned sadly.

It is a special wonder, then, that God chose this man, this "Grabber" of blessings, to be his own—for God loved Jacob in spite of his sin. God went with him wherever he went. And God worked a change in this man, so that he became a blessing to his family. God was his God, too!

Centuries later—when Jacob's children and his children's children had grown into a huge and mighty family—they ever remembered that their God was "the God of Abraham, the God of Isaac, *and the God of Jacob!*"

The Brothers Are Born

Even as Abraham and Sarah had to wait a long time before their son Isaac was born to them, so Isaac and Rebekah had to wait. Rebekah, like Sarah, was an older woman when finally she conceived, when finally life began to grow in her.

At first she was glad, and she laughed. But as the months went by, she began to groan. Hard it was to carry the life inside of her. She lay down, hurting.

"O Lord!" Rebekah cried in her pain. "O God, I will die before my time is come!"

The Lord heard her and answered that not one but two children grew in her womb. Twins! They struggled inside of her. They crushed each other, and their movements brought the pain which she endured.

"Their struggle," said the Lord, "is a sign of their future. Both your sons shall be fathers of great nations. These nations shall clash, shall fight until the nation of the second son defeats the nation of the first."

At the end of nine months Rebekah did not die. She delivered her twins, one at a time.

The first child was ruddy and covered with red hair. He was named Esau. The second came out grabbing his brother's heel in a tight grip, as though he wanted something, as though he wanted to be first! So the second child was named Jacob, for the name means "grabs the heel."

Now, Esau grew into a cunning hunter, ranging the fields and the forests to catch all manner of animals. But Jacob grew into a quiet man, one well contented to dwell in tents.

Isaac loved his rugged son the most, because he ate what the hairy Esau hunted. But Rebekah loved Jacob.

Jacob Grabs Esau's Birthright

In those days a father always bequeathed his wealth—his herds, his flocks, and his authority—to the *eldest* son. Always, the eldest was to become the head of the house when a father died. This was his right by birth, the birthright of the firstborn.

One day Jacob was quietly boiling a bowl of vegetables when Esau came stumbling toward the tent. "Jacob!" Esau gasped. "Food!" During a long, futile hunt Esau had caught nothing and now he was starving.

"Jacob, let me eat something," he pleaded.

"With all my heart," Jacob said, stirring the stew. "But first," he said slowly, "first—sell me your birthright."

"Take it!" said Esau. "Take it! What good is it to me if I die? Just let me eat!"

"No, brother," Jacob said. "I want you to swear that you give it to me."

Esau swore. He sold his birthright for a pot of stew, which he ate and by which he lived. But Jacob made a fortune by this trick; and by the next he made an enemy.

Jacob Grabs Esau's Blessing

Now there was a custom in those days: A father when he was old blessed his eldest son so that he would then receive God's protection. When Isaac had grown very, very old, he called Esau to his side and stroked his son's strong arms. "I love you," he said. Isaac needed to touch the wild hair on Esau's arms, because the old man was stony blind, and the touch was a comfort.

"I love you, Esau," he said, "but I am dying and will soon be taken away from you. Who will watch over you then? I want to bless you, son; then my God will be your God—and *God* will protect you hereafter as he has protected me."

He touched the hair on Esau's neck. "Go into the fields," he said. "Hunt, kill, and cook one final feast for me. I will eat it, and then I will bless you."

Esau touched his father's face and left.

The walls of a tent are thin. Rebekah had heard all of Isaac's words, and she was jealous for her favorite son, Jacob. Immediately she ran to him and spoke in a low, urgent voice.

"We are not going to let this thing happen," she said. "Slaughter a goat, Jacob. I will cook it to taste like wild meat and you will carry it to your father as if you were Esau come back from the hunt. Pretend that you are Esau! Your father will eat, and then he will bless you. Hurry! Go!"

"Wait," said Jacob. "What if my father should touch my smooth skin? He will know the truth. He will give me a curse instead of a blessing."

"Curses! Curses!" Rebekah pushed her son away. "Let any curses come down on me. Go, Jacob! Do what I say!"

While the meat of the goat was cooking, Rebekah covered Jacob's neck and arms in its hairy skin. Then she dressed him in Esau's clothes and sent him with the food to his father.

Old Isaac heard a footstep. "Who's there?" he said.

"I am," Jacob said, "Esau, your firstborn son. Here is the food for your feast, and here is my head for your blessing."

"Already?" Isaac was puzzled. "How did you find the game so quickly?"

"God helped me," Jacob said. "Eat, Father. Eat quickly, then bless me."

But the blind man stretched out his hands. "Come here," he said. "Let me touch you." He wondered if the rough goat hair was Esau's hair. "Are you truly Esau?" he asked.

"Yes, I am," said Jacob. "Please, Father, eat!"

"Closer," Isaac said. "Come and let me kiss you." It was a long time that Isaac embraced his second son, and while he did, he sniffed. Finally he raised his blind face and said, "The smell of these clothes is the smell of the fields. You must be Esau. So let me eat your food, my son."

"For no other reason did I hunt it," Jacob said, "but that you might eat it."

When he was done eating, Isaac put his hands on Jacob and blessed him. "Whole nations shall bow down to you," he said. "You will succeed by the mighty power of God so that your brothers, even your own brothers, shall serve you, because you, my son, shall be their master!"

He stroked Jacob's arm and sighed. "I love you, Esau," he said, "and now I may be

Isaac stroked the hairy arms of his son. Surely this was Esau. So it was that the old man gave to Jacob the blessing that rightfully belonged to Esau.

gathered to my people in peace because it is done. I have blessed you, and you shall be blessed."

No sooner had Jacob left his father than Esau came, happy and holding another feast.

"Father, the hunting was good," he said, "and the food is better. But best of all is the blessing you have for me!"

"Food? Blessing?" the old man said. "Who are you?"

"Why, Esau. I am Esau, your firstborn son!"

Then Isaac trembled all over and cried out, "Whom did I bless? Was your brother here?"

Esau raised his own voice in a great and bitter cry. "You have blessed someone? Jacob? Jacob was here in my place? Oh, my father, my father," Esau wailed. "Bless me too!"

The old man turned his head from side to side. "I cannot, my son. Your brother took your blessing, and he shall be blessed."

"But I am the eldest! There has to be something for the eldest," Esau cried. "What have you got for me, *for me?*"

"I have made your brother your master," Isaac said miserably.

"Father, Father, make me something!" Esau lifted up his voice and wept.

The old man took his eldest son to himself and held him. And though nothing could change the prophecy that one day Jacob's children would rule over Esau's, yet Isaac did speak a quiet blessing for this his most beloved son. "In time," he said, "your children shall fight and free themselves from Jacob's rule. In time. In God's good time."

And so it was that Esau hated Jacob.

He breathed a dreadful vow. "When my father is dead, I will kill my brother; I will murder Jacob!"

How thin the walls of tents! Rebekah heard her son's threat. She ran to Jacob and, in words both low and urgent, she told him to escape. "To Haran," she said. "To my brother Laban's house, where you will be safe from your brother's angry hand. Go, Jacob. Go!"

God's Promise, Jacob's Dream

Sudden and light on his feet, lonely, apart from his family, and frightened by the brother behind him, Jacob fled from his home in Canaan toward the northeast, where his uncle Laban lived.

But the journey was a long one. At nightfall Jacob came to a holy place, though he did not know its holiness. He knew only that he was broken by exhaustion, so he lay down to sleep. For a pillow he took a stone of that place.

Then he had a dream.

Jacob dreamed that there was a ladder set on earth, a ladder so high that its top went into heaven. Down this ladder came the angels of the Lord, and up they went again. At its topmost rung stood the Lord God himself.

"I am the Lord," he proclaimed, "the God of your fathers Abraham and Isaac. I am the Lord, who shall be your God, too. The land that you lie on I will give to your children and to your children's children; and your family shall be as countless as the dust on earth, and a blessing for all the families of the world. Jacob! Jacob! I am with you!"

When Jacob awoke, he was trembling with fear. "The Lord!" he whispered. "The Lord is in this place, and I did not know it!

Jacob fled from Canaan. At nightfall, weary and fearful, he lay down to sleep. He dreamed of a ladder and of angels on that ladder. On the topmost rung stood the Lord God. He made a promise to Jacob.

Why, this is none other than the house of God!"

Indeed, the Lord had begun to seize his man, to change him, and to make him his own.

In the morning Jacob set up the great stone that had been his pillow, and poured oil over it, and bowed down to pray.

"O God, I have heard you. Keep me, as you promised it to me. Take me one day back to my father's house in peace. Be with me, and you shall surely be my God."

Jacob stood up and named the place where he had slept, where he had dreamed, where he had seen God, Bethel. *Beth-el:* "the house of God."

Jacob Meets Rachel

Laban, Rebekah's brother and Jacob's uncle, was a man with many flocks in his possession. He had, as well, two daughters, one of whom watched the sheep. Her name was Rachel, and Rachel was lovely to behold.

Now it happened that when Jacob came to the end of his journey, he saw this woman leading her sheep to a well for water. The sheep were thirsty; but the well was covered

With the strength of several men, Jacob moved the stone from the well and drew water for Rachel's sheep. Rachel, his cousin, was beautiful to behold.

by a flat stone so heavy that it should have taken several men to move it.

When he looked upon this beautiful shepherd, and when he saw the thirst of her sheep, young Jacob felt stronger than several men together. All by himself he moved that stone aside! All by himself he drew water for Rachel's sheep. And then he sat down to gaze into her face.

"Who are you?" he asked.

"I am Rachel," she answered.

"Rachel," he said, "this is your flock?"

"Oh, no. It belongs to my father," she replied.

"And who is your father?" he asked.

"His name," said Rachel, "is Laban—"

"Laban!" Jacob leaped to his feet. "Laban!" And tears began to warm his eyes. "Oh, Rachel, don't you know who I am? I'm Rebekah's son! Jacob! Your father's kinsman! Your cousin!" He kissed her and hugged her, and he wept, so glad was he to see her.

Soon thereafter he fell in love with her. Rachel was lovely to behold.

Laban Tricks Jacob

The young man loved the young and lovely woman. Moved by his love, Jacob went to his uncle and asked him: "Sir, will you give me your daughter Rachel, that I might marry her?"

In those days a man first proved himself worthy of the woman he would marry; and in those days a man gave something to a father in return for his daughter. So Jacob said, "I will work for you a full seven years. At the end of them, let Rachel be my wife."

Laban agreed to the seven years.

Seven years! It might seem a long time to labor and to wait. But such was the love which Jacob had for Rachel that the years melted into days, and the seventh seemed done before the first had begun.

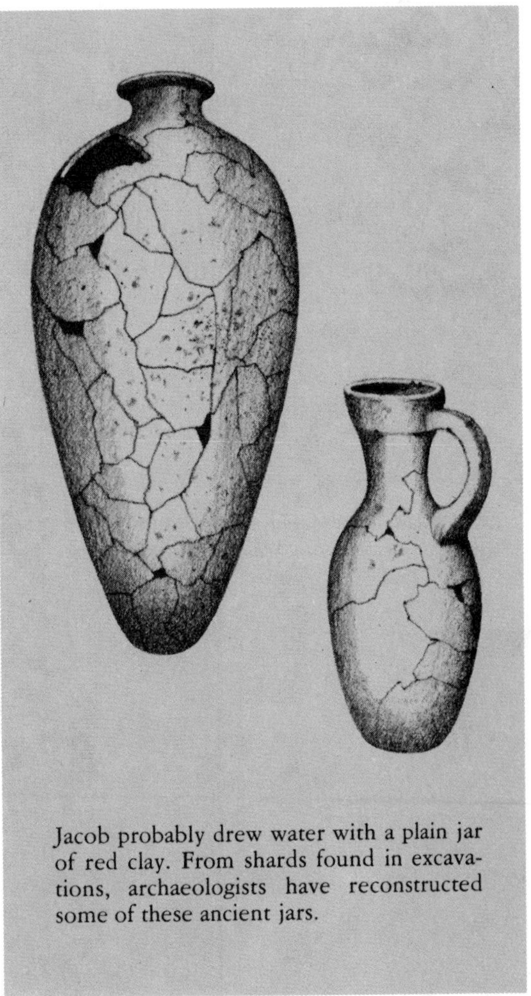

Jacob probably drew water with a plain jar of red clay. From shards found in excavations, archaeologists have reconstructed some of these ancient jars.

During those seven years Laban saw that Jacob was an excellent worker. For him, too, the time went quickly—too quickly, because he did not want to lose this good shepherd! So Laban thought of a plan to keep Jacob with him longer.

Soon Jacob was standing in front of Laban ready to receive the woman he had worked for.

"Now, sir," Jacob said, "I have fulfilled my side of the bargain. Let me marry your daughter."

They made ready for the marriage.

But there was also the custom in those days to separate the bride and groom throughout the wedding ceremony. A veil hung between Jacob and his bride, so he could not see her till the morning sunlight.

By this custom Laban tricked Jacob. It was not Rachel on the other side of the veil. It was Leah, her older sister, the sister less beautiful, the sister of dull, unlovely eyes whom Jacob married!

In the morning Jacob saw the switch.

"I asked you, sir," he said to his uncle, "for Rachel! For Rachel I have labored these seven years! And Rachel I thought I married. But—"

"But," said Laban, "it was a true marriage made yesterday, wasn't it?"

"It was," said Jacob.

"And a marriage it shall be: Jacob and Leah. A fine marriage, and a right one, too, because in our country the oldest girl must always marry first. Now," said Laban, smooth Laban, "if you still wish to marry Rachel, we can strike another bargain, nephew. Work for me a second seven years, and you may marry the younger daughter too."

That was the custom. In those days a man might marry more than one wife. So Jacob agreed. "It is a bargain," he said.

A wedding feast took place. As was the custom in those days, a veil hung between Jacob and his bride.

Twice seven is fourteen years. Laban's plan had worked, and Jacob stayed to labor with his uncle a long, long time.

Jacob's Children

It was Rachel whom Jacob loved best. That was obvious to both of his wives, and so Leah suffered. But the Lord eased her suffering by letting her bear children easily. Four sons she carried, and she bore them one right after the other! Reuben, Simeon, Levi, and Judah.

Now Rachel watched this fruitfulness, and she suffered, because she bore no children at all.

Rachel said, "Give me children, Jacob, or I shall die!"

Jacob said, "Woman, am I God? I'm not the one who made you barren."

"Then take my maid," said Rachel. "If she has children, I will call them my own."

Rachel's maid did have children, two boys whom she named Dan and Naphtali.

When Leah saw that she had stopped bearing children, she brought her maid to Jacob, that the maid might have children whom Leah would call her own. So the seventh and the eighth sons were born, Gad and Asher.

And still Rachel bore no children out of her own body; but Leah did—the ninth son and the tenth, and then a daughter. She named them Issachar, Zebulun, and Dinah.

Finally God remembered Rachel. He

heard her prayer. He blessed her and she bore a son.

"The Lord has taken away my shame!" Rachel said. And she named the boy Joseph.

So Jacob's family grew, eleven sons and a daughter in the time that he lived with his uncle Laban.

Jacob Flees

In all the years Jacob lived with his uncle there came to be less and less love between them. Yet Laban needed his nephew's skills.

When Jacob asked whether he could take his family and go, Laban made him an offer. "Stay," he said. "Keep working for me, and you can have all the spotted and striped animals born in my flocks and herds."

Jacob agreed to this wage; but Laban was not going to let Jacob have anything more than he had to. Laban removed every spotted and striped animal from his herds and gave them to his sons, hoping that *no* new animals would be born this way.

But Jacob knew a trick of his own. When the ewe sheep and the cows had life within them, he put spots and stripes in front of their eyes, so they bore striped and speckled young in spite of Laban's plans.

Jacob became rich. Laban's sons became angry with him. And Laban himself had not a kind word for him. Jacob became rich and miserable at once.

Finally the Lord God spoke the word that Jacob had been waiting for. "Go home again," said the Lord. Jacob rejoiced at the command. He waited till his uncle had gone to shear sheep; then he gathered his wives, his children, and his flocks, and he fled away.

Jacob's Name Is Israel

When Jacob drew near to his brother's land, there came a message to him out of that land. "Esau is coming to meet you, and he brings with him four hundred men!"

O Lord God! thought Jacob. *He comes to*

"Go home again," said the Lord. So Jacob gathered his family and his flocks and fled. Troubled, fearful, he returned to Canaan, the land of his brother Esau.

smite me, my wives, and my children! I know that I am not worthy of all the mercies that you have given me. I left alone; I am returning rich. Yet I remember your promise to me, and I pray that you deliver me from the hand of my brother.

Then Jacob gathered out of his goods a present for his brother Esau: sheep and rams, camels and cows, bulls and donkeys. All these he sent ahead of him into Esau's land.

Then the rest of his goods, his wives, his maidens, and his children, he sent across the brook Jabbok. He himself was left standing alone in the night.

A man came to Jacob in that night. The man wrestled with him. From midnight till morning the two of them sweated and fought in grim silence. Like a giant Jacob gripped his adversary; like lightning the other slipped and struck him back. Jacob's thigh was wrenched out of joint. But Jacob locked so tight a hold on him that the other cried out, "Let me go!"

"No!" Jacob hissed in his ear. "Not until you bless me."

"What is your name?" the other said.

"I am Jacob."

"Ah, the Grabber!" breathed the other. "Grabber, listen to me. Your name is Jacob no longer. It shall be *Israel,* for you have striven with God and with men, and you have prevailed."

With God! Jacob had striven with God!

He dropped his hold and wondered at the words. "I have seen God face to face," he said, "yet my life was preserved!"

With the morning Jacob, no longer fearful of the meeting, arose and went forth gently to meet his brother. He walked with a limp. He walked, now, with a wise humility. And when he saw Esau, he bowed himself seven times to the ground. Much, much had passed this man's eyes and his spirit, and he was changed.

"Jacob! Jacob!" Esau cried. They ran together, and Esau fell on his brother not in anger, but in love. They embraced. They wept at the meeting. And Jacob—who was no longer Jacob, but Israel—said, "Truly, to see your face is like seeing the face of God, my friend, my brother! No longer my enemy."

Israel. His name would stay with his family, even when they had become the multitude that God had promised they would be. Hereafter they knew themselves as his children, the children of Israel.

JOSEPH: THE FAMILY COMES INTO EGYPT

Joseph was Israel's eleventh son; yet he was also the firstborn of Rachel, Israel's most beloved wife. Therefore, to the great bitterness of all his brothers, Joseph became his father's favorite. He and Benjamin, the last child and Rachel's child too, were dear and cherished in their father's eyes.

When Joseph was seventeen years old, Israel gave him a special coat, a coat ornate and beautiful. And when his brothers saw that their father loved Joseph more than the rest, they hated him and could not speak peacefully to him.

Joseph Dreams Two Dreams

Joseph's brothers heard of certain dreams their brother dreamed, and their hatred grew dangerous. In the dreams he seemed to scorn them.

"We were in a wheat field, tying up the

As Joseph approached his brothers, his beautiful coat billowing, their hatred boiled and spilled over. "Let's kill him!" they muttered. "Kill him!"

sheaves," Joseph told them. "Mine stood up straight while yours drooped. It looked to me as though your sheaves were bowing down to mine."

"So it looks to you!" they sneered at him. "It looks to you as if you will one day rule over us? Little brother, that is not how it looks to us!"

Soon Joseph was back with another dream.

"I dreamed—" he said.

"What, again?" they cried. "Dream, dream! And forget your dreams!"

But Joseph did not forget them. He told them instead.

"I dreamed about the sun and the moon and eleven stars; they were all bowing down . . . to me."

His brothers burned with hatred against him, and even his father was hurt. "Are you telling me, Joseph," said Israel, "that your mother and I shall bow down to you as well?"

Joseph Is Sold into Slavery

Israel trusted Joseph more than he did his other sons. When the older ten were far afield and watching the sheep, he would send Joseph after them to return with the news of their doings.

One day, not long after his dreams, Joseph left on such an errand, never to return.

His brothers saw him coming, a slow dot on the horizon, and they recognized him by his curious, dazzling coat.

"Look!" Ten faces turned in one direction. "Our little brother!" they jeered. "Whom our father loves so well!" they spat. "Come to see us and to spy! Come to carry tattle home again!"

"Look! Look!" The more they growled, the greater their hatred became. "The dreamer, come to tell us his dreams! The sweet little king, come to rule over us! The rotter!" They had worked themselves into a rage. "Let's kill him!" they cried. "Let's kill him and see what comes of his dreams!"

Not all of Joseph's brothers despised him with the same fire. None of them liked him, to be sure, but Reuben, who was the eldest, and Judah, who was kind, both cringed when the others cried "Kill him!" That was too terrible a payment, even for Joseph.

"Kill him and pitch his body in a pit," they cried. But Reuben bought time by turning the plan around. *"First* pitch him in the pit," he said, "then kill him *later."*

And that is what they did. They seized Joseph, they stripped him of his coat, they dragged him and dropped him into a cistern. Then they left him imprisoned for a while.

Reuben wanted to free Joseph later, when his brothers were not looking, so he went off alone while the rest of them sat and talked. But their talk was evil and it turned again to murder. Judah spoke up, then, with a sudden plan to save the boy's life. "If you murder your brother," he said, "what good is that to you? What gain do you get? Satisfaction fills no purses. But if you *sell* him into slavery, why then he is gone altogether and as good as dead—and you have made some money besides! Sell him, brothers, and he will suffer all the longer! He will suffer the rest of his life!"

One brother, Reuben, prevailed upon his brothers not to kill Joseph at once, but to hold him prisoner for a time. Joseph's brothers stripped him of his coat and dropped him into a cistern.

When the evil talk of murder began again, another brother spoke up. Judah said, "Sell him into slavery. He will be gone, and you will have money as well." And so Joseph was sold and taken away into Egypt.

Simeon, Levi, Dan, Gad, Asher—all the brothers liked the plan. When a band of Midianite traders came by on their regular route, nine brothers jerked one from his hole in the ground. Nine brothers sold one into slavery. Nine heard the ring of coins in their purses, while one heard the ring of chains round his neck. The traders had Joseph; and Joseph was gone—gone as a slave into Egypt.

Suddenly there arose a cry of anguish. Reuben had returned to the pit. "It is empty!" he wailed. "The boy is gone. What will I tell my father?"

That night they brought to their father Israel the beautiful coat he had given his son, now torn and covered with blood.

"See what we found?" they said.

"My son!" the old man cried. "Joseph! My son! You have been torn into pieces by some wild beast! My son! I will never see you again!"

All his sons and his daughters tried to comfort Israel, but he would not be comforted. For none of them told him the single thing that might have given him peace—that the blood was *not* the blood of his son; that the coat had been dipped in the blood of a goat and that Joseph was living—in Egypt.

In Egypt, into Prison

Whatever his brothers thought of him, Joseph was a gifted lad—obedient, handsome, thoughtful, wise, reliable. So the traders had no trouble selling him, and that they did to one Potiphar, a captain of Pharaoh's guard.

But such gifts are sometimes a blessing and sometimes a curse. When Potiphar recognized Joseph's wisdom, he put him in charge of all his household; that was a blessing. On the other hand, when Potiphar's *wife* saw Joseph's beauty, she loved him, and that was trouble. She would not leave the young man alone.

"Love me," she whispered.

Joseph was shocked.

"My lady," he said, "your husband trusts me with all that is his. Into my hands he has placed everything—everything except for you. How can I break that trust? How can I do this great wickedness and sin against God?"

But again and again she called to Joseph, "Love me!"

For a long time Joseph simply ignored her plea. Then one day she laid hands on him, winding her fingers into his cloak. "Now!" she demanded. "Love me!" But Joseph slipped out of the garment and dashed outside.

The woman stared at the empty cloth hanging from her hand; then suddenly she started to scream. She was humiliated! She would hurt this slave for hurting her! "Save me, save me, save me!" she shrieked.

Servants burst into the house, and she waved the empty cloak in their faces.

"See this?" she cried. "Proof! That slave named Joseph—it is his! He caught me here and told me to love him, demanded that I love him! I screamed, and he ran away, but he left his cloak. Do you see this? This is the proof!"

Everyone believed her story. Her husband, when he heard it, was so enraged that he had Joseph taken from his house and thrown at once into prison.

Down the poor young Joseph had come, from being a son to being a slave. And down he had come again, from slavery to imprisonment. Yet in all this time the Lord God never left his side, for the Lord loved Joseph.

The Dreams of the Butler and the Baker

Joseph—a most talented young man! He could read dreams and well interpret them.

He was a prisoner, yet the keeper of the prison saw his obedient reliability and put all the prisoners in Joseph's care, and Joseph prospered. He came to know every man in

Even in prison, Joseph's obedience and wisdom shined. The prison keeper put all the prisoners in his care.

the place, and every man came to trust him.

It was no surprise, then, when two of the other prisoners—one the Pharaoh's butler, the other his baker—came to Joseph. Each was distressed by a dream he had dreamed in the night.

"Please tell me what it means," the butler said. "I dreamed of a grapevine with three branches, and the branches bore buds, and the buds became flowers, and the flowers fattened into grapes. I picked the grapes. I squeezed their juice into Pharaoh's cup. And behold! the juice was wine already. All of this happened in a moment."

"Friend, be at peace," Joseph said. "In three days Pharaoh will lift you out of this low and dirty place, lift you up to your high office and make you his butler again. That is the meaning of your dream. But, please," Joseph said, "when your dream does come true, remember my name to Pharaoh. Speak a good word for me."

"My dream is not much different," said the baker. "I was going to Pharaoh with three bread baskets on my head. The birds pecked the pastries out of the top one."

"I am sorry for you," Joseph said. "In three days Pharaoh will lift you up, too—but he will lift you up to hang you, and then he will leave your body to the birds."

On the third day it happened all as Joseph had interpreted. A baker died, and a butler lived. But the butler, when he was set free, forgot about Joseph in prison.

Pharaoh's Dreams

Two years later the king of Egypt woke from a deep sleep, roaring and sweating and wiping his face.

"My magicians!" he thundered. "Get me my magicians and all the wise men of the land!" Something had terrified the man.

When the magicians had gathered, and when all the wise men of the land had come into his room, Pharaoh told them the nightmares he had dreamed. Then he glared at the men around him. "What do they mean?"

Mumbles and silence and halfhearted answers were all they gave back to him.

Pharaoh wiped his face the harder. "I pay frogs to be my wise men," he growled. "They blink at me! They croak and they hop in circles, and I am none the wiser! Is there no one?" he cried. "Is there no one to tell me my dreams?"

"When I was in prison—"

"Yes?" Pharaoh commanded his butler to continue.

"When I was in prison, there was a young man," said the butler, finally remembering Joseph, "who told me the meaning of my dream, and it came true just as he—"

"Get him!" Pharaoh commanded.

Get him! That command shot from Pharaoh's room, from his house, through the city and into the prison like a desperate bird: *Get him!* Instantly the keeper released Joseph. Quickly the young man washed, shaved, changed his clothes. And within the hour Joseph stood straight and calm in the presence of the king of Egypt.

"It is said," said Pharaoh, staring at the slave, "that you can interpret dreams. Can you?"

Joseph said, "No."

"What?"

"No, it is not in me to interpret. But God will speak what he wishes to speak *through* me."

"So," said Pharaoh, nodding. Here was a man and not a frog. Here was someone both bold and obedient at once. "So—good. Then listen to my dreams," said Pharaoh.

Pharaoh dreamed. And Pharaoh was terrified. "Bring me my magicians," he thundered. "Call together the wisest men in the land."

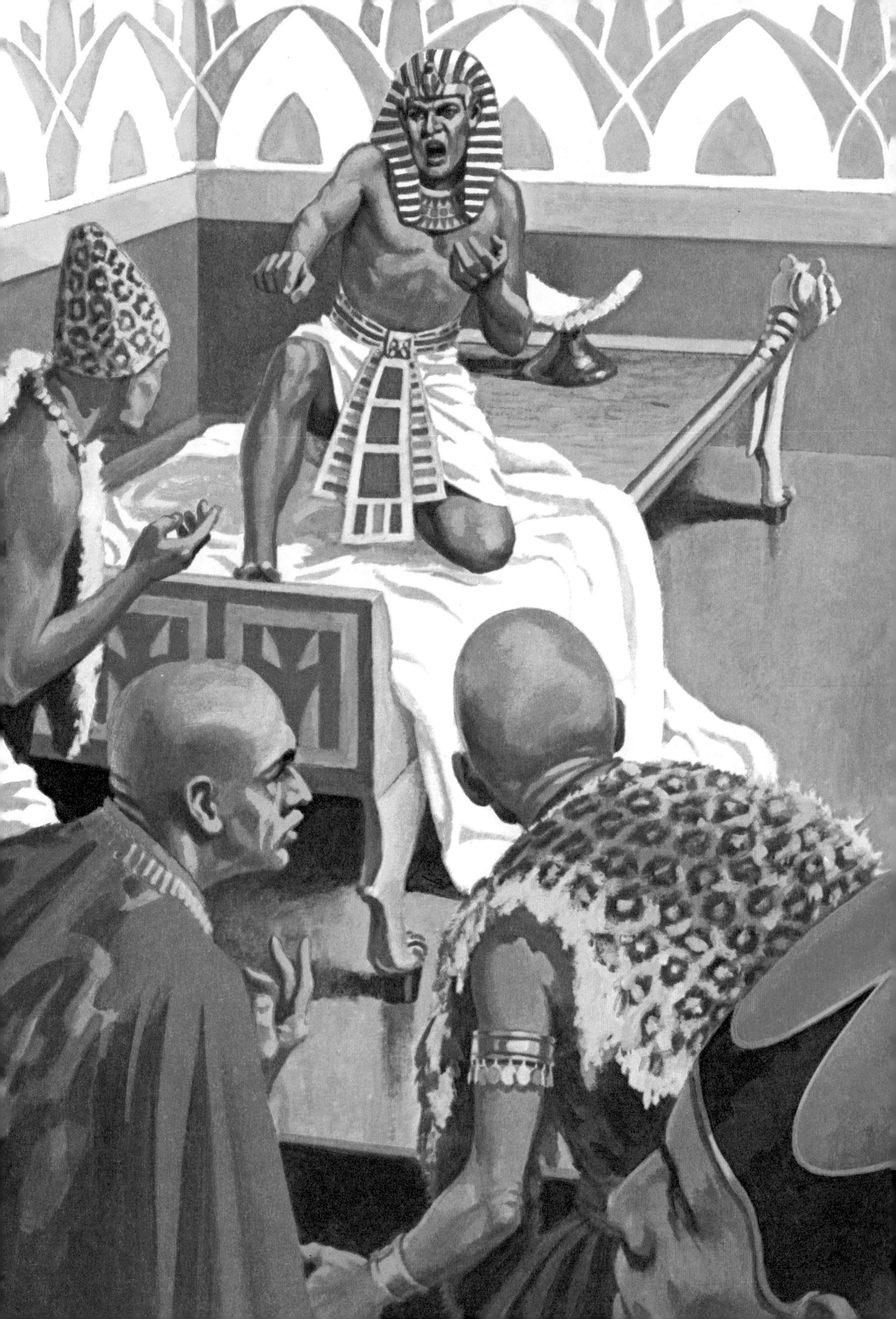

Soon Joseph, the prisoner, stood before Pharaoh.
"Can you interpret dreams?" demanded Pharaoh.
"No," said Joseph. "God speaks through me."
Pleased, Pharaoh told his dream to Joseph.

"I stood on the banks of the Nile River. Seven cows, healthy and fat, climbed up out of the water and began to graze on the grass. Then seven more cows came up; but these were the skinniest, most unhealthy cattle I have ever seen. They ate up the seven fat cows! Yet when they were done, they were as miserably thin as before. In the second dream I saw a cornstalk with seven good ears and full. Soon seven more ears grew out, blighted, withered, and wretched. Then the bad swallowed down the good ears, and that was an end to them—to the good cows, to the good ears, and an end to my dreams. Slave, look at me! What does your God say about my dreams?"

Joseph: Second in Command of Egypt

"God has shown you what he is about to do," Joseph said. "Out of the waters of the Nile shall come seven years of plenty, and the land will be fat with good growing. Those years are the fat cows and the full ears of corn."

Pharaoh nodded, and Joseph continued.

"But immediately afterward shall come seven years so dry, so dusty, and so dire that no one will remember the good any more. Famine, Pharaoh, shall follow the plenty, and that very soon."

"Your God says as much?" Pharaoh was thoughtful.

"He does," said Joseph. "And a word of counsel besides. Pharaoh, today set someone in charge of all the harvest of Egypt. Today! Let him store a fifth of all that the good years yield; then full bins shall feed Egypt when the bad years come."

Pharaoh gazed a long time at this slave, and he whispered his wonder. "Surely, the Spirit of God is in this man."

"What is your name?" he asked aloud.

"Joseph," the young man answered.

"You, Joseph," Pharaoh said with a sudden, regal certainty. "You shall yourself do what you advise. I command it!"

He stepped toward the young man. "Put this on," he said. He gave Joseph the ring by which the king sealed laws for all the land. "Wear these!" The royal linens were draped from Joseph's back. "Hang this about your neck." A fine gold chain dangled at Joseph's chest.

Pharaoh stepped back and said, "And when you ride through Egypt, ride, Joseph, in my own chariot. Before you they shall cry 'Attention!' so that all the people shall bow, all the people shall know that you are second in all this realm only to me, and all the people shall obey your command as though it were mine. Slave, you are a slave no longer! You, Joseph, are the man to plan for the famine you foretold!"

So Joseph, the eleventh son of Israel, went out into the land of Egypt with power in his right hand, with wise, unbending authority in his eye, with talent, and with the blessing of Almighty God. He was the second in command; the people did as he ordered them to do. For seven years they stored their wonderful harvests in bins in every city of Egypt. The grain piled up beyond the measuring of it, until it seemed like sand on a seashore, and Joseph managed everything with a godly skill. Surely, the Lord God was with his servant Joseph!

Joseph's Dreams Come True

Then came the famine. The skies went white and hot and stayed that way; never a drop of rain did they send to the land. The land cracked, and the dry wind ripped it of dry dust. The river shriveled, and the people starved.

Famine was everywhere. Year after year all the lands suffered. And in Canaan, too, the people were dying. They stumbled about in hunger and stared at one another with a dim light in their eyes.

Israel was a very old man, now, but he was still the father of his family.

"I have heard," he said to his sons, "that there is food to be bought in Egypt. Take money, my sons. Go, and buy Egyptian food, that we may live and not die. Let ten of you go while one of you stays with me—for I will never let Benjamin out of my sight, as once I did Joseph."

Reuben, Simeon, Levi, Judah, Dan, Gad, Asher, Naphtali, Issachar, Zebulun—ten of them went, trudging from Canaan to Egypt, to the city that sold the food.

They went with their heads down, not only for hunger, but also in humility because they knew they had no right to ask for this food: They were Hebrew and not Egyptian. And they went with their heads bowed because they had heard stories about the mighty man who governed the food, how shrewd he was, how bright and noble, hard and powerful, how talented he was! They feared to meet him face to face.

In that city they sought the man who governed the food. And then not a little way, but all the way down to the ground the ten brothers bowed in the presence of this governor.

This governor—Joseph—spoke sharply to them: "Where are you from?" he asked.

"From Canaan, sir; to buy food, sir."

Joseph knew very well that these were his brothers now bowing before him. Yet he pretended ignorance and sharpened his words.

"That is a lie!" he snapped. "You are spies!"

The brothers looked up first in surprise, and then in fear. "My lord! We are not spies. We are sons of an honest man!"

"I have evidence," Joseph repeated, "that you are spies."

"No, sir! No, my lord! We are a family! We are twelve brothers, that's all! The youngest is with our father, and the other is—gone. But—"

"But you are liars as well as spies!" Joseph accused them. "Youngest brother, indeed! What is the name of this youngest brother?"

"Benjamin! Benjamin! He is at home!"

"Bring him here. Produce a Benjamin before me," Joseph said, "and then I will believe your story about twelve brothers. Only then will I think you anything other than spies."

The brothers stood with their mouths open at the governor's proposal.

"Well, do you hear me?" Joseph demanded. "I am giving you the chance to prove your words true. But if you do not bring this Benjamin back with you, I will know for a fact that you are lying spies, and you shall, for a fact, see my face no more!"

They were silent. Each brother was thinking of his father.

"It would kill our father to see Benjamin go," Reuben said in his own language. He did not know that the governor could understand Hebrew because, of course, he did not know that the governor was his own brother.

"He lost Joseph," Reuben whispered. "Our father cannot lose another."

"But what else can we do?" they all said.

"Oh, why did we sin against Joseph so long ago?" said Reuben. "Don't you see that our guilt comes back again? This is the punishment."

Suddenly Joseph had to turn his face away. Reuben's words had pierced him to the heart, and he wept.

He did still love his brothers. But as governor in Egypt, he kept a hard face before them. He had Simeon tied up and put into prison to await their return. He ordered that their sacks be filled with food, and he sent them away. "Benjamin!" he reminded them. "I will see this Benjamin, or else you will not see me!"

Ten came, but nine went home again.

A Year Passes: The Brothers Return

Buy food in a famine, and it is food soon gone. Then death comes closer than before.

Soon old Israel was preparing his sons for another trip into Egypt. "My bins, my hands, our sacks, and our stomachs are empty again," he said. "We will die if we do not eat. Let nine of you go back to buy food, and let Benjamin stay with me."

"Father," Judah said sadly, "we will die if we do not bring Benjamin with us. The governor solemnly warned us that we would not see his face again if he could not see Benjamin. We will not get food; we will not eat; and we will surely die."

"Die?" the old man wailed. "There are many ways a man may die! My Joseph is gone. Simeon sits in prison. If I should lose the son of my old age, if I should lose Benjamin, *that* will kill me. *Then* I will surely die!"

"Let me be responsible for my brother," said Judah. "If Benjamin does not come back, then let me bear the blame forever. But Father, he has to go with us!"

And so it was that the old man stood lonely in front of his tent, hiding his sorrowful eyes so that he would not see them leav-

All of Israel's sons set out for Egypt. All. Not one was left to comfort the old man.

ing. Ten went to Egypt; two were already there. Israel was left standing alone.

The Whole Family Comes to Egypt

When they met the governor, everything seemed to go well.

Joseph welcomed all ten of the brothers into his own house. He spoke kindly to Benjamin; no one noticed the tears in his eyes as he spoke to his own true brother. He brought Simeon before them, and he invited them to eat with him before they filled their sacks with food and began the journey homeward.

Then they left the governor's house feeling light and cheerful. All eleven of the brothers were together again. Their father would rejoice at their success. . . .

But Joseph had hidden his personal silver cup in Benjamin's sack!

"They have stolen my cup!" Joseph said to his steward. "Go after the Hebrews. Identify the thief, and bring him back to me!"

Soon the steward transfixed eleven men with a stern accusation. "Why," he demanded on the open road, "have you returned evil for good?"

"But we've done nothing," said Judah.

"One of you is a thief!"

"No, sir! No, sir!" cried Judah. "We want too much to be home to steal anything—"

"One of you has taken the silver cup of the governor!"

"His cup? But why—?" So close to going! So close to gone again, and to their father! Judah was in anguish over the trouble that stopped them at the last minute. "Look," he said, "if any one of us has taken that cup, let him die. The rest of us will be slaves in Egypt. But I know that none of us—"

"Empty your sacks," commanded the steward, high and hard in his chariot. "The governor wants no death, nor does he need a scattering of Hebrew slaves. The one who has the cup, he alone will be slave. Empty your sacks! The rest of you can go home. Empty the sacks!"

They did. Trembling, they spilled their sacks onto the ground. Then, out of Benjamin's sack, rolled a bright silver cup.

The brothers gasped. The steward nodded and seized Benjamin. With the youngest he rode away. And Judah cried out, "Father!"

On foot ten men followed a fast chariot back to the city, back to the governor's home, grieving and weeping as they went, wailing as though someone dear had died. Twice they had come to Egypt, twice had met with distress. Why couldn't they slip in and slip out like anyone else?

They begged an audience with the governor. When he relented, when they found him surrounded by his servants, and Benjamin in the middle, Judah wrung his hands and said, "We cannot! Sir, we cannot go back to our father without his youngest son!" Then he bowed his head.

Long, low, and slow Judah began to plead with Joseph. He said, "Once our father had another son, whom he loved as if the boy were his own heart. Joseph. But, God forgive us the sin, we envied Joseph. We sold our father's son into slavery; and we let our father believe the boy had been murdered. That was a stroke that crippled our father and made him old. Sir, he hasn't the strength for a second stroke. Without Benjamin, the man will die. Sir, I swore on my life to care for my brother. Therefore, take me. Let me be your slave and you will save two lives: my brother's, which is precious to my father, and my father's, which is precious to me."

With his head bowed Joseph listened to all that Judah said. He was moved by the words, and he could not control himself. He wept.

"Leave the room," he commanded his servants. And when he was alone with his brothers, he burst into loud sobbing. He raised his face. He went to Judah and embraced him; he went to Benjamin and kissed him, and then to each of his brothers one after the other.

"But *I* am Joseph," he said. "Look at me, Reuben—*I* am your brother! Judah, I am not dead, not dead at all, but alive. Levi, Dan, Simeon, it is Joseph! And you do not need to be ashamed any more for what you have done, because I have been in the hands of God from the beginning. Gad, go tell our father that this has been the plan of the Lord. Asher, run to him! You meant evil against me, but God meant it for good, so that many people should be kept alive as they are today. Naphtali, run! Issachar, Zebulun, race! Hurry! Haste! Run! And you, Benjamin, tell our father to come down and live with me!"

And so it was that all the sons of Israel, and the old man himself, settled together in Egypt, in the land of Goshen. They raised families. They prospered. They grew wonderfully in numbers. They became a multitude, a vast and countless family, and they named themselves by the name of their father, Israel.

For Israel himself, his last years were his loveliest. Twelve sons were twelve again. He looked upon them all. He blessed them. And he died in peace.

"Benjamin is my slave," said Joseph. The brothers thought of their father and cried out in anguish.

Israel in Slavery — God Sets the People Free!

OPPRESSION IN EGYPT

"YOU SHALL FEAR the Lord your God; you shall serve him and worship him, and by his name you shall swear. He is your glory; he is your God, who has done for you these great and terrible things which your eyes have seen. Your ancestors went down to Egypt seventy persons, and now the Lord your God has made you as the stars of heaven for multitude."

In the centuries after Joseph invited his fathers and his brothers to live with him in Egypt, God kept his promise; he increased the children of Israel. Seventy persons swelled into a vast family, a multitude.

They filled the land! And finally they frightened the king of Egypt, who did not remember Joseph, who had forgotten the good he had done some hundreds of years before.

"They are too many, too mighty for us," this new king said. And he determined to hurt them first before they could hurt him.

Slaves

The king of Egypt commanded that all of the rights of the Israelites be taken away. They were no longer equal to the citizens of Egypt; they were less! They were no longer free; they were slaves!

"We will break their spirits with slavery, and their backs with burdens," said the king, "and they will be too weak to threaten us by their numbers."

He sent taskmasters among the Israelites. The taskmasters carried whips, and the whips cut any slave too slow to do his work.

To work! To work! And the work that the king demanded of his slaves was deadly.

Quarry stone, and cut it!
Cut stone and drag it!
Drag the stone a hundred miles
and heap it into piles!
Place a block and mortar it!
Build a wall and plaster it!
Make a house! A thousand bins
to store the Pharaoh's harvest in!

Whole cities did Israel build for the king this way, cities named Pithom and Raamses. At the same time the slaves were driven into the fields to grow the grain that the cities would store.

Yet the Lord was with Israel, and a marvelous thing happened: The more that Pharaoh oppressed the people, the more they multiplied! And the more they multiplied, the more they terrified Egypt!

"Midwives, Kill Their Babies!"

So Pharaoh conceived a still more dreadful plan to ruin Israel.

No woman could give birth to a baby alone. She needed the help of another woman, and those who were trained to give such help were called midwives.

"When you help an Israelite to bear her child," Pharaoh commanded the midwives, "you shall see whether it is a son or a daughter. If the baby is a boy, kill him!" For Israel could not grow without sons. Its people could only diminish in numbers, in strength, and in spirit.

But the midwives feared God, and they simply ignored Pharaoh's command. Israel kept growing.

"Didn't I tell you to kill them?" Pharaoh demanded.

"Oh, yes, sir!" the midwives said. "And we've done our best. But it takes time to rush to a woman's house, and these Israelite women are so strong that the baby is born before we get there."

"By the sun! By the sun and the river!" Pharaoh raged. He turned away from the midwives and made his command to all the people of Egypt.

"Each boy born to the Israelites," he roared, "shall be cast into the Nile! Do you hear me? Drown him!"

A Child Escapes Drowning: Moses

These were violent times, when women feared for the lives of their sons. To save the babies they hid them and hoped they would not cry. Pharaoh had the power to strike great fear in his people.

But what could a mother do when her son grew too large to tuck in a cupboard?

One woman wove a basket of bulrushes, just the size of her child. She covered it over with tar to make it watertight, then put her son in the basket and slipped it into the river. There it rocked among the reeds like a tiny boat, hidden from anyone who passed on the shore. The baby's sister watched over this treasure from a distance.

It seemed to be in an excellent hiding place, yet by accident it was soon discovered because Pharaoh's daughter always bathed in this same spot.

Soon the lady came with her maidservants. She undressed and waded into the river until she herself was hidden among the reeds.

"Oh!" she cried. She had spied the basket there, and she heard small noises from inside.

On shore they opened the basket. The small noises turned to tears as the baby came into the sunlight, and from the start Pharaoh's daughter loved the child she looked at. "It's one of the Israelite children!" she whispered. "This is one who is not going to die."

Then the baby's sister ran forward. "Should I," she asked, "should I find a nurse for the child?"

Pharaoh's daughter said, "Please do." Already she thought of the boy as her own.

Quickly the girl ran and returned with her mother, who was also the baby's mother.

"Woman," said Pharaoh's daughter, "you may nurse the boy. But I shall adopt him, and in my own house will I raise him up to manhood."

Then this high-born, important lady glanced from the river to the basket and said, "I will name him Moses, because I drew him out of the water."

Moses Suffers with His Family

Moses grew to manhood in an Egyptian house with Egyptian education. He walked under Egyptian eyes in Egyptian riches. But he had been borne, nursed, and cuddled by an Israelite! With his mother's milk he learned that his family was Israel, that Abraham, Isaac, Jacob, and Levi were his great-great-grandfathers, and that he himself was not, nor could ever be, Egyptian.

His heart was with the slaves.

One day, as he moved among his own people, grieving to see the difficult life that they lived, he heard a cry of pain. Among the stones an Egyptian taskmaster was whipping an Israelite. Moses caught his breath; his eyes flashed. "No!" he cried in a perfect fury. He threw himself on the Egyptian and killed him. Then he hid the body in the

Israelite mothers feared for the lives of their boy babies. One mother concealed her child among the reeds of the Nile. As the baby's sister watched from afar, Pharaoh's daughter found him, loved him, and vowed to raise him as her own. She called him Moses.

---

sand. He wondered if someone had seen the murder.

On the following day Moses went out again, and this time he found two Israelites fighting together.

"How can you do this?" he pleaded as he pulled them apart. "You are brothers, not enemies! We have enemies enough!"

But one of the men jerked away. "Moses, the most high judge of us all!" he sneered. "What will you do, kill me as you killed the Egyptian?"

Moses stared at the man and thought, *The murder is known! Pharaoh will look to execute me!*

Before nightfall Moses had fled the land of Egypt altogether. He went to Midian, where he hid himself and lived for many years as a shepherd.

GOD FIGHTS PHARAOH FOR HIS PEOPLE, ISRAEL

Many years Moses lived in Midian, the quiet, unassuming life of a shepherd.

During that time one Pharaoh died in Egypt and another took his place—but there was no change at all in the hardship of the Israelites, for the second Pharaoh was as hateful as the first. The people of Israel groaned in bondage; they cried out for help. Their cry went up to God, and God remembered his covenant with their first father, Abraham.

The Lord God now moved to set the children of Israel free from slavery. And whom should he use to lead them? Moses!

The Call of Moses

One day Moses saw a sudden and marvelous sight. On the side of a mountain, a fire! A single bush was burning there—but though it burned, it never burned up!

Moses began to climb the mountain, the better to see this wonder. But as soon as he touched ground near it, the Lord God called out of the bush: "Moses! Moses!"

The man stopped short. "Here I am."

"Do not come nearer, but take your shoes off your feet," said the Lord. "The place on which you stand is holy ground!"

Moses hastened to do the Lord's will, then stood very, very still. This bush burned with no common fire; it was a fire divine!

"I have seen the affliction of my people in Egypt. I know their sufferings," said the Lord, "and I have come to deliver them, to give them the land that I promised their fathers. And you, Moses! I will send you to Pharaoh, to my people, to lead Israel out of slavery."

But Moses was conscious of his weaknesses, his fears, and his failings. Even now

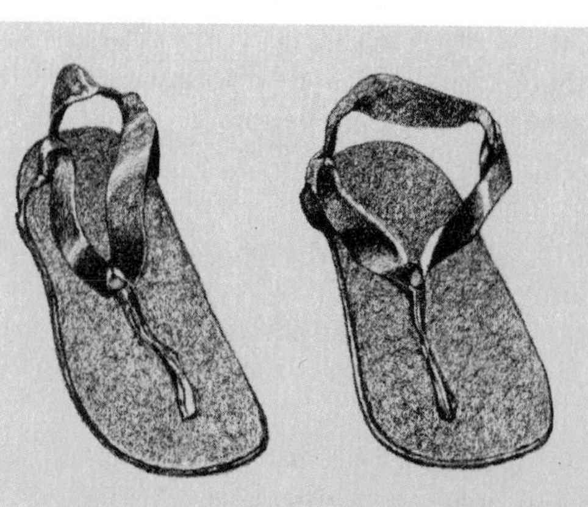

Possibly Moses wore tough leather sandals tied with thongs. It is thought that soles were made of wood, cane, or palm bark and then nailed to the leather.

he stood with his face covered, frightened by the nearness of his God. Therefore, he shook his head. This task was too much; it was more than he could do. He—Moses—squirmed before God!

"No," he said. "If I come to Israel in Egypt with such mighty news, and if the people ask who sent me, I will not know your name to say it."

God said to Moses, "I AM WHO I AM." God said, "Tell them I AM sent you." And God said, "Say, the Lord, the God of your fathers—of Abraham, Isaac, and Jacob—has appeared to me. He promises to set you free from slavery, to give you a good land."

But Moses continued to shake his head. "No," he said, "they will not believe me."

The Lord said to Moses, "What is that in your hand?"

"Why," said Moses, "my shepherd's rod."

"Throw it to the ground," said the Lord.

Moses did. Instantly it curled and turned into a snake. Moses ran back, the more afraid.

"Now take it by its tail," said the Lord.

Moses did, and the snake was a rod again.

"Do that, and they will believe you," said the Lord God.

But still the man Moses was shaking his head. Still he said, "No, they will not believe me." And this time he added, "Because I cannot speak well, Lord. I stutter."

"Who made the mouths?" God said. "I will be your mouth."

"O Lord God!" Moses burst out. "Send someone else!"

Then the anger of the Lord burned against Moses. "Your brother Aaron," he said, "speaks eloquently. Your brother Aaron shall speak for you. But you, Moses, shall go down. And you, Moses, shall gather my people. And you, Moses, shall most certainly lead them out!"

So it was that Moses bowed his head before the commands of the Lord. He said farewell to those whom he had come to love in Midian, and he turned back to Egypt, to the task too great for him.

The First Word of the War

Moses met Aaron his brother, then together they revealed to Israel all that the Lord had spoken upon his mountain.

From a bush burning with a fire divine, the voice of God spoke to the frightened Moses. "Moses, Moses! I will send you to my people to lead Israel out of slavery." But Moses knew his own weaknesses and protested.

The children of Israel rejoiced. They were glad to learn that God cared for them, that he grieved over them and planned to set them free. They bowed their heads. They worshiped. And they watched as Moses and Aaron went to speak with Pharaoh....

"The Lord, the Lord God," Aaron said before Pharaoh's face, "the God of Israel says, 'Let my people go, that they may hold a feast for me in the wilderness!' "

Pharaoh looked on the two men standing in front of him and chuckled. "What God did you say this was?" he said. "I have not heard of this God before."

"He is the God of Israel," said Aaron, "and he shall fall on Egypt by disease or by the sword if his word is not obeyed."

"Do you mean," said Pharaoh, "that I should obey a little deity—and at the same time give my slaves a rest? Get out of here! You and your little God, get out of my sight!"

But the word had been spoken: "Let my people go." And though Pharaoh did not acknowledge it, the war had begun!

Pharaoh Fights Back

As soon as Moses and Aaron had left him, Pharaoh demanded to speak to the taskmasters of Israel.

Together, Moses and Aaron faced Pharaoh, who looked on them with contempt. Aaron spoke eloquently. "The God of Israel says, 'Let my people go, that they may hold a feast for me in the wilderness!' " But Pharaoh only laughed and ordered them out of his sight.

"It seems," he said, "that our slaves have too much time on their hands. They want to offer sacrifices to some God of theirs. Well, we will busy those hands, and we will break that people for good, forever! From now on, provide no straw for their bricks, yet demand that they make the same number of bricks nonetheless! From now on they will gather the straw themselves; and if it is stubble they have to use, why then stubble they shall use. Yet not one brick less shall they make for all of that!"

So the taskmasters went out among the people with Pharaoh's order, and the people were scattered across the land, picking bits of stubble for their brick.

"Do it! Do it! *Do it!*" the taskmasters cried, cracking their whips across the Israelites.

At the end of a day there were fewer bricks than before, for the job was impossible. At the end of the day the Israelites were beaten like beasts for their failure. So they carried their complaint to Pharaoh.

"Why?" they said. "Why are we beaten when it's not our fault? We can't make bricks without straw!"

"Fault?" said Pharaoh. "Of course it's your fault. Did not your own leaders say you want the time to sacrifice to your God? Excuses come from laziness, slaves! Well, we'll see how lazy you can be!"

When the Israelites saw Moses and Aaron again, they were angry. "You've made trouble for us with Pharaoh," they cried to Moses. "This isn't setting us free! This is putting the sword into Pharaoh's hands that he might kill us!"

They would listen no more to Moses, and Moses himself wondered how God would deliver the people. He wondered why God had sent him at all. For here, at the beginning, it looked as though Pharaoh was winning!

Great Acts of Judgment: The Ten Plagues

"Speak as I command you to speak," said the Lord God to Moses. "Do as I tell you to do. And the Egyptians shall know that I am the Lord, when I stretch forth my hand upon Egypt and bring out the people of Israel from among them!"

Then began the signs, the wonders, the war, the terrors, the mighty acts of God before the eyes of Israel and of Egypt.

The Lord God turned all the water in the Nile River into *blood.* And the canals, and the ponds, the pools, the water in jugs and the water in cups—all of it went to blood.

The Israelites made bricks from clay or mud mixed with straw to prevent crumbling. Workers kneaded the mixture, molded it, and dried the bricks. An ancient mural depicts the process of brickmaking.

But when Pharaoh found that his magicians could do the same thing by their magic, he ignored Moses. He hardened his heart, and he did not let the children of Israel go anywhere.

Then God sent *frogs* into the land of Egypt. The earth bounced with them. The waters swarmed with them. The houses, the bedrooms, the pots, and the ovens were full of them.

This time, though Pharaoh's magicians could also do this thing, they could not *un*do it. They could not rid the country of frogs.

So Pharaoh called for Moses and Aaron. "Is your God great enough to stop what he has started?" he demanded. "Tell him to take the frogs away, and I will let the people go."

And Moses said, "That you may know that there is no one like the Lord our God, it shall be done tomorrow."

And it was. On the morrow the frogs died wherever they were. People shoveled them into piles as high as houses, and the piles stank.

But Pharaoh hardened his heart again, and he did not let the people go.

Therefore God turned the dust of Egypt into *gnats,* and the gnats covered the living—both men and beasts.

This the magicians could not do. "Surely this is the finger of God!" they said.

But Pharaoh's heart remained hardened, so that he would not even listen to his own people.

"Let my people go!" the Lord God said through Moses. "Or I shall infest the land with *flies!*"

Pharaoh did nothing. The Lord God did something. He blackened Egypt with crawling, buzzing flies. But in the land of Goshen, where the children of Israel dwelt, there was not a fly to be found.

"Stop them!" Pharaoh cried to Moses. "Clean the country of these flies, and you can worship your God here."

"No!" said Moses. "We must sacrifice to the Lord in the wilderness, not in Egypt."

"The wilderness, then!" cried Pharaoh. "Only kill these damnable flies!"

God did remove the flies. But Pharaoh hardened his heart and did not let the people go.

The hand of the Lord fell on the flocks and the herds of Egypt, and the animals died from fearful *diseases.* But Pharaoh sat like a stone, his heart still hardened.

The hand of the Lord made *boils* to cover the bodies of the Egyptians themselves. Even the magicians suffered from running sores. But Pharaoh's heart was a rock. He did not let the people go.

"Pharaoh!" the Lord God said through Moses. "By now I could have cut you off from the earth. But I have not. I have let you live to show you my power, so that my name may be declared throughout all the earth."

And God said, "Behold, tomorrow I shall cause a heavy *hail* to fall, such as never has been in Egypt from the day it was founded till now!"

On the next day Moses stood high and stretched forth his rod toward heaven.

BOOM!

The Lord sent thunder. Hail. Flowing fire ran down to the earth, while a fire more brittle did flash in the midst of the hail. The hail cracked and battered everything that stood in the open—men, beasts, and crops.

BOOM! BOOM! BOOM!

Only in Goshen, where the children of Israel lived, there was no hail.

"I have sinned!" Pharaoh cried to Moses. "Your God is right, and I am wrong! Plead with your God to stop the hail, and I will let you go!"

But when the violence in heaven ceased,

Seven plagues had God sent to Egypt, and seven times had Pharaoh broken his word and hardened his heart. For the eighth plague, God sent dense, buzzing clouds of locusts to settle on the land and devour the green fields. And still Pharaoh did not let God's people go.

Pharaoh sinned again. Again he did not let the people go.

Not when the Lord God sent clouds of *locusts* by a hard east wind did he let the people go.

And not when the Lord God cloaked the whole of Egypt in a *darkness* so thick that it could be felt.

"Please," Pharaoh said to Moses after three days of such darkness. "Please go away. Go serve your God. Just leave your cattle here in Egypt, and you can go."

But Moses said, "When we go, we go with all that is ours. Not a hoof nor a horn shall be left behind, since it is our cattle that we sacrifice to the Lord."

"No! No! No! No!" Pharaoh was on his feet and shaking. "When do you stop asking?" he cried. "I will tell you when. Now! Get out of my sight! Never see my face again! See me again, troubler, and you die!"

Moses said, "Just as you say, Pharaoh. I will never see your face again."

The Last Plague, the Passover

Plague after plague the children of Israel had watched in wonder. Awesome was the grand power of their God. Nine signs, nine wonders, the mighty hand and the outstretched arm of the Lord their God had turned their hearts again, and they did not doubt the words of Moses. They trusted him, the servant of God.

Therefore, when Moses called the elders of Israel to himself, they came. When he cried silence and demanded their attention, they gave it. When he urged them to prepare for the final, most terrible plague of all, they did.

"At midnight," Moses cried, "the Lord God shall confound Pharaoh, and Egypt, and the whole of the land! Not a house stands but that there shall be weeping in its walls—except for the houses of Israel! The houses of those that prepare themselves shall go untouched! God shall pass over the prepared. Therefore, Israel, O Israel—prepare!"

And Israel did prepare.

Every household among them took a lamb, one without spot or blemish, a male one year old. In the evening each father slaughtered his lamb, caught the blood, dipped a brush of hyssop into it, and smeared it—still glistening—on the doorposts and the lintels of his house. *Prepare! Prepare!* The blood was a sign for the Lord, a sign that the houses of Israel had prepared....

For the rest of the evening, the people did not go outside their houses, but roasted the lamb and ate it with unleavened bread and with bitter herbs. They were dressed, shod, and ready to go. They ate their meal in a hurry! For the last plague came at midnight.

At midnight the angel of destruction descended on the land. At midnight the angel

At midnight the final and most terrible plague fell on Egypt, and a sorrowful cry rose up, lasting the night long. As Pharaoh watched in horror, helpless to save his firstborn son, the people of Israel, who had prepared, were spared the angel of destruction.

of death did blast through Egypt, smiting the firstborn of every family. Of Pharaoh, the firstborn son was slain! Of the captive who sat in the dungeon, the firstborn son! Of the maid who worked at the mill, the firstborn! Of all the fathers and all the mothers throughout all of Egypt, the eldest son did die, and there was not a house where one was not dead.

A cry rose up in Egypt, then. Wailing, weeping all the night long, tears and swollen sorrow.

And Pharoah cried to Moses and Aaron, "Away! Away! You and the people of Israel, your flocks and your herds, go away and serve the Lord God as you have said!" And he mumbled, "And bless me also."

And all the Egyptians prayed for Israel to get out of their land at once, for they said, "We are dead men."

The children of Israel clapped their hands at the freedom that lay before them! Not one of their sons had died. The children of Israel grabbed the bread dough before it had time to rise, and yet while the night was upon them they left their houses. They left the cities and the land of Goshen. Thousands and thousands of people, they went out of Egypt. After four hundred and thirty years, they got up and went out of Egypt. Free, free, and a people of God! The children of Israel went into the wilderness free!

Pesach

And so, in those days, by the command of the Lord, the children of these children of Israel ate the same meal on the same day of the same month. They ate a lamb that had no blemish, that had not a bone broken. And they ate this meal as an everlasting reminder of all that the Lord God did for them in the night he led them out of Egypt.

That observance is called the Passover: *Pesach*.

Israel in the Wilderness

"THE LORD WILL FIGHT FOR YOU! ONLY, BE STILL!"

SUDDENLY ISRAEL was free. The wide wilderness stretched all around, and to the Lord alone were the people beholden. God was their God; him alone should they serve!

Israel was free, suddenly. But only slowly did the people learn to trust the God who freed them. Slowly—through much suffering in the wilderness, sometimes grumbling against the Lord and sometimes turning toward him in a panic, sometimes proud and sometimes humiliated, sometimes sinful, sometimes obedient—slowly, did Israel come to know the Lord God as God, the God of Israel.

"Hear, O Israel, the Lord our God, the Lord is one. And you shall love the Lord your God with all your heart, and with all your soul, and with all your might!"

These words became their creed and their command. But it took forty years of wandering in the wilderness before they learned well to accept this creed.

Yet as they learned it, as they came to accept the Lord for their own God, as they grew to trust him, then Israel was transformed—changed! No longer a family small among the nations, Israel became a nation itself, mighty, prosperous, and the possession of God!

"For you are a people holy to the Lord your God! The Lord your God has chosen you to be a people for his own possession, out of all the peoples that are on the face of the earth. Not because you were great in numbers has he brought you out with a mighty hand; but because the Lord loves you, because he is keeping the oath which he swore to your fathers has he redeemed you from bondage to Pharaoh, the king of Egypt!

"Know therefore that the Lord your God is God, the faithful God who keeps covenant and steadfast love with those who love him and keep his commandments, to a thousand generations, and requites at once those who hate him, by destroying them."

Suddenly free, slowly learning, for a full forty years Israel wandered the wilderness. And that learning surely did begin with their first step into the wilderness—across the Red Sea.

From the Very Beginning, God Leads Them

In the days following their escape from Egypt, the children of Israel seemed lost, seemed not to know where they were going.

First they traveled south and east, to Succoth. Next, by a long turning, they went north again to Baal-zephon. Finally they stalled in a useless place, a dead-end backwater from which there seemed no exit. They gathered on the marshy shores of the Red Sea, and the mud and the water of the place dragged them to a stop.

Israel seemed baffled of direction. But God was not. The Lord knew what he was doing, and it was he who led them!

He went before them by day in a pillar of cloud. By night he led them in a pillar of fire to give them light. Always he was near, and always he was in front of them.

Pharaoh's Pursuit

Pharaoh of the narrow eyes, Pharaoh of the deep suspicions, Pharaoh of the fierce, unstable, hateful heart, had changed his mind again.

"We must have been mad," he raged, "to let Israel go! Why did we do such a thing?"

He paced and he trembled in his wrath.

But when the news was carried back to him that Israel was bogged on a marshy shore, then the Pharaoh of evil intent smiled. He conceived a plan.

"They are entangled in the land," he said, "and their confusion is our opportunity. Arise! After them!"

With six hundred of his finest chariots, with horses and warriors, knives, swords, and bristling arrows, Pharaoh entered the

Pharaoh's army behind them, the waters of the Red Sea before them, the children of Israel moaned in despair. Then, through Moses, God performed a wonder. The surging waters parted. The Israelites walked to safety.

field. Eastward he rode, his army massed and flashing behind him. Toward Israel he glared—and it was more than the wind and the sunlight that narrowed his eyes. It was hate.

Israel's Terror

Thousands and thousands of people stood milling like cattle at the edge of the Red Sea—but they were no army. Never trained to fight, crowded into an unlikely spot, slipping on the mud, and stalled by the water in front of them, Israel was helpless.

Suddenly the ground itself began to tremble. Then they saw yellow dust on the horizon. Fear made them mute, and they watched the yellow cloud swell.

Sunlight glinted from a weapon. A woman screamed: "Pharaoh!" And another: "Egypt!"

Water on the one hand, Pharaoh on the other. All the people began to lift their voices, and to cry, "Moses! Moses! Aren't there graves in Egypt? Did we have to come here to die? O God! We are all going to die!"

"Do not be afraid!" Moses cried in a ringing voice.

"But there is nothing to do!" they shrieked.

"Then do nothing," cried Moses, "but trust! Stand firm and see the salvation of the Lord! The Lord will fight for you! You have only to *be still!*"

The pillar of cloud rose up. It moved from the sea to a space between Israel and Egypt. It settled. It hid the army from the people, and there it stayed till the night was come.

Then, during that night of blind, furious confusion, God performed a wonder.

Crossing the Red Sea

At the command of the Lord God Almighty, Moses stretched his hand over the sea. A strong east wind began to blow, screaming past the ears of Israel and slapping the whole water of the sea. Hard did that wind blow the long night through. It drove the waters to the left, and they piled up; it swept the waters to the right, and they piled up. It scoured the seabed dry. And while yet the wind was blowing, all the children of Israel crossed the Red Sea. They went between two walls of water. They *walked!*

As soon as the morning light appeared, Egypt saw where Israel had gone.

"After them! After them!" Pharaoh roared above the streaming wind. "Arrow bite, and sword destroy them! After them!"

He gave head to his chariot horses. Their eyes rolled, their necks strained forward, and they charged into the midst of the sea. Six hundred chariots followed, horses and warriors with violent weapons in their hands.

"After them!" Pharaoh howled, even as the wheels of his heavy chariot began to clog in the mud. Foot soldiers rushed past. "After them!"

Moses stood on the other side, watching the coming armies.

"Now!" the Lord God whispered. "Now, Moses, stretch your hand above the sea."

Moses stretched forth his hand above the sea, above Pharaoh, above the whole host of Egypt—and the east wind died.

In the terrible silence that followed, the walls of water, both left and right, came down. Down! The sea slammed back to its regular course, and the sea did cover Pharaoh in white water and a swirl. The sea swallowed his chariots, his horses, his armies, his officers to the last man, till not a soul was left alive. Now there was water only, the still, smiling water, and Israel standing on the farther shore.

When the children of Israel, beyond harm, stood on
the far shore, another miracle did God perform.
Moses stretched his hands above the sea. The walls
of water came down, and the sea swallowed
Pharaoh, his chariots, his horses, his armies.

Moses' Song—and Miriam's

Moses looked at the place where Egypt had been. Slowly, he lowered his hand. Then his heart grew light, and his eyes filled with tears, and this was for joy.

"Who is like thee, O Lord, among the mighty?" He whispered it. Then he said it. Then he sang it in a loud song of jubilation:

"Who is like thee, majestic in holiness, terrible in glorious deeds, doing wonders? Thou didst stretch out thy right hand, and the earth swallowed the enemy!"

Moses' sister Miriam took a timbrel. All of the women went out after her, striking their timbrels and dancing. And Miriam sang:

"Sing to the Lord, for he has triumphed gloriously! The horse and rider thrown into the sea!"

And Moses sang:

"The Lord is my strength and my song; he has become my salvation. This is my God, and I will praise him! My father's God, and I

Pharaoh was destroyed, and the Israelites were freed at last from the bonds of Egypt. Moses lifted his voice in thanksgiving, but Miriam and the women danced their joy, each step in praise of the Lord.

will exalt him. The Lord is a man of war! The Lord is his name!"

Thus the Lord saved Israel that day from the hand of the Egyptians, and Israel saw Egypt dead upon the seashore. Israel saw the great work which the Lord had done, and the people feared the Lord. They believed in the Lord, and they believed in his servant Moses.

"What Shall We Drink?"

The people believed in the Lord and in his servant Moses—for a little while.

It was a dry land and a hot dust that they traveled now. Under a white, hot sky they went. They left behind the Red Sea. They entered the Wilderness of Shur.

A day and a night; a day and a night; a day and a night. Three days and three nights they walked without relief and without water. Soon their high spirits drooped, their tongues thickened, their glad mood turned sour, and the children began to whine, "Thirsty!"

And as the children whined, so their parents complained, "What are we going to drink?"

At Marah they discovered water, but it was a bitter, brackish stuff, and no one would touch it. "Thirsty! Thirsty! Thirsty!" cried the children.

So Moses took their grievance before the Lord. The Lord, their faithful God, did answer him. He showed Moses a tree, which Moses cut and threw into the waters of Marah.

The waters sweetened. The people drank and were satisfied. And that should have been the end of complaining but it was not.

"Hungry!"—"Manna"

For another month and fifteen days the people of Israel traveled the wilderness, the days and the nights, the days and the nights so hard on them, muscle and bone.

Soon the children were putting hands on their bellies, whining a different word, "Hungry! Hungry!"

And soon their parents turned the word into a vile accusation. "You, Moses," they said, "brought us into the wilderness to kill us! Would that we had died in Egypt, where we sat next to the fleshpots and ate! Here we are starving! Here, weeping, we can count numbers on our children's ribs!"

Moses said, "Your grumbling is not against me, people. It is against the Lord!" But God, their faithful God, did hear their complaint, so that Moses was able to say to the people, "In the morning you shall see the glory of the Lord, and *you shall know* that he is the Lord your God!"

In the morning...

In the sweet beginning of the day, the children of Israel arose to a delicate sight. The wide face of the wilderness was lacy white, as if it had snowed in the night, as if a light frost had formed on the ground. But the ground was not cold, and the fine, flake-like thing that lay everywhere at Israel's feet was not cold. Not frost, not snow—"What is it?" they asked.

"Taste it."

They tasted it and found it like coriander seed, like wafers made with honey. "What is it?" they asked—and in their language, the question sounded like *Manna?*

"Manna?" the children of Israel asked.

"It is the bread which the Lord your God has given you to eat," Moses answered them. "Gather as much as you can eat in a day. Gather no more than that, nor try to save any until the next day, but trust the Lord to rain some more tomorrow."

Those people who did not listen to Moses, who stored up manna against the morrow, found, on the morrow, that their manna had bred worms and stank.

Mediterranean (The Great Sea)
E G Y P T
Rameses
Baal-zo
GOSHEN
Pithom
Succoth
Nile River
The Lands of the Exodus
• City
? Probable site
Land of Shinar
Area of this map
ASSYRIA
Euphrates River
Tigris River
Babel
LAND OF SHINAR
Ur
0 50 100 150 miles

TO THE NORTH
Canaan
Ararat
Assyria
Haran
Bashan
Shechem
Gilgal
Bethel
Jordan River
River Jabbok
Mount Moriah
Jerusalem
Mount Nebo
Dead Sea
Hebron
MOAB
Gomorrah?
Sodom?
Zoar
WILDERNESS OF SHUR
AMALEKITES
EDOM
WILDERNESS OF PARAN
Marah?
SINAI
MIDIAN
Rephidim?
Mount Sinai?
Mount Horeb?
N
10 20 30 40 50 miles
Red Sea
TO THE SOUTH
Sheba

"But on the sixth day of the week," Moses said, "you *shall* gather more, enough to feed you for two days. That gathering will not spoil, and you will not have to work on the Sabbath day."

Morning by morning the people gathered manna, and ate, and were full. Year after year, through all the years they wandered the wilderness, they lived on what they ate. And that should have been the end of their complaining—but it wasn't.

"Thirsty! Thirsty!"

By stages Israel traveled until they had come and encamped at Rephidim. Again there was no water, and again the children tugged at their parents with whimper and whine.

"Thirsty! Thirsty! Thirsty!" they cried.

And again the parents confronted Moses. But this time they were so twisted, angry, and frustrated that they picked up stones and threatened to stone him to death.

"Why did you bring us out of Egypt? To kill us and our children with thirst?"

"No," Moses said, "that is not the question. The question is, why will you still put God to the test, you faultfinders? The question is, how can you doubt whether he is among us?"

Yet, despite their murmuring, God, their faithful God, did satisfy them with drink. At the Lord's command Moses took the elders of the people to the rock at Horeb. This rock he struck with his rod—once, lightly. Water poured out of the rock, and the people drank, and that should have been the end of complaining—but it wasn't.

"HAVE NO OTHER GODS BESIDES ME"

Early in their freedom, early in their wilderness wanderings, the Lord God made a covenant with his people, even as he had with their father Abraham. And under this covenant he gave them his law.

Israel, special unto the Lord God, was asked by God to behave in a special way.

At the Mountain Sinai

On and on the children of Israel traveled through the wilderness until one month had become two, and two, three. Finally they entered a land out of which there rose a singular mountain. In sight of this stony majesty they paused....

God had led them here. This was a holy mountain, the mountain of God, Sinai.

"Tell Israel," God said to Moses, " 'You have seen how I bore you on eagles' wings and brought you to myself. Now therefore, if you will obey my voice and keep the laws of my covenant, you shall be my own possession. For all the earth is mine, and you shall be to me a kingdom of priests, a holy nation!' "

Moses faced all the children of Israel, who were facing great Sinai. He lifted up his voice to them. "And you shall be to God a kingdom of priests, a holy nation! Behold!" he cried. "Now this thing is happening! The Lord God himself is coming to us in a thick cloud. And shall we not prepare to meet him?"

Israel cast glances at the high, hard mountain. Then, with nervous fingers, the people began to prepare.

They washed their clothes, every one of them.

They built a boundary altogether round the mountain so that no wandering child or

Wandering in the wilderness, Moses at last led his people to majestic Mount Sinai. For two days the people prepared for what was to come. On the third, thunder rolled from the peak, lightning split the gloom, and God commanded Moses to climb the mountain.

---

any stray beast could touch it. It was God's mountain: Any mortal who touched it would die.

By careful ceremony, Moses consecrated all the people.

On the first and second days Israel prepared. At the dawning of the third, the time was done. It had begun. God was coming down to meet them.

Thunder cracked; lightning blazed like glory round the mountain head. A thick, rolling cloud descended till the terrible rock was wrapped in it. The blast of a trumpet ripped the air, and the people shivered in their camp.

But Moses brought them out of the camp to the foot of the mountain, where they took their stand before the Lord.

Fire! Black, scarlet fire and smoke poured up from the mountain. And the mountain shook till its roots were moved, and the blast of the trumpet never ceased. The blast swelled louder, a gleaming sound. And Moses roared. And the Lord did answer him in thunder, *"Come up!"*

With no companion to comfort him, Moses went up onto Mount Sinai. Hidden from the eyes of his people, he was to receive God's commandments.

Then Moses ascended the mountain alone. And Moses was swallowed in cloud.

The Law of the Covenant

And God spoke all these words, saying,

"I am the Lord your God, who brought you out of the land of Egypt, out of the house of bondage. You shall have no other gods besides me.

"You shall not make for yourself a graven image, or any likeness of anything that is created. You shall not bow down to any image or serve it. For I the Lord your God am a jealous God, visiting the iniquity of the fathers upon the children to the third and fourth generation of those that hate me, but showing steadfast love to thousands of those who love me and keep my commandments.

"You shall not take the name of the Lord your God in vain.

"Remember the Sabbath day, to keep it holy. Six days you shall labor; but the seventh is a Sabbath to the Lord your God. In it you shall rest, even as the Lord rested after the six days of creating, even as he rested and hallowed that day.

"Honor your father and your mother, that your days may be long in the land which the Lord your God gives you.

"You shall not kill.

"You shall not commit adultery.

"You shall not steal.

"You shall not bear false witness against your neighbor.

"You shall not covet your neighbor's house, shall not suffer secret desire for his wife, his servants, his cattle, or for anything that is your neighbor's."

These ten commands the Lord God spoke in Moses' hearing, that the people might obey and be his people.

And then the Lord gave Moses many other ordinances, laws, and rules so that the people might live peacefully with one another.

He spoke of slaves—gently.

He spoke of crimes deserving death, and of lesser crimes. He said, "You shall give life for life, eye for eye, tooth for tooth, hand for hand, foot for foot, burn for burn, wound for wound, stripe for stripe."

He spoke of the ownership of things—wisely.

He spoke of moral duties, of religious practices, and of justice.

All these laws came from God, from his own mouth for his holy people, Israel.

Israel's Vow Before the Lord

Then Moses returned and told the people all the words of the Lord. And all the people answered with one voice and said, "All the words which the Lord has spoken, we will do!"

Moses wrote the words down, that they might be preserved.

Next, he built an altar at the foot of the mountain, and twelve pillars, one for each of the twelve tribes of the family of Israel.

Before this altar he made a sacrifice of oxen, catching the blood in basins.

"This," he cried as he threw half the blood against the altar, "is the blood of the covenant. The covenant," he cried, throwing half of the blood upon the people, "which the Lord has made with you!"

So the people of Israel and the Lord God were united in a sacred fellowship.

The thing was done.

The Tabernacle and Its Furnishings

But still the almighty mountain, Sinai, rolled with smoke; still the glory of the Lord flashed, burned, and rumbled at the top of it like a devouring fire.

"Come up to me," God called again to Moses—for he was not yet done. "I myself will give you two tablets of stone, whereon I have with my own finger written the law and the commandment."

Moses left the people behind, again to enter the cloud alone. This time he was gone

Moses wrote down the commandments and laws for his people. Then he built an altar and raised twelve pillars—one for each of the twelve tribes of Israel.

long, long from the people—forty days and forty nights upon the mountain.

Then God began to speak.

Steadily, carefully, the God of the covenant ordered that Moses should build him a tent for worship, a TABERNACLE. And it should be furnished with an ARK, in which the tablets of the law would be kept, on which would rest the golden MERCY SEAT.

"For I will dwell in the midst of my people!" said the Lord. "My wings shall encompass and keep them."

There should be a TABLE for sacred bread, a LAMPSTAND, and ALTAR for the burning of incense; and outside the tent an altar ornate and large for burning sacrifice; and around the whole, a court to the length of 150 feet and 75 feet wide.

Then the Lord made clear before Moses the holy festivals which the Family Israel was to keep year after year forever, everywhere: that the Passover be hallowed by the Feast of UNLEAVENED BREAD, when Israel would offer to God the first fruits of the barley harvest. Fifty days later, let Israel gather again to celebrate the harvest of wheat, in the Festival of WEEKS.

On the tenth day of the seventh month of the year, let Israel be cleansed in the Day of ATONEMENT, that Israel be hallowed from all iniquity. In that day, one goat shall be killed as a sin offering for the people; but one goat shall be kept alive. Over the living goat the priest shall confess the people's sins, so that bearing their transgressions this beast may go out into the wilderness, go out into a solitary land and be gone.

Then the Lord, who had measured before Moses the tabernacle; the Lord, who had appointed the days of feasting and of convocation—the Lord told Moses as well how he expected his people to BE and to behave.

"You shall be holy," he said, "for I the Lord your God am holy.

"When you reap, you shall not strip a field or vineyard bare, but leave behind both grain and grapes for the poor and for the wanderer: I am the Lord your God.

"You shall neither oppress your neighbor, nor rob him, nor curse the deaf, nor trip the blind; but fear me. I am the Lord.

"You shall do no injustice to scorn the poor or scrape to the great. You shall not hate your brother in your heart nor take vengeance nor bear grudges. But you shall love your neighbor as yourself: I am the Lord.

"Rise before the hoary head. Honor the face of the aged. Fear me. I am the Lord your God."

And when he had made an end of speaking on the mountain, God finally gave to Moses the two tablets of stone, the tablets of the testimony, whereon the Lord God himself had written the law.

The Golden Calf

"Where is Moses?"

"Gone! Maybe he's lost, and maybe he's dead—who knows?"

"But we cannot go after him. If any of us touches the mountain, we will surely die."

"I'm afraid of the mountain."

"Where is Moses?"

"Gone! And I think the man has forgotten us! I think he doesn't care!"

"How long has it been?"

"Too long! Longer than a month!"

"Oh, where is Moses?"

"Gone! *Gone!*"

Thus spoke all the people of Israel among themselves. Worried, lonely, frightened, and full of woe, they suffered in the absence of the man who made decisions for them.

"Where is Moses!"

"Aaron!" they said, when finally they had made up their minds. "We can't go on like

A month passed. Moses did not come down from the mountain, and the people grew anxious. At last Aaron fashioned a golden calf. This the people worshiped.

this. We need gods who will go before us and lead us. Aaron, make us gods!"

Aaron, the brother of Moses, agreed.

He picked up a child and gathered the hair back from one ear. He removed the golden ring that hung there, then the other from the other ear and set the child down.

"These are only ornaments now." He held the earrings where everyone could see them. "But as soon as I have all the rings from all of your ears, I will fashion a god to lead you!"

Suddenly all the people of Israel were plucking gold ornaments from their bodies and bringing them to Aaron.

Aaron melted all this gold. He shaped it, graved it, carved it, and made from it a molten calf.

When he brought the calf before the people, they clapped their hands and cried, "Here is our god, that led us out of Egypt!" Then they worshiped the thing they had made. Early in the morning they offered offerings. In its presence they sat down to eat and drink; in its presence they rose up to dance.

Punishment for the Sin

"Go down!" God said to Moses. "Go down to that people and take them from my sight!" God's voice was dark, heavy with anger and sorrow. "Go down to that people! Tell them I will have nothing to do with them any more!"

As Moses descended the mountain, he heard a curious noise. It was a wine-driven cry from the camp below, but he feared he heard a battle. A little closer, and he changed his mind: This was not the shout of victory. A little closer, and he knew that neither was it the weeping of defeat. Closer still, and he recognized the sound. "Why are

Moses returned and anger burst in him when he saw the people reveling before their idol. He flung down the stone tablets. They smashed at his feet.

they singing?" he wondered. "What do they have to sing about?"

Suddenly he was out of the cloud, and he saw the golden calf, and he saw Israel dancing around it, and the anger exploded in his soul.

Moses raised the two tablets of stone above his head. Down they came with a mighty crack! He broke them on the foot of the mountain—and the people knew that Moses had returned.

"You will drink it!" the prophet roared as he strode through the people to their idol, his eyes flashing. "By God, you shall *drink* your god of gold!" He seized the calf, he burned it with fire, he ground it to powder and scattered it upon the water. "Drink!" he commanded, and the people of Israel drank.

"Now, who is on the Lord's side?" cried Moses at a distance from the people. "Come to me!"

All the men of the tribe of Levi stepped away from the people and gathered around Moses.

"This is what the Lord God of Israel says," Moses told the Levites. "Take your swords. Go to and fro from gate to gate throughout

the whole camp and slay every man, his brother, his companion, and his neighbor!"

As God commanded, so did the sons of Levi do. And there fell dead three thousand men that day—because the sin that Israel committed had been serious. And it had been dangerous. They had broken loose from all laws. By their golden calf they had broken loose from God himself!

Forgiveness for the Sin

It is possible for a man to be angry, to punish someone for a sin, and still to love the one he punishes. Moses hated the golden calf, but he hurt for his people and grieved for the harm they had done to themselves.

So the prophet of God went back up the mountain of God and sought to speak with the Lord again—to pray for Israel.

The Lord said to him, "I have seen this people, and behold, it is a stiff-necked people. Let me alone that my wrath may burn hot against them and I may consume them. But of you I will make a great nation."

But Moses did not let God alone. He prayed. "Lord, Lord, turn from your fierce wrath. Remember the promise that you made to the fathers of this people, and consider that this nation is *your* people. Egypt will laugh to see that you saved a people only to slay them on the mountain. Alas, they have sinned a great, terrible sin; but now forgive their sin. And if not, then blot me, I pray you, out of the book you have written."

Moses, a man more obedient than any other on the earth, and a prophet of God, found favor in the sight of the Lord. The Lord repented of the evil which he thought to do to his people; he forgave Israel.

Then, to show Moses how much he loved him, God took the man and placed him in a cleft of rock. And God himself passed by, so that Moses might see with his own eyes the glory of the Lord. Not *all* the glory, for that would have been too wonderful for him, and he would have died. But the little part that Moses did see was enough to make his own face shine as bright as any sun.

"The Lord, the Lord God!" God proclaimed his own name as he passed by. "I am a God merciful and gracious, slow to anger and abounding in steadfast love and faithfulness, forgiving iniquity and transgressions and sin, but a God who will by no means clear the guilty!"

And then, to show that he had truly forgiven Israel, God told Moses to cut two more tablets of stone, just like the first. Upon these tablets Moses himself again wrote the Ten Commandments. These, then, he carried down to the people.

When Moses drew near to their camp, the people covered their eyes and backed away from him.

"Your face!" they cried. They were terrified. "Your face is too bright to look at!"

So Moses hung a veil in front of his face, and the people relaxed. The veil hid the light that came from speaking so closely with God.

God in the Midst of His People

Now the children of Israel, under Moses' direction, built the tabernacle and its furniture precisely as God had described it. And Moses was pleased.

"Is it not in your going with us," he said to the Lord, "that we are made different from all of the people on earth?"

The children of Israel brought more than ever was needed to build the tabernacle exactly as God had described it to Moses. Everything—the lampstand with its six branches, the veil of the screen, the altar of incense, and the altar of burnt offering—everything was made from the finest the people could give. And Moses was pleased.

Indeed, God went with them in this tabernacle. For when the work was complete, the cloud covered it, and the glory of the Lord filled the place. Throughout all their journeys, Israel moved when the cloud moved, and Israel stayed where the cloud stopped. By day the cloud of the Lord was on the tabernacle; by night it was fire in the sight of all Israel.

And Moses said to the people, "Now, Israel, what does the Lord your God require of you, but to fear the Lord your God, to walk in all his ways, to love him, to serve the Lord your God with all your heart and with all your soul, and to keep the commandments and the statutes of the Lord? Behold, to the Lord belong heaven and the heaven of heavens, the earth and all that is in it. Yet he set his heart upon your ancestors and chose their descendants, you above all peoples! Love him, therefore! And be no longer stubborn. For the Lord your God is God of gods and Lord of lords, the great, the mighty, the terrible God. Yet he is your glory. He is *your* God, who has done for you these great and wonderful things! Your ancestors went down to Egypt seventy persons—just seventy—and now the Lord your God has made you as the stars of heaven for multitude."

"HOW LONG SHALL THEY MURMUR AGAINST ME?"

Eleven months—not quite a year—the children of Israel encamped at Sinai, and the cloud remained on the tabernacle.

But then the cloud rose up and removed itself. Quickly the tent was dismantled, and the priests began to carry its pieces. The ark of the covenant went first of all, to follow the cloud and to lead the people.

Then came each of the twelve tribes of the Family Israel, one by one in perfect order.

The nation was moving. And though none of them knew it yet, they were moving toward the land that God had promised to Abraham so long ago. Canaan. The Promised Land! They were going home.

Manna's Not Enough!

Now the Lord God had promised that manna would cover the ground every dawn of their trek through the wilderness. Faithful the word of their merciful God! The morning earth was always white with the sweet, melting food. The people always ate. The people never went hungry.

But some of the people grew bored.

"Leeks!" somebody grumbled. "Leeks, onions, garlics, *something else!*" And someone, with a faraway look in his eyes: "Melons! Cucumbers!" And somebody else said, "Fish!" And they all began to moan, "Meat! We want meat! We want to chew and taste the stuff we eat. Meat!"

Soon they were patting their bellies, and rubbing their eyes—and crying! The whole lot of them, weeping for self-pity!

They made their Lord angry with them.

"Do they want meat?" God said to Moses. "Then they shall have meat. I will give them meat—not for a day, meat! Not for two days, nor ten, nor twenty days. They shall have meat for a whole month! Meat till it comes out of their nostrils! Meat till it is loathsome in their throats!"

Moses was confused. "Where do we find such meat?" he asked. "Must we slaughter our flocks just to fill a belly?"

But God said, "Is the hand of the Lord shortened? Now you will see whether my word comes true or not."

An eastward wind began to blow. It crossed the sea, the wilderness, and drove with a pounding force toward the children of Israel. But the wind was more than a wind: It carried a cargo.

Stunned, fluttering, and helpless, millions and millions of quail were blown straight at Israel, and all around Israel the birds dropped out of the sky. Meat!

Meat piled up to the people's waists! Quail lay on the ground so far around the camp that a man would have to walk a full day before he came to the end of them. Meat for the picking. Meat for the eating. Meat so abundant that it made some sick, and some of the people died.

Ever after that, the name of this place remembered the sin of the people. It was called Graves of Craving.

Men went into Canaan to seek out the good and the bad of this Promised Land. When they returned, they brought with them some of the goodness.

"Spy Out the Land of Canaan"

In the heat of the summertime, the children of Israel entered the Wilderness of Paran, some distance south of Canaan. There they stopped, there they encamped, and there an excitement jumped from tribe to tribe like sparks.

"Moses wants men!" they said. "He wants a man from every tribe to go spy out the land of Canaan. Soon, now! Soon we'll enter the Promised Land and live!"

Among the men that Moses gathered around himself were Joshua the son of Nun, whom he trusted dearly, and Caleb.

"Cross the desert," Moses ordered them. "Go into the hill country and see whether the people are strong or weak, whether the land is good or bad, whether the cities have walls or not. . . ."

The spies left. Forty days they were gone while the people waited for news.

An Evil Report

When the spies returned, the people laughed for joy at what they saw: grapes in bunches so heavy that two men had to carry them on a pole between them! Pomegranates! Figs!

And the land! How was the land?

"A good land," the spies reported. "A land flowing with milk and honey."

All the louder the merry people laughed—until it was noticed that none of the spies had joined in their laughter. Instead, the spies were shaking their heads and stubbing their toes in the dry desert dust.

"It is no good," they said.

The people stopped laughing and stared at the spies. "No good?"

"Oh, the land is good," said the spies. "But the men are a terror. Their cities are walled and dangerous. And the fighters who dwell in those cities stand so almighty huge that we felt like grasshoppers bouncing about their ankles. It is no good, no good! We cannot conquer giants!"

The joyful day was suddenly gray and empty. The people stood with their hands loose at their sides.

But Joshua and Caleb were distressed by the report. "We were there, too," they cried. "We saw the good land, too, and the huge men who live in it. *Listen to us!* The God who is with you will make those men as soft as bread before your attack. Get up and conquer them in the name of the Lord, and do not be afraid!"

But the people had been discouraged. They believed the evil report sooner than the good, and the more the doomsayers among the spies hung their heads saying, "No good, no good," the sadder the people became.

"We should have died in Egypt," they wept. "We should have died in the wilderness!" Tears rolled down their cheeks. "The Lord brings us to a land where babies will die on the point of a sword, and women will die by the edge of it. Let's go back! Let's go back to Egypt!"

They began to look for a captain to lead them back—not Moses, not the man who brought them into so much trouble.

Joshua and Caleb were so grieved by the people's grumbling that they tore their clothes and cried: "A good land! A good God to lead you into the land! How can you rebel against your God this way? Trust him! He will fight for you!"

But Joshua and Caleb were suddenly an irritation to the people because they disagreed with the new plan to return to Egypt. The people decided to get rid of irritations: They picked up stones to stone them to death.

Then it was that the glory of a watching God, the brilliance of a furious God, burst from the tabernacle like streaks of lightning.

The Punishment for Faithlessness

"How long will this people despise me?" the Lord God thundered. The people threw up their hands and covered their heads. "How long will they not believe in me, in spite of the signs which I have worked among them? I will strike them with diseases. I will cut them off. And of you, Moses, I will make a nation greater, mightier than they!"

Moses was a man more obedient than any other on the earth, yet though he was obedient he was also bold before God.

"O Lord," he prayed. "You spoke a promise, and I heard the promise, and I remember the promise, and I believe in it. You said you are slow to anger! Abounding in steadfast love, you are! One who forgives iniquity, transgression, and sins. I do not say these things of you; you said them of yourself. Now, Lord, God of these people, forgive them according to the greatness of your love. Again, again—forgive them!"

Then the Lord said, "You, Moses. Your word. According to your word I do pardon this people."

There was a long silence, as the people wondered what God and Moses had to say to one another.

Then the Lord said to Moses, "As I live, not one of the men who have seen my marvelous works and who yet have not believed in me—not one of them shall see the land which I promised to their fathers! As I live," said the Lord, "their dead bodies shall fall in this wilderness. Those who have murmured against me shall wander forty years, and year by year they shall die, tired, until the last of the number is gone and their children have grown. Their children shall enter the land of promise—and Caleb, and Joshua—but not the men who murmured."

Sadly Moses turned and told the people all the words that the Lord had spoken. A vast groan arose from the whole congregation, and with it their hands went up to God, beseeching him, pleading with him. But he did not change his mind.

"I, the Lord, have spoken!"

Yet, still—he remained with the children of Israel.

"We Have Sinned"

Forty years, a full generation, the children of Israel wandered the wilderness. Some of them died on the way. Some were born. Often they repeated their rebellious ways, and when they did, the Lord drew them back to himself and disciplined them.

He humbled them, testing them to know what was in their hearts, whether they would keep his commandments or not. He taught them that man does not live by bread alone, but by everything that proceeds out of the mouth of the Lord.

Once more, people lost faith in the Lord God. Although some of the men had brought proof of the goodness of the Promised Land, others brought tales of unconquerable warriors. The people believed the stories and wished to return to Egypt. They picked up stones to throw at those who wished to enter the good land. God's wrath came upon them.

Their clothing did not wear out. Their feet did not swell those forty years.

Once, near the end of their wandering, they repeated the old and faithless complaint. They became impatient.

"Moses," they said, "why have you brought us here to die? No food. No water. And the food we do have—why, we loathe this worthless food."

Suddenly, silently, no word of warning, the Lord sent poisonous snakes to slide among the people. There was fire in their bite, and the people suffered a burning in their blood. And the people began to die.

"We have sinned!" they wailed. "We spoke against God, and we spoke against you," the people said to Moses. They confessed, "We have sinned! Pray to the Lord that he take the snakes away!"

As he had so often before, Moses did pray for the people. And the Lord said, "Make a snake out of brass like the snakes that are moving among you. Hang it high on a pole. Then anyone bitten can look on it, and he will live."

Moses did as the Lord directed him, and the words of the faithful Lord came true. When someone was bitten by the living snakes, he had only to look toward the brass snake, and he lived.

So it was that slowly, slowly the children of Israel learned to turn to the Lord their God, to look toward him, to trust in him, to know him for their God, and to live.

Sihon, Og, and the Terror of Moab

And so it was, too, that the children of Israel were changed!

For the more they trusted the Lord their God to lead them, the mightier was their sword! The more frightful their armies!

They went into the wilderness a trembling family. They came out of it a hard and fateful nation!

What was the king of the Amorites, Sihon, against them? Nothing! He came with his men to fight Israel and to keep that nation out of his land. But Israel was traveling northward, now, and sure of the plan to turn west and to enter Canaan by crossing the Jordan River. And Israel would not be stopped. Israel fought Sihon's men and slew them with the edge of the sword and took the whole land of the Amorites for themselves.

Northward still they went like a creeping fire. Og, the king of Bashan, came out with all his people to stop Israel, but under the leadership of the Lord, Israel hit him hard, and his sons, and his people, until not one was left alive.

Then the people turned their faces to the west. Only the land of Moab lay between them and the Jordan River. Balak, the king of Moab, looked out at the nation of Israel, and he was terrified.

"They cover the face of the earth!" he said. "Like oxen licking the grass of the field, they are licking up everything in sight!"

Too frightened to fight the nation of Israel, Balak sent for a soothsayer named Balaam. "Cast a spell on these people," he commanded Balaam. "Curse them, and maybe then I can defeat them. I will pay you for the curse. Curse Israel!"

But when the soothsayer stood next to the king and looked out on Israel, he could not curse them! Instead, by the command of the Almighty God, he blessed them.

"The Lord their God is with them," he said, "and the shout of a king is among them. God brings them out of Egypt. They have the horns of the wild ox!"

King Balak heard the blessing, and he was miserable. "Curse them!" he cried. "What do I pay you for? Curse them!"

But Balaam could not. Every time he

At last only the land of Moab lay between the Israelites and the Jordan. King Balak looked out over the people and sent for a soothsayer to curse them. But the soothsayer could only speak blessings. Enraged, Balak ordered him away—and still he spoke blessings.

---

opened his mouth, blessings came out.

"For there is no enchantment against them, no divination against Israel," he said. "Behold, a people! As a lioness it rises up and as a lion it lifts itself. It does not lie down till it devours the prey and drinks the blood of the slain."

"Then shut up!" King Balak cried. "Don't curse, don't bless, don't say anything!"

But Balaam could not even be quiet; he *had* to bless Israel. "Israel shall eat up the nations, its adversaries," he said, "and break their bones in pieces, and pierce them through with his arrows."

King Balak was slapping his hands together in a perfect fit. *He* was the adversary to be eaten. *His* were the bones to be broken! "I called you to curse my enemies and three times you have blessed them! Get out of here! Go away! Go home and leave me alone!"

And still Balaam continued to bless Israel. "A star shall come forth out of Israel, and a scepter shall rise out of Israel. It shall

crush the head of Moab and break down all the peoples around!" said Balaam the soothsayer.

Israel, under God, had become a mighty and dangerous nation!

The Death of Moses

So Israel stood ready to enter Canaan, the land of promise. But Moses, one hundred and twenty years old, was not to go along. His time and his duties were done—well done. And Joshua the son of Nun was appointed by the Lord God to lead Israel into the land itself.

Yet one more time before his old eyes closed, and one more time before he died, Moses lifted up his voice and spoke to the whole people together.

"Hear, O Israel! You are to pass over the Jordan, to go in and dispossess nations greater than yourselves, cities great and fortified up to heaven, a people great and tall. Know that he who goes before you as a devouring fire is the Lord your God. He will destroy them and drive them out before you!

"But never, never say in your heart, after the Lord has thrust them out, 'Because of my righteousness the Lord has brought me to this land.' Israel, you are and you have been a stubborn people! You have been stiff-necked before the face of your God—and not once, but again and again!

"Not because of your righteousness, but rather because he has chosen to love you in spite of yourselves!

A hundred and twenty years old, having said farewell to his people, Moses climbed Mount Nebo to the very peak. And the Lord showed him the land that would belong to his descendants, the land on which Moses would never set foot. Then Moses, leader of Israel, died and was buried, his faith ever strong.

"Now, therefore," said Moses as he gazed upon the multitude, remembering the times both good and bad, the triumphs and the sorrows he had had with them. "Now, therefore, obey the commandments which I have commanded you. Love the Lord your God. Serve him with all your heart and with all your soul. Then he will give the rain for your land in its season, the early rain and the later rain, that you may gather in your grain and your wine and your oil. And he will give grass for your cattle. Walk in the ways of the Lord your God; cleave to him. Do not turn aside to worship other gods! Then every place on which you step shall be your own. No man shall be able to stand against you! The Lord your God will lay the fear of you upon all the land where you walk."

Moses fell silent. The people stood silently looking at him. Here, at the edge of time, when the people were soon to take their own land and to cease their wanderings, when Moses was soon to leave them and to cease his life—here they stood, and they loved one another.

Then Moses raised his hands and blessed them.

"Blessed are you, O Israel!" he said. "Who is like you, a people saved by the Lord? The eternal God is your dwelling place, and underneath are the everlasting arms."

Then Moses left them on the plain, and for the last time he climbed a mountain alone. Up Mount Nebo he went to the very peak. From this high place the Lord showed him all the land that Israel would possess, the land that had been promised to Abraham, to Isaac, and to Jacob.

Moses died, then, and was buried in a place unknown to any man. And there has never arisen since then a prophet in Israel like Moses, whom the Lord knew face to face.

The Lord, the Commander and King of Israel

"PASS OVER THE JORDAN! POSSESS THE LAND!"

EAST OF THE Jordan River the children of Israel sat encamped—waiting. The valleys and the hills were covered by this multitude, this vast quilt of people, and the kings in the lands nearby were filled with fear. For who could fight so many? Who could stop this massed congregation once it stood up and began to move? God, even the Lord their God, was with them!

Israel was ready to conquer the land which God had promised to Abraham. Israel was a nation, hardened in the wilderness, hungry for its home. Israel lacked but one thing: a leader to speak for the Lord.

Joshua

"My servant Moses is dead," the Lord God said to Joshua the son of Nun. Joshua bowed his head. The voice of God is a terrible thing.

"Be strong, Joshua! Be of good courage!" said the Lord. "For you shall lead this people into the land which I swore to their fathers to give them. Be strong—careful to do all the law which Moses commanded you. Be courageous—for no adversary shall be able to stand before you all the days of your life. As I was with Moses, so shall I be with you. I will not forsake you!"

"Command us, and we will be commanded," said the people of Israel to Joshua the son of Nun. They bowed their heads. Taking a leader is a solemn thing.

"Wherever you send us," they said, "we will go. And just as we obeyed Moses in all things, so we will obey you. Only, may the Lord your God be with you, as he was with Moses! Be strong!" they said. "Be of good courage!"

So Joshua the son of Nun stood on a high place above the people; thousands and thousands of faces were spread before him. "Prepare your provisions!" he cried out. "Within three days you are to pass over the Jordan, to go in to take possession of the land which the Lord your God gives you to possess!"

In three days!

Women turned away, hid their faces in their sleeves, and wept. Some of the men stood still, blinking and grinning at Joshua. The young men leaped high into the air and shattered the sky with their cheering. Israel cried. Israel laughed, Israel danced. And Israel sang, "Praise the Lord! Praise, O servants of the Lord, praise his holy name!"

For Joshua the son of Nun had said "three days."

Crossing the Jordan

In three days Joshua led the people to the eastern shore of the Jordan River. Here their singing ceased, and they stared at the river in silence.

It was spring. The northern snows were melting. And the river that cut between them and the land of promise was flooding! Its waters ran high and hard, growling at the banks and swelling in the middle. There was no bridge. There was no shallow place for fording it.

God forced back the Jordan that his people might pass. Joshua now led them, the twelve tribes. As they crossed the dry riverbed, they picked up twelve rocks. These they set in pillars on the far shore, twelve reminders of what God had done.

But the Lord spoke to Joshua, "This day will I begin to exalt you in the sight of all Israel, that they may know that as I was with Moses, so I will be with you."

That word of God was Joshua's strength, his courage. So he did not hesitate to give the people a strange and dangerous command.

"Hereby you shall know that the living God is among you," Joshua cried. "Priests!" he commanded. "Carry the ark of the covenant to the brink of the river—to the brink and beyond! Even into the water! People!" he commanded. "Follow behind! Come at a distance of a thousand yards!"

The priests obeyed.

With the ark between them, the priests dipped their feet in rushing water—and suddenly the river shrank! They walked farther, and the river diminished in front of them! The Jordan became a stream. The Jordan became a creek before the toes of the priests. The Jordan became a gentle brook. And when they had reached the middle, the Jordan was nothing more than a trickle, and all of its stones were bare.

For behold! Look to the north! Priests, look to your right! There the river had backed up, stood up, piled up on itself—and stopped!

What ails you, O Jordan, that you turn back? Tremble, O earth, at the presence of the Lord, at the presence of the God of Israel!

Now Joshua continued his commanding. "Priests!" he cried. "Stand still until the whole nation has passed to the other side. People!" he cried. "Go!"

In a great hurry, glancing at the mountain of water to the north of them, the people of Israel ran across.

And Joshua among them was still commanding.

"You!" he called to a man of the tribe of Reuben. "Grab a rock. You!" to one of the house of Simeon. "Lift a rock from the riverbed. You!" to a Levite. "Carry a rock to the other side!"

Twelve orders; twelve men; twelve rocks for the twelve tribes of Israel.

And when all had passed over, Joshua called one more time, "Priests! Come up out of the Jordan!"

In the same moment that the soles of their feet left the riverbed, the mountain of water broke down, and the Jordan was a river again, a furious, flooding, rushing river again—just as it was before.

On the westward side, at a place called Gilgal, Joshua had his twelve men set up their twelve stones in pillars high and visible. "So when, in time to come, your children see these, and when they ask their fathers, 'What do these stones mean?'" Joshua said, "you will be able to tell them the whole story of all your God has done for you—from Egypt to the drying up of the Jordan."

And then the children of Israel—ready to conquer the land of promise—celebrated the feast of the Passover, *Pesach,* exactly as Moses had told them they ought to celebrate. They remembered the Lord who had remembered them for so long. They remembered his wonderful works, his miracles, and the judgments that he uttered.

And in that same day, manna stopped. No more did God drop down this bread from heaven; for now they had the fruit of a fat land. Israel had come home. Joshua looked toward Jericho with strength and courage—toward the first battle of the conquest. . . .

Spies to Jericho

Joshua called two men to himself. "Carefully, quietly," he said, "like whispering shadows pass through the land, slip into the city Jericho. See its strength and its weakness, then bring your report to me."

The men melted into darkness and stole to Jericho. There they found the walls to be a thick protection all around the city—so thick, in fact, that people dwelt between an inner and an outer wall. The walls: They would be a problem.

They met one of these wall-dwellers, a harlot, a woman named Rahab, who heard their mission and befriended them. In the dead of night she let them into her house.

But someone saw them enter there and recognized them. That someone rushed to the king of Jericho. "Two Israelites, prowling the city!" he puffed. "Spies! Enemies! They're with Rahab the harlot."

Soon there was a pounding in the night, a beating on Rahab's door. *"Open up!"*

Rahab jumped and pointed to a ladder. "Quick! Climb it!" she whispered, and the spies went up the ladder.

"Open up! Open up!"

On the roof of her house Rahab had laid out stalks of flax to dry. "Lie down!" she hissed. She began to cover the men with flax.

"Open up!"

"I'm going to hide you," Rahab said to the spies, "because I know you will win this war. We have heard of your God, of his mighty deeds. The men of this city are shivering rabbits on account of you—"

"Rahab! Open this door or we'll break it in!"

The flax now covered the spies. Rahab stood at the top of the ladder. "Now swear to me," she whispered, "as I save you, so you will save me. When you come again you will not put my family to death!"

BOOM! BOOM! The pounding had turned to battering on the door below.

"Our life for yours," the spies said. "You keep our secret, and we'll keep our promise to let you live—"

Instantly Rahab was down the ladder and at the door. She opened it. Soldiers burst into the house. "Where are they?" they snarled, staring about.

"Who?" Rahab asked sweetly. "Where are who?"

Joshua sent spies to Jericho to seek out its strengths and weaknesses. Its strengths, they found, were its walls—double, thick. But its weakness, a small one, an unexpected one, was Rahab. She gave them shelter, hid them, helped them escape. All she asked was their promise: As she had saved them, so would they one day save her.

"The two men you took in, spies for Israel!" They tossed her bed. They scrambled up the ladder.

"Oh, is that who they were? Spies? Then you'd better hurry, or you'll miss them."

"What?" The soldiers came down from the roof and stared at her.

"Two men were here, yes," she said, "but just before the city gate was closed they slipped out. They are an hour ahead of you, but they suspect nothing and they are walking slowly. If you run—"

The soldiers were gone, running. Rahab

closed her door and locked it, then climbed to the spies again. She took them into a room whose window looked out of the wall. There she tied a stout rope and hung it outside.

"Run to the hills," she said, "where you can hide three days until the soldiers have returned. Then go your way."

One of the Israelite spies gave her a scarlet cord. "We will remember what we have sworn to you," he said. "Bind this cord to this window. When we return to take the city, be sure that your family is gathered here in this room. Those in the room shall live; those out of it shall die."

Rahab said, "So be it." And the spies swung down the rope and left.

Three days later they made their report to Joshua. "Truly, the Lord has given all the land into our hands. The inhabitants are fainthearted because of us."

"Commander of the Army of the Lord"

On his own, alone, Joshua went to study the walls of Jericho, to measure their strength with his eye, to plan his battle strategy.

As he was pacing secretly outside the city, he saw a man standing in front of him. The man drew his sword.

Joshua stood absolutely still.

"Are you for us," Joshua said, "or against us?"

The man answered in a rumbling voice. "As commander of the army of the Lord, I have now come."

Joshua, by the words alone, was struck to his heart. He bowed his face to the very ground and worshiped. "What does my Lord bid his servant?" he asked.

The commander of the Lord's army said to Joshua, "Put off your shoes from your feet, for the place where you stand is holy."

And Joshua did so.

The Fall of Jericho

So, then, it was not Joshua, but the Lord who planned by peculiar stratagem to crush the city Jericho. The battle was one of almighty power and almighty mystery....

The gates of Jericho were shut tight, and the walls were unbreachable. No one could get in; no one was coming out. There would be no clash of swords, no swinging, stabbing battle in an open field. And certainly the people of Jericho had great stores of food inside; they could wait a long time before they needed to come out. A siege would take a long, long time.

One morning, the watchmen of Jericho leaned over the walls to see a strange sight. Israel's warriors were marching—but not to the attack!

In perfect order, in dreadful silence, and staring straight ahead, the warriors marched *around the city.* In their midst was carried the ark of the covenant, and before the ark marched seven priests dressed in white. All at once the seven priests raised curved rams' horns to their lips.

BRAAA! BRAAA!

The trumpets blew a chilling sound. Jericho gasped. But the warriors of Israel did not break stride. Marching, marching under the horns of the glory of God, surrounding the ark of his presence, marching, until once they had circled the city, then silently marching away again, marching back to their camp—and that was it.

The day was still again. The plains outside the city were empty: footprints, but no feet; memory of the mysterious procession, but no warriors, no priests, no ark visible any more.

What was Israel doing?

On the next day the warriors and the priests of Israel appeared again, marched the same course full round the city, blasting the rams' horns but uttering no human sound, no shout, no word, no whisper. The ark of the Lord compassed the city once, then the ark of the Lord was carried back to camp—and silence.

What was Israel doing?

And on the third day, and on the fourth, and the fifth, and the sixth, the same mysterious march.

Israel—*what?*

But for the seventh day the Lord had given other instructions to his warriors, and on the seventh day his terrible might burst forth upon the city Jericho.

At sunrise Israel emerged from camp and marched as they had marched before, but this time once around was not enough. They circled the city a second time, a third, a fourth—

Then, at the seventh round, Joshua threw back his head and called, "Shout! Warriors, shout! For the Lord has given you the city!"

The warriors raised a great shout. They roared. Their voices cracked the air with human cry—and the walls of the city fell down flat. Then every warrior turned his face toward Jericho. Every warrior leaped the crumbled stone in front of him, entered, and fought—and utterly destroyed all in the city.

Only Rahab and her family were brought out alive before Joshua burned the city and cursed it forevermore.

A mighty wonder of God: Jericho was a dead thing. The door to Canaan, the way into the land of promise, was open to Israel.

So the Lord God was with Joshua, and his fame was in all the land.

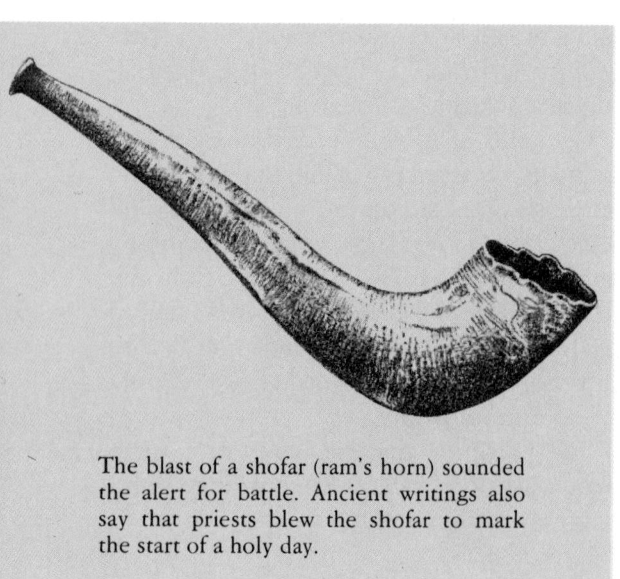

The blast of a shofar (ram's horn) sounded the alert for battle. Ancient writings also say that priests blew the shofar to mark the start of a holy day.

Truly, Jericho's walls were unbreachable. But God had a plan for his people. Israel circled the city six times, and on the seventh, Joshua commanded, "Shout, warriors!" They raised their voices in a powerful roar, and the walls began to crumble.

Achan's Sin

But for all the joy of victory, an evil thing had happened during the fall of Jericho; an Israelite warrior had sinned.

The Lord had made his commandment very clear: that all the treasures of Jericho belonged to him and to no man. Yet one man, Achan, saw an exquisite robe and gold and silver, and the desire for these things broke his obedience. During the fighting he stole them and buried them under his tent.

So when Joshua sent three thousand warriors to defeat the next city, the Lord did not go with them.

Ai was a tiny town. Israel should have cracked it with a single blow. Instead, as soon as the men of Ai charged out of the city, Israel turned in fright and made a miserable retreat. The enemy chased these scrambling warriors until thirty-six of them had perished and the rest had fallen exhausted into Israel's camp.

Joshua was astonished at the failure. He tore his clothes. He covered his head with dust. He fell down before the ark of the Lord. "O Lord, what can I say when the people of Israel have turned their backs to the

With the victory, God had given Israel a commandment: Jericho's treasures are mine. But Achan had seen a fine robe, gold, and silver. Overcome with greed, he stole them and hid them.

enemy?" he said. "The Canaanites will hear of this. They will surround us and cut us off. And what will you do for your great name?"

But the Lord said to Joshua, "Get up! Israel has broken my commandment and cannot stand before the enemy. Until the disobedient man is found, until he is utterly separated from you, I am with you no longer."

Early the next morning Joshua approached every tribe of Israel, and then the families, and then the households, and then the men. He narrowed the multitude until one man stood before him, his head hanging, his lips quivering, his knees weak; this man was Achan. And Achan, standing alone, apart from the people, confessed his sin. And having confessed his sin, he was punished, cut off from Israel, cut off from the earth.

Now Joshua and the warriors of Israel returned to Ai. And God went with them.

In darkness half the army lay down and hid behind the city—each man seemed only a bush—while the other half took up an open position in front. With the morning, then, the men of Ai saw no more than a part of Israel's army. "Oh, ho! The rabbits!" They laughed at what seemed a pitiful collection of warriors. "The rabbits are back for more!"

Out of the city the men of Ai charged; every last man shot through the gates. Joshua waited a moment, then commanded his men to retreat, to run away! The men of Ai ran after Israel, and across the fields.

But when the city was empty, Joshua raised his spear—a signal! Now the men who were in ambush leaped out. They entered the naked city and set it afire. Then *they* charged after the charging men of Ai.

The men of Ai saw the smoke, turned to look at their burning city, and screamed! Here was a new army descending on them, sudden and savage. They turned again, and knew they were lost, for the warriors they had been chasing were running no more. Sudden and savage and keen as a sword, they were coming back to fight. Israel's two armies met together, and Ai was caught between.

Because of their value, exquisite robes tempted Achan and other soldiers. Garments worn by the rich and powerful were often adorned with gold thread and gems.

This time the Lord God had commanded his people, and this time Ai died. Only the king of Ai was left alive.

Canaan Conquered

Jericho and Ai were at the heart of Canaan. These two cities had sat in the middle of it, and now, by Joshua's victories, the land was cut into two parts, and fear spread like fire through the southern part, through its cities, its kings, and its fighting men, and through the northern part as well.

Joshua attacked these two pieces one at a time in two driving thrusts.

To the south he turned his grim and brilliant face. Five kings and five armies came out to meet him all at once. But the Lord said, "Not a man among them shall stand before you!" And Joshua defeated them, king and soldier alike.

Hear the names of the cities that Joshua besieged. And hear the names of the cities that fell before him in the south: Makkedah and Libnah; Lachish, yea though Horam king of Gezer came to help its king; Eglon and Hebron and Debir. So Joshua defeated the hill country, the Negeb and the lowland, and the slopes. Then he turned his face to the north.

There a mighty host of armies was drawn up to meet him at the waters of Merom, armies from all over northern Canaan, as far east as the Jordan, as far west as the Great Sea. They were like sand on the seashore. But the Lord said, "Do not be afraid; I will give them over, slain, to Israel!"

So Joshua released a sudden attack upon this host, as though a spring had shot every one of his men into the midst of them. He terrified them. He cut them down, slaughtered them to the last man. Then he hamstrung their horses and burned their chariots with fire. They were no more, neither the warriors nor their weapons. And after them, he brought their cities down as well.

A long time Joshua made war against all those kings. He took the whole land, according to all the commandments that the Lord had spoken. And when he was done, the land was divided among the tribes of Israel. And the land had rest from war.

The Wish and the Warning of Joshua

"Thus says the Lord, the God of Israel, 'I gave you a land on which you had not labored, and cities which you had not built,

Long did Joshua lead Israel in battle, until the land was theirs. When the Family Israel had settled, he called them together and exacted their pledge to fear the Lord and ever serve him. These were his last words. And the people were witnesses to their own promise to be faithful to God.

---

and you dwell therein. You eat the fruit of vineyards and oliveyards which you did not plant!' "

These were Joshua's last words to the children of Israel. When he was an old man, and when all the people of Israel had settled snugly into their new home, he called them to Shechem, where he spoke these final words to them.

"Therefore, fear the Lord," he said, "and serve him in sincerity. Put away false gods. And if you be unwilling to serve the Lord, choose this day whom you will serve, whether the gods of the days before Abraham or the idols once served in this land. But as for me and my house, we will serve the Lord."

The people answered, "Far be it from us to forsake the Lord to serve other gods. We also will serve the Lord, for he is our God!"

Joshua said to them, "Ah, he is a jealous God! If you forsake him, he will turn and do you harm, after having done you good."

The people said, "No, but we *will* serve the Lord!"

Joshua said, "Then you are witnesses against yourselves, that you have chosen to serve him."

And they said, "We are witnesses."

After these things, Joshua died—Joshua the son of Nun and the servant of the Lord, a man full of strength and courage, one hundred and ten years old. His bones were buried in his own land. And this is a wonder—that after so many centuries of slavery and wandering, a man of Israel should be buried in his own land!

GOD'S ANGER, HIS PITY: THE JUDGES OF ISRAEL

"When Israel was a child, I loved him," the Lord God said, "and out of Egypt I called my son." By his calling, by his loving, his people now lived in a good land. By the might of the Lord they had conquered Canaan and made it their own.

But matters did not always stay so calm and so righteous, for Israel did not clear the land of *all* the Canaanites! In pockets throughout the land, in cities and on the high places, the enemy continued to dwell side by side with Israel and continued to worship their own gods, the Baals.

"The more I called them," said the Lord with sorrow, "the more they went from me. They kept sacrificing to the Baals, and burning incense to idols."

That was the evil Moses had commanded them not to do; that was the gross wickedness that Joshua had warned against. Yet the people did it. They forsook their God. And God, in his anger, withdrew his protecting arms from around them.

When the Lord no longer stood before Israel, enemies unkind and murderous swept down on his people, marauding the land and killing them. So Israel bled. Israel groaned. And Israel cried out to the Lord God for mercy.

"Yet it was I who taught Israel to walk," said the Lord out of his infinite love. "I became to them as one who eases the yoke on their jaws. I bent down to them and fed them." Hearing the cry of his people, God sent his mighty spirit and raised up among the people a JUDGE, someone to gather them together in a hard army. Then the JUDGE of the Lord, and the army of Israel by the strength of the Lord, defeated this enemy. And the land was at peace again—for a little while.

Only a little while. For this is the poor story that was repeated again and again—over and over for two hundred years. That Israel would anger God by forsaking him; that God would permit an enemy to grieve Israel; that Israel, oppressed, would plead with God for mercy; that God would save the people of Israel through the leadership of a JUDGE—and then that Israel would anger God by forsaking *him*. . . .

Evil Brings Evil: The Canaanites

And the people of Israel did what was evil in the sight of the Lord. And the Lord sold them into the hands of the Canaanites.

Jabin, a Canaanite, king of Hazor, grew grim and powerful in the very midst of Israel. His commander, Sisera, had nine hundred chariots of iron, a terrible war machine that utterly crippled poor Israel, because the fighters in Israel fought only afoot. Jabin ruled! Jabin crushed the people. Under Jabin, crime and robbery ran through the land like hungry wolves, and the people were terrified. Farmers hid in the forests; nobody worked the fields. Travelers avoided the highways, creeping from place to place on the back roads, and nobody brought goods into the land for Israel to buy. No food. No provisions. No going out, no coming in. No peace, no freedom—no hope!

The people of Israel cried out to the Lord God for help.

Deborah

In those days the spirit of the Lord lived in a woman named Deborah. This remarkable prophetess spent her days seated beneath a palm tree, whither came all the people of Israel with their arguments, and she settled them. They came with their fears, and she calmed them. They came with their yearning questions, and she answered them. They came with their hunger for some word of the Lord, and she spoke it!

Deborah was a JUDGE.

Now Deborah summoned Barak, whose name means "lightning."

"This is what the Lord says to you, Barak!" Deborah's eyes flashed with a divine fire. "He says, 'Gather ten thousand men of Israel at Mount Tabor. I will draw Sisera and his nine hundred chariots to meet you, to fight with you, by the river Kishon. And I will give him into your hand!' "

Barak said to Deborah, "If you will go with me, then I will go. But if you will not go with me, then I will not go."

Deborah looked at this general and spoke softly, "I will go with you, Barak. But there will be no glory for you in this war. Not by your hand, but at the hand of a woman shall Sisera die."

The Women Defeat the Enemy!

When Canaanite Sisera heard that Barak had gathered an army on Mount Tabor, he smiled at the shuffling challenge of the Israelites.

"Your hands against my iron," he said. "Your legs against my horses! Your feet and my nine hundred chariots! And your leader," he sneered, "is a woman! A mother in Israel!"

Into the field he sent his chariots of iron and his fighting men. They marched in the valley along the river Kishon, rumbling eastward to Mount Tabor, to meet and to murder Israel.

Heavy, gray clouds filled the sky above them. Another rumbling came from that place: thunder. Drops of rain spat against

But the Israelites forgot their promise, and God gave them to the Canaanites, until they pleaded for help. Then led by Deborah, Israel waited on the mount to face the chariots of the terrible Sisera.

their armor and their iron chariots. The air tightened. It would storm soon.

Deborah looked down from the mount and saw the enemy coming. A chill wind began to pull at her robe.

"Now!" she cried to Barak. "This is the day! The Lord has given Sisera into your hand, and he goes before you. Attack!"

NOW!

Barak and ten thousand men swept down the face of the mountain and charged across the valley floor.

BOOM!

Lightning ripped open the belly of heaven. Rain fell down in a thundering flood. The river swelled, tumbling in a furious white water, until it burst its banks and covered the valley with water. And the water made mud. And the mud sucked nine hundred chariots into it, so that they could not move. Sisera's army was helpless before Israel's attack. The dripping swords of Israel slashed his men down and down until not one was left alive.

The river swelled with furious rain, and Sisera's chariots sank deep into mud. Sisera leaped from his chariot and fled, splashing through the water, seeking a place to hide from Israel's swords.

But Sisera himself had jumped from his chariot and fled away on foot.

He ran hard and searched for some place to hide.

At last he came near the tent of a man named Heber, and there he saw Jael, Heber's wife, beckoning to him.

"Here, my lord!" she called. "Hide here, and don't be afraid!"

Sisera slipped into the tent, for Heber, he thought, was a friend of his. He fell down on the floor gasping for breath. "Thirsty, thirsty," Sisera breathed. "Give me some water!" And all the rain of heaven pounding on the tent skins!

Jael brought him milk to drink, and Sisera relaxed. She covered him with a rug. "Guard the door," he sighed. And the man, exhausted, fell asleep.

But Jael did not guard the door. With a stake and a mallet a woman killed the mighty general of the Canaanite army.

And when Barak came in pursuit of Sisera, Jael met him. "Come," she said. "I will show you the man you are seeking."

The Song of Deborah

In that same day, Deborah raised her voice. She laughed at the triumph of God, and she sang:

"Hear, O kings! Give ear, O princes; to the Lord I will sing!

"He came among us, and the earth trembled. The heavens dropped, yea! the clouds dropped water! The mountains melted before the Lord!

"The torrent Kishon swept away the enemy! The onrushing torrent, the torrent Kishon!

"So perish all thine enemies, O Lord! But thy friends be like the sun as he rises in his might!"

After that, the land had rest for forty years.

Sin Turns to Suffering: The Midianites

The people of Israel did what was sin in the sight of the Lord. And the Lord gave them into the hands of the Midianites seven years.

Out of the east this enemy came, riding the loping camel. Whenever Israel had planted a crop, the Midianites seized that crop and ate it themselves. Wherever the grass grew thick and good, the Midianites mowed it with the teeth of their beasts till none was left. The wheat, the fruit of the land, its food in every form, the Midianites gobbled, and the Israelites starved.

And when Midian put the point of his sword to Israel's throat, the people ran to the mountains and lived in hiding. Their houses were caves, and their doors were holes in stone.

Israel was brought very low because of Midian. And the people cried out for help to the Lord God.

Gideon

Crouched inside of a winepress, so that he could work in secret, a man was busy threshing a little wheat from his harvest.

"Gideon," said a voice outside the press.

Gideon, hunched over his wheat, didn't move. Who wants Gideon?

The voice came again. "The Lord is with you, you mighty man of valor!"

Slowly Gideon raised just his eyes above the wooden wall. "Mighty man? Valor?" He saw another man sitting under an oak tree, and this man was an angel of the Lord, but Gideon didn't know that.

The angel smiled at Gideon's eyes. "Go in this might of yours," he said, "and deliver Israel from the hand of Midian. I send you."

Gideon stood up. His head and his neck appeared above the wooden wall. "How can I deliver Israel?" he said. "My clan is the weakest in the tribe; and I am the weakest in my family."

"But I will be with you," said the angel. "You will smite Midian as one man."

Gideon thought for a while. "I need a sign," he said. "Please—wait here till I come back with a present."

The angel of the Lord nodded, and Gid-

The people cried to the Lord for delivery from Midian's hand. Then God sent an angel to Gideon—weak Gideon, Gideon who asked for signs and certainties. He peered out of a winepress at his visitor.

eon leaped out of the winepress and ran to prepare a dinner.

"Put your dinner on this rock," the angel said when Gideon brought it out to him. "Pour the broth over it."

Silently, Gideon did.

Then the angel reached out the tip of his staff and touched the meat. Immediately fire sprang out of the rock and burned the dinner away. And the angel of the Lord disappeared.

Gideon clutched his head. "Oh, no!" he wailed. "Now I have seen the angel of the Lord face to face!"

But the Lord said, "Peace be with you, Gideon. You will not die!"

And the Lord said, "Behold! The Midianites, and the Amalekites, and the people of the East are all encamped in the Valley of Jezreel. By your hand, Gideon, I will deliver the people of Israel from this enemy!"

There was much for Gideon to think about, so he thought hard. Between the winepress and the house, between the morning and the evening, he thought about the Lord's promise. Then he said to the Lord, "I need a sign. I am laying some wool on the threshing floor. If by morning there is dew on the wool alone, and if the floor around be dry, then I shall know that you will deliver Israel by my hand."

In the morning Gideon ran and grabbed his wool. He squeezed the fleece and wrung enough dew from it to fill a bowl; but the floor was dry.

Yet still he thought about the Lord's command, and by evening he spoke to the Lord once more. "I need a sign," he said. "I will put the same wool on the same floor. If by morning the wool is dry and the *floor* is wet, then I shall truly know your victory over the enemy."

And God did so that night. The wool was dry, the floor all around was wet—and the Spirit of the Lord took possession of Gideon, and he became a JUDGE of Israel.

Gideon's Army Is God's

Gideon sounded the trumpet! The startling ram's horn! The call to arms! And the call went through Israel.

From the tribe of Manasseh came warriors to fight under him; from the tribes of Asher, of Zebulun, and of Naphtali they came, thirty-two thousand men at arms. They gathered beside the spring of Harod, south of the Midianite camp.

It was a powerful force.

But the Lord said to Gideon, "They are too many for me! If this army murders Midian, then Israel may become proud, saying, 'My own right hand delivered me!' Make it clear that I am fighting," said the Lord. "Reduce the numbers, Gideon!"

So Gideon cried to his army, "Whoever is afraid, whoever is trembling before this war, let him go home!" Twenty-two thou-

Signs and more signs Gideon demanded, proof that it was to be he who would save Israel. In the morning he received God's answer: Wet with dew was the fleece on the floor, but dry the ground around it.

sand men took their gear and left; ten thousand remained.

But the Lord said to Gideon, "They are still too many for me! Take them to the water to drink, and we will make a test of it."

At the water's edge, ten thousand men drank.

"Separate them," said the Lord. "Those that lap the water like a dog, place here. Those that kneel to drink, there."

The two groups, when they formed, were unequal. Those that knelt numbered nine thousand seven hundred; those that lapped the water were a tiny band of three hundred.

And the Lord said to Gideon, "Done! With three hundred will I deliver you!"

So Gideon dismissed the men who knelt, and a tiny band watched as a good-sized army marched away and left them alone.

"I Need a Sign"

"Arise!" said the Lord to Gideon. "Attack the camp of Midian, for I have given it into your hand!"

But Gideon did not arise. And Gideon, with his little band of men, did not attack. Instead he stared at the enemy in the valley below him—forces, fighters, and frightening camels in such numbers that they covered the valley floor like locusts.

"Then if you fear to attack," said the Lord, "go down in the darkness, you and your servant alone. Go, listen to the men of Midian. Their fears will strengthen your courage."

So Gideon slipped into the valley, stealing close to the outposts, where he lay hidden, and listened.

"I had a dream," said one Midianite guard. "A little biscuit tumbled into our camp. It rolled up to a tent and hit it, and the tent fell down! It just flipped over and lay flat!"

The other guard shivered in the darkness.

"That little biscuit is Gideon!" he said. "God has given this whole camp into his hands."

Quietly Gideon praised the Lord for what he had heard, and he slipped back to his little bunch of men.

"A Sword for the Lord and Gideon!"

Gideon divided his band into three companies, a hundred each. Into each man's hands he put a trumpet and a jar with a torch inside.

"Watch me!" he commanded them. "When we come to the outskirts of the camp, do exactly what I do."

Then he separated the companies, so that they spread out in the darkness and surrounded the enemy camp.

Gideon waited. He waited till the first watch was done. He waited till the guards for the second watch had taken their positions in the camp—

Then, suddenly, he smashed his jar! All round the camp the jars began to shatter, and the noise was like swords on swords. Gideon blew his trumpet, and three hundred trumpets blared in the night. Torches flared everywhere around Midian. "A sword for the Lord and Gideon!" roared Israel. "A sword for the Lord and Gideon!"

And the Midianites, and the Amalekites, and all the people of the East started from their tents horrified. In utter confusion they fell on each other, each man screaming, each man stabbing at his friend!

"A sword for the Lord and Gideon!"

The camels snapped their traces and charged through the camp. The armies of Midian took to their heels in a wild panic and fled. Soon the enemy was in full and ragged retreat—and *now* Gideon sent messages to his greater forces, to pursue Midian across the land, to slay, and to drive them out!

In the weeks that followed, the land was cleansed of the enemy, and its kings were killed. Gideon, the little biscuit, commanded with force, with faith, and with absolute courage, and all Israel came to see that the Spirit of the Lord was upon him.

"Rule over us," Israel said to Gideon when the fighting was over and everyone was home again. "You and your son and your grandson, be our king!"

But Gideon said to them, "I will not rule

Gideon led his army, loud with the crash of jars and the blare of trumpets, into the Midianite camp. The Midianites fell on each other in confusion, friend stabbing friend, fleeing through the night.

over you, nor will my son. It is the Lord God who is your king!"

So Midian was subdued before the people of Israel, and the land had rest for forty years, while Gideon was yet alive.

The Birth of Samson

The people of Israel did what was evil in the sight of the Lord, and the Lord gave them into the hands of the Philistines for forty years.

There was a certain man named Manoah who lived with his wife just a few miles from the land of the Philistines, a man and a woman who had borne no children. To Manoah's wife now appeared an angel of the Lord.

"You shall conceive and bear a son," the angel told her. "Rejoice! And rejoice again, because this child shall be separated from all others. He shall be holy to the Lord—the Lord's man! From the moment of his birth, and for his whole life long, no razor shall cut a hair of his head; neither shall he drink wine nor any strong drink; neither shall he eat any unclean thing. For he shall begin to deliver Israel from the hand of the Philistines!"

"A man of God came to me!" Manoah's wife told him. "His face was an angel's face—very terrible!"

In time the woman bore her son, even as the angel had said, and called his name Samson. The boy grew. The Lord blessed him. And the Spirit of the Lord dwelt mightily in Samson.

The Lion and the Riddle

Now the Lord God looked for a chance to bring his mighty man, Samson, against the Philistines—to hurt them, to embarrass them, and to triumph over them, for they were a plague on Israel. God would demoralize them through the single Samson! But he began this work with a simple and common event. Samson saw a Philistine woman and wished to marry her.

While he was traveling to her town to talk with her, a young lion leaped suddenly into

A mighty man was Samson, his power a gift from God. One day, in the countryside, a lion barred his way. Samson brought down the beast with his bare hands.

his path. The lion roared and crouched to spring at him. But the Spirit of the Lord came with such power upon Samson, that *he* sprang instead! He attacked the lion bare-handed and tore it apart as if it had been a bleating lamb.

Some time later Samson was walking the same road. This time he was going to marry the woman; it was the week of his wedding. He turned aside to see that lion's carcass—and behold! a swarm of bees had built a hive in its hollow chest! Samson scraped the honey into his hands and went on, eating as he went.

Now there came to his wedding feast thirty Philistine guests. When everyone was eating, laughing, enjoying the feast, Samson stood up.

"Let me ask you a riddle," he said. "If you can answer it in seven days, I will give you each two fine robes. But if you cannot answer it, then each of you will give me two, and I shall have sixty."

"What is your riddle?" they asked.

And Samson said, "Out of the eater came something to eat. Out of the strong came something sweet."

In the next three days the laughter of the Philistines died away, and there was much muttering instead. They were upset. Every answer that they could think of for Samson's riddle was wrong.

On the fourth day they went to his wife. "Look," they said. "Either you find the answer to your husband's riddle, or else we will burn your father's house down."

So Samson's wife went to him and turned her back to him. "You hate me!" she said.

"No, I don't," said Samson.

"You hate me, you don't care about me, you don't love me," she said, and she was weeping.

"I just married you!" Samson said.

"What is marriage?" she wept. "A chance to mock my countrymen with a riddle? What is marriage when a husband keeps secrets from his wife?" Then she turned and kissed him and stroked his forehead. "Please, please tell me the answer to your riddle," she pleaded.

But Samson said, "I haven't even told my parents, so should I tell you?"

She jerked away from him and turned her back. "You hate me!" she said.

Day and night the young wife wailed and pouted before her husband; day and night, until his will was broken. The answer he gave her was not a simple one; it was another riddle. Immediately she told it to her countrymen, and before the seven days were up, they came to Samson, grinning.

"What is sweeter than honey? What is stronger than a lion? Now, pay us the price of the bargain."

Samson was furious. "If you had not plowed with my heifer," he said, "you would never have figured my riddle!"

And now began the Lord's destruction of the enemy by one man. For the angry Samson went to another Philistine town where he killed thirty men. The robes of the dead men he threw at the wedding guests, and then he returned to his own town in a rage, leaving his wife behind.

Foxes, Torches, and Fields of Wheat

After a while, at a time when the wheat fields were yellow and ready for harvest, Samson's anger cooled, and he went to visit his wife again.

"No!" said her father. "You can't."

"She's my wife," said Samson.

"Not any more," said her father. "I thought you despised her, so I gave her to your best man. *They're* married now. But I have a younger daughter, much prettier than she—"

In a flash Samson's whole rage was back again. "This time," he growled, "I am blameless in what I do to them!"

He went and caught three hundred foxes. He tied them tail to tail. To each pair of foxes he bound a torch stick soaked in oil. Then he lit all the torches and sent the flaming foxes through the wheat fields of the Philistines. Like wakes behind boats, the fire spread out behind the foxes, burning the wheat to the ground, and burning the olive orchards too.

"Who did this?" the Philistines cried. And when they heard that it was Samson, they went after his former wife and her father, and burned them.

"I swear," Samson roared when he heard of this murder, "I will be avenged on you!" Samson smote the murderers hip and thigh; he killed them in a hard and hectic slaughter. Then he went into hiding from the Philistines.

Thus the Lord continued to hurt the enemy by the arm of one strong man.

The Jawbone of an Ass

So the Philistines entered the land of Israel, looking for Samson. When they could not find him, they began to plunder cities of the Israelites.

"And we will not stop this," they said to Israel, "until Samson is our prisoner, tied up and helpless, so we can do to him what he has done to us!"

The Israelites knew where Samson was hiding. His own countrymen came to him, then, in a great force, determined to deliver him to the enemy. They would rather save their cities than Samson's skin.

"The Philistines are our rulers!" they told Samson, as if he never knew this.

"I have only done to them what they did to me," Samson said.

"But now they are coming up against us, too!" his countrymen whined. "So we've come to tie you up and to give you into their hands."

Samson said, "Swear to me that you will not kill me."

"No, we will only bind you," they said. And Samson let them do it. With two new ropes, three thousand Israelites bound one; then they brought him to the Philistines.

When they saw their mighty enemy tied up like a captive, the Philistine army shouted with laughter and delight. They ran

To save the cities, Israel delivered Samson to the enemy. But Samson took vengeance on the Philistines.

forward to meet him, clapping their hands and hooting.

But the Spirit of the Lord came upon Samson, and his strength bulged, and the ropes snapped like thin flax. He found a jawbone of an ass, curved, with terrible teeth at the end of it. He seized it and ran forward; he swung his weapon and slew one thousand fighting men of the Philistines.

"With the jawbone of an ass," he cried, "heaps upon heaps! With the jawbone of an ass I have slain a thousand men!"

Delilah, Delilah!

For twenty years, Samson judged Israel. In all that time his great strength bewildered the Philistines. He hurt them, embarrassed them, and struck them down. They hated this mighty man of God.

Therefore, when Samson began to love a woman of the Valley of Sorek, the lords of the Philistines saw a chance to humble him. They knew his weakness.

Her name was Delilah, this woman of Sorek.

They came to her secretly and offered her money. "A great deal of money. Eleven hundred pieces of silver from each of us," they said, "if you will discover the cause of his great strength and tell us what will overpower him."

Delilah gazed at this fortune in her mind; and Delilah agreed.

In the evening she touched the thick muscle of Samson's neck and shoulders. "Look at me," she said, and he did. Then she said, "Please tell me, dear Samson, wherein your great strength lies. However could some poor someone bind you so that you would stay bound?"

Samson's eyes twinkled. "If someone

The Philistines vowed to destroy Samson. They went to Delilah, whom he loved, and promised her money if she would discover the source of Samson's power. Delilah wheedled and begged. Samson smiled.

would bind me with seven new and undried bowstrings, then I would be weak and be like any other man," he said.

So at Delilah's whisperings, the lords of the Philistines brought her seven new and undried bowstrings. They hid themselves in an inner room of her house and waited.

When Samson fell asleep that night, Delilah tied him in the bowstrings. "The Philistines! The Philistines!" she sang out. But Samson stretched and the bowstrings snapped as if they had been touched by fire. The secret of his strength was still not known.

Delilah pushed out her bottom lip. "You have mocked me," she pouted. "My Samson has told me lies. Please let him tell his Delilah how he might be bound."

"If someone should tie me with new ropes that have never been used," Samson said, his eyes dancing, "then I would be weak and be like any other man."

Delilah had no trouble getting such ropes, and in the night she tied Samson up with them. She stepped backward. "Samson, look out!" she cried. "The Philistines are here!"

But the sleepy Samson shrugged, and the new ropes snapped like old thread. The secret of his strength was not known.

A third time Delilah tried her trick; a third time Samson tricked her in return. "Weave seven locks of my hair into a loom, as if the hair were thread," he smiled. He was enjoying the game. "Tighten the weave with a pin, and then I will be weak."

When he was sleeping, then, Delilah did just that. "Samson!" she screamed. "The Philistines have got you!"

But when he stood up, he pulled the posts of the loom out of the ground by his hair; the pin, the loom, and the web all clattered after him, for he was not weak.

Now Delilah began to cry. This was no game for her! "How *can* you, Samson?" she wept, turning her back to him. "How can you say you love me when you mock me so hatefully? Three times I've asked you a serious question; three times you've laughed at me." For days and days the woman pressed the man, wailing and weeping, spurning him and nagging him by turns—urging him, until he was vexed to death. Finally he shared his whole secret.

"A razor has never touched my head," he said. And his eyes were not smiling; they were closed in weariness. "If I be shaved, then my strength will leave me, for my special vow to God shall have been broken. I will be weak, like any other man," Samson said.

Again Delilah called the lords of the Philistines, who came with her money in their hands. They hid in a back room while she took Samson's head upon her lap. Songs she sang to him, then; gentle words and soft caresses of love she gave to him, until his eyes drooped and he fell asleep, his head upon her knees.

"Now!" Delilah hissed, not moving a muscle. A man appeared in the room. This man quietly cut off the seven locks of Samson's hair. Then Delilah gave Samson a savage pinch. "The Philistines have got you *now*, Samson!" she said.

He woke. He tried to break free as at other times, because he did not know that the Lord had left him.

But the Philistines grabbed Samson. They gouged out his eyes, and they bound him with bronze fetters. To Gaza they dragged their enemy, where they set him to work turning a millstone to grind their wheat.

The man, the prisoner, the judge of Israel, would raise his head, some mornings, to look toward heaven; but he saw nothing, not even the sun, for he had no eyes.

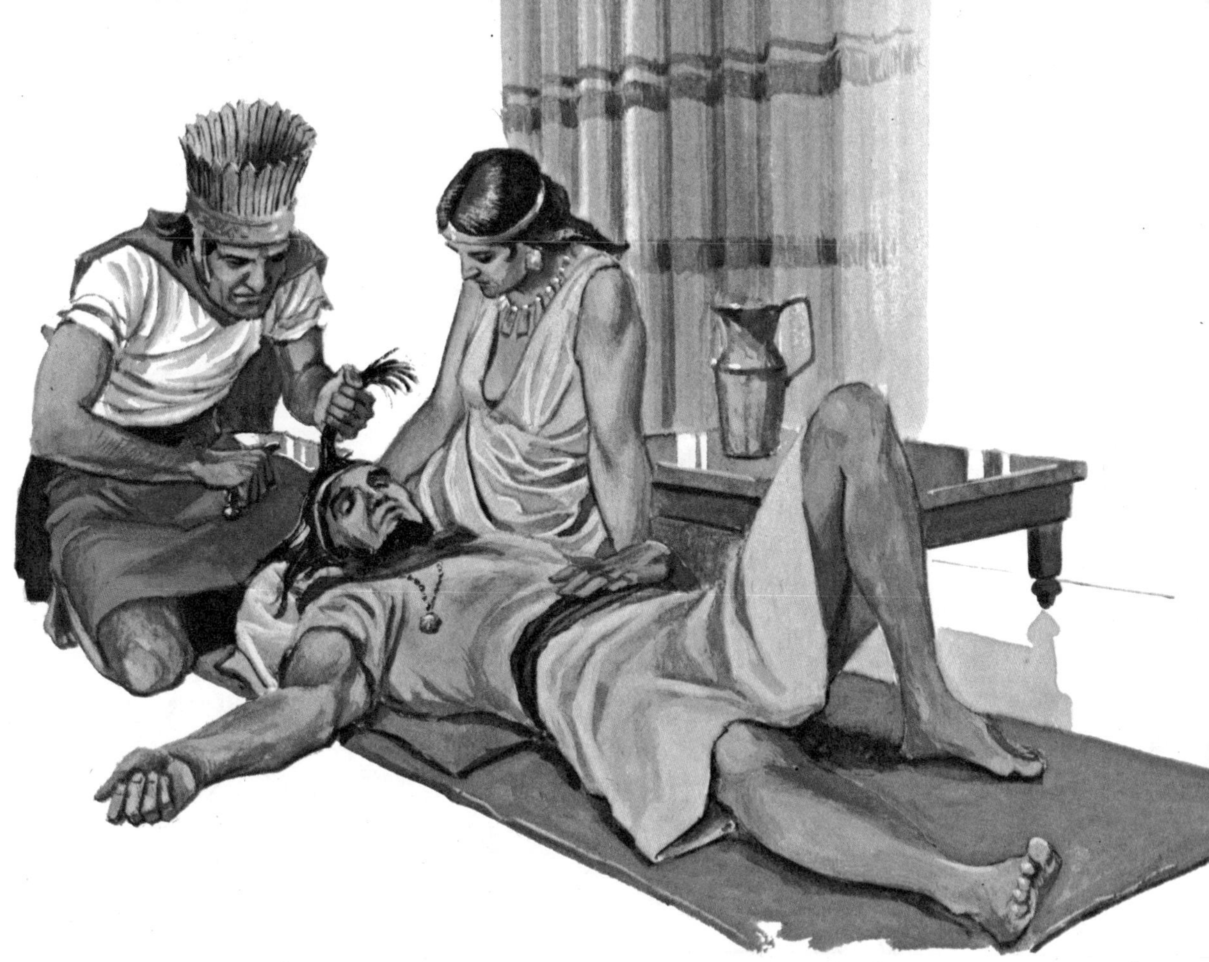

Long, long, did Delilah persist, and finally Samson broke his vow to God. He revealed to Delilah that his strength lay in his hair. Then while he slept, the Philistines took their revenge.

The Death of Samson

Yet the hair of Samson's head began to grow again.

Now there came a day when all the lords of the Philistines gathered together in their temple to celebrate their victory.

"Praise be to Dagon!" they cried. "Praise him, for he has given Samson into our hand! Praise be to our god, Dagon!"

As the day drew on, their celebration became wild, and they called for Samson. They wanted to see their enemy blind and bound. They wanted him in the middle of the courtyard, all surrounded by the many terraces of the temple, so that the people could laugh at him.

Samson came; the mighty man was led into the courtyard by a small boy. A roar went up from the people while he stumbled and felt his way to a spot between two pillars.

"Ahhh, Samson!" thundered three thousand voices from the roof. All around Samson, on every side, the temple was full of the sound of confident, mocking voices. "Ahhh, Samson! Cut and cut down!"

But Samson leaned on the boy and whispered in his ear, "Let me feel the pillars on which the temple rests. Let me lean against them," he said.

Then Samson raised his eyeless face. He

Helpless Samson was blinded and imprisoned. At last came the Philistines' victory celebration. Amid jeers and laughter, he was led to the courtyard. No one noticed that his hair had grown long again or that he prayed. With renewed strength, he avenged the wrongdoings of his captors.

felt—he did not see—the ring of twisted, shouting mouths that overhung the roof. But his attention was higher than the roof. Blind Samson was staring toward heaven. Weak Samson was praying.

"O Lord God, remember me," he prayed. "Strengthen me only this once, O God, that I may be avenged upon the Philistines for one of my two eyes."

And Samson grasped the two middle pillars upon which the temple rested, and he leaned his weight upon them, his right hand on the one and his left hand on the other.

"Let me die with the Philistines," Samson said.

Then he bowed with all his might, and the temple fell upon the lords and upon all the people who were in it. So those whom he slew at his death were more than those he had slain during his life.

He had judged Israel for twenty years.

RUTH

Naomi in Moab

In the days when the judges ruled, there was a famine in the land of Israel. So a man named Elimelech left his town of Bethlehem and went to seek greener land. He took his two sons and his wife with him; and his wife's name was Naomi.

They settled in Moab.

Soon Elimelech died. Then Naomi's sons married Moabite wives, one named Orpah, and the other named Ruth.

After about ten years both of Naomi's sons died, too, so that the woman was bereft of sons and husband.

She heard that the Lord had visited Israel and had given the people food, so she set out from Moab with her daughters-in-law and began to return home.

But Naomi said to her daughters-in-law, "Go back, each of you, to your mother's house. May the Lord deal as kindly with you as you have dealt with the dead and with me." Then she kissed them, and they lifted up their voices and wept.

They said, "No. We will go with you to your people."

Naomi said, "Please go back. I have nothing else to give you, my daughters. I am too old to have a husband, too old to bear sons. And even if I did bear sons, how could you wait until they were men, and how could you wait so long to marry again? Go back, my daughters."

With tears Orpah kissed Naomi and left.

But Ruth said, "Entreat me not to leave you or to return from following you. For where you go I will go, and where you lodge I will lodge. Your people shall be my people, and your God my God. And where you die I will die, and there will I be buried."

When Naomi saw that Ruth was determined to go with her, she said no more. So Naomi returned to Bethlehem with Ruth the Moabitess, her daughter-in-law. They came at the beginning of the barley harvest.

"Look! Here is Naomi come back!" the people said.

But Naomi said, "Do not call me Naomi.

Call me Mara. Call me bitter, for the Lord has dealt bitterly with me."

Boaz of Bethlehem

Now Ruth saw the harvesting in the fields. So she said to Naomi, "Let me go follow the harvest. Let me gather what the reapers leave behind them in the fields."

Naomi said, "Go, my daughter."

As Ruth stooped in the fields, gleaning barley ears, there came a man who owned some of the land.

"The Lord be with you," he said to his reapers. And they answered, "The Lord bless you." His name was Boaz. He was a man of wealth.

Then Boaz said to his servant, "Whose maiden is this?"

The widow Ruth returned to Bethlehem with Naomi, her mother-in-law. There, Ruth gleaned in the fields of Boaz, Naomi's kinsman. Boaz made sure that the reapers left barley in the field for Ruth.

"She is the Moabitess come back with Naomi," said the servant. "She has been gleaning from early morning till now without a rest."

Boaz went and spoke to Ruth. "Listen, my daughter," he said. "Glean only from my land. I have charged the young men not to hurt you, and when you are thirsty, you may drink from their water."

Ruth bowed down before him and said, "I am a foreigner. Why should you notice me?"

"Naomi is my kinswoman," Boaz said. "I know all you have done for her, and I pray that you be rewarded by the Lord, under whose wings you have taken refuge."

"You are a gracious man," said Ruth.

At mealtime Boaz fed her bread, wine, and parched grain. And in the afternoon he saw to it that his reapers left extra barley for her in the field.

"Blessed be the man who took notice of you!" said Naomi when Ruth had shown her what a fine success she had that day.

"The man's name is Boaz," said Ruth.

"Ah, blessed be he by the Lord, whose kindness has not forsaken the living or the dead!"

Ruth gleaned in the fields of Boaz until the end of the barley and wheat harvests.

Meeting

Naomi said, "There is a law, Ruth, that when a man dies his next of kin should marry the widow and care for her. Is not Boaz our kinsman? Tonight he is guarding his grain on the threshing floor. Wash yourself; anoint yourself; put on your best clothes, and go to him."

That night, after Boaz had eaten and drunk, and when his heart was merry, he lay down at the end of the heap of grain. Then Ruth came softly and uncovered his feet and lay down, too.

At midnight the man was startled. A woman lay at his feet! "Who are you?" he said.

"I am Ruth," she said. "Protect me, sir, for you are next of kin."

"Well, this is a kindness," he said, "that you have not gone after young men, either rich or poor." Then he said, "Do not be afraid, my daughter. I will do for you all that I should. But there is a closer relative to you than I am. If he is not willing to do what he ought for you, I will."

So she lay at his feet until morning, but she arose before it was light, and he sent her back to Naomi with a present, six measures of barley.

Marriage

Boaz went that day and sat in the gate of the city until he met Naomi's closer relative. Then he called ten other men to be witnesses of what they said, and they spoke together.

Did this man, Boaz asked, want to buy a parcel of land that Naomi was selling?

Yes, said the man.

Well, then, he must also marry Naomi's daughter-in-law, Ruth the Moabitess, Boaz explained.

No, said the man, he didn't want to do that, too. Boaz could do that.

"You are witnesses this day," Boaz said to the ten men, "that I am permitted to make Ruth the Moabitess my wife!"

So Boaz took Ruth and she became his wife. And the Lord blessed her and she bore a son.

By the mercy of the Lord, Naomi's bitterness was taken away. The child was comfort to her old age, and she became his nurse.

The boy's name was Obed.

Obed became the father of Jesse.

And Jesse became the father of David, the great king of Israel.

In time, Ruth and Boaz were married, and a son was born to them. Ruth and Boaz and Naomi rejoiced. All of Israel would have cause to celebrate, for Obed would be grandfather to Israel's great king.

Monarchy! Israel's Most Glorious Days

"GIVE US A KING!"

FOR THE LAST two centuries, there had been no king in Israel. The Lord God alone was king for all his people. When an enemy arose to trouble Israel, the Lord and no king had led his armies and destroyed that enemy. When the times were peaceful, the Lord and no king had asked peaceful obedience from the people. Israel was different from the nations that surrounded it, because Israel's king was the Lord!

But now there came an enemy that would not be destroyed. And the people of Israel lived in dread both day and night, and year after year. So the people of Israel became urgent with their God. They demanded from him what he had never before given them. They demanded to have what even now the Lord considered hurtful. They prayed for a perilous thing. . . .

THE ENEMY lived along the Great Sea, south and west of Israel. They fought with iron weapons and with chariots; and, like no enemy before, they fought with a purpose. They didn't want food; they didn't want tribute money; they wanted to possess the whole land of Israel. They were the *Philistines,* and they had created a hard, military tyranny in the long years after the death of Samson. Israel, from the north to the south of its borders, trembled.

THE DEMAND which the Israelites made of the Lord God was this: "Appoint for us a king to govern us like all the nations." They said, "Give us a king to govern us!" They cried, "Let us have a king over us, that we also may be like all the nations, and that our king may govern us and go out before us and fight our battles!"

God heard their prayer. God would give them their desire. Through the last judge, Samuel, the Lord God would give them a king.

The Birth of Samuel

There was a man in Israel who had two wives and trouble. One wife, whose name was Peninnah, had borne him children, both sons and daughters, but the other wife, whose name was Hannah, had borne him no children at all.

Now, the man, Elkanah, loved Hannah the most—and that was the trouble. For Peninnah, seeing this love for the other, shivered with an everlasting jealousy.

"Look at you!" she would hiss to tease Hannah. "Not a baby, for all of your effort. You may be a wife, Hannah, but what good is that if you can't be a mother, like me?"

This chatter went on year after year, so that Hannah bowed her head and suffered because she had no child.

Every year Elkanah took his family to Shiloh, where he made a sacrifice to the Lord, and every year they ate a meal together in that place. It was there that the teasing finally became too much for Hannah to bear.

As Elkanah passed the portions of food around, Peninnah whispered, "Let's count them, Hannah. How many portions for you, and how many for me? There's one for you;

here's one for me. Oh, look! Here's another for me! And another, and another, and another, all for me! But no more for you? Why, that's because I have children to feed, isn't it? But you—poor Hannah! Poor, childless Hannah!"

Hannah stared at her one portion of food, listening to this insistent whispering; and then her heart broke. She burst into tears and could not eat.

"Why, Hannah!" said her husband. "What is this sorrow? Why is your heart so sad?"

"Poor, dear Hannah," said Peninnah. "The Lord has given her no children."

"So?" said the man, still looking at his dearest wife. "Am I not more to you than ten sons?"

Hannah rose and left her food untouched. She went to the temple of the Lord, where she prayed and wept bitterly, both at once.

"O Lord, if you will look on my suffering," she prayed, "and if you will give me a son, then I will give him back to serve the Lord for all the days of his life."

Hannah's distress was so deep that she prayed without making a sound. Her lips moved, but her voice could not be heard, because it was her heart that cried out to God.

So the priest of that place, when he noticed her praying, thought that she was drunk.

Peninnah had many children; Hannah had none. Year after year, Peninnah taunted Hannah until, at Shiloh, Hannah's heart broke. She prayed silently to the Lord, not knowing that one day he would bless her with a son who would become judge of Israel.

"Woman!" he said. "Put wine away from you!"

"Oh, no, sir," Hannah said. "I haven't had any wine. But you have seen my great anxiety. I have been pouring out my soul before the Lord!"

Then Eli, the priest of that place, looked kindly on her and said, "Go in peace, and the God of Israel grant you your prayer."

Hannah's face did become peaceful at that. "Thank you, sir," she said, and she returned to eat her food.

In due time the Lord God remembered Hannah. She conceived and bore a son, and she called his name Samuel. And when he was old enough, she brought him with great joy back to the old priest Eli.

"For this child I prayed," she said, "and the Lord has answered my prayer. Therefore I have lent him to the Lord. As long as he lives, he is lent to the Lord!"

So the boy Samuel stayed with Eli, while Hannah returned to her home. The Lord blessed her five times over, with three sons and two daughters.

But Samuel grew in the presence of the Lord.

Evil Priests in Israel

Eli was an old man, growing older. He had two sons who were priests in Israel, one Hophni and the other Phinehas. They were utterly worthless men. Eli grieved at their sinning, but he could not control them.

When the Israelites brought meat to sacrifice to God, Hophni and Phinehas took to themselves not only the priest's portion, but the people's portion as well.

"Why do you do such things?" their father said.

Such things, and worse things yet, they did, for even the portion of the sacrifice that belonged to the Lord God they demanded for themselves. And if someone argued with them, they threatened violence. Thus they treated the offering of the Lord with contempt.

And their father said to them, "No, my sons! If a man sins against a man, God will mediate for him; but if a man sins against the Lord, who can speak for him, or who can help?"

Eli was a sad man, growing sadder, for he spoke, but his sons would not listen to him.

"Speak: Thy Servant Hears!"

The word of the Lord was precious in those days. Visions were not frequent.

Samuel ministered under Eli most obediently, performing even small services for the poor man. Old man Eli, nearly blind! Sad man Eli, very fat—he was growing helpless, and he needed the quick, strong arms of the boy. So Samuel slept close to the priest's chambers, always ready to wake, to run, and to serve.

One night, when it was almost dawn, the Lord called, "Samuel! Samuel!" The boy said, "Here I am." He ran to Eli and said, "Here I am, for you called me."

But the priest said, "No." He touched the boy's shoulder in the dark. "No, I did not call you, son. Lie down again."

So Samuel went and lay down.

"Samuel!" the Lord called a second time. "Samuel!"

The boy got up and ran to Eli. "Here I am," he said. "You called me."

The priest reached and hugged the boy and patted his back. "Shhh," he said in his ear. "I did not call you, my son. Go lie down again."

A third time the Lord called to Samuel; and a third time Samuel rose up and went to the priest. "Here I am," he said, "for you called me."

But this time Eli knew that it was the Lord. Therefore he said to Samuel, "Lie

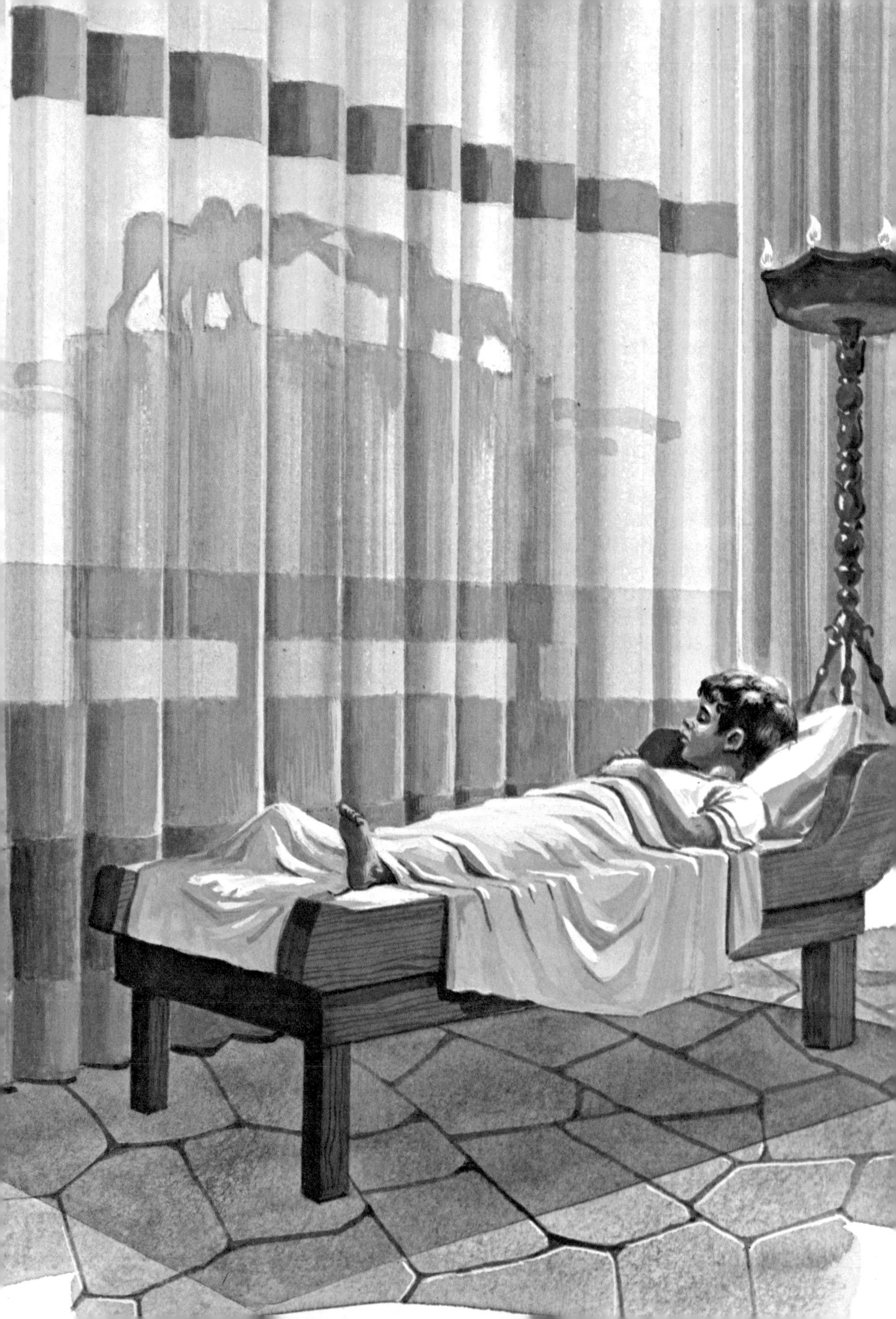

down and wait. And if he calls you, you shall say, 'Speak, Lord; thy servant hears.' "

So Samuel went and lay down and waited in the night. He was lying near the ark of God. The lamp of God made a dim, flickering glow.

And the Lord came and stood forth, calling, "Samuel! Samuel!"

The boy whispered, "Speak, for thy servant hears."

Then the Lord said, "Behold, I am about to do a thing in Israel, at which the two ears of everyone that hears it shall tingle! I am about to punish the house of Eli forever, for the iniquity which he knew, because his sons were blaspheming God and he did not control them. Both Hophni and Phinehas shall die on the same day, and there shall not be an old man in Eli's house forever!"

Samuel lay very still until morning. Then he got up silently and began to do his duties, opening the doors of the temple as he always did, as if it were just any other morning of the year. He was afraid to tell Eli his vision.

But Eli called to him, "Samuel, my son."

Samuel said, "Here I am."

"Well?" said Eli. And Samuel was silent.

"Whatever it was that he told you," Eli said gently, "do not hide it from me. Samuel, tell me."

So Samuel told him everything and hid nothing from him. And Eli said, "It is the Lord. Let him do what seems good to him."

And Samuel grew, and the Lord was with him. All Israel, from Dan to Beer-sheba, knew that Samuel was established as a prophet of the Lord, that visions now most rare were granted unto Samuel at Shiloh. The word of Samuel went everywhere in Israel.

A Thing to Tingle the Ears

Then it happened that the enemy of Israel prepared for open warfare. From their five cities the Philistines streamed north to Aphek. From Ashdod and Ekron came armies coldly organized, troops trained from childhood to fight under clean, concerted orders. From Ashkelon and Gaza and Gath marched forces in unison, forces and horses and chariots of iron—a host like none that Israel had ever seen before. None had been so military; none had planned so well; and none had stayed with such tenacity. Israel was already bowed before them; now the Philistines wanted to break Israel altogether!

The Israelites encamped at Ebenezer. Men from every tribe gathered to fight, but they were a ragged force that fought in bunches.

In an open field the armies met, the Philistines' lean battle line, the Israelites' running clumps of men. When the battle spread among them, Israel was defeated. The survivors retreated to the camp, having lost about four thousand men—and out of their blackened, bloody faces came the cry: "Oh, why? Why has the Lord put us to rout?"

Then the elders of Israel thought of a way to bring the presence of the Lord into this war.

"Let us," they said, "bring the ark of the covenant of the Lord here from Shiloh, that the Lord may come and save us!"

So the priests left Ebenezer for Shiloh. The priests brought back the ark of God. The priests' names were Hophni and Phinehas.

Such a mighty shout went up in the camp

Near the ark of God, in the dim flickering light, Samuel lay down and waited for the word of the Lord. The old priest Eli knew who had called the boy, and soon all Israel would know that Samuel, son of Hannah, was the Lord's prophet.

of Israel when Israel saw the ark that the whole earth resounded—and the Philistines looked at one another and trembled.

"What does the shouting mean?" they asked. And when they heard that the ark had come, they were afraid. "A god is among them!" wailed the soldiers. "Woe to us! These are the gods who smote the Egyptians with every sort of plague! Woe to us!"

"No! Take courage, O Philistines!" their commanders cried. Hard orders went out from the generals: "Fight like men, lest you become the slaves of Israel as they have been of you. Acquit yourselves like men, and fight!"

So the Philistines and the Israelites met a second time upon the Plain of Sharon, between Aphek and Ebenezer.

Ever since his sons had taken the ark from the temple, old Eli had been sitting on his seat by the gate, his heart trembling for the ark of God.

Now a man returned to Shiloh from the war. His clothes were torn, and his head was covered with earth. But Eli was blind and could not see him. The man began to tell his news. All the city raised a sorrowful voice and cried out.

"What?" called Eli from his seat. "What is this uproar?"

Then the man came to Eli. "I am he who has come from the battle," he said. "I fled the battle today."

Eli said, "How did it go, my son?"

The man said, "Israel was defeated. The armies ran in the face of a great slaughter."

And the man said, "Your two sons Hophni and Phinehas are also dead."

And the man said, "The ark of God has been captured."

When the man mentioned the ark of God, Eli fell over backward from his seat by the gate. And his neck was broken, and he died, for he was an old man and heavy.

He had judged Israel forty years.

"We Will Have a King over Us!"

A long time passed, now—about twenty years—in which the people of Israel were sorry for their sins, repentant before the Lord.

And Samuel was their judge.

"If you are returning to the Lord with all your heart," he said, "then put away the foreign gods from among you. Turn to the Lord. Serve him only, and he will deliver you out of the hands of the Philistines!"

Yet, though the Lord did help them against the Philistines, this enemy did not pass away. These tyrants of five cities would not pass away! Neither could Israel finally defeat them.

Therefore, it was under a stormy cloud that Samuel worked and judged the people, the skittish Israelites.

Year after year he traveled among four cities, comforting the nervous, admonishing the wayward, deciding disputes, administering justice—judging.

But in Bethel a request was made which Samuel ignored for a while. And in Gilgal, and in Mizpah, the same demand was put to him. But Samuel shook his head. Even in his own hometown, even in Ramah, the people said, "Appoint a king for us!"

When Samuel was old he made his sons to be judges over Israel. But his sons, like the sons of Eli, were men both greedy and perverse. So Israel's demand grew shrill in Samuel's ears.

"Appoint a king to rule over us!" they said. "Behold, you are old, and your sons do not walk in your ways. So give us a king to govern us like all the nations!"

Samuel was displeased. "Do you know what a king will do?" he said. "He will drive your sons to war! Do you know what a king will do? He will force your children to work for him as plowmen, as smithies and carpenters, as cooks and bakers! He will take for himself. For himself he will take the best of your grain and your grapes, the best of your cattle, your donkeys, your flocks. And they shall be his, and you shall be slaves. Do you know what a king will do? In that day you will cry out because of your king!"

But the people refused to listen to Samuel. Again they demanded. "But we will have a king over us, that our king may govern us and go out before us and fight our battles!"

Samuel prayed to the Lord, and the Lord said to him, "Listen to the voice of the people." The Lord said, "They have not rejected you; they have rejected me from being king over them. Listen to them," said the Lord, "and make them a king."

The Israelites demanded a king. Samuel, old and wise, warned that a king would make slaves of them.

SAUL: FIRST KING OF ISRAEL

Saul Is Anointed King

There was a man in Israel, of the tribe of Benjamin, who was the son of Kish, who was born the son of a farmer, and who might have been a farmer all his days—except that the Lord chose him.

Saul was handsome. When he walked out among the people, his head and shoulders rose higher than the head of any other man. There was a wild and urgent fire in his face, so that he could charm people, he could excite them, he could inspire them. When this tall man said, "Do!" the people heard him, and they did!

Yet, for all his marvelous talent, Saul began life as a humble man.

In humility he heard the news that he was to be king of Israel. Samuel said to him, "All the wonderful things in Israel are coming to you and to your father's house!"

And Saul said, "Am I not a Benjaminite, from the least of the tribes of Israel? And is not my family the humblest in that tribe? Then why do you talk this way to me?"

These two, the judge and the future king, had met when Saul passed near Ramah, looking for certain of his father's donkeys which were lost.

Samuel asked to speak to Saul in private. When they were alone, he took a vial of oil and poured it on Saul's head and kissed him. "The Lord has anointed you," said Samuel, "to be prince over his people. You shall reign over the people of the Lord, and you shall save them from the hand of their enemies round about."

No one knew that this was taking place, for Saul's servant had gone ahead of them. For the moment, it was a secret matter.

"Now watch for your chance, Saul, son of Kish," Samuel said. "When the time is right for men to know that you are their king and leader, then do whatever your hand finds to do, for God is with you!"

When Saul turned to leave Samuel, God gripped his heart, and God filled Saul with courage.

Oh, he was a handsome man, with earnest fire in his face! And he would, for all of his

Humble, handsome Saul knelt before Samuel. And from this anointing, Saul was to be king of Israel, heroic in battle and loved by the people. In time, Israel would know Saul's courage had come from God; Israel would have its long-awaited king.

life, be a driven man. Right now it was the Spirit of God that drove him, mightily, so that when he was among his own people, he rolled his eyes and prophesied, and his friends were astonished. Later, a darker spirit would drive him, and the people would be grieved.

But for now Saul returned home and watched for the chance to reveal his kingship to Israel. One month after Samuel had anointed him, that chance came. . . .

Israel Accepts Saul As King

Nahash, the leader of the Ammonites, brought his warriors to an Israelite city named Jabesh-gilead. He circled the city with his men. Since the people of Jabesh knew that they could not defeat him in fighting, they offered Nahash food and money if only he would leave them in peace.

But Nahash had come for something more sinister. Vile, ugly, was his purpose, for it was not food that he wanted, or money from Jabesh. "I am going to humiliate you," he said. "I am going to cripple this population so that it cannot fight again! I am going to gouge out all your right eyes!"

When that news spread through Israel, the helpless people wept aloud, a helpless lot. And Saul—even in the fields, where he was plowing behind a team of oxen—heard the noise. "What ails the people?" he asked.

"Nahash! Jabesh! Right eyes! Gouged!" someone lamented. But Saul did not weep! This was his chance, and the Spirit of God came mightily upon him. That fire blazed in his face. Rage flashed from his eyes. He slaughtered his team of oxen on the spot, then cut them into pieces—roasts and ribs, shanks and livers. He sent the butchered meat everywhere in Israel, and this is what he said: "Whoever does not come to fight

with Saul and Samuel against Nahash, he will find his oxen slaughtered the same as these!"

Then the dread of the Lord fell upon the people, and they came out as one man. Under Saul's leadership there gathered three hundred and thirty thousand warriors. Under Saul's leadership this massive army went to Jabesh-gilead, where Saul launched a three-pronged attack against Nahash, defeating and scattering his warriors so terribly that it was as if a hammer had hit glass!

The people of Jabesh burst with joy; nor would they ever forget Saul's rescue of their city.

"King!" the people of Israel cried. "Let Saul be our king!" For they had seen the Spirit of God moving within him.

Then Samuel made the announcement: "Behold, I have listened to your voice in all that you have said to me and have made a king over you. And now, behold," said Samuel, "the king walks before you.

"Come," the old judge said, "let us go to Gilgal and there renew the kingdom."

So all the people went in high spirits to Gilgal, and there they made Saul king before the Lord. The private anointing of Saul had become public, and all of the people now knew: THERE WAS A KING IN ISRAEL!

The Reign of King Saul

When Saul became king, he created a standing army of three thousand men—men who did nothing but fight, or else train to fight. Two thousand were under his own command; one thousand he placed under the command of his son Jonathan.

Then Saul fought against all his enemies on every side, against Moab, against the Ammonites, against Edom, against the kings of Zobah—and most particularly against the Philistines.

In one battle against the Philistines Jonathan performed a heroic deed, so that the battle was won. But his father performed a sin, so that the Lord began to be displeased with him—the good and the bad together, all on a single day!

On the north side of a deep gorge the Philistines had encamped their armies. Again and again they raided the towns nearby, so that the Israelites took to the caves. They hid in holes, among the rocks, in tombs, and in cisterns.

On the south side of the same gorge Saul had encamped his own armies, and he waited for Samuel to come so that a sacrifice might be burned to the Lord before any attack.

When Samuel did not come, Saul grew nervous. The wild light in his face flashed fiercely, and he could not control it. His troops began to desert him—so Saul himself seized wood and meat, and Saul himself burned the offering to the Lord. Immediately Samuel appeared in the camp, angry. "What have you done?" he demanded. And he said, "You have done foolishly! You have not kept the commandment of the Lord your God! You took rights unto yourself, King, that were not yours for the taking! You have sinned!" Saul had sinned.

In one way, Jonathan was like his father: He, too, was impatient. But he acted differently from Saul.

Quietly he left the camp of Israel. He and his armor bearer slipped down into the gorge between the two camps, and then he began to climb the northern side.

From a private anointing to a public proclamation, Saul stood tall beside Samuel—the time had come. Before the Lord and the happy throngs of Israel, humble Saul became King Saul. But, growing bold and brash, he would one day lose God's blessing.

The Lands of the Old Testament

- City

? Probable site

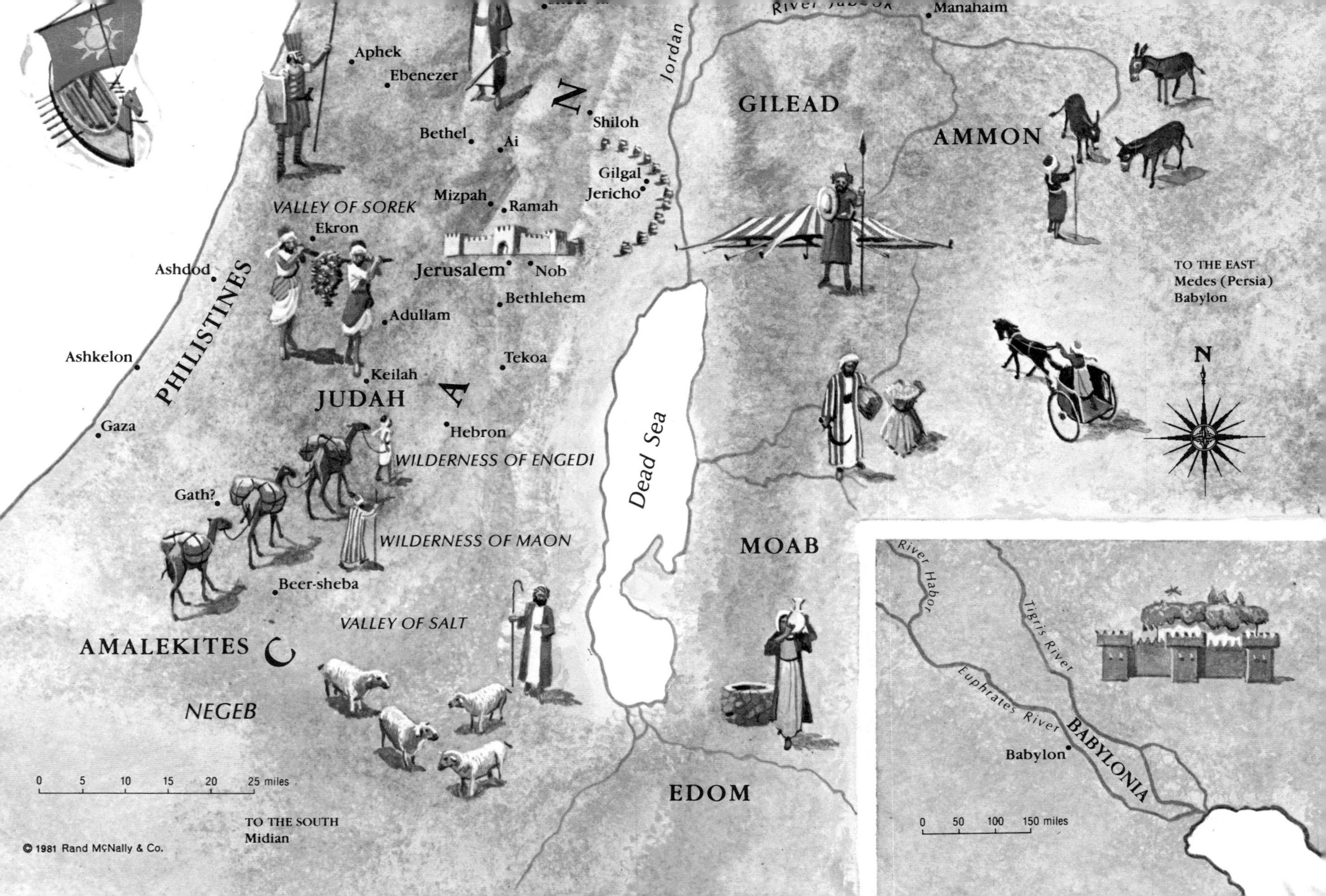

Aphek
Ebenezer
Bethel
Ai
Shiloh
Jordan
Manahaim
GILEAD
AMMON
Gilgal
Jericho
Mizpah
Ramah
VALLEY OF SOREK
Ekron
Jerusalem
Nob
Ashdod
Bethlehem
Adullam
PHILISTINES
Ashkelon
Tekoa
Keilah
JUDAH
Gaza
Hebron
WILDERNESS OF ENGEDI
Dead Sea
Gath?
WILDERNESS OF MAON
Beer-sheba
VALLEY OF SALT
AMALEKITES
NEGEB
MOAB
EDOM
TO THE EAST
Medes (Persia)
Babylon
N
0 5 10 15 20 25 miles
TO THE SOUTH
Midian
River Habor
Tigris River
Euphrates River
BABYLONIA
Babylon
0 50 100 150 miles

Impatient for battle, Jonathan and his armor bearer scaled the north wall of the gorge. They would soon surprise and defeat the Philistines.

The Philistines never expected an attack to come out of the gorge, for the wall was straight up and as smooth as a tooth. They were confident of protection on that side, and they were shocked when Jonathan suddenly stood tall on the rim of the cliff. Shocked, confused, frightened, and after that, dead! For Jonathan struck them down, and his armor bearer killed them: one, two, ten, twenty men in a slaughter! The whole camp began to panic. Then the Lord God shook the earth in a quake, and the Philistines ran back and forth in terror. Saul, on his side of the gorge, heard the howl and saw the enemy surging to and fro. He dispatched his armies to the weakened Philistine camp. And the Israelites, when they saw how matters stood in their favor, leaped out of their holes and hiding places to join the fight.

So the Lord delivered Israel that day; but the Lord, that day, was displeased with Saul because he chose to sacrifice on his own.

And the mighty spirit of God began to pass away from him.

The Disobedience of King Saul

Not once, but again and again Saul listened to his own heart first, and to the Lord second.

"Go," the Lord said to him during his reign, "smite Amalek. Utterly destroy all that you see. Spare neither man nor woman, ox nor sheep, camel nor anything that is theirs!"

Saul went and fought the Amalekites, and Saul defeated them. But then Saul and the people spared the king. And the best of the sheep and the oxen and the fatlings and the lambs and all that was good he did not destroy!

The word of the Lord came to Samuel. "I repent that I have made Saul king! He has turned away from me, and has not performed my commandments!"

It became Samuel's sad duty, then, to speak this hard word to Saul.

When they met—the judge of God and the first king of Israel—Saul was smiling on account of his victory over Amalek. Samuel was frowning.

"I have done God's bidding!" said Saul.

"Then why," said Samuel, "do I hear the bleating of sheep and the lowing of oxen?"

Saul lost his smile. "The people," he said, "it was *they* who brought these things from the Amalekites. And they want to sacrifice them to God," he mumbled. "But *I* utterly destroyed—"

"Stop!" cried Samuel. "Hear what the Lord said to me this night."

Saul lowered his head and said, "Say on."

"Behold, obedience is better than sacrifice," said Samuel, "and hearkening to God is better than the fat of rams. Because you have rejected the word of the Lord, he has also rejected you as king."

Samuel turned to go, but Saul reached out and grabbed his robe with such a pitiful appeal that it tore.

"Do not leave me!" Saul pleaded.

But Samuel only gazed at the rip in his clothing. "So," he said. "The Lord has ripped the kingdom of Israel from you and has given it to one who is better."

Then Samuel himself went and killed the king whom Saul had not killed, and after that he went home to Ramah. Samuel did not see Saul again until the day of his death, but he grieved over him, because Saul's life would be one of torment from now on.

Saul had not followed the commandments of God. Now he was rejected as king. Now he suffered.

DAVID: GREATEST KING OF ISRAEL

David Comes to Saul

The urgent fire that once burned so boldly in Saul's face did not go out. But it changed. It grew dark. It turned inward, and sometimes it caused him a most desperate pain. An evil spirit tormented him, and Saul did double over in sad agony.

One thing alone did ease the poor king's soul: music. Sweet, gentle music, played upon a lyre, could soothe him, so that he might lay his head upon a pillow and rest.

"Where is the man," Saul cried, "who can touch my soul with his music?"

"I have seen a son of Jesse," said a servant, "who is skillful in playing the lyre. He lives in Bethlehem. He is someone careful in his speech; and the Lord is with him."

Therefore Saul sent messengers to Jesse, and Jesse gladly sent his son David to Saul.

So much did Saul come to love the boy, that he asked David to work for him, to be his armor bearer. And whenever the evil spirit burned in Saul's soul, David took the lyre and played it with his hand, and Saul was refreshed.

Saul did not know that this same boy, David, had already been anointed with oil by Samuel. Ruddy David; young David of the beautiful eyes; David, comely in appearance, was to be the next king of Israel.

Saul, king in name but rejected by God, writhed in dark agony. Then David of Bethlehem was brought to serve him—David, a boy whom Saul grew to love and need, for David's music brought peace to Saul.

Daily Goliath, the Philistine giant, mocked and challenged Saul's armies. And, daily, Israel's finest warriors grew more fainthearted. None would approach the towering figure.

Goliath of Gath

Now the Philistines gathered again for war. (Saul was never, in all his days, able to crush this enemy for good.) They drew up their armies on one mountain, while Saul drew up the armies of Israel on another; and a valley was between them.

"Ho, Israel!" there boomed a voice from the Philistine mountain everyday. "Ho, you insects of Saul! Ho, you grasshoppers!" The men of Israel heard the voice everyday, and everyday they trembled.

Because it was the voice of a giant. "I am Goliath of Gath!" he roared. Nearly ten feet tall, a helmet of bronze on his head, a coat of mail, greaves of bronze upon his legs, a javelin of bronze slung down between his shoulders, a spear whose shaft was like a weaver's beam and whose iron head was over twenty pounds—this was Goliath of Gath!

"I defy the ranks of Israel!" he thundered from his mountain. "Give me a man that we may fight together! Israel, send me your champion!"

But there was no champion in Israel willing to look at the giant close up.

It was only David who finally approached King Saul in his tent. "Let no man's heart fail because of him," David said. "Your servant will go and fight with this Philistine."

"My servant," said Saul, "is no more than a boy! My servant is nothing but a shepherd. But this loud man on his mountain has been a man of war all his life. No, David. You cannot fight him."

"I have been a shepherd," David said. "But that means that I have saved my sheep from bears and from lions by fighting them and killing them. This uncircumcised Philistine has defied the armies of the living God. The Lord who delivered me from the paw of the lion and the paw of the bear will certainly deliver me from the hand of this Philistine!"

Then Saul agreed to let him go. He dressed the boy in his own armor and girded a sword at his waist. "The Lord be with you," he said. But David could not move. All that metal was more than the boy could bear. So David took it off again, picked up only his staff, his shepherd's bag, his sling, and, from the brook in the valley, five smooth stones. Lightly he crossed from one mountain to the other.

Goliath came out to his shouting-place on the mountain, opened his mouth to thunder again—then suddenly saw the boy walking his way.

He might have laughed at the little figure, as if this were a joke. Instead, the giant glared, insulted. "Am I a dog," he growled, "that you come to me with sticks?" He began to curse David by all his gods, but the boy walked on with his sling, his staff, and no fear in his face.

"Come, then! Come to me," the giant roared. "I will give your flesh to the birds and the beasts for their dinner!"

Then David spoke. "You come to me with a sword and a spear and a javelin," he said. "But I come to you in the name of the Lord of the armies of Israel. This day the Lord will deliver you into my hand, that all the earth may know there is a God in Israel! The battle is the Lord's," said David. "The battle is the Lord's."

The giant was silent, now. Goliath was striding toward the battle line to meet David.

David ran quickly, lightly, to meet the Philistine. He put his hand in his bag, took out a stone. The sling made a small buzz as David whirled it round his head, a snap when he let it go. The stone struck Goliath on his forehead and sank into his skull, and he fell like lumber to the ground.

David had no sword. He ran and stood over the Philistine, and drew his sword out of its sheath, and killed him and cut off his head with it.

When the Philistines saw their champion dead, they broke and ran. And the men of Israel pursued them as far as Gath and the gates of Ekron. David brought the head of the giant back to camp.

Jonathan's Dear Friendship

It was then that Saul's son Jonathan saw David clearly as more than a mere boy, and his soul was knit to the soul of David with a profound love. He made a pledge of his friendship to David, stripping himself of his robe and giving it to David, together with his armor, his sword, his bow, and his strap for wearing the sword.

None would respond to Goliath's challenge—none but a boy. Armed with faith, a sling, five smooth stones, and a staff, David ran forward. He whirled the sling, snapped loose a stone, and Goliath of Gath fell—a giant cut down by a simple shepherd.

Saul's Suspicion and His Hatred

In time Saul came to love David less, for the young hero inspired praise in the people. Saul brooded. How dare David—boy become man, shepherd turned soldier—replace the king in people's hearts!

And it was then that King Saul began to love David less, for all of the people praised the hero who had killed the hero of the Philistines—but few of the people praised their king.

Wherever Saul sent David in the wars, David succeeded. No enemy could beat the boy—the boy that had now become a man. And when David returned from slaying the Philistines, the women came out of all the cities of Israel, singing and dancing. "Saul has slain his thousands," they sang, "and David his *ten thousands!*"

Saul heard the difference in the numbers, and he was angry.

One morning, when the black and gloomy fire was smoldering in his face, and when David was playing the lyre to soothe him, Saul suddenly curled his lips and screamed. He grabbed a spear and threw it at David. *I'll pin him to the wall!* he thought. But David evaded him twice.

Saul was afraid of David, for the Lord God, who had left him and left him so desolate, was now with David. *David* was the mighty one in Israel! *David* received the dear praise of the people. David and not Saul!

Saul tried to persuade certain people—including his son Jonathan—to murder David. But their love for David was too great, and they whispered to him the sinful plot instead. In grief David fled from the presence of the king.

"The Lord Be Between Me and Thee!"

"What have I done? What is my guilt?" David asked Jonathan. The two friends had met in secret in a field. "What is my sin that your father seeks my life?"

Jonathan hung his head. "Aye, my father wants to harm you. But I don't know why."

"If there is guilt in me," David cried, "slay me yourself!"

"God forbid!" said Jonathan. There were tears in his eyes. "When my father saw that you were gone, he cursed me for loving you and demanded that I bring you back to him. I asked him why you should die. I asked him what you had done. David, he gave me no reasons and he named no sin. He didn't even answer me with his mouth, but with his hand: He threw a spear at me. My father tried to kill me, too."

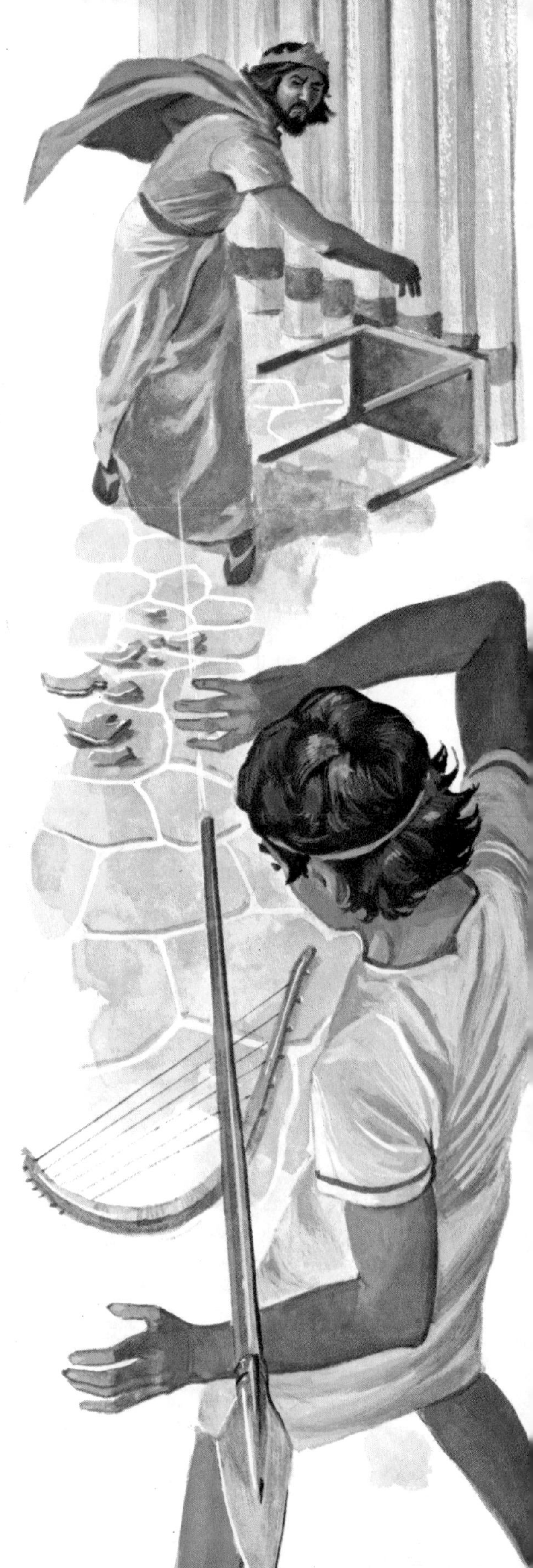

David played God's music for Saul, but Saul was deaf to the sweetness. Each note kindled his jealousy, and his love for David turned to hatred. He would rid himself of this rival! He would kill David!

David gazed in sorrow at his friend. Then he embraced him and the two men wept together.

Very softly Jonathan said, "When the Lord cuts off all of the enemies of David from the face of the earth, O let not the name of Jonathan be cut off from the house of David."

David kissed Jonathan. "Never," he said. "I swear, Jonathan, that I love you as I love my own soul. Never shall you be cut away from me."

Jonathan, son of Saul, and David, servant of Saul, embraced in sorrow. David must leave. No longer was he safe near the king. Neither friend could understand the depth of the danger that would follow David from that day forward.

So then they stood back from each other. "It is time," said David.

Jonathan said, "Go in peace."

David said, *"Shalom aleichem."*

Jonathan said, "The Lord be between me and you, and between my children and your children forever."

And David, without another word, left.

The War Between David and Saul

In his flight, David stopped with a few men at Nob, where he told the priest that he was on the king's business and that he was in a great hurry. Could they have something to eat? The priest, Ahimelech, served them holy bread, and then they left to hide.

David ran to the hills, to the cave of Adullam. It was there that he made his stronghold.

When the word spread through the countryside that David was a fugitive, hiding in Adullam, people began to gather around him. His brothers came. Those who were in debt, those who were discontent, the criminals, and the ragged came to him, so that David was able to build a small army of about six hundred men, and he was their captain.

Hotter and hotter burned the black fire in Saul's face. The man was nearly mad with yearning to see David dead. So every time that someone said, "David is here!" or "David was there!" Saul took an army and rode out to pursue his enemy, to hunt him and to kill him.

"David was at Nob," someone told the king. "And the priest fed him food!"

At Nob! Soon the king was standing in front of the priest, Ahimelech, questioning him. The priest said that he thought David was loyal (and Saul's face flashed like lightning). The priest said that he had often helped David in the king's name (and Saul ground his teeth). The priest said that, in any case, he knew nothing, much or little, about this matter of David's flight—and Saul exploded. He commanded that this priest be killed—with all his family, with all his cattle and flocks, and with all in the city of Nob. It was done.

"David is in Keilah," someone said.

In Keilah! Soon the king was marching to Keilah, demanding that the people of that place surrender David at once. But the Lord had told David of Saul's approach, and he had already escaped.

"David is in the Wilderness of Maon."

The Wilderness of Maon! Soon Saul was marching into that wilderness, breathing threats. But there was a great rock, almost a mountain, in the middle of it. As Saul and his men marched on one side of the rock, David and his men marched on the other side, the blind side. This silly chase stopped only when a messenger came and told Saul that the Philistines were raiding the land again. Saul, not knowing how close was his enemy, left. So the place was called the Rock of Escape.

"Behold! David is in the Wilderness of Engedi!"

David commanded a ragged army, which Saul pursued to the Wilderness of Maon. There Saul marched on one side of a mountain, David on the other, neither knowing how close to battle they had come.

Engedi! Soon, with three thousand men, the king was marching in that wilderness, in front of the Wildgoats' Rocks. At evening Saul entered a cave there to relieve himself.

Deep within the same cave were David and his men, all silent in the dark.

"Now," whispered the men to their captain. "The Lord has given him into your hand!"

But David said, "The Lord forbid that I should put forth my hand against the king, the one whom God anointed."

He did not hurt Saul. He merely slipped through the dark close enough to cut off the hem of Saul's robe.

When Saul had left the cave, when he and his three thousand men had marched some distance in the night, David came out and cried, "My lord the king!"

The sound of marching stopped.

"Why do you listen to people," David

Saul's hatred grew ever greater, yet David hated not in return. While Saul slept in a cave, David approached and cut the hem of Saul's robe. Surely now Saul would believe David wished him no harm.

cried, "who say that David wants to hurt you? I do not! I would not hurt the Lord's anointed! My lord, look at your robe. Look for its hem—and see that I could have killed you here in my cave. Look! The hem is in my hand! I cut nothing more on my king than a little cloth!"

Saul cried back, "Is that your voice, my son David?"

And David said, "It is my voice, my lord, O King! Why does my lord pursue his servant? What have I done? What is my guilt?"

Saul said, "I have done wrong. Return, my son David, for I will no more do you harm, because you could have killed me today but did not!"

But David did not return, and it was well that he did not. For—

"David is hiding on the hill of Hachilah," they told the king thereafter. And soon the king was on the march again, with three thousand picked men, to *Hachilah.*

The Death of Saul

It was in the southern part of the kingdom that Saul had pursued David, but now the king and his armies were drawn to the north, as far as Mount Gilboa. For there the Philistines began to gather their forces for war, to fight against Israel.

From his place on the mount, Saul looked down and saw the Philistines, their hundreds and their thousands. He trembled at the sight. The king was afraid.

Again and again Saul prayed to the Lord, that he be given some word about the war to come. But Saul received no answer. Neither by dreams nor by the prophets would God break his silence before this king. The Lord had left him, and Saul was utterly alone.

He remembered Samuel, who had died some years ago.

God no longer spoke to Saul. The terrified king begged a witch to bring Samuel's spirit before him—and so learned, from the old judge, what his fate would be.

Desperate, frightened, the old fire flickering behind his eyes, Saul went to a witch who lived in Endor. "I want to talk with a dead man," he said. "I want to talk with Samuel the judge."

The next day Saul lay sprawled on the battlefield, wounded unto death. Dead, his son Jonathan. Destroyed, his armies. He commanded his armor bearer to kill him, but the boy refused.

The witch said, "It is against the law."
Saul said, "Forget the law! Help me!"
So the witch did what she had to do.

Suddenly Saul grabbed her arm. "What do you see?" he hissed.

"I see a god coming up out of the earth," she said.

"What does he look like?"

"He is an old man," she said. "He is wrapped in a robe."

The king put his face down to the dirt and whispered, "Samuel. Samuel."

Then Samuel, dead these many years, spoke. "Why do you disturb me?" he said.

Saul clapped his hands together. "Oh, what shall I do?" he cried. "The Philistines are warring against me. God has turned away from me. He answers me no more. I need you, old man! I called you to tell me what to do!"

"If the Lord has turned away from you," said Samuel, "then there was no need to call me, because I will have no new word for you. The Lord is doing what he said he would do. For your disobedience he is taking the kingdom away from you. And tomorrow he shall give the army of Israel into the hand of the Philistines, and tomorrow you and your sons shall be with me."

Tomorrow! Tomorrow! Saul collapsed at the word.

But the next day it was as the judge had said it would be. The Philistines fought against Israel, and the men of Israel fled and fell dead on the face of Mount Gilboa. Dead were the sons of Saul. Dead! And dead lay Jonathan among them.

Saul himself was grievously wounded by arrows and found that he could not escape.

"Draw your sword!" he cried to his armor bearer. "Draw your sword and thrust me through with it. I will not be caught by these uncircumcised Philistines. I will not have them make sport of me!"

But the armor bearer was a boy. How could he kill his king?

Therefore Saul drew his own sword and fell upon it. And when the armor bearer saw that the fire had gone out of the king's face, and when he saw that Saul was dead, he did the same.

Then all Israel began to flee the cities. Only the men of Jabesh-gilead, remembering what good Saul once had done for them, came and took his body and buried it.

David, too. David, when he heard of the terrible defeat and of the death of the king, took hold of his clothes and tore them. He mourned for Saul, and for Jonathan he wept.

"Saul and Jonathan, beloved and lovely!" he cried. "In life and in death they were not divided. They were swifter than eagles, and stronger than lions! Ye daughters of Israel, weep over Saul!

"And Jonathan lies dead on the high places," he wept. "Oh, I am distressed for you, my brother Jonathan. Your love to me was wonderful, passing the love of women.

"How the mighty are fallen!" he shouted. "How the mighty are fallen down!"

David Becomes King

David, the son of Jesse, born in Bethlehem, of the tribe of Judah—David had a strong right arm, a shrewd mind, and a heart. . . .

A generous heart. In all the time that he ran from the wrath of King Saul, he had also protected the cities of his own tribe, Judah, and he gave them gifts, clothing, arms, and wealth, the spoils of his wars. Therefore the people of Judah, at the death of Saul, anointed him to be their king. David took his wives to Hebron, where he reigned for seven years as king of Judah.

And David had a heart. . . .

A sensitive heart, a forgiving and a righteous heart. He grieved at the death of Saul—yea, though Saul had sought his life. And when Abner, the captain of Saul's armies, was murdered—again, David mourned for the loss of the man. And when Ishbosheth, Saul's son, whom the other tribes in Israel had made their king, was also murdered—again, David wept and lamented the death of his rival!

All the people of Israel saw fair love and fair justice in David. They saw his arm, how strong it was; his mind, how keen; and most especially his heart, how great it was.

Therefore, all the tribes of Israel came to him at Hebron. "We are your bone and flesh," they said. "In times past, when Saul was king over us, it was you that led us out and brought us in again. And the Lord said to you, 'You shall be shepherd of my people Israel.' "

So all the elders of Israel anointed David their king. He was thirty-seven years old. He reigned until he was seventy.

King David Acts: Jerusalem

There was a city, strong and fortified, that sat between the eleven tribes of the north and Judah on the south. In all the time that Israel had dwelt in this land, from Joshua down to David, no one had been able to capture this city. Now David decided that this was to be his own city. From its hill, from Zion, he would reign over the people of God. This city's name was Jerusalem.

"Ha, ha!" laughed the inhabitants of Jerusalem. "Our walls are so strong that the lame and the blind could fight you off!"

But David did not attack the walls of this city. Instead, he entered like a spider, crawling up the water shaft and surprising the

Saul's death freed David from pursuit, but David did not rejoice. He mourned the lives lost in war, for his heart was great, his justice fair. God had chosen him, and now arrived the time for David to be king of the twelve tribes. The elders anointed him.

A mighty fortress was Jerusalem, but David made it his. And from atop Zion, David governed his people. God worked through him to free forever the twelve tribes from Philistine attacks.

people at their very backs. He took the city after all. He lived on Zion, and ever after that, Jerusalem was called the city of David.

King David Acts: The Philistines

The Philistines heard the news that David had been anointed king over Israel. They knew that he was a foe more deadly than Saul had been. Therefore, they did not wait till David came to them; they gathered their armies and went after him first.

Northwest of Jerusalem, David met the attack. Through him and through his armies, the Lord God burst like a flood upon the Philistines, and they were beaten back.

Again the Philistines arranged themselves for attack, spreading out through the Valley of Rephaim. But this time David did not meet them face to face. The Lord said to him, "Go around to their rear. Come on them opposite the balsam trees. And when you hear the sound of marching in the tops of the trees, then move! For then the Lord has gone out before you to smash the army of the Philistines!"

David did as the Lord had commanded him. He hit them hard, then chased them back into their own territory. He gathered their idols and burned them. He broke their strength. He broke their spirit. He broke this enemy forevermore, so that never again did the Philistines injure Israel—but rather they shrank and shrank until they were five tiny cities lost among the nations of the earth.

King David Acts: The Ark of God

Now there was a place for the king; and now there was peace for the people. Now was an excellent time to bring the ark of God, the sign of his presence, into Jerusalem, into the city of David, to Zion, the center of the kingdom. It was time for the ark to be home.

So David went in person, he and thirty thousand men of Israel, to the house of Abinadab, where the ark was kept. On a new cart they carried it back to Jerusalem. And David danced before the Lord with all his might. There was joy at the coming home of the Lord's ark. There were lyres and harps and tambourines and castanets and cymbals—music! There was laughter and shouting and the sound of the horn. And David offered burnt offerings and peace offerings before the Lord.

The ark of the Lord was in Jerusalem!

"Your Throne Shall Be Forever"

There was a prophet in Jerusalem whose name was Nathan. Through this man, the Lord God now made an everlasting promise to King David.

"I took you from the pasture," said the Lord, "from following the sheep, that you should be prince over my people Israel. I have been with you wherever you went, and have cut off all your enemies from before you. Now I shall make your name as great as the great names of the earth. And when you lie down to die, I shall raise up your son after you to be king, and his son after him, and his son, so that your house and your kingdom shall be made sure forever. Your throne, David, shall be established forever—and never shall I take my steadfast love away from it!"

Jerusalem, the city of David, now witnessed a joyous celebration. Laughing, singing, dancing, King David and his men brought the ark of God to Jerusalem. King David made burnt offerings before the Lord, and all within the city's walls feasted.

David Sings Songs

Then King David picked up his lyre. He struck the strings with a vigorous, dizzy joy; and he sang this song:

"Bless the Lord, O my soul; and all that is within me, bless his holy name! Bless the Lord, O my soul, and forget not all his benefits, who forgives all thine iniquities, who heals all thy diseases, who redeems thy life from destruction, who crowns thee with loving-kindness and tender mercies, who satisfies thy mouth with good things, so that thy youth is renewed like the eagle's!"

And David sang this song:

"I waited patiently for the Lord, and he inclined to me and heard my cry. He drew me up from the horrible pit, out of the muck and the clay, and he set my feet upon a rock, making my steps secure. He put a new song into my mouth, a song of praise to our God. Many shall see and fear and trust in the Lord!"

And David sang this song:

"I love thee, O Lord, my strength! The Lord is my rock! My fortress! My deliverer! My God! My strength in whom I trust! My shield and the horn of my salvation! My high tower! I call upon the Lord, and I am saved from my enemies! For this I will shout thy name, O Lord, among the nations, and sing praises to thee. Great triumphs he gives to his king, and mercy he shows to his anointed, to David and his house forevermore!"

And David sang this song:

"O Lord, our Lord, how excellent is thy name in all the earth! Out of the mouths of babes and sucklings thy glory is sung above the heavens! When I consider thy heavens, the work of thy fingers, the moon and the stars, which thou hast established, I think: What is man that thou art mindful of him, and the son of man that thou dost visit him? Yet thou hast made him a little lower than the angels, and hast crowned him with glory and honor! Thou hast given him dominion over the works of thy hands! Thou hast put all things under his feet, sheep and oxen, and the beasts of the field, the birds of the air and the fish of the sea, and everything that passes on the paths of the sea. O Lord, our Lord, how excellent is thy name in all the earth!"

And David sang this song:

"The Lord is my shepherd; I shall not want. He maketh me to lie down in green pastures; he leadeth me beside the still waters. He restoreth my soul. He leadeth me in the paths of righteousness for his name's sake. Yea, though I walk through the valley of the shadow of death, I will fear no evil; for thou art with me; thy rod and thy staff, they comfort me. Thou preparest a table before me in the presence of mine enemies; thou anointest my head with oil; my cup runneth over. Surely, goodness and mercy shall follow me all the days of my life; and I will dwell in the house of the Lord forever."

With all of his heart, and with all of his soul, and with all of his might, King David loved the Lord.

The Wars of David

Not only did David defeat the Philistines, but year after year he expanded his little kingdom by defeating all the peoples round about Israel.

He defeated the Moabites southeast of Israel.

He defeated Hadadezer the son of Rehob, king of Zobah. And when the Syrians of Damascus came to help Hadadezer, he defeated them, too. Soon he had taken the whole land north-northeast of Israel.

He defeated the Edomites in the Valley of Salt—south; and the Ammonites—due east; and the Amalekites. They all became his servants, for the Lord gave victory to David wherever he went. And the Lord made Israel, under David, an empire that ruled lands north and east and south, for as far as the eye could see.

Thus did the Lord God keep his promise which he made a thousand years before, to Abraham: Arise, walk through the length and breadth of the land, for I will give it to you and to your descendants forever!

So David reigned. And David administered justice and equity to all his people.

David's Sin Against Uriah

Hiram, the king of Tyre, had given David, the king of Israel, a present. It was a house built of cedar trees and stone upon the eastern ridge of Zion, in Jerusalem.

In the cool of the evening David would stroll on the roof of his house and gaze down upon his city.

Uriah the Hittite also had a house in Jerusalem. His house was wrapped around an open courtyard and a pool; his house was built on a level lower than the king's. From his roof, David could see Uriah's pool.

One evening, when Uriah was gone with the armies of Israel to fight the Ammonites, David glanced down to Uriah's pool. There was a woman bathing there—a woman slim and beautiful. "Who is she?" David asked a servant.

A victor in battle, just, and good, King David sinned against the Lord and against Uriah, his loyal soldier. David loved Bathsheba, Uriah's wife.

"Somebody's daughter and somebody's wife, my lord," his servant said. "She is the wife of Uriah the Hittite."

David said, "Bring her to me." Her beauty had melted his eyes.

So Bathsheba was brought to the king, who loved her. For a little while she stayed in his high cedar house, and then she returned to her own lower house. A little while longer, and David received a very short letter from Bathsheba. The letter said: "I'm going to have a baby."

Now the king became nervous—not because he had sinned with another man's wife, but rather because somebody might *find out* that he had sinned. So he conceived a plan to hide his sin. He commanded that Uriah be sent home from the wars.

When Uriah stood stained, sweated, and dirty in the presence of the king, David smiled at him. "And how is my general Joab doing?" he asked.

"Well," said Uriah the Hittite.

"Well," said David the king. "And how do my soldiers fare?" he asked.

"Well," said Uriah.

"Well," said the king of Israel. "And how," he asked, "how does the war prosper?"

"Very well, my lord," said Uriah.

"Ah, *very* well," said the king. "Good, good." He paused for a moment, and then he said, "Well, thank you, Uriah, for the good news. Now, go down to your house. Wash yourself. Be with your wife—what is her name? Bathsheba? Yes, be with your wife for a while, and rest."

Uriah left the king, and he did wash. But he did not go down to his house. He said, "Why should I lie at ease with my wife, when Joab and all the soldiers of Israel must sleep in open fields?" Uriah slept that night with David's servants.

So David was more nervous than before. But though his plan had failed the first time, he would *make* it work the second. He invited Uriah to dinner, and there he gave the Hittite wine and made him drunk. "Go! Go rest with your wife," he pleaded.

But again, Uriah the Hittite would not go near Bathsheba.

King David panicked. His plan had failed. No one would think that the baby was Uriah's, and someone might suspect that it was the king's. Therefore David created a foul, unseemly plan to save his reputation. He sent Uriah back to war, and in the Hittite's hand he sent a letter for Joab.

The letter read: "General! Set this man in the front line, in the place of the hardest fighting. Then, when the sky is dark with arrows, fall back from him, so that he stand alone there, so that he be struck down and die."

Uriah fought valiantly. But who can fight an army alone? Uriah the Hittite fell before many swords, and he died.

This plan worked.

King David waited until Bathsheba was done mourning the death of her husband, and then he sent her a letter. "Come up to my cedar house," it said. "Come up as the wife of the king."

So when the baby was born, no one saw anything wrong with the birth, for his mother and father were married, after all. And David had hidden his sin....

But the Lord saw the sin, and the Lord God was displeased!

"You Are the Man"

Nathan the prophet came to David, now, with a matter that needed the king's judgment. "It involves two men," Nathan said.

"Tell me," said the king.

"One man is rich. He has many flocks and herds, and he lives in a high cedar house. The other man is poor, owning but one ewe lamb, which once he loved and raised in his house as though it were a daughter. Food from his table, drink from his cup, and a place by his side at night were all hers.

"Now this," said the prophet, "is the matter. A traveler came to the rich man, but the rich man was unwilling to kill any of his flock to feed his guest. Instead, he took the poor man's lamb, killed *her,* and fed his guest upon her sweet flesh—"

David stood up, angry with the rich man. "As the Lord lives," he said, "that man deserves to die. My judgment? That he restore the lamb fourfold, because he did what he did without pity!"

Nathan said to David, "You are the man." David sat down again. "You have many wives," said the prophet. "Uriah the Hittite had but one. Yet you struck him with the sword of the Ammonites so that his one wife might add to your many! You have utterly scorned the Lord, David, and therefore the son born to you by Bathsheba shall die."

"I Have Sinned Against the Lord"

The child that Bathsheba bore to David became sick. David therefore prayed to God for the child. He fasted and he lay all night on the ground.

"Have mercy on me, O God, according to thy loving-kindness," he prayed. "According to the multitude of thy tender mercies, blot out my transgressions. For I acknowledge my transgression, and my sin is ever before me. Against thee, thee only, have I sinned and done this evil in thy sight!"

David's sin was grave. By his command, Uriah was killed in battle. By his desire, Bathsheba became his wife and bore the son conceived in sin. Through Nathan the prophet, the Lord told David of his displeasure. The son would die, and David would grieve and plead for forgiveness.

The people of his house tried to raise David from the ground, but he would not rise up. Neither would he eat food with them. For seven days the child was ill; for seven days David prayed.

"Create in me a clean heart, O God, and renew a right spirit within me! Cast me not away from thy presence, and take not thy holy spirit from me. Restore unto me the joy of thy salvation, and renew in me a steadfast spirit."

On the seventh day, the child died. But David's servants were afraid to tell him, because they thought he would do harm to himself. He was praying.

"Thou desirest not sacrifice, else I would give it. Thou delightest not in burnt offering. The sacrifices of God are a broken spirit. A broken and a sorry heart, O God, thou wilt not despise."

Then David saw his servants whispering together, and he understood that the child was dead.

Nathan the prophet said to David, "Yes, your sin has had its consequence; the boy is dead. But in his mercy the Lord has not turned away from you, King David. Instead he has put your sin away, and he is with you. You are forgiven."

Then David arose from the earth. He washed himself, changed his clothes, and went to his wife to comfort her.

When Bathsheba bore the king a second son, they named him Solomon. This one the Lord loved dearly. David was indeed forgiven.

Absalom

For all the glory David won, for all the lands he conquered and all the kings he defeated, for all the wealth and honor he brought to Jerusalem—yet David had trouble at home, for all of that. David suffered the sins of his own family.

He had a son named Absalom, who was exceedingly shrewd, but who put his fine brains to no good work. Absalom, when somebody hurt him, could hate that somebody hard and mean and forever. But Absalom would hide his hatred behind thin grins and propriety, waiting for the right time to reveal the hatred like a naked knife. When that time came, there were no grins any more. There was murder; there was vengeance. And only then would Absalom cease to hate—when his enemy ceased to be.

In this way did Absalom hate his father David, for something David had done some years ago. And in his heart of hearts, behind grins and proprieties, Absalom was convinced that *he,* not David, should rule, king over Israel.

So day after day and year after year shrewd Absalom would rise early in the morning and sit by the gate of Jerusalem, smiling.

"You, sir!" he would cry whenever a man came through the gate to see the king. "What city are you from?" Smiling, he said it.

The man would tell him. Indeed, Absalom was such a beautiful figure, his smile so wide, his hair so long and flowing, that no man could resist the greeting.

"And why do you wish," Absalom would ask, "to see the king?"

The man would tell him. Then Absalom would begin to shake his head as if in great sorrow. "Ah, sir!" he would sigh. "Your claim is good and right, and you *should* put it to the king. But the fact is that you can't. The king is busy, you see, and he has never appointed anyone to hear such claims as yours. I'm sorry. I am so sorry for you."

And when the man began to look as woebegone as Absalom himself, then Absalom would jump up and cry, "Oh that I were king in the land! Then *every* man could come to me and I would give him justice!"

This speech would inspire the man so much that he would come and kneel in front of Absalom, but Absalom would have nothing of kneeling. Instead, he would hug the man and kiss him, so the man went away hating David and loving Absalom. And thus did Absalom steal the hearts of the people.

During these years Absalom got himself horses and a chariot and fifty soldiers to run before him—the seeds of his own army!

And at the end of four years he went to King David himself, smiling, with a request. "Please let me go to Hebron," he begged, "that I might worship the Lord there. I vowed that I would do so."

David said, "Go in peace." And Absalom went—but not in peace.

He spread the word! To all the men whom he had hugged these many years, he spread the word. To all who were discontent with David's ruling, he spread the word. Through all the tribes of Israel he whispered, "As soon as you hear the trumpet, then shout: 'Absalom is king at Hebron!'" That was the word. Rebellion!

Absalom was smiling no more. Grim was the face he wore, and hard. Hatred hung on every part of it. And all around him gathered men of Israel, even some of the king's own counselors.

It was a real army, now, marching toward Jerusalem. "Absalom is king!"

Flight, Fight, and a Grievous Death

King David heard of his son's coming, heard, as well, of the size and the bitterness of the army that marched with him. Sadly he spoke to his servants and to those most loyal to him. "Arise," he said quietly, "let us flee the city, or else there will be no escape from Absalom."

So the king went forth, and all his household with him, his general Joab, and his own chosen army.

This was a day of testings, for to many who followed him David turned and said, "Go back. Shall I make you wander about with me, seeing I know not where I go?" He was standing on the Mount of Olives, barefoot, weeping, his head covered for sorrow. Some went back—but they would only pretend to be with Absalom; others would not go back at all; still others brought food and drink for the journey.

Weary, sorry, cursed by some who ran along beside his men, David arrived by nightfall at the Jordan River; but even there he could not wait. Absalom had entered Jerusalem. At any time he could muster an army of twelve thousand to pursue his father. So David crossed the river all that night and came to the city Mahanaim.

Not immediately, but within a few days, and not with twelve thousand, but with thousands upon thousands, Absalom crossed the Jordan after his father, encamping the army of Israel in Gilead.

King David saw the conflict coming; he was sick at heart for what he saw. "I am going to the fight with you," he told his general Joab.

"Don't, my lord," Joab said. "If half of us die, they won't care about us. But you are worth ten thousand of us. Stay in the city."

So David stood at the gate and watched his soldiers marching out before him, marching out against his son, his enemy. At the very last moment he grabbed Joab.

"For my sake," he said, "deal gently with the young man Absalom!" Everyone heard the king's earnest word, but no one heard Joab give answer.

So the army went out into the field against Absalom and his army. It was a rout and a slaughter. Absalom's army turned from the King's forces under Joab and ran—over hills and into the forest. They streamed away!

Absalom himself was riding a mule in furious retreat through the forest, when the mule went under the thick branches of a great oak. His hair caught fast in the branches, the mule that was under him went on, and Absalom was left hanging between heaven and earth.

A soldier saw the sight and ran to Joab. "Absalom's hanging in an oak!" he cried.

"What, you saw him!" Joab snapped. "Why didn't you kill him?"

"I heard the king's command," said the soldier. "I wouldn't hurt the king's son!"

"You waste my time!" sneered the general. He took into his own hand three darts, and he himself went and killed Absalom where he was hanging.

Now David was sitting between the two gates of the city, and a watchman was on the roof of the gates.

"Here comes a man running," called the watchman to the king.

David said, "If he comes alone, he comes with news of the battle."

Then the watchman called, "I see another man, running behind him!"

"He has news, too," said David.

Death was Absalom's reward for his treachery against King David. Through his own planned battle against his father's armies, he met his fate.

Another enemy had been vanquished. No longer was there a threat to the throne. But there was no joy in the victory, for another son had been lost. David wept. Absalom, O Absalom.

"I think the first man is Ahimaaz," called the watchman.

"A good man!" said David. "He will have good news."

Then Ahimaaz cried out to the king, "All is well! All is well!" And when he was close to the king, he bowed and said, "Blessed be the Lord your God, who has given you the victory today."

David said, "How is the young man Absalom?"

Ahimaaz said, "I do not know. I saw a tumult, but I don't know what it was."

King David said, "Then wait. Stand over here." Ahimaaz stood and waited.

Then the second messenger ran up, gasping for breath and crying. "Good news for my lord the king!"

David said, "How is the young man Absalom?"

The messenger smiled. "May all the enemies of the king die as he has died."

Then David the king was deeply moved. He backed away from the messenger and went up to his room over the gate, and as he went, he wept and said, "O my son Absalom! My son, my son Absalom! Would God I had died for thee! O Absalom, my son, my son!"

The Death of David

King David grew old and his shoulders bent down under the glory and the grief of his reign. He became cold, so that his servants covered him with robes and blankets. But the chill was age; nothing could warm him again, not even the young woman Abishag, whom they sent to hold him and to nurse him. David was dying.

He called Solomon to his side.

"My son, I am about to go the way of all the earth," he said. "By my promise to you and your mother, by the anointing of Zadok the priest and the word of Nathan the prophet, by the choosing of the Lord, you shall rule this land after me.

"Solomon, be strong. Show yourself a man. Keep the charge of the Lord your God, walking in his ways and keeping his commandments as they are written in the Torah, the teachings of Moses, and you shall prosper—and the promise of the Lord shall most certainly be established, that never shall a son of David not be sitting on this throne."

Then David slept with his fathers and was buried in the city of David.

Solomon sat upon the throne of David his father, and his kingdom was firmly established.

SOLOMON: RESPLENDENT KING OF ISRAEL

Solomon's Prayer

The Lord appeared to Solomon in a dream by night, and God said, "Ask what I shall give you."

"Ah, my Lord," Solomon said, "you have shown loving-kindness to David my father, for you have given him a son to sit upon his throne this day.

"O Lord my God, I am like a little child. I do not know how to go out or come in. Yet you have placed me in the midst of your people, your chosen people, a great people that cannot be numbered.

"Now show me your loving-kindness. Give me an understanding mind to govern your people, that I might distinguish between good and evil."

It pleased the Lord that Solomon had asked this. "Not long life," said the Lord. "Not riches for yourself, nor for the lives of your enemies have you asked! Behold, I do according to your word. I give you a wise and discerning mind, so that there has never been, nor shall there ever be, one like you in all the world. And I give you also what you did not ask, riches and honor."

Solomon awoke, and behold, it was a dream.

The Wise Judgment of Solomon

Two women came to the king. One bore a baby in her arms; the other's arms were empty.

"But I used to have a baby, too," the second woman told the king. "We both had children, until she took mine from me."

"I did not!" said the woman with the baby.

"O King, she did!" said the other. "One night when we were both sleeping with our babies in the same house, she rolled over on hers and killed it. Then, while I was still sleeping, she carried the dead child to my

Solomon's wisdom inspired awe in Israel. Two women came to him, each claiming to be the mother of a certain child. Solomon judged which was the true mother. So worked God through the king.

bed and took the living for herself. In the morning I wept because I thought my baby had died, but when I looked closely, I saw that it was hers. King, the baby she carries in her arms is mine!"

"No, it is not!" cried the other, squeezing the infant to her bosom. "It is mine!"

"Mine!" said the lady with empty arms.

"Silence," said Solomon. He gazed at the women for a moment. Then he said quietly, "Bring me a sword."

A sword was brought to the king.

To his servant, Solomon delivered his judgment as a command: "Divide the living child in two," he said. "Give half to the one and half to the other."

"No! Don't!" cried the one, pressing her empty arms to her empty bosom. Her heart was breaking for the baby. "Let her keep the living child!"

But the other woman gave the baby to Solomon's servant. "I won't keep it, and you can't have it," she said to the woman. And to the servant, "Divide it."

Then the king said, "No, do not kill the infant. Give it to the woman with the empty arms. She is its mother."

All Israel stood in awe of Solomon, because they saw that the wisdom of God was in him.

The Proverbs of Solomon

"The fear of the Lord," said King Solomon to his people, "is the beginning of knowledge, but fools despise wisdom and instruction!"

Solomon did not keep his wisdom to himself. It was a gift from God which he yearned to share with all of the people of Israel, a gift which he hoped would last long after his death. So he wrote a book.

"Wisdom is like a woman," he wrote, "who calls to all the children of men. 'O foolish people,' she cries at the gates of the city, 'pay attention!' And then she says, 'All the words of my mouth are righteous. There is nothing twisted or crooked in them. Take knowledge instead of silver or gold, for wisdom is better than jewels! I have counsel; I have insight; I have strength. By me kings reign, and rulers decree what is just. By me princes rule and nobles govern the earth. I walk in the way of righteousness and in the paths of justice, but pride and arrogance and evil and evil speech I hate!' "

Throughout his long life King Solomon continued to write his book, always adding to it the understandings which the Lord God granted him.

He wrote: "A wise son makes a glad father, but a foolish son is a sorrow to his mother. A wise son hears his father's instruction, but a scoffer does not listen to rebuke. He who is often reproved, yet continues to stiffen his neck, will suddenly be broken past healing! Poverty and disgrace come to him who shuts his ears against instruction, but the one who listens to reproof is honored. Train a child in the way that he should go, and when he is old he will not depart from it."

Solomon wrote: "A worthless man plots evil. His speech is like a scorching fire, his twisting tongue starts fights, and his whispering gossip turns friends into enemies! Hatred makes war! But love covers all offenses. A harsh word stirs up anger; a soft reply turns wrath away. He who is slow to anger is better than the mighty, and he who controls his passion controls much more than a city."

Solomon wrote: "The thoughts of the wicked are an abomination to the Lord; the words of the pure are pleasing to him. A good man has his favor, but a man of evil designs, God finds guilty!"

Solomon wrote: "Pride goes before destruction, and a haughty spirit before a fall. He who trusts in his own mind is a fool. Many are the plans in the mind of a man, but it is the one plan of the Lord that shall take place. Therefore, commit your work unto the Lord, and it shall surely be established."

So wrote Solomon, the wise king of Israel. And besides these, he wrote many another saying—for *It is the glory of God to conceal things,* he thought, *but the glory of kings is to search things out.*

The Temple of the Lord

In Solomon's day the whole land of Israel in the north and the tribe of Judah in the south had peace with their neighbors round about them. The king had rest on every side; therefore he could do what his father David could not.

He brought in chariots for his armies; and for the chariots, he bred horses; and for the horses, he built stables: Forty thousand stalls he built. He built fortresses in many cities, and a wall around Jerusalem. He built a palace for himself, and a magnificent throne of ivory all covered in gold.

He sold to countries east and west of him, and he bought from them. He traded by land, and the camels were like a river in the desert. He traded by sea, and the ships of Tarshish were common in his ports.

Silver became as common in Jerusalem as stone, cedar wood as plentiful as kindling, and visitors as many as the citizens of the city. For all the world sought Solomon, to wonder at his wealth and to marvel at his wisdom.

In those days Solomon said, "By the kindness of the Lord my God I have neither adversity nor misfortune. I will build a house to the name of the Lord my God!" And he did.

Solomon would build a house to honor the Lord.

The best of cedar, silk, ivory, came by land and sea.

From Lebanon came cedar and cypress timber, and craftsmen to cut and to carve it. From all Israel Solomon levied laborers, the burden bearers and the hewers of stone. Thus the foundation was laid; and the walls went up and were covered; and the ceiling was made, by beams and by planks. In the four hundred and eightieth year after the people of Israel came out of Egypt, Solomon began to build this house. And when he finished, he overlaid it everywhere in gold—a building ninety feet long, thirty feet wide, and forty-five feet high, overlaid in gold. Its rooms and its furniture he built to be like those of the tabernacle, which went through the wilderness with the children of Israel. But with how much more cost! With how much more beauty, skill, and intricacy did Solomon build these things!

And when all of the building was done, Solomon assembled the elders of Israel and the heads of the twelve tribes and the leaders of every house in Israel, and together they brought the ark of the covenant out of the city of David. With joy and with high sacrifice they brought it into the Temple, into the most holy place, where they set it underneath the arching wings of two magnificent cherubim. Then a cloud filled the

Craftsmen of all kinds came: carpenters and carvers.

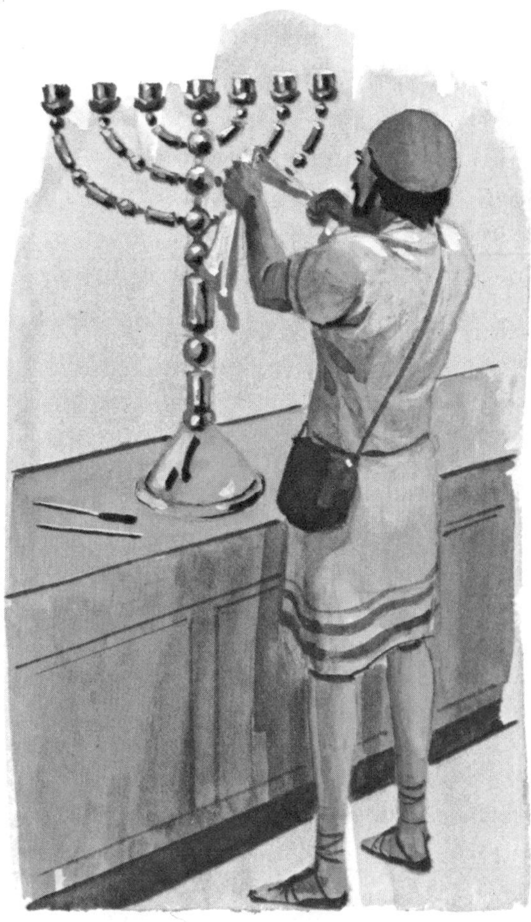

Every skill, every beauty, went into the Temple.

whole house of the Lord, so thick, so glorious that the priests could not stand to minister there. A cloud! It was the presence of God.

Solomon cried out to the Lord, "I have built thee an exalted house, a place in which to dwell forever!" He went and stood before the altar and spread forth his hands to heaven and prayed.

"But will God dwell on earth? Behold, heaven and the highest heaven cannot contain thee! How much less this house which I have built. Yet listen to my prayer, O Lord. Let your eyes be open night and day toward this house, that you may *always* hear the prayers which your servants offer in this place. Yea, hear in your heaven, your dwelling place, and when you hear the thing they ask of you, then, O Lord our God, give and forgive!

"And hear this prayer, too," prayed Solomon. "O Lord, God of Israel, keep the promise that you made to David—that so long as they walk in the way of righteousness, his sons shall always rule from the throne of Israel."

The Lord answered Solomon:

"As for this house, I have consecrated it. I put my name there forever, and my eyes and my heart shall be upon it always. Solomon, I have heard your prayer.

"As for you, if you and your sons will walk before me in righteousness, doing all that I have commanded you and never turning aside to worship other gods, then I shall keep my covenant with you. Your sons shall sit forever on the throne of Israel!

"But if you do not follow me, either you or the sons that shall be kings after you, then I shall cut you off. This house will crumble into such a heap of ruins that everyone passing by will hiss and say, 'Because they forsook their God, their God brought evil upon them.' And *Israel,* that lovely name, will be a byword, a mock among the nations."

The Queen of Sheba

Solomon, so glorious! Solomon, so glittering, resplendent in his riches and famous for his wisdom! The kings and the queens of the whole world heard of his name and wondered that there should be such a man. Were the reports of him really true? Or were they just the chatter of addled travelers?

One monarch, the queen of Sheba, chose to go herself to Jerusalem, to see Solomon with her own eyes, and to discover the truth.

With camels bearing spices and gold and precious stones, she entered the city of David. With sharp, hard questions she tested King Solomon's wisdom. And with awe she heard him answer every one. Then she looked at the Temple he had built, and at the king's palace. She saw the food on his table, the number and the clothing of his servants, and the breath went out of her.

"Not half of the truth was told me in Sheba," she said to him. "Sir, your wisdom and your prosperity are even more than the reports which I heard. Blessed are these servants who stand ever before you and hear your wisdom."

She gave him the spices and the gold and the stones she had brought. And after her came many who gave presents to Solomon: silver, gold, clothing, myrrh, spices, horses.

Those were wonderful, glorious years for Israel, the chosen people of the Lord God!

At last the ark of the covenant was brought to Solomon's magnificent Temple, and his fame spread through the world. In wonder came the queen of Sheba, to judge for herself the wisdom of this extraordinary king and to witness Israel's prosperity.

Israel Declines – and the Prophets Cry Out

HOW OFTEN THE LORD ASKED OBEDIENCE!

FROM THE EARLIEST days of Israel, even from the days when the people stood shivering at the foot of Mount Sinai, the Lord God had said to them: "Obey my voice. Keep my covenant, and you shall be my own, among all peoples!"

And Moses, when Israel stood ready to enter the Promised Land, had cried to the people, "Behold, I set before you this day a blessing and a curse: the blessing, if you obey the commandments of the Lord your God; and the curse if you do not, but turn aside to go after other gods which you have not known."

And Joshua—when Israel had conquered that land of promise, and when he was an old man about to die—Joshua had pleaded, "If you forsake the Lord and serve foreign gods, then the Lord will turn and do you harm, even after having done you good." At that time the people had said to Joshua, "We will serve the Lord!" And Joshua had warned them, "You are witnesses against yourselves that you have chosen the Lord." And the people had answered, "We are witnesses!"

And Samuel—when *he* was old and when, sadly, he had bowed before the wishes of Israel to give them a king—Samuel also had said, "If you will fear the Lord and serve him and not rebel against his commandment, both you and the king who reigns over you, all will be well. But if you will not listen to the voice of the Lord, then the hand of the Lord will be against you and your king."

And to King David, God had said it, and to King Solomon as well: "Walk in my ways. With integrity, with righteousness, do all that I command you. . . ."

From the earliest days of Israel this family had heard the word. And they *would* hear it forever! But now begins a woeful chapter in the story of the chosen people, for they chose to break that word. Many of their kings turned away from the Lord their God. And though many of their kings were faithful, yet it was the faithless king who had the greater power, finally. Him the people followed. They too broke the word. But God kept *his* word: At the end of this dolorous chapter he let the kingdom, and the city of David, and the Temple itself fall flat before its enemies. The people were sent into exile.

Many a king turned away from the Lord. But the first was Solomon himself.

The Lord Is Angry with Solomon

Though the Lord had appeared to Solomon twice, commanding him not to go after other gods, yet he did just that.

Throughout his reign, Solomon had married many foreign women. They brought into Israel, into Jerusalem, and into his own house their foreign gods. And when the king was an old man, his love for his wives overpowered his love for the Lord. A part of his heart went to the goddess Ashtoreth; a part of his heart to Milcom; a part to Chemosh; a part to Molech—and to these last two gods he built places of worship. Solomon's heart was not true to the Lord God.

For the third time, God spoke to Solomon: "Not in your lifetime," he said, "but close after your death, Solomon, I will tear the kingdom from your throne. One tribe alone shall be left unto your son. Judah and Jerusalem alone shall be his."

And so it was.

After Solomon slept with his fathers, the northern tribes all rebelled against his son Rehoboam. They were furious at the taxes Solomon had laid on them during his lifetime. They were outraged at the labor he had demanded of them so that he might build his buildings. And their fury doubled when they considered that they lived in the north, but Solomon had come from the south! From Judah!

Since Rehoboam was not as shrewd as his father Solomon, nor as courageous as his grandfather David; since he was a weak, arrogant, and childish king, the northern tribes succeeded in their rebellion against him. They set up a new kingdom with a new king. And so there was a divorce in the Family Israel, which had, in times before, been one.

The northern kingdom called itself Israel. The southern kingdom called itself Judah. The Lord still was God for both of them, but the brothers no longer loved one another as once they had.

Kings Do Evil in the Sight of the Lord

Especially in the northern kingdom of Israel the kings welcomed the false god Baal. Especially there the Baal worship grew like a mildew on the souls of the people, though even in Judah people made room for other gods.

But God—who grieved to see his people turn away—the Lord God did not cease to love them!

"What shall I do with you, O Israel?" he said. "What shall I do with you, O Judah? Your faithful love is like the morning cloud, like the dew that goes early away!"

What the Lord did was this: *He kept speaking the word even now unto them!* The same word which he had spoken from the beginning. But now it was not Moses, nor Joshua, nor the judges, nor the priests, nor the kings who carried that word for the Lord. *It was the prophets!*

"I have hewn them by the prophets!" said the Lord. "I have slain them with the words of my mouth and my judgment goes forth like the light."

The prophets. Individual men who loved God mightily, who agonized over the sin of the people, and who cried God's word unto them. The prophets. . . .

THE PROPHET ELIJAH

Ahab

The seventh king of the northern kingdom did evil in the sight of the Lord. Yea, more than all the kings that went before him. Ahab, the son of Omri, took Jezebel to be his wife. Jezebel was the daughter of the king of Sidon. The king of Sidon was also a priest of Baal, and as Jezebel was a woman of powerful will, she convinced her husband to build for Baal an altar in the capital city of Israel.

Not only the queen, but King Ahab himself and the people of Israel worshiped Baal!

Ahab did more to provoke the Lord God of Israel to anger than all the kings of Israel who were before him.

Drought!

So Elijah the prophet went to King Ahab and demanded to speak with him.

"As the Lord God lives," said Elijah, "the Lord before whom I stand, there shall be neither dew nor rain these years—until my word calls them back again."

And so it was that the land became dry, and baked like a cake in an oven.

Elijah withdrew himself. He hid by the brook Cherith, east of the Jordan, and drank its water to survive. While he was there, the ravens brought him bread and meat both morning and evening, for the Lord God commanded them. But soon even the Cherith dried up in the withering drought.

A Little Flour, a Little Oil

So the Lord sent Elijah altogether out of the country, to Zarephath. "I have commanded

After Solomon's death, his kingdom was torn apart. In the lands to the north, King Ahab and Jezebel led the people in worship of the idol Baal.

a widow there to feed you," said the Lord. Elijah went.

When he came to the gate of that city, he saw a widow stooping, gathering sticks.

"Please bring me a cup of water," he called. She glanced at him with weary eyes, then straightened and turned to bring the water.

But Elijah called again, "And bring me a bit of bread!"

Now the widow stopped, turned, and spoke to him. "I have no bread," she said. "A little flour in a jar, a little oil in a cruse, a few sticks in my hand—these are all that I have, sir. And even now I'm going to burn the sticks and bake the last of everything, that my son and I may eat and die."

"Widow, don't be afraid," Elijah said to her. "Go, do as you have said. But first do what *I* have said. Bring me the bread from your flour, and the Lord will watch over you."

So the widow went and did as Elijah said, and he ate. So did she. So did her son. And not one meal only, but they ate for as many days as the drought lasted, for the jar never emptied of its little flour, nor the cruse of its oil. The Lord watched over them, even as Elijah had said he would.

"Now I Know You Are a Man of God!"

After a while the widow's son became sick with a sickness so violent that finally there was no breath left in the boy.

"Is this why you came?" the poor widow wept before Elijah. "So that God should see my sin and punish me with the death of my son?"

Elijah said, "Give me the boy." He took the limp body from the widow's lap, then carried it to his own room on the roof and laid it on his own bed.

He cried to the Lord, "By your own com-

The prophet Elijah foretold of a drought that would sear the earth in punishment of Ahab's sins. Then the prophet withdrew to Zarephath where a poor widow gave him shelter. When her son sickened and died, Elijah prayed over him, and the boy lived.

mand this widow has helped me! And now you want to kill her son?"

Elijah stretched himself three times upon the boy, crying out, "O Lord my God, give him life again! Life again! Life again!"

And the Lord listened to Elijah. The boy coughed and came alive.

So Elijah picked him up and carried him back down to his mother. "See," he said, "your son lives."

"Now I know you are a man of God," the widow said. "And the word of the Lord in your mouth is truth!"

The Contest of the Prophets

For three years the drought burned the land. The grass turned yellow and died, and no more grew to feed the cattle, so the cattle turned over and died. King Ahab began to worry about his purebred horses and mules, for if the grass was gone and the cattle but corpses across the land, horses and mules were surely the next to go!

Therefore the king himself went out into the land to look for grass. "Maybe I can save some of the breed," he said.

He found no grass. Instead he saw a singular man standing in the distance—long, tangled hair falling down the man's back, a goatskin girdle at his waist, a sheepskin mantle thrown over his shoulders, ropy muscles in his arms and legs. Ahab squinted, because it seemed to him he recognized this bitten, solitary figure.

"Is that you," he cried, "you troubler of Israel?"

And the man cried back, "I have not troubled Israel. You have—because you have forsaken the commandments of the Lord and have followed Baal!"

Ahab shuddered. It was just as he thought: This was Elijah, suddenly reappearing after three years of utter silence.

Elijah cried again, "Now gather all Israel to me at Mount Carmel, and also bring the prophets of Baal, those four hundred and fifty mouths that eat at Jezebel's table!"

Ahab did as he was told, and when the people of Israel and the prophets of Baal crowded Mount Carmel, standing on a windy ridge above the shores of the Great Sea, Elijah appeared.

"How long," he cried to the people, "will you hop from foot to foot? How long will you split yourselves between two gods? Choose one or the other! If the Lord is God, follow him. And if you choose Baal," said Elijah, glaring at the prophets of Baal, "then follow him."

The people answered him not a word. His eyes narrowed to knives—some of the sharpness for Israel, some for the prophets of Baal. And he said, "I, even I alone, am left a prophet of the Lord. But Baal has four hundred and fifty mouths to prophesy for him. So, let two bulls be brought. You choose one, cut it to pieces, lay it on wood, but put no fire to it. I will cut the other and lay it on wood and put no fire to it. Then call on your god. I will call upon the Lord. And the god who answers by fire, he is God!"

The people agreed to Elijah's challenge, so he sat down and wrapped his mantle around himself. "You are so many," he said to the four hundred and fifty, "please go first."

The prophets of Baal prepared their bull. Then, from morning till noon, they called upon their god, "O Baal, answer us!"

But there was no voice, no answer.

At noon Elijah said, "Cry louder! He is a god, surely. But maybe he is lost in thought, or maybe he just took a walk, or maybe he took a whole trip. Cry louder! Maybe your god has gone to sleep, and you have to wake him up. Try crying louder!"

So the prophets of Baal cried louder. And besides that, they cut themselves with swords and spears till the blood spilled out. On and on they raved, until the middle of the afternoon—

But there was no voice. No one answered. No one listened to them.

Then Elijah stood up and called the people of Israel to himself: "Watch." He built an altar with twelve stones, one for each of the tribes of Israel. He dug a trench around the altar, put wood on top of it, put the meat on top of the wood, then commanded the people to pour four jars of water over the whole. They did. "Do it again," he said. They did. "Do it a third time," he said. They did, and the water not only soaked the altar, it also filled the trench.

"Now O Lord, God of Abraham, Isaac, and Israel," Elijah prayed, "show that you are God in Israel, that I am your servant, and that I have done everything only according to your word. Answer me, O Lord God, answer me—that this people may know that you are indeed God."

Then the fire of the Lord fell, consuming the meat, and the wood, and the stones, and the dust—and licking the water up out of the trench.

The people fell down on their faces, crying, "The Lord, he is God! The Lord, he is God!"

But immediately Elijah commanded them to grab the prophets of Baal. "Don't let even one of them escape," he ordered.

Four hundred and fifty prophets were captured and brought down from the ridge to the brook Kishon. In that place Elijah had them killed.

Rain!

Elijah turned now to King Ahab and said, "Can you hear it?" But the mute king could only stare back at the prophet.

"No, of course you can't hear it," said Elijah. "But I can. It's the sound and the roar of

Elijah challenged the priests of Baal. The priests cried out to Baal to flame their offering. But it remained untouched. Then Elijah called to the Lord, and fire descended upon his offering, consuming all—meat, wood, stones, dust, and water.

a great downpour, because the drought is over. Go eat and drink, King Ahab. The drought is over."

While the king prepared to eat, Elijah went up to the top of Mount Carmel and sat on the ground. He bowed his head, he put his face between his knees, and he said to his servant, "Look out over the Great Sea."

The servant went and came back saying, "There's nothing there but the hard blue sky."

Elijah said, "Then look again. Look seven times again."

At the seventh time, the servant said, "I see a little cloud, like a man's hand, rising out of the sea."

"A little cloud," said Elijah. "Go tell Ahab to harness his chariots and to leave now. Now—or the rain will turn this earth to black mud and he will not be able to move."

The little cloud swelled. The heavens frowned—dark, full, ready. The wind cracked the earth and the sky. And there was a great rain.

Elijah at Sinai

Ahab, speechless before the prophet Elijah, had a long speech ready for his wife when he came home to her. He told Jezebel of the murder of her four hundred and fifty prophets, mouths never again to eat at her table.

In white fury Jezebel sent a message to Elijah: "May the gods murder me if I do not murder you as you murdered them!"

And Elijah, hearing the pagan rage in the queen's threat, feared for his life. He went south, out of Israel, across Judah and into the wilderness, where he threw his mantle down upon the ground and fell on it. He was tired in his bones, sick in his soul, and utterly alone.

The people had seen the power of the Lord. They worshiped him. And now the drought ended. The sky darkened, and a mighty rain fell.

"Enough. Enough!" he groaned. "O Lord, let me die. I am no better than my fathers." Underneath a broom tree, the prophet fell asleep.

But then an angel touched him. "Wake up and eat," the angel said. Elijah blinked and saw both water and a biscuit. He ate and lay down again.

And the angel touched him a second time, and said, "Wake up and eat, or else the trip will be too much for you." Again Elijah ate—and with the strength of that food he went forty days and forty nights, deep south, to Sinai, the grand mountain of God.

"Elijah! Elijah!" God called to the prophet in that place. "What are you doing here?"

"Ah, Lord," said Elijah, "my feeling for you has been hot, like a fever. For the people have forsaken you, and shattered your altars, and murdered your prophets. I, even I alone, am left, and they seek my life as well."

"Elijah, stand in the mouth of a cave," said the Lord. Then the Lord God himself passed by.

A screaming wind ripped the mountain, whipping trees and pounding the stones into pieces. But God was not in the wind.

An earthquake shook the mountain to the roots of it. But God was not in the earthquake.

Fire broke out, dancing up the mountain face like salamanders in full jump, but God was not in the fire.

Then, after the fire, a still, small voice—a sound of gentle stillness.

When Elijah heard this vast quietness, he wrapped his face in his mantle, for the Lord was very near.

"Go, Elijah," said the Lord. "Return to the north. Anoint a new king over Israel; and to be prophet in your place, anoint Elisha the son of Shaphat. Know, Elijah," said the Lord, "that I will keep a remnant for myself, seven thousand faithful, whose knees have never bent to Baal, whose lips have never kissed him."

Elijah to Elisha

The prophet did go north again. He found Elisha the son of Shaphat, who was plowing with twelve yoke of oxen.

As Elijah walked by him, he cast his mantle over the young man. Immediately Elisha understood. He ran after the prophet with a request: "Let me kiss my mother and my father, and I will follow you."

Elijah turned clear eyes upon the young man. "Do it quickly," he said. "For you know what I have done to you, don't you?"

Elijah Is Taken into Heaven

Many other things happened in the life of the prophet Elijah, and the man Elisha learned from them all.

But the time came when the Lord was about to take Elijah up to heaven.

As they were traveling from Gilgal, Elijah said, "Stay here, for the Lord has sent me to Bethel."

But Elisha said, "As the Lord lives, I will not leave you!"

So they came to Bethel, where certain men took Elisha aside and whispered to him, "Do you know that today the Lord will take your master away from you?"

Elisha said, "Hush! I know it, but hold your peace."

Then Elijah said to his follower, "Elisha, stay here, for the Lord sends me to Jericho."

But Elisha said, "As the Lord lives, I will not leave you!"

So they came to Jericho, and again certain men mumbled to Elisha about the prophet's departure; and again Elisha told them to hush, that he knew what he was doing.

For the third time Elijah said, "Stay here,

At God's command, Elijah anointed Elisha. Elisha followed Elijah, learning from him. When at last Elijah's days were done, he was lifted into heaven in a flaming chariot. Because Elisha saw, he knew that Elijah's spirit would remain with him.

Elisha. The Lord has sent me to the Jordan."

"Then he has sent both of us," said Elisha, "for I will not leave you!"

So the two of them went on. And when they came to the Jordan River, Elijah rolled up his mantle and struck the waters. The river parted to one side and to the other, so they crossed on dry ground.

Now Elijah said to Elisha, "Ask what I shall do for you before I am taken."

"I pray you," said Elisha, "let me receive a double share of your spirit."

"It is a hard thing you ask," said Elijah. "But if you see me in my going, it shall be for you. If you do not, it shall not."

And as they were still walking and talking together, behold! a chariot of fire and horses of fire separated them. Elijah was seized. His mantle fell backward to the earth, and he himself rose up by a whirlwind into heaven.

Elisha saw it. "My father, my father!" he cried. "The chariots of Israel and its horsemen!" And he saw him no more.

THE PROPHETS AMOS AND HOSEA

Jeroboam II

The thirteenth king of the northern kingdom, Jeroboam the son of Joash, did what was evil in the sight of the Lord. Indeed, he did not depart from all the sins of his fathers.

He made his kingdom powerful, to be sure. He made it wealthy, and the rich slept on beds of ivory, and the rich owned two homes, one for the winter and one for the summer. He made his kingdom *seem* religious, for the rich brought rich sacrifices to be burned, and the rich ate rich food on many a holy feast day during the year. It seemed to them, under King Jeroboam, that all things were secure: money and luxury, peace, and the kindly presence of a kindly God that would last forever. . . .

But all this wealth was wealth without justice! The people had turned from the commandments of the Lord, and instead of caring for the poor within their gates, they trampled on the poor man. They forced him to pay impossible taxes; when he could not pay, they either forced him to work or else sold him into slavery for silver—sometimes they sold him for no more than a pair of sandals.

And all this religious ceremony was religion without righteousness! The people had turned from the love of the Lord, and instead of worshiping him alone, they mixed him up with other gods, they spoke of him in terms much too familiar, they took it for granted that he would protect them forever.

But the Lord said, "I hate, I despise, your feasts, and I take no delight in your solemn assemblies. Even though you offer me your offerings, I will not accept them; I will not look at them. Take away from me the noise of your songs. Instead, let justice roll down like waters, and righteousness like an everlasting stream!"

For the sake of his wayward people, for the sake of Israel, the Lord God cried out to them again through his prophets.

Through Amos "the Lord roars from Zion and utters his voice from Jerusalem—and the top of Carmel withers!"

The Hard Prediction of the Prophet Amos

Near the tiny village of Tekoa, twelve miles south of Jerusalem, there lived a shepherd named Amos, a man busy with sheep and with the poor fruit of the sycamore tree. The soul of this man was as hard and as craggy, as clean and uncompromising, as the rocky land in which he lived. And he might have lived there all the days of his life—except that the Lord came to him.

The Lord said, "Amos, what do you see?"

Amos looked and saw a plumb line hanging down, a string to judge whether a wall stood true, straight up from the ground.

"I see a plumb line," said Amos.

And the Lord said, "I am hanging a plumb line in the midst of my people, judging them, testing them. Amos, I will never again pass by them. The sanctuaries of Israel shall be laid waste, and I will come against the house of Jeroboam with a sword!"

Thus the Lord spoke to Amos. With this message he changed him from a shepherd into a prophet and sent him into the northern kingdom.

Amos went and cried out to the people of the northern kingdom.

He stood in their holy places and he said, "Hear this word that the Lord has spoken against you, O people of Israel. The Lord says, 'You only have I known of all the families on earth; therefore I will punish you for all your iniquities!' "

He shouted, so that whole cities could hear his voice, "Woe to those who lie upon beds of ivory and eat lambs from the flock, who sing idle songs and drink wine in bowls—*but are not grieved over the ruin of Israel!* For the Lord says, 'The end has come upon my people Israel; I will never again pass by them. The songs of the palace shall become wailings in that day,' says the Lord, 'and the dead bodies shall be many.' "

Louder and louder Amos lifted up his voice in the streets and in the marketplaces. "Seek the Lord," he roared. "Seek the Lord and live, lest he break out like fire in Israel. Seek good, and not evil, that you may live, and so the Lord will be with you. Hate evil, love good, establish justice! It may be that the Lord will be gracious to the remnant of Israel that may survive."

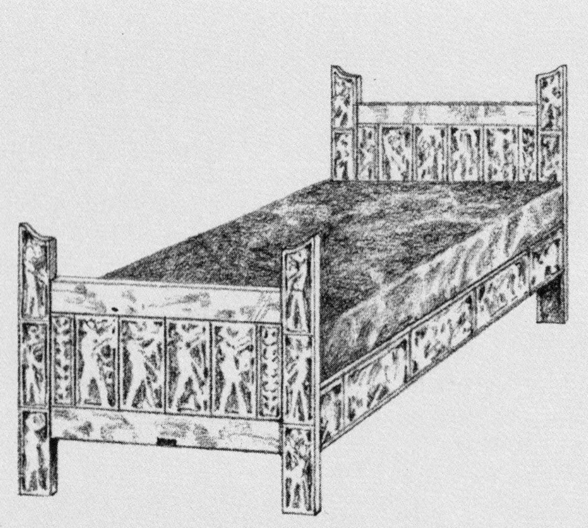

"Beds of ivory" were often elaborately carved and decorated with gold and precious stones. Excavations have also uncovered ivory chairs, couches, and jewelry.

Amos Goes Home

The people of the northern kingdom hated Amos, who stood in their city gates and scolded them. They loathed him, because he spoke the truth. And some of them, like the priest Amaziah, feared him, for his words raked the people like iron prongs.

This priest sent word to King Jeroboam, saying, "Amos is plotting against you. The land is not able to bear his words, for he predicts your death, O King, and the exile of Israel."

With the king's authority, then, Amaziah brought bitter accusation against the prophet. "Get out of here," he said. "Go home! Go back to Judah! Prophesy there. But never again prophesy in this place!"

Amos waited until the priest was done, and then he spoke. "Not by my own will have I said these things; the Lord sent me to say them. Therefore, though I go away, and though you hear my voice no more, yet the prophecy shall linger and the truth come true: You, priest, shall die in an unclean land, and Israel shall surely go into exile!"

So saying, Amos took his leave and went home.

The Merciful Word of the Prophet Hosea

Still during the reign of King Jeroboam in the northern kingdom, God spoke to his people a different word. Through a different prophet. Through Amos, the Lord had said, "Watch out!" Through Hosea, he said,

After Elijah and Elisha came other prophets. One, Hosea, told of his wife who had betrayed him. But he loved her and had taken her back into his house. In the same way, said Hosea, God had not deserted his people when they had turned to false gods.

"But I love you." This is how he said it.

Hosea married a woman named Gomer. In the early years of their marriage she bore him three children. The oldest son was called Jezreel, because the Lord said, "I will put an end to Israel!" Their daughter was called Not Pitied, because the Lord said, "No longer shall I have pity on Israel! On Judah alone will I have pity." And their youngest son, too, had a name that meant something. He was called Not My People, because the Lord said, "You are not my people, and I am not your God!"

Hard words had Hosea for the people when first he prophesied. But then a hard thing happened in his own life, and that made a difference.

Gomer ran away from him. His wife went after other men, other lovers. She broke their marriage covenant. For food and wool and flax and oil and drink, she sold herself and shamed her husband Hosea.

"No," the man said, first to himself, and then to others. "No," he said before witnesses to make the word an official divorce. "No! She is not my wife any more, and I am not her husband!" He was angry; he was wounded; he was full of grief, all at once, for what his wife had done.

But then the Lord spoke to Hosea and said, "Take her back again. Go after her, Hosea. Find her sitting in her sin; wash her; bring her into your home; love her. Love her again. Your love alone can help her, now, and save her. Hosea, love her."

So Hosea went out and found Gomer. He set her free from the bleak life that had entangled her, for she had become a slave. He bought her, and he brought her back again. And though there seemed nothing lovely in the woman, yet he loved her.

"This!" cried the Lord to Hosea. "This!" cried Hosea before all the people of Israel. "This is what happens between you and me," said the Lord. "For you are my wife, and I am your husband," said the Lord. "And I have loved you dearly. From the day that I led you out of Egypt have I loved you. It was I who gave you the grain, the wine, the oil; I who shed gold and silver on you. But what have you done to me? You forgot me, my law, my covenant. And you ran away from me! Look! There is no faithfulness, no kindness, no knowledge of God in the land! There is swearing, lying, killing, stealing, adultery; and murder follows murder! So what shall I do to you, O Israel?

"I shall divorce you," said the Lord. "The pagan Assyrian shall be your king; the sword shall rage against your cities and eat you in your fortresses! You are bent on turning away from me—so you shall be bent like an ox under a yoke, and no one shall remove it! I will destroy you, O Israel—who can help you?"

And then the Lord changed his voice and made it new. Then, suddenly, the Lord spoke gently to his people. "How can I give you up?" he said. "How can I hand you over, O Israel? My heart twists within me; my mercy grows warm and tender. After your sin, after the punishment, I will whisper to you as a husband whispers to his wife. I will bring you to my home and speak tenderly to you. I will not again destroy you—for I am God and not man!

"I will have pity on Not Pitied; and to Not My People I will say, 'You are my people.' And in that day you shall say to me, 'Thou art my God.' "

The Fall of the Northern Kingdom

"Return, O Israel, to the Lord your God," Hosea pleaded. But they did not.

After King Jeroboam died, his son Zechariah reigned over Israel for a bare six months. And he did what was evil in the sight of the Lord. He was assassinated by Shallum, who himself reigned as king but a single month before *he* was assassinated by Menahem. After Menahem, Pekahiah reigned; after him, Pekah; after him, Hoshea—and he was the last.

With an army like none that Israel had ever seen before, the Assyrians came out of the east and overwhelmed Israel. The king of Assyria carried the Israelites away and put them in Halah, and on the Habor, the river of Gozan, in Mesopotamia, and in the cities of the Medes to the east.

Still the people sinned, and the words of the prophets came true. The Assyrians swept out of the east and led the sorrowing people away.

THE PROPHETS ISAIAH AND JEREMIAH

Hezekiah

In the southern kingdom, Judah; in the city of David, Jerusalem; and from the house of the king, a young man watched the destruction of the northern kingdom. He was eighteen years old.

He listened closely to the words of a prophet who also dwelt in Jerusalem, for the words explained this tragedy, and the young man understood.

The prophet said, "The people did not turn to the Lord, nor seek him out. So the Lord cut off Israel, head and tail, in a single day. Every one is godless and an evildoer, and every mouth speaks folly," said the prophet. "For all this, the Lord's anger is not turned away and his hand is stretched out still."

And his hand is stretched out still!

The young man heard those warning words. He took them into his heart. Therefore, when seven years later he was made the king of Judah, Hezekiah did what was right in the eyes of the Lord, according to all that David had done nearly three hundred years before him.

Hezekiah yearned to protect his people against the Assyrians. Therefore he broke down all the places in Judah where other gods were worshiped. He held fast to the Lord God and kept the commandments which the Lord commanded Moses, and the Lord was with him.

The Hopeful Word of the Prophet Isaiah

Other words rang in the young king's ears, good, blessed words spoken by the same prophet, Isaiah. King Hezekiah yearned to see these words come true.

"The people who walked in darkness have seen a great light," Isaiah cried out. "Those who dwelt in the land of deep darkness, on them the light has shined! For the yoke of their burden," Isaiah cried to the Lord, "and the rod of their oppressor you have broken as in the day when you helped Gideon!" Then Isaiah spoke to the people: "For to us a child is born, to us a son is given; and the government shall be upon his shoulder, and his name shall be called Wonderful Counselor, Mighty God, Everlasting Father, Prince of Peace!"

Good days for Judah under a good, anointed king! King Hezekiah himself wanted no less than that. And if, as Isaiah promised, "through the performance of justice and righteousness by the ruler, the zeal of the Lord of hosts will accomplish this," then Hezekiah felt confident that it would be done.

But the prophet Isaiah had even more to say. He saw in the future perpetual peace. He saw, first, a king who would rule with the Spirit of the Lord upon him. This king would not judge by what his eyes saw nor decide by what his ears heard, but with righteousness he would judge the poor, and with equity he would decide for the meek of the earth. "He shall smite the earth with the rod of his mouth," Isaiah prophesied, "and with the breath of his lips he shall slay the wicked!" And when such a king shall rule, then, *then* would come a remarkable peace for all the earth.

Isaiah said, "The wolf shall dwell with the lamb, and the leopard shall lie down with the kid, and the calf and the lion and the fatling together—and a little child shall lead them."

The prophet said, "The cow and the bear shall feed while their young lie down together; and the lion shall eat straw like the ox. The sucking child shall play at the hole of the cobra, and the weaned child shall put his hand on the viper's den."

Isaiah cried out, "They shall not hurt or destroy in all my holy mountain! For the earth shall be full of the knowledge of the Lord as the waters cover the sea."

For King Hezekiah—indeed, for all of Judah and for all time—there were two messages. One was a warning: "Turn to the Lord! Seek him out!" And the other was a promise: "Peace! Peace! With joy you will draw water from the wells of salvation!"

Thus did the young king Hezekiah begin to rule in Judah. And this must be said of him: For many years he was a very good king, faithful unto the Lord God. But there came a time when he put greater faith in the nations around him than in God, and that was a disastrous decision.

The Political Word of the Prophet Isaiah

The years of Hezekiah's reign passed by. Every year he paid a little gold, a little silver, to the Assyrians—tribute money—so that they would not attack his kingdom. This was something his father had begun, and he himself despised the doing of it.

So when the Egyptians planned to fight the Assyrians, and when they invited kings like Hezekiah to join in the attack, King Hezekiah thought he might. Perhaps it would be good to put faith in Egypt, a far greater nation than Judah.

"Put faith in Egypt?" The prophet was shocked. "Rather, put faith in God! Look," said the prophet Isaiah. "Look at me! The way that I am is the way that Egypt shall be when Assyria is done with it!"

The king looked and saw that Isaiah was walking barefoot, stripped naked but for a loincloth. "Ashamed, dismayed, confounded, *naked* will Egypt be led away by the enemy," said the prophet. "Put your hope, O King, in the Lord!"

Hezekiah listened to Isaiah this time; and though nations round about Judah fell before the Assyrians, Judah did not. Judah paid a little gold, a little silver yearly.

But the day came when Hezekiah, still yearning to be rid of the Assyrians, did not listen to Isaiah.

When one king in Assyria died and another took his place, Hezekiah decided to

King Hezekiah of the southern kingdom, Judah, meant to join Egypt in war against Assyria. But the prophet Isaiah warned him against such a plan.

In time, Hezekiah refused to hear Isaiah, and soon the Assyrians were at Jerusalem's gates. The king cried out to God, and the Lord heard his prayers. That night an angel smote the enemy in their camp.

send no more tribute. Let the Assyrians come! He would join with other kingdoms in his area, and together they would resist the foe! Into his own hands Hezekiah would take the sword, and by his own might he would fight!

"Woe!" cried the prophet Isaiah. "Woe!" was the word of the Lord through Isaiah. "Woe to the rebellious children who carry out a plan, but not mine! Who make an alliance, but not of my Spirit!" said the Lord.

"In returning to *me* and resting in *my* care shall you be saved," said the Lord. "In quietness, in trust you will be strong. But no! You say, 'No! We will ride and fight in our own strength.' Therefore, ride. Therefore, fight. But a thousand of you shall ride away from one of them. And five of them shall chase you all until you are left like a lonely flagstaff on top of a mountain!"

So spoke Isaiah. But this time Hezekiah did not listen—and the Assyrians came. All of the allies of Judah fell, one by one. And then the cities of Judah began to fall before the advance of the enemy. Finally they stood outside the very walls of Jerusalem, crying, "Your God cannot save you, Judah!"

Hezekiah heard the threat. He saw the armies scratching at the door. And now he was afraid.

The king tore his clothes in grief and went into the Temple. In the holiest place he knelt down. "O Lord God of Israel, you are God, you alone, of all the kingdoms of the earth," he prayed. "Do you hear the mockery that the Assyrians make of you? Save us, O Lord, from their hand. Show all the kingdoms that you are God alone!"

Then Isaiah came to Hezekiah. "The Lord has heard your prayer," he said. "Not an arrow nor a shield of Assyria shall come into the city. For thus says the Lord, 'I will defend this city, for my own sake and for my servant David.' "

That night the angel of the Lord killed a hundred and eighty-five thousand in the camp of the Assyrians.

"The Lord waits to be gracious to you," said Isaiah. "The Lord is a God of justice. Blessed are all those who wait for him."

Josiah

When Hezekiah died, his son Manasseh ascended to his throne and ruled for a long time. But Manasseh did what was evil in the sight of the Lord—as did his son, Amon.

Both permitted the worship of other gods in Judah; both continued to strip the glory and the wealth from the Temple of the Lord, to send it to Assyria. And in their day innocent blood stained the streets of Jerusalem.

"I will," said the Lord, "wipe Jerusalem as one wipes a dish, wiping it and turning it upside down!"

And the Lord would; soon, soon he would let Jerusalem be broken even as the northern kingdom had been broken, conquered, ruined. But not yet!

For Amon's son was different from his father. King Josiah did what was right in the eyes of the Lord, and the Lord withheld the punishment. To Josiah the Lord said, "Your eyes shall not see all the evil which I shall bring upon this place."

Josiah repaired the bare Temple of God with timber and stone. And when the book of the Torah, God's teachings, was found under the rubble, Josiah had it read to him. And when he heard all the words therein, he ripped his clothes in shame, he wept in an almighty sorrow, and he cried out, "Great is the wrath of the Lord, because our fathers have not obeyed the words of this book!"

King Josiah loved the Lord; therefore the Lord held back the hurt of Judah.

To all the men of Judah, to all the people of Jerusalem, to the priests and the prophets, to the children and the grown, King Josiah himself read this book of the Torah. And then in their hearing he vowed to follow its commandments, its testimonies, and its laws with all his heart and soul. Then he burned every vessel in Judah that had the taint of Baal. Those who worshiped the sun and the moon he drove out of the land. Idols he burned and beat to dust, and the dust he cast on common graves. Altars and pillars and gates and buildings dedicated to false gods Josiah smashed into pieces. Witches went. Wizards were no more seen in the land. And the king commanded that the Passover be kept with a greater faith, a more intense righteousness than ever before. And so it was that in the eighteenth year of King Josiah the Passover was kept in Jerusalem.

Before Josiah there had never been a king equal to him, one who turned to the Lord with all his heart and with all his soul and with all his might, according to all the teachings of Moses.

And after he died, never again did a good

Archaeologists found two temples at Ugarit dedicated to Baal, the god of the sky and rain. They also found bronze statues of Baal and clay tablets inscribed with myths.

king arise in Judah. He was the last. He was the last.

A New Enemy: Babylon!

After Josiah died, a new enemy showed his face, grim on the eastern horizon. He was Nebuchadnezzar of Babylon, whose empire had swallowed up even the Assyrians. Westward he marched with his forces, into Judah, up to the walls of Jerusalem. Josiah's grandson, King Jehoiachin, simply gave up.

Then Nebuchadnezzar plundered the house of the Lord, taking its wealth, its gold and silver. And the warriors of Judah, and the craftsmen, the smiths, the king himself,

---

The evils of kings of the southern kingdom were many. But King Josiah loved the Lord, and God withheld Judah's punishment. Josiah rebuilt God's Temple and read the Torah to all young and old.

and all his family Nebuchadnezzar took away to Babylon.

Yet even then Judah would not be still. Even then—though the prophet Jeremiah pleaded for surrender to Babylon—Judah raised a shaky, skinny fist against its enemy. Even then Judah trusted in itself.

The Words and the Troubles of Jeremiah

For a few years Nebuchadnezzar fought wars far away from Judah. He left the people alone under their last king, Zedekiah, so the people had time to think that they were strong still. They decided to fight the mighty enemy Babylon.

It was a proud, foolish decision, and the prophet Jeremiah knew that. He tried to change their minds. He put the yoke of an ox on his own neck, then tied it to himself by leather thongs and walked through Jerusalem crying, "Wear the yoke of Nebuchadnezzar! Submit to him! Serve Babylon! For the Lord himself has given him power, and the Lord himself will consume any nation that does not wear his yoke!"

But there were other prophets at that time who said, "Don't serve Babylon!" who said, "The Lord will bring our wealth back home again!" These false prophets were enraged by Jeremiah's yoke. One of them, Hananiah, ripped the yoke from Jeremiah's shoulders and broke it, saying, "Thus the Lord *breaks* the yoke of Babylon!"

Jeremiah said, "How I wish that were true. But you are making the people to trust in a lie. Not of wood, but of iron shall be the yoke that the Lord puts on the neck of the people!"

Neither did the leaders of Jerusalem like to hear what Jeremiah prophesied. They, too, were enraged by words that frightened the people instead of encouraging them for war. In a little while, then, they arrested him for desertion and locked him in dungeon cells.

But King Zedekiah was nervous. It was no small undertaking to challenge Babylon, and he wanted assurance from everyone—especially from the hard prophet Jeremiah—that he was right. Therefore he brought Jeremiah to himself and met him secretly. "Is there any word from the Lord?" he asked.

"There is," said Jeremiah. It was a simple pronouncement: "You shall be delivered into the hand of the king of Babylon."

Zedekiah did not receive assurance from Jeremiah. He prepared to send him back to the dungeons. But Jeremiah pleaded with him, "Don't send me back. I will die there."

So the king committed him to the court of the guard, where he had more freedom, and where he was given a loaf of bread a day.

But still the prophet would not hold his peace. He said, "He who stays in this city shall die by the sword and by famine. But he who goes to the Babylonians shall live." He said, "This city shall surely be given to the king of Babylon!"

Finally the leaders of the city could stand this discouraging talk no longer. They went to the king and demanded that Jeremiah be put to death. "He is frightening our soldiers," they said, "and weakening our people."

King Zedekiah said, "He is yours. Do what you want with him."

Immediately they seized Jeremiah and let him down by ropes into a cistern. There was no water in this pit—just mud. Jeremiah sank into the mud, and the leaders left him there, expecting him to die.

But a friend of Jeremiah went to the king and pleaded for his life. So the king changed his mind and said, "Take three men and lift him out before he dies."

With old rags and worn-out clothing, the friend went to Jeremiah's pit. "Tie these under your arms," he said. Then he pulled the prophet out to safety.

Again Zedekiah called for Jeremiah. "Please, tell me the truth," he said.

"If I tell you the truth," said Jeremiah, "you will kill me."

Zedekiah said, "As the Lord lives, I will not put you to death. Listen: I am afraid of the Jews who have deserted to Babylon, that they will take me and abuse me."

Jeremiah said, "You shall not be given to them. King, obey the voice of the Lord, and

---

After Josiah, Judah fell to Babylon. And still the people would not obey God's will. The prophet Jeremiah tried to guide them, but his were hard words, and none would listen. To silence him, the leaders of the city left him to die in a cistern.

it shall be well with you. Surrender to Babylon and this city shall be spared. But if you do not surrender, then this city shall be theirs, and they shall burn it with fire, and you shall not escape from their hand!"

It was the same word, repeated all over again. There was nothing new in it. Yet even now King Zedekiah would not listen to the prophet Jeremiah. He did not surrender. He did not submit. He tried to fight—and he failed.

The Fall of the Southern Kingdom

So Nebuchadnezzar returned and burned the city Jerusalem. He burned the Temple built by Solomon. He burned the palace built by David. Every house of the city he burned to the ground: black, sooty graves where laughter once had been. He destroyed the wall around the city. Whatever had value, that was taken. Whatever was living, that was carried away. And the people themselves, the chosen people, those who were left of the family of Israel, the remnant—they were driven into exile. Nebuchadnezzar went home to Babylon with full hands. With full and breaking hearts the chosen people watched their home disappear behind them.

"My anguish! My anguish! I writhe in pain! Oh, the walls of my heart! My heart is beating wildly, I cannot keep silent. Where are you, Jerusalem?"

The Hopeful Word of the Prophet Jeremiah

He had tried for years to turn the people's hearts, and he had failed. He said, "O Jerusalem, wash your heart from wickedness, that you may be saved!" They did not, and they were not. He said to the king, "Serve Babylon and live." The king would not, and so he did not. Always Jeremiah had spoken

Jeremiah survived his trial, but Jerusalem did not. King Nebuchadnezzar returned. He burned the city and led the people of Judah away to Babylon.

The kingdoms of the north and the south were destroyed. But Jeremiah saw hope in the days ahead. The Lord's people would triumph.

what the people did not want to hear.

And now, remaining behind in Jerusalem, he sang what they did not expect to hear.

"A voice is heard in Ramah, lamentation and bitter weeping. Rachel is weeping for her children, and she refuses to be comforted, because they are not.

"But thus says the Lord: 'Hush your weeping; dry your eyes; for your work shall be rewarded, and they shall come back from the land of the enemy.

" 'Behold, the days are coming,' says the Lord, 'when I will make a new covenant with the house of Israel and the house of Judah, not like the old one which I made with their fathers when I brought them out of Egypt, my covenant which they broke. But this is the new covenant: I will put my law *within them.* I will write it upon their hearts. And I will be their God, and they shall be my people, and they shall all know me! For I will forgive their iniquity, and I will remember their sin no more.' "

So sang Jeremiah, words of comfort even in the days of weeping. And he sang, "They shall come back from the land of the enemy. 'There is hope for the future,' says the Lord."

Israel in Exile

FAITH IN THE TIME OF TRIAL

THE GREAT NATION brought down! The free people conquered and bound! The people of a Promised Land ripped from that land and carried into Babylon! The multitude made small, the chosen of the Lord now but a bare remnant in a foreign land. The issue of Abraham, the wanderers of Moses, the armies under Joshua and Deborah and Gideon, the citizens of David's reign and Solomon's, the ears that tingled to the prophets' messages—Israel! Israel sat in desolation. Israel sat in exile.

It was a wonderful history of the saving acts of the Lord God that they could remember and rehearse together. But when they raised their eyes and looked at the city of Babylon, the story was all a memory. For now it was not the salvation of the Lord, but his punishment, that they were experiencing.

Sad Songs

Did David sing songs of joy and dance when the ark was brought into Jerusalem? Well, the ark was gone, and the Temple that housed it was gone. And the city of David itself was rubble. So joy was gone, too. Israel sang sad songs.

"How long, O Lord?" they sang. "Wilt thou forget me forever? How long wilt thou hide thy face from me? How long must I suffer this sorrow in my soul all the day? How long shall mine enemy walk on my neck?

"Answer me, O Lord my God! Lighten mine eyes, lest I sleep the sleep of death, lest my foes rejoice because I am shaken.

"I have trusted in thy strong, strong love. My heart shall rejoice in thy salvation. I will sing to the Lord, because he will deal bountifully with me!"

Sad, yearning songs. But in these songs, Israel's faith began to return. In exile, Israel began again to fear the Lord!

"Out of the depths have I cried unto thee, O Lord," they sang. "Lord, hear my voice! Let thine ears be attentive to my cries and my pleadings!

"If thou, Lord, shouldst mark iniquities, O Lord, who could stand? But there is forgiveness with thee, that thou mayest be feared.

"I wait for the Lord, my soul waits, and in his word do I hope. My soul waits for the Lord more than they that watch for the morning—more than they that watch for the morning!

"O Israel, hope in the Lord! For with the Lord there is mercy, mercy and forgiveness. And he will redeem the people Israel from all their iniquities!"

Dry Bones! The Healing Vision of Ezekiel

During these hard years in exile, the merciful God of Israel was not silent. He continued to speak to his people and to soothe them through the prophets, especially through the prophet Ezekiel.

"Listen to what the Lord did, and hear what he said unto me," Ezekiel said to the woeful people.

"He set me down in the middle of a valley. And I looked, and the valley was full of bones. The bones of dead men. A hundred thousand bones. And behold, they were very dry.

"And he said to me, 'Son of man, can these bones live again?'

"And I answered, 'O Lord God, thou knowest.'

"Again, he said to me, 'Prophesy to the bones. Say to them, O dry bones, hear the word of the Lord. Tell them that I shall cause breath to enter them, and they shall live!'

"So I prophesied as the Lord commanded; and while I did, I heard a noise. A rattling! The bones were coming together, bone to bone! Then there were sinews between them, and meat came upon them, and skin began to cover them! But there was no breath in them.

"Then the Lord said to me, 'Prophesy to the breath, son of man. Cry to the breath that it must come from the four winds and breathe upon these dead, that they may live!'

"So I prophesied as the Lord commanded, and the breath came into them, and they lived! They stood up on their feet, an exceedingly great company of people!

"Then the Lord said to me what now I say to you, Israel. He said, 'Son of man, these bones are the whole house of Israel. They grieve that they are dried up, lost, and clean cut off. But, O my people, I will open your graves and raise you from your graves!' said the Lord. 'And I will put my Spirit in you, and you shall live, and I will place you in your own land again. And then you shall know that I am the Lord!' "

DANIEL

Boys for Nebuchadnezzar

When the king of Babylon had brought the best of Judah to his land—the noble folk, the priests, the educated, the wealthy, the craftsmen—then he wanted the best of the best for himself.

"I want," he commanded his servant, "boys both handsome and smart, boys skillful and ready to learn. Raise them on my food in my palace, educate them, and at the end of three years, they will serve me."

So his servant searched and found the best. Among those who sat down to eat the king's rich, delicious food was Daniel, and on either side of him, three others: Shadrach, Meshach, and Abednego.

When the boys got up from the table, four plates had been untouched.

"Eat it!" said the king's servant.

"Sir, we cannot," said Daniel. "It is unclean."

"Why, it is the king's own food, washed and seasoned and full of goodness. Eat it!"

"But it is not the Lord's food, sir," said Daniel. "Some things our God will not permit us to eat, and whatever we can eat must be prepared in a particular way. This is unclean, and for love of the Lord our God, we will not eat it."

"Don't you understand," the poor servant said, "that if you don't eat, and if you grow sallow and skinny, then Nebuchadnezzar will blame *me?* He'll have my head!"

"Then bring us vegetables," said Daniel.

"You can't live on vegetables," said the servant. "A growing boy needs meat, and besides that, he will only pick at a green leaf."

"Bring us vegetables and water for ten days," said Daniel, "then compare us with the others and see if we are healthy or not."

Ten days of onions; ten days of lentils, leeks, and garlics; ten days of radishes; and now and then a fig. But when the ten days were done, these four boys of Judah looked fatter and more fit than any who had swallowed a piece of seasoned meat.

So they kept their faith, Daniel, Shadrach, Meshach, and Abednego. They ate vegetables, and they grew in wisdom, learning the letters of the Babylonian language. Daniel, it was discovered, could interpret dreams as well as his ancestor Joseph once did while in bondage in another country.

The Fiery Furnace

After the Jewish boys had completed their three years of training, had grown up and had been given positions in government, King Nebuchadnezzar decided to make an image of gold. *Make* is too small a word for what he did. He constructed, he erected, he *created* a monument that rose full ninety feet above the Plain of Dura—an idol, glowering from proud, majestic height. Then, when the thing was done, Nebuchadnezzar sent out a decree through all the land:

"Satraps, prefects, governors, counsel-

Daniel, Shadrach, Meshach, and Abednego loved the Lord their God and kept their faith. Though they sat at Nebuchadnezzar's table, they would not eat the king's rich food. They ate only vegetables.

ors, treasurers, justices, magistrates, every official of Babylon, come! Come worship the image of my own making!"

And they came. In colorful, noble dress, they came. Striding and riding with the dignity of power, they came. Servants buzzing round each almighty personage, like flies around oxen, they came to the Plain of Dura. And when a clash of music filled the air, every official went down on his face before the idol to worship—

Every official but three. Shadrach, Meshach, and Abednego of Judah—Jews—stayed standing.

When Nebuchadnezzar heard of their civil disobedience, he was furious. "Bring them to me!" he roared.

"Is it true that you do not worship my god?" he demanded of the three.

They nodded. It was true.

"Do you know the punishment waiting for those who will not worship my god?" he demanded. "Have you heard of my burning, fiery furnace?"

They nodded. They knew and had heard.

"Then are you ready now to stand before the image that I have made, and at the sound of music to fall down and worship it?"

They stood quiet awhile, then said, "We needn't answer you that, O King. Our God himself will answer you. He will deliver us from your hand. And if not, we still will not worship either your god or the image."

The king's face swelled, purple with the burning rage inside of him. "The furnace!" he roared. "Stoke that furnace to seven times hotter than it has ever been before!" And, "Mighty men!" he shouted. "I want my mightiest men to bind these three and to cast them into that furnace! Into the fire!"

Still dressed in all their clothing, Shadrach, Meshach, and Abednego were tied, dragged, and thrown into the furnace. So hot was the white, whipping flame in the furnace that the mighty men who came near it perished on the spot.

All the high and mighty of Babylon came to worship the great golden idol King Nebuchadnezzar had made. On the Plain of Dura all bowed down before it—all but three. Shadrach, Meshach, and Abednego would not worship the glittering image.

Though red-hot flames surrounded Shadrach, Meshach, and Abednego, not a hair was burned upon their heads. They trusted in their God, and he delivered them from Nebuchadnezzar's fiery furnace.

After a while Nebuchadnezzar himself came to witness the execution. He stooped down to see whether bones or only dust was left of the stubborn Jews.

Suddenly he stood up again. He stared at his counselors. "How many men did we cast bound into the furnace?" he asked in a low, trembling voice.

"Three, O King," they said.

"But I see four men," said the king. "Loose. Walking in the midst of the fire. Unhurt. And the fourth looks like a son of the gods!"

Then he turned to the furnace. "Shadrach!" he called. "Meshach, Abednego! Servants of the Most High God, come out! Come here!"

They did. And when they did, a long gasp of wonder went up from the people. For the satraps, the prefects, the governors, the counselors, treasurers, justices, magistrates—all saw that not a hair on the young men's heads had been singed. Their clothing was still clean, and no smell of smoke was on them.

The king said, "Blessed be the God of Shadrach, Meshach, and Abednego! They trusted in him, giving their bodies to be burned rather than worshiping any other god—and his angel delivered them! Therefore, I make a decree: If anyone speaks against this God, he shall be torn limb from limb! For no other god can deliver in this way."

Handwriting, and the End of Babylon

A long time later, when Nebuchadnezzar had died and when Daniel was an aging man, Belshazzar, king of Babylon, gave a great feast for a thousand of his lords. And he drank wine in front of the thousand.

Now, Nebuchadnezzar had been a proud, vainglorious king, and his vanity had been a sin in him. But his son Belshazzar was the same and worse. He added sin to sin by drinking from the vessels that once were in the Temple of the Lord, cups dedicated to the Lord God only, and holy unto him. From these the king and his concubines drank wine with giggles and dribbling.

As the king was drinking, he looked over the rim of the cup and saw a sight that chilled his blood.

"Look!" he whispered, and his thousand lords fell silent.

The fingers of a man's hand had appeared. They were writing on the wall of the king's palace, opposite the lampstand.

"What is that?" the king whispered. His arms and legs felt weak; his knees knocked together. "What is that?" he screamed. "Who can read that for me?"

The astrologers and the wise men of Babylon came one after the other; but none could either read or understand the words written on the king's wall.

Belshazzar paced the hall that only a little while before was filled with laughter. His face was white. He was terrified. He roared, "What is that! Who can read that for me?"

The queen heard his roaring and came. "Don't be afraid, King. There's a man in your kingdom whom your father respected, who can interpret dreams, explain riddles, solve problems—a wise man named Daniel—"

"Get him!" cried the king.

Belshazzar, king of Babylon, saw handwriting on the wall. None of his seers could tell him the meaning of the writing.

When Daniel came into the room, he looked at the king before he looked at the wall.

"Hear my words first, O King," he said, "before I tell you those. You have," said Daniel, "gone even further than the pride of your father. You have set your face against the very Lord of heaven, insulting the vessels of his house. You praise gods of silver and gold, of bronze, iron, wood, and stone, but you do not honor the God in whose hand is your life. *Therefore* the fingers, O King: They are from heaven. And *therefore* the words which they have written on your wall."

And Daniel read them: *"Mene, Mene, Tekel,* and *Parsin.*

"Mene!" said Daniel. "God has numbered the days of your kingdom and brought it to an end.

"Tekel!" said Daniel. "You have been weighed in the balance and found wanting.

"Parsin!" said Daniel. "Your kingdom is divided between the Medes and the Persians."

And so it was that that very night Belshazzar the Babylonian king was slain. Darius of the Medes received his kingdom.

After Belshazzar, Darius ruled the kingdom. He intended to place Daniel above all other officials. But some of the leaders plotted against Daniel.

Daniel in the Lion's Den

It pleased Darius to set a hundred and twenty satraps over his whole kingdom. Over the satraps he set three administrators, of whom Daniel was one, and because Daniel was filled with such an excellent spirit, the king planned soon to set him alone over the entire kingdom. So the satraps and the administrators together despised him and looked for some fault in him that would dishonor him.

But Daniel was faithful. No fault was found in the man.

Therefore they conceived a plan by which to break him and to bring him down.

"King," they said to Darius, "we have studied the matter together, and we believe that you are equal to any god."

Darius smiled.

"Therefore, make a law that any man who worships another god besides yourself shall be cast into the den of lions."

Darius mused, smiled, and nodded.

"Good! Here is the law written out, O King," they said. "Sign it, so that it cannot be changed."

Darius signed the law. It could not be changed.

Several of the satraps went and hid outside of Daniel's window.

And Daniel, although he came to know of the law, never once broke his custom. Daily, three times a day, he continued to kneel in a window open to Jerusalem, praying and giving thanks to the Lord his God. No law, not even that of the Medes and the Persians, would break his faithfulness to God.

"Ah-ha!" cried the satraps. "The man of Judah sneers at the law of the king of the Medes!" They had him taken and held, while one of them went to Darius.

"King!" he said. "Didn't you sign the law that no one could worship any god but you?"

Darius said, "I did."

"And wasn't the punishment that such a one be cast into the den of lions?"

"It was," said Darius, "and it still is so. I signed it. It cannot be changed."

"Good!" said the satrap. "That Daniel, that fellow from Judah, ignores your law. Three times a day he prays to his own God!"

The king, when he heard this, was distressed. The whole day through, until the sun went down, he tried to think of ways to rescue Daniel.

But the satraps said, "You signed the law." And the satraps said, "It cannot be changed."

Finally Darius muttered the command, and Daniel was brought and cast into the den of lions. It was a pit with a narrow hole at the top, a wide floor at the bottom, and lions. And Daniel.

"May your God deliver you," said Darius as a stone was pushed over the opening. "May your God, dear Daniel, deliver you," as he sealed the stone with his own ring. Then the king went to his palace, where he spent the night restless, unable to eat or to sleep.

At the break of day Darius ran back to the den. Anguish in his voice, he cried, "Daniel! Daniel! Daniel! Has your God been able to deliver you from the lions?"

And Daniel, in the hollow of the pit, answered, "King, my God sent his angel to shut the lions' mouths. Because I am blameless before him, they have not hurt me."

Darius smiled with relief—and commanded those who accused Daniel to try a night themselves in the den of lions. And then he decreed that all men tremble before the God of Daniel.

Going Home Again!

Seventy years God's people were in Babylon, seventy years bowed down under the rule of foreign kings in foreign lands. But then the Persians utterly defeated the Babylonians—and a prophet rubbed his eyes; a prophet raised his head. And then a new king, Cyrus, took the whole empire into his own hand—and a prophet grinned; a prophet stood up. And then this Cyrus revealed that he was not as cruel as the kings who went before him—and a prophet clapped his hands; a prophet opened up his

The satraps of Babylon tricked Daniel and Darius. They knew Daniel was faithful to God despite the king's law. Daniel was thrown into the lion's den. But God protected him, and in the morning, Daniel, unharmed, greeted the anxious king.

mouth and shouted. And this is what that prophet said.

"Comfort ye, comfort ye my people, saith your God! Speak ye comfortably to Jerusalem, and cry unto her that her exile is ended! That her iniquity is forgiven!"

For Cyrus, this prophet knew, was about to send the people of God back home again! Back to Jerusalem! Back to the land of their ancestors and of their God!

"A voice cries out: 'Prepare in the wilderness the way of the Lord! For he is coming to his people. Therefore, make straight in the desert a highway for our God. Every valley shall be lifted up, every mountain and hill cut down, that the road be smooth. And the crooked places shall be made straight, and the rough places planed, that the road for him be smooth!' "

This prophet was very happy. The Lord was coming like a king to lead his people through the desert by a straight road home again. It was over. The time of trial was over. They were going home again.

Cyrus's Decree

A buzzing in the homes of the Jews. Exiles whispering in one another's ears. The raising of grateful hands to heaven. The exiles have heard the message. God is at work in the affairs of the peoples! God has moved the king of the vast empire of Persia to make a decree. The decree is law, and it shall be. For thus says Cyrus, king of Persia:

"The Lord, the God of heaven, has charged me to build him a house at Jerusalem, which is in Judah. Let all his people go up to Jerusalem and rebuild the house of the Lord, the God of Israel. Let the cost be paid from the royal treasury. And also let the gold and silver vessels, which Nebuchadnezzar took from the house of God, be brought back to the Temple, each to its place!"

Now there is hasty labor in the homes of the Jews, and happiness. The fathers of the families gather them together. The priests, the Levites, and the Temple servants gather themselves together. Many of the Jews who were captive in Babylon gather in a great assembly—and go.

The Temple Is Begun and Left Undone

When the seventh month came, and the people were in their towns and homes again, they all gathered as one man in Jerusalem. Near the ruined, gutted house of God they built the altar of the God of Israel, and there they began again to offer their burnt offerings to the Lord. Daily, morning and evening, according to the laws, they offered burnt offerings, and they kept all the appointed feasts of the Lord.

But the foundation for a new Temple had not been laid.

Two years and two months later, they began that foundation. Money was drawn from the Persian treasury for masons and carpenters, for food, drink, and oil, and for the cedar trees of Lebanon. Workers were assigned, and supervisors were appointed over them. . . .

When the builders laid the foundation of the Temple of the Lord, then came the priests in their vestments, with trumpets and cymbals and joyful song, praising and giving thanks to the Lord, singing, "For he is good, for his steadfast love toward Israel lasts forever!"

And all the people shouted a thunderous shout.

But many of the heads of the families, the elders who had seen the first Temple, wept to see this foundation. They wept so loud that weeping and shouting were mixed, and the people could not tell one from the other. And the sound was heard afar.

It was no secret, then, what the people were doing. Their enemies soon learned that a new Temple was begun in the place of the old. And because they feared a strong Judah too close to them, these enemies tried every trick to trouble the Jews and to stop the building. When Cyrus was alive, very little was added to the foundation. Then, when he died and another king reigned over the Persians, work stopped altogether. For Judah's enemies wrote a letter to this king, reminding him that Jerusalem had always been a rebellious city, proud, restless, and quick to fight its governors. If the Jews built their Temple again, said the letter, then they would surely rebel again.

So the new king of Persia sent out a new decree which said, "Stop!" And the enemies

---

For many years the Jews lived in exile. Then the decree rang out—to Jerusalem! Home at last! Mothers, fathers, sons, and daughters happily piled high their carts. In one great assembly they left.

came into Jerusalem with this decree and with swords, and they said, "Stop!"

Their Temple was barely above the ground. But the Jews did stop. Sad and discouraged, they returned to their homes.

The Temple Completed

"Each of you has built *himself* a house! And each of your houses has a roof, and panels on the inside! But where is the wood and the roof for *my* house? And when will you give *me* a house again, that I may take pleasure in it and appear in my glory?"

The Lord God sent a new prophet to his people to pinch them in their lethargy, to wake them, move them, and set them to building the Temple again. The prophet's name was Haggai.

"Your return to Jerusalem has been miserable," said Haggai, "and do you know why? You looked for much, and lo! it came to little. Then even that little was made less in a drought—and do you know why? Because the house of the Lord still lies in ruins!"

First Haggai, and after him Zechariah, preached to the people. They roused Zerubbabel, who led the people—and the sound of the hammer on stone rang out again in Jerusalem. A new spirit! They began again to rebuild the Temple.

Immediately enemies sent another letter to the king of Persia. But this was still a different king, the third since Cyrus. He did not say, "Stop." Instead he went back to the records of Cyrus's reign. There he found the law which said specifically that the Jews should rebuild the house of God. "Not only," said this king, "shall they build the Temple, but we will also pay for it! And you," he said to the enemies, "will help!"

Now the Jews were laughing again. Now the people of God bent their backs to the work. Now the house of the Lord rose with diligence and with speed.

And when the Temple was completed, they gathered with a holy and careful joy. They sacrificed hundreds of lambs, rams, and bulls to the Lord, and goats as sin offerings for each of the twelve tribes. Then they celebrated the Passover in remembrance of all the merciful acts the Lord had done to save them throughout their history.

Joy burst the hearts of the Jews. Tears overflowed their eyes. For the Lord had made them glad again—the Lord, the God of Israel!

The Jews began to rebuild Jerusalem. Slowly the rubble around the city grew into a wall. It was a low wall at first, only waist-high. But under the hands of builders strengthened by purpose and faith, it rose to towering heights—a massive defense.

The Wall of Jerusalem

In those days many a fine weapon was used in war, both for attack and for defense: horses and chariots, swords, spears, shields, bows, arrows, slings, fire, and the battering ram. But no weapon was more important than the one most massive: the wall around a city.

Without a wall, a city could not be defended. Without a wall, no effective attack could be prepared and launched upon a nearby enemy. Without a wall, a city was sadly vulnerable, soft, and easily beaten.

Jerusalem, when the people returned to it, was without a wall.

This knowledge was a great sadness for a man named Nehemiah. He was a high official in the Persian court, and he lived far away from Jerusalem. But his heart was there, for he was a Jew.

Day after day the worry tightened in his face, and fear for his people made him weep. He mourned; he fasted; he prayed to the Lord. And his soul became so heavy that the king himself asked Nehemiah the cause of his sorrow.

"A wall broken down," said Nehemiah. "Gates burned to the ground. My people are in danger, O King, so long as Jerusalem stands naked before the enemy."

The king said, "Make a request."

And Nehemiah did. He asked leave to go to build the wall again.

And the king said, "Go."

Building the Wall

As long as the wall was a crumbled mound around the city of Jerusalem, the enemies of the Jews were happy. There was no threat to them. They could, if they wished, simply march into the city and harass it with a sword and a little knife.

Therefore Nehemiah kept his plan a secret when he came to Jerusalem. Hidden by the night he went to the old wall. In darkness he inspected it, touched it, and measured the damage there. And then, when he knew precisely what must be done, he called the leaders of the Jews to himself.

By a quiet persuasion he convinced them of the need for a wall and of his own right to supervise their building it. For he had a plan, and he had the blessing of the king—and he had the guidance of God.

The leaders of the Jews said, "Then let us build it!"

The work began.

The work was spread, by families, all around the old wall. The Sheep Gate, the Fish Gate, the Old Gate, and the Valley Gate, the gates called Dung and Fountain and Water and Horse and East—someone worked rebuilding each of these. And others worked to repair the walls between the gates. The Tower of the Hundred, the Tower of the Ovens—both began to rise again.

And the enemies of the Jews were no longer happy.

At first they sneered at the labor. "What are these feeble Jews doing?" they said. "Ha! Even a fox could knock through such a wall!"

But the work went on. And the wall kept rising. And mockery soon turned to anger and to fear.

So the enemies plotted to join their armies and to fight Jerusalem before it could finish and fight back.

The wall was at half its height when the workers heard of the plot. They were weak from lifting and pushing the stone; so how could they find strength to lift a sword and swing it?

Yet Nehemiah encouraged them. "Do not be afraid of them," he said. "Remember the Lord, who is great and terrible, and fight for your brethren, your sons, your daughters, your wives, and your homes!"

Workmen became soldiers! Even a low wall is something. So when the enemies heard that Nehemiah had set a guard all around Jerusalem, their plot broke down, and they did not attack.

From that day on, Nehemiah divided his workers into two groups, half to build and half to guard the building. And he gave the guard a signal. "Wherever there is trouble," he said, "the trumpet will blow. You come to that place and fight, and our God will fight for us."

To the workmen, too, he gave each a short sword to wear at his belt. The trumpet would change them immediately into soldiers, rushing to the point of trouble, rushing to fight.

No one left the city by night. No one took off his clothes to sleep. And everyone kept his weapon in hand.

The work went on. The wall kept rising.

And now the enemy, afraid to fight, tried tricks to shatter Nehemiah's confidence.

Four times they invited him to a harmless meeting in a little town outside Jerusalem. Four times Nehemiah replied, "Thank you, no. I am busy about a great work, and I cannot come." For he knew that such a meeting would end in his murder.

A fifth time the enemy called him out, saying, "We know you plan rebellion against the Persians! We know you plan to set yourself up as king in Judah! Come talk with us, or we will tell the king your plans, and he will come to talk with you!"

"You know nothing but what you yourselves made up!" Nehemiah answered. "There are no such plans in Jerusalem."

Finally, they sent a priest to Nehemiah, who spoke to him as a friend. "Hide in the Temple," this priest said, "because they are coming to kill you at night. At night they will kill you!"

"Sacrilege!" said Nehemiah. "It would be sacrilegious for me to enter the Temple! And what would the people think of me then? They would hate me instead of following me. No, you are no friend of mine, you and your warning words. You were paid by the enemy!"

So the work went on. And the wall kept rising. And on the fifty-second day it was done!

When the enemies heard this last, crushing report, all the nations round about Jerusalem were afraid. For they understood that there would have been no wall except by the help of the Lord. But there was a wall! The Lord, the God of Israel, had seen to it.

The Reading of the Torah

Then all the people of Judah were gathered in the walled city, Jerusalem. Early in the

When the wall of Jerusalem was completed, the people made a great feast. In booths of leafy branches—of olive, myrtle, and palm—they lived for seven days. They listened to the law read from the Torah scroll. And there was much celebration.

morning a man named Ezra stepped out in front of them. He climbed a wooden pulpit, so that he might be seen by everyone, and he opened a scroll. When he opened the scroll, all of the people stood up and waited.

Ezra was a scribe skilled in the Torah, the teachings of Moses, which the Lord God of Israel had given. The scroll opened before him was that Torah.

Ezra began to read. Clearly, in a ringing voice, in familiar language, Ezra read; and all the people heard him. Then the Torah was explained, and all the people understood it.

And when they heard the ancient teachings, and understood, they wept. They confessed their sins—theirs and the sins of all their ancestors. And Ezra gathered their confession in a prayer before the Lord.

Then Nehemiah made a firm covenant—wrote it out and signed it with all the leaders of the people—to walk in God's law which was given by Moses, the servant of God, to observe and do all the commandments of the Lord, his ordinances, and his statutes.

And in that day Nehemiah and Ezra said to all the people, "This day is holy to the Lord your God. Do not mourn or weep. Do not be grieved, for the joy of the Lord is your strength!"

By their gentle directing, the people changed. Tears turned to joy, and sorrow into thanksgiving. And the people began to celebrate a feast. For seven days they dwelt in booths made of leafy branches; and day by day Ezra read from the scroll of the Torah. And now when they heard his reading, there was great rejoicing.

Matthew
Mark
Luke

The New Testament

JESUS

IN THE BEGINNING *was the Word,*
and the Word was with God,
and the Word was God.
He was with God at the beginning of things.

All things were made through him,
not one thing made which he did not make!
Life itself was in him,
and this life was the light of men,
and this light still shines in the darkness,
for the darkness has not overcome it!

He was in the world,
the world that was made through him,
yet the world refused to know him.
He came to his own,
yet his people refused to receive him.

But to those who received him,
to those who believed in his name,
he gave power to make them the children of God!
So these children were born not of blood;
not of the will of the flesh were they born,
nor yet of a human will
but of God!

And the Word became flesh
and he dwelt among us,
blazing with grace and truth!
And we saw his glory,
the Son in his glory,
the singular Son of the Father,
whose fullness has given us
grace upon grace upon grace!

For Torah was a gift through Moses,
but true grace came through Jesus Christ.
For no one has ever seen God:
The only Son,
who leans on the breast of the Father,
he has made him known. . . .

A Jew and A Descendant of Abraham

ABRAHAM WAS THE FATHER of Isaac, and Isaac was the father of Jacob, whose name was changed to Israel. Jacob, or Israel, had twelve sons, all of whom had many children and who went to live in Egypt. These children, with all their descendants, were called the children of Israel.

Jesus was one of the children of Israel, a descendant of Abraham.

Jacob's fourth son was Judah. When all of the children of Israel crossed the Red Sea and returned to the Promised Land, the descendants of Judah began to live in the southern part of that land, and the place where they lived was called the land of Judah. They themselves were finally called Jews, because of the name of their land, because of the name of their father.

Jesus was a Jew, for Jesus was born in the tribe of Judah.

After the children of Israel had lived in the Promised Land for several hundred years, a man named Boaz, who was of the tribe of Judah, married a foreign woman named Ruth, and they had a son named Obed. Obed, when he grew up, had a son named Jesse; and then Jesse had a son named David. David became the greatest king of Israel.

Jesus was of the house and lineage of David, a descendant of that great king, and therefore he was called "Thou Son of David!"

King David had a son named Solomon, who became king after him. Solomon's son Rehoboam also reigned as king over Judah; and then Rehoboam's son, and his grandson, and his great-grandson followed one another as kings in Judah to the seventeenth generation. Hezekiah was among those kings. So was Josiah. And the last of all to reign as king over Judah was Jehoiachin.

Then it was that the children of Judah, the Jews, were carried into exile and lived in the far land of Babylon. But the family line continued, generation after generation. Throughout the centuries people watched the house of David; they watched the coming of the new generations, and they prayed, "How long, O Lord? How long before you send another king like David here to save us? How long before we see the one who is to come, the anointed of the Lord?"

After the return from exile, a man of the house of David, whose name was Eleazar, had a son named Matthan. Matthan became the father of Jacob, and Jacob was the father of Joseph. This Joseph, in the course of his life, betrothed himself to Mary; and Mary bore the child named Jesus, who was called Messiah, the Christ!

The story of Jesus begins with Abraham. The story of the Family Israel continues when Jesus appears. There are, after all, not two stories, but one—the whole of the Bible, the Old and the New Covenants together.

The Word Became Flesh

PREPARATIONS FOR THE BIRTH OF JESUS

WHEN THE EVENING sacrifice had been offered, a young priest took fire from the altar of burnt offering and entered the Temple. An elder priest, an old man whose hair was white and whose eyes were filled with quiet joy for the thing he was about to do, stood without, watching the people. The people, the worshipers that evening, were moving away from the Temple porch until they all stood on the far side of the altar of burnt offering, and the white-haired priest was left alone.

This was the custom in those days, and a very common practice indeed, since it happened every evening the same way. Yet for the white-haired priest it was a peculiar joy, for he had never done this thing before. And for the white-haired priest it would be a shock as well, for God himself was about to do a new thing.

Now the younger priest stepped out of the Temple and nodded toward his elder. By this he meant, *The fires are burning, and everything is ready.*

The old priest raised his hands before the people, and they fell silent. Several hundred faithful stood still in the Temple court, praying in absolute silence.

May the God of mercy enter his sanctuary and be pleased to accept the sacrifice of his people. Such was the bidding of a hundred hearts, though no one spoke it aloud. They must hold their peace in reverence until the priest's return.

The old priest lowered his hands and, taking with him a small box, went into the Temple—alone. He crossed the room now lit by the burning lamps along the walls and went straight to the farthest side of that room, where there hung a heavy veil, and in front of the veil, an altar with glowing coals. He opened the box. His nostrils flared at the scent that arose, for this was incense mixed of stacte, onycha, galbanum, and pure frankincense. No hesitation now! If he took too long in the Temple, the people would fear that he had been struck dead as one unworthy to burn incense to the Lord. The old priest put forth his hand and sprinkled the spices onto the coals. Smoke puffed, then arose in clouds as white as his hair.

He thought he was done. He began to bow toward the veil. He began to step backward—

But suddenly a light more terrible than he had ever seen filled the place, and he blinked furiously, his hands before his face, and he saw to the right of the altar the bright angel of the Lord!

"Zechariah," said the angel, "do not be afraid, for your prayer has been heard by the Lord—"

Prayer? Prayer? The old man's mind was muddled by unusual circumstance and his memory was weak for the closeness of holiness. This was an angel of the Lord! What prayer?

"Your wife Elizabeth will bear a son, even as you desired it," said the angel, "and you will call his name John—"

Oh, *that* prayer! The old priest pulled at his white hair. *That* prayer? They had ceased to pray that prayer a long time ago, when their age had made it unreasonable. Old people do not have children!

"You will have joy and gladness, Zechariah," said the angel, "for your son will be great before the Lord. No wine, no strong drink shall he drink; but he will be filled with the Holy Spirit from his mother's womb. And he will turn many of the sons of Israel to the Lord their God. He will go before them in the power of Elijah to prepare the people for the Lord!"

Now Zechariah trembled and smiled and bowed and smiled and spoke. "Forgive me," he uttered tiny words to the angel of the Lord, "but how shall I know this? I am an old man, you see. My wife is old, too. Old people do not have children."

The angel paused a moment, his fierce brightness seeming to reduce the words of Zechariah—and his tongue, and his throat, and his lungs—to dust.

"I am Gabriel!" said the angel. "I am one who stands in the presence of God, whom God sent to speak unto you this good news!"

Good news, to be sure; but the messenger had suddenly a stern and boding look about him. "Behold!" he announced from a seemingly great distance. "You shall be mute, unable to speak till the day that these

An angel of the Lord appeared to the old priest Zechariah and told him that his wife Elizabeth would bear a son. His name would be John.

things come to pass. Not a word from you, Zechariah, because you did not believe my words, which will be fulfilled!"

The people outside in the courtyard had been silent long enough. Now they began to mumble among themselves because the priest was taking so long inside and they worried for his safety. "It is a fearful thing to come into the presence of the Lord," they whispered, by which they meant, *To burn incense.*

Then Zechariah stepped onto the porch, and they were relieved. But when he opened his mouth, not a word could he speak to them, and they were anxious again. "He did!" they said to one another. "He saw a vision!"

Finally, the old man waved his arms in a silent blessing and silently waved them away—for he was, indeed, mute.

Silently he went home, when his term of service was fulfilled. Silently he met his wife Elizabeth, and silently he lived with her. And then it was in silent wonder that he discovered that she had conceived and they were to have a child.

But Elizabeth was not silent.

"Ah, the Lord looked down on me!" she sang in exultation. "He has taken away my shame!"

Zechariah nodded.

Angelic News for the Virgin Mary

North of Jerusalem, where the Temple was—north of the whole territory of Judea, in which Jerusalem was—north even of the territory of Samaria, in the province of Galilee, in a small city of that province called Nazareth, there lived a young woman whose life was gentle, kind, and unassuming, and whose single expectation was that she would one day marry the man to whom she was betrothed.

It was a common expectation indeed, and a good one—neither more nor less than any woman of her day was given to expect: to marry, then to nurture and to raise a family. But God would change that. This woman's family would contain a most uncommon wonder—beyond all expectations! By this young woman every family everywhere could anticipate extraordinary blessings, for through this ordinary woman God himself was about to do a new thing.

The man to whom she was betrothed was Joseph, the son of Jacob, of the house of David. He was a carpenter. The woman's name was Mary. And she was a virgin.

Six months after he had appeared to Zechariah in the Temple, the angel of the Lord appeared also unto Mary, flooding her little house with light.

"Hail, thou woman so favored of God!" he gave her celestial greeting. "The Lord is with you!"

Young Mary forgot altogether that she was holding a cup in her hands. She trembled and wondered what sort of greeting this was.

But the angel said to her, "Do not be afraid, Mary. You have indeed found favor with God. Behold, you will conceive in your womb, and you will bear a son whose name you shall call Jesus—"

The cup rose up to her breast, where she pressed it against her heart as if to keep it from beating so hard. But she did not know what she was doing. Mary was listening.

"Your son will be great," said the angel. "He will be called the Son of the Most High. The Lord God will give him to sit on the throne of his father David, and he will reign over the Family Israel forever. Forever! To his kingdom there will be no end!"

"How—?" Mary began, but then she hesitated, and dropped her eyes to the cup. It was blue.

Oh, these were grand pronouncements

from the bright and shining messenger of God, and she could dearly believe them. But one small, utterly common fact seemed overlooked, something so obvious—

"How can this be?" she asked. And then she said, "I have no husband."

"The Holy Spirit will come upon you," announced the angel, "and the power of the Most High will overshadow you. Therefore, the child to be born of you will be called holy, the Son of God. Mary, with God nothing is impossible. Even your kinswoman Elizabeth, whom everyone called barren and who should have been too old for children, even she is now with child."

Mary smiled, and the cup at her cheek made the smile a delicate and lovely thing.

"Behold, I am the servant of my Lord," she said. "Let it be for me according to your words."

Then the angel departed, and it was Mary alone in her house, and the cup—a plain piece of earthenware gone suddenly sky-blue and beautiful because of the news she had heard.

Mary Runs to Visit Elizabeth

Wash a cup and set it away—your heart is dancing while you do. Straighten a room, sweep the floor; take food to the neighbors, latch the door—none of this is work for you. For the news is bursting in your breast. No time to talk! No need to rest!—you're off to tell your cousin, too!

Soon after the angel had gone, Mary closed her house and left the city of Nazareth to travel south as fast as she could go. Into Judea she went, and then to the town

Mary of Nazareth was betrothed to a carpenter, Joseph. One day an angel came before Mary and told her that she would bear a son, Son of the Most High. His name would be Jesus.

and the house of Zechariah. But it was not Zechariah whom she went to visit.

"Elizabeth! Elizabeth!" she cried when she saw her kinswoman. "Do you know what has happened to me?"

Old Elizabeth gasped. She felt her side for just an instant, smiling, then threw her arms around Mary and wept.

"Oh, blessed are you among women!" she cried, for by the Holy Spirit she understood everything in an instant, and she was not a woman to be silent about her understandings. "And blessed the fruit of your womb!" she shouted. Then she sat down and delivered herself to grateful tears. "I am so happy," she said. "I am so honored that the mother of my Lord should come to visit me here."

Mary touched the old woman and said, "You know already?"

"Oh, my dear, the moment that you spoke to me my own child leaped in my womb, and I knew," said Elizabeth, dabbing her eyes. "Yes, blessed is the woman who believed that the Lord would keep his promises!"

"Who believed that the Lord would keep his promises," Mary whispered after her. "Oh, Elizabeth!" Mary sang, clapping her hands. She could no longer restrain her joy. "Elizabeth, my soul magnifies the Lord! My spirit rejoices in God my Savior! For you know I was nothing, was merely a maidservant before him; but he looked down on me, and he who is mighty has done great things for me, and I will be called blessed by all of the people hereafter! Holy is his name!

"You know the strength of his arm. He scatters the proud; he drops the mighty from their thrones; but the low are lifted up and the hungry are filled with good things!

"Our God is helping Israel, Elizabeth, even as he promised Abraham and all of his children forever! Ah, believe it, believe it, my lady—the Lord is keeping his promises!"

After that memorable meeting between two women carrying two promises of God, Mary stayed with Elizabeth for about three months—

—and Zechariah nodded.

The Birth of John

The news went out to the whole town—not by angels this time, but by knocks on doors and by word of mouth: "The Lord has shown great mercy to the priest's wife!" was the news. "Our neighbor, old Elizabeth, wrinkled Elizabeth—she has had a son!" That was the news. And the people of the town were genuinely happy to hear it.

On the eighth day after the baby's birth—when the child was to be circumcised and given his name—they gathered with great joy at the house of Zechariah, where they made much talk and much laughter.

"How gentle he is!" they said, patting the baby, pinching his cheek.

"Not at all gentle!" said Elizabeth, removing their hands and their fingers. "He has a will of iron!"

"Well, that's true," they said, putting their noses close to the baby's nose. "Great children are born to the barren. Think of Isaac and Jacob and Samuel—"

"Great children," said Elizabeth, pulling the baby's nose far away from their hairy nostrils, "are born by the promise of God!"

"He looks like his father," they said.

"That may be," said Elizabeth, though she had ideas of her own.

"And of course, he will be named after his father," they said, tugging at the baby's toes.

"He will not," said Elizabeth, catching both of his feet and all ten toes in one protecting hand.

"Elizabeth, how can you say such a thing?" They turned from the child to attend directly unto his mother—who needed, it seemed, some attention. Their smiles were stretched a little thin, but they smiled nonetheless, since the woman was old, after all, and she had only lately given birth. "Surely you want him named Zechariah. It is the custom, and it gives honor to—"

"He shall be called John," said Elizabeth.

"John?" All of the eyes blinked. All of the smiles faded away. "John? John? None of your family has that name."

Elizabeth rocked her child in her arms and smiled. She seemed, suddenly, quite content to say nothing.

"Woman," they said in a businesslike manner, "this is not a matter for women. We will take it up with the father of the child!" And they did. They made signs to Zechariah, to ask him what *he* would call his son.

The old man motioned for a writing tablet, and when he had it in hand, he wrote "His name is John."

Elizabeth rocked her baby John, silently.

The people marveled in a new silence of their own.

But Zechariah—that man suddenly found his tongue, and he opened his mouth, and the words tumbled forth with a fine noise and with high praise for God. Wonderful was the change in him, so that the people became afraid and were filled with an awestricken feeling: *Something is about to happen!*

Through the whole hill country of Judea the news of these wonders went out, and the people said, "What then will this child be?" For it was clear that the hand of the Lord was upon him.

But Zechariah, moved by the Holy Spirit, understood fully what was to be, and he sang of it.

"The Lord is remembering promises sworn to our father Abraham! He is deliver-

John, son of Zechariah and Elizabeth, prepared himself to preach. He lived in the wilderness, and his food was locusts and wild honey.

ing us from the hands of our enemies that we without fear might serve him! That we might in holiness live before him, all of the days of our life!"

Zechariah picked up his son and sang. "You, child! You will be called the prophet of the Most High, for you will go before the Lord to prepare his ways, to give knowledge of salvation in the forgiveness of sins. You, child! You will point to the rising of the sun, to the dawning from on high, when light will shine on those who sit in darkness and in the shadow of death. You, my child!"

And Elizabeth, when she heard what her husband had to say, nodded.

After that John grew, matured, became strong in spirit, and went to live in the wilderness until the day when he began to preach to Israel and to baptize.

Angelic News for Joseph

Mary and Joseph were not yet married, nor did they live together. But they were betrothed to each other, and in those days that was a very solemn thing. It meant that they had promised their lives to each other, their hearts, their bodies, and all their days. They had made this promise before God and in the presence of their families, and now they were waiting for the wedding day—when Mary would move into Joseph's house as his wife.

Joseph was a good man, stable, honorable, dependable, and, like Mary, both quiet and devout. Joseph was a good man.

He did not mind that Mary went alone to visit Elizabeth. Neither did he mind that she was three months gone from him. Nor did he complain, when she returned, that she had changed somewhat, being a little more giddy than usual, a little more given to tears, and much more secretive. He did not ask her what her secret was.

But when her secret began to tell itself, when her womb began to grow, and when it became evident that she was with child, then the good man became a sad man, for it seemed that Mary had broken her promise to him. Joseph thought long and decided that there was nothing for it but to divorce her. Tomorrow.

But Joseph was a good, just man. The law said that because of her sin he could shame Mary before all of the people, but he hated the thought of Mary in humiliation, so he determined, rather, to divorce her quietly. Two witnesses and a piece of paper were all that he would need, and there would be an end to it. Tomorrow. He would do the deed tomorrow.

It was a fitful sleep that he slept that night. It was also a divine sleep, for an angel came into it, and his dreams were filled with the light of the messenger from God.

"Joseph, son of David!" said the angel, and the good man, sleeping, listened with a wholehearted faith.

"What, my lord?"

"Do not be afraid to take Mary as your wife, for the child in her is of no sin but is of the Holy Spirit. She will bear her son; and you, Joseph, shall call his name Jesus—because he will save his people from their sins."

There was no divorce on the morrow, nor shame nor any sorrow. In Nazareth, there was a wedding! And for Mary, the fulfillment of expectation.

Good Joseph arose from his bed, prepared both himself and his house, sent a message of his own, gathered his friends, and strode through the city to Mary's house, whence he brought her home to be his wife.

Here was the promise! God was fulfilling what he had promised so long ago through the prophet Isaiah.

"A virgin shall conceive and bear a son, and his name shall be called Emmanuel."

Now was the right time! Now was the Lord God keeping that promise! The virgin about to bear her son was Mary; and although his given name would be Jesus, yet his whole being was *Emmanuel*—"God with us"!

THE BIRTH OF JESUS

Now the birth of Jesus happened this way.

Caesar Augustus, the emperor of the whole Roman Empire, commanded a counting of all of his people.

"Count them by families!" the order went out. "Count them in the cities of their ancestors. And record the count that we may tax them hereafter!"

So it was ordered. So it was done.

All over the world people began to travel hither and yon, short distances and long, to the homes of their heritage. In Spain near the Atlantic, in Gaul, in the deserts of northern Africa, as far east as the Euphrates—and even in little Nazareth of Galilee, the people bagged their belongings and traveled.

One good man also obeyed the order, though his wife was heavy with her child, being in the ninth month and in no condi-

Joseph the carpenter claimed Mary as his wife. Amid song and dance, he took her to his home.

tion to travel. By slow stages Joseph and Mary moved south from Galilee, into Judea and round the city of Jerusalem. They continued south until they came to the tiny town of Bethlehem, which was the city of David, and there they meant to stay.

But it was late, and the town was full of the family of David; the inn had no rooms available, and the rooms had no beds unoccupied. But the birth pains were hurting poor Mary, and she whimpered softly while Joseph searched for some shelter, some soft place where she might bear her baby.

There was so little time.

Then he said to her, "I have a place," and he led her round to the back of an inn, where there was a low stone fence and a rough thatched roof against the wall. Here the innkeeper shut up animals for the night. Here Joseph lodged his Mary for the night. But Mary asked no questions.

There was no time.

She shaped a little bed in straw, then leaned into her labor and strained for dear life. The sweat on her forehead was no different from the evening dew now fallen on the grass and all that countryside—or else the sweet earth sweat with her.

Mary delivered her baby—a son. She washed him and wound him in swaddling clothes; and then it was a mother's hands, somewhat swollen and tired, but infinitely gentle, that laid him in a manger.

Angelic News for the Shepherds

Night—and a dog barked far away, barked and kept on barking. But it must have been a private matter between him and the stars, for no one else was disturbed. The shepherds' own guard dog raised his head once and twisted his ears, then lay down again. The sheep themselves were sleeping. The fields near Bethlehem were still, dark outlines against a deep blue and starry sky—all signs of peace. And the shepherds were concerned only to keep awake and to keep a watch over their flocks till the morning.

They were lying on the ground, leaning on their elbows, and talking of common, forgettable things—

When suddenly the whole night lit up with a furious light. The bright glory of God blazed all around them, and an angel of the Lord stepped forward, and the animals were stunned cold, and the shepherds threw up their arms in fear and shouted, "Oh!"

"No, do not be afraid," said the angel, but none of the shepherds lowered his arms.

"Good news!" said the angel. "Behold, I bring you good news of great joy, and joy it shall be for all of the people! For to you is born this day, in the city of David, a Savior who is Christ the Lord! And this shall be a sign for you—"

There was no room at the inn in Bethlehem. Jesus was born in a stable. Mary wrapped him in swaddling clothes and placed him in a manger.

Two of the shepherds lowered their arms the better to listen. A sign! They would want a sign to ratify such news as this and such a vision!

"You will find the babe wrapped in swaddling clothes and lying in a manger."

All at once the deep sky was filled with angels—as many as there had been stars before. They were praising God in a thrilling voice, and saying,

"Glory to God in the highest,
And peace to the people with whom he is
pleased!"

Then the angels returned into heaven, and the chorus was over, and the chill stars shined like ice again, and the night was vastly dark.

The sheep began to shuffle and to bleat. The shepherds shook their heads and stared at one another.

There was a moment of absolute silence among them—till one man whispered, "Did you—?"

"I did! I saw it!" said another.

"Angels and good news!" cried a third.

"And a sign!"

Then the shepherds, every single one of them, threw back their heads and burst into long, loud, and joyful laughter. A little band of men under the infinite sky, they thumped

An angel carried the news of Jesus' birth to the shepherds. Wonder, joy, laughter, overcame them.

one another and slapped their knees and laughed till the tears rolled down their cheeks—and the sheep blinked at them.

"Why not?" roared the shepherds. "Why shouldn't we go to Bethlehem to see what the angel has told us about?"

And when their happy laughter had settled somewhat, they did.

"Oh, this night!" said one as they rushed to the city. "What a beautiful night this is!"

Beautiful and fine! They found the manger. They found Mary and Joseph. And they found the babe, whom the angel had called Christ the Lord.

And again they were laughing. But this time they woke people with their laughter, and they told everyone who would listen what the angel had said about the child, and the people were amazed. Then they went back to their sheep in the dawning light, but they did not stop glorifying God and praising him for all that they had heard and seen.

Mary, who had borne the child; Mary, who had watched the shepherds come, who understood the source of their rough laughter, and who had seen them go; Mary turned to the child and picked him up and closed her eyes. Even so did she keep these things as a treasure in her heart and remember them.

Simeon's Song

On the eighth day after his birth, the baby boy was circumcised, and his name was given unto him:

Jesus.

On the fortieth day after his birth, his parents gathered him up and walked the distance from Bethlehem to Jerusalem. There they purchased two turtledoves in order to perform the appointed sacrifice; and then, for the first time in his life, Jesus was taken into the Temple of the Lord, the house of God.

After a little while they thought to leave the Temple again—but a man came in whose eyes were so bright with a burning hopefulness that they paused. This man glanced around the sanctuary, one hand on his chin, the other on his forehead, until he spied the babe in Mary's arms. At once he stepped forward and stretched out his hands.

"Woman," he whispered. His voice trembled. "Is the child yours?"

"Yes," said Mary.

"And may I," whispered the man, "woman, may I hold him awhile?"

Mary said, "Yes," and the man took Jesus to his own breast as though he were a starving man and the child were bread for him.

"Forgive me," he said, for he wept.

This was Simeon. And this particular moment in his life, this holding of the baby Jesus, was all that he ever lived for. Long ago the Holy Spirit had promised him that he would not die until he had seen the Christ of God. And for all his years Simeon had led a devout and righteous life, waiting, waiting for the consolation of Israel.

Now here it was. And here he was. And he wept with a joy fulfilled.

Suddenly he began to chant a song over the child.

"Now you may let me die, my Lord, in peace according to your word, for my own eyes have seen the bright salvation which you sent for all the people. Light enlightening the nations! Glory for your people, Israel!"

Simeon turned his wet eyes to Mary and Joseph, who marveled at the song he sang. He blessed them both. But for Mary alone he chanted another verse.

"Ah, Mother, by your child shall many stumble and fall. And many in Israel shall rise by him. Bitter will be the arguments surrounding him, for he will reveal the se-

cret thought of many hearts. And a sword," sang Simeon. "Yes, and a sword shall pierce through a mother's soul—yours, dear Mother of the Child. Yours."

Just then a commotion broke out on the other side of the sanctuary.

"There he is!" cried an old, old woman. "Oh, thank the Lord, his people, there he is!"

She lowered her head and bustled across the floor, making great haste slowly, for she was very excited but very old. She was Anna, a widow and a faithful lady who worshiped in the Temple night and day, fasting and praying.

"This is the one!" she announced when she had peeked at the baby's face, and immediately she began to speak of Jesus to everyone who yearned for the redeeming of Jerusalem.

One single child did Mary and Joseph bear in their arms as they returned that evening to Bethlehem. But in their hearts they bore a thousand thoughts about him. And they walked in silence by the way.

Wise Men and a Wicked King

At that time the king of Judea was an old, embittered, and suspicious man named Herod, a cunning man and a man quite willing to murder in order to keep his crown—although he was not long for the world, for death sat on his shoulders. Herod was sick with a killing illness, but that did not soften him. Instead, it made him desperate and sharpened his wickedness. Beware old men who do not want to die!

This King Herod was not happy to hear the news that certain visitors had come to Jerusalem from the East.

"They are wise men," he was told, "men who study the stars to discover the meanings of mankind."

"Why do you tell me this?" asked Herod. "Visitors are common in Jerusalem, wise men and fools in the thousands. Stargazers are no special matter."

"Well, sir, that is true. But they are asking for the king."

"Here I am!" snapped Herod. "Here I sit. Let them look and they will find me."

"Well, sir, that is true, too. But they are not looking for you."

"What?" Herod fixed the messenger with a narrow stare. "What other king is there?"

"Well, sir," said the messenger, "they are asking for one who was recently born King of the Jews. They say they saw his star in the East, and they have come to worship him."

"Stand right there, little man!" roared the king. "Don't move a muscle while I think!"

Herod paced the room a moment, twisting his beard and growling like thunder.

Herod was brought news that wise men were seeking an infant king. A new king? Herod was enraged.

Suddenly he stopped and pointed at the messenger.

"The Messiah!" he cried.

"That is true," squeaked the messenger, though he had no idea what the two of them were talking about.

"They think," cried Herod, still pointing at the poor man, "that they are going to see the Messiah, the one whom the Jews expect to set them free! Well, we will give them the Christ. What do you think about that?"

"Well, sir, I think—"

"Get out of here!" Herod shouted. "Bring me the chief priests and the scribes at once!"

The *scribes* whom Herod called for were men who devoted their lives to a thorough study of the Scriptures of Moses. They were scholars, profoundly learned in the text of the Torah and the prophets. They knew very much.

"Where," Herod demanded of them, "does the Scripture say that the Christ is to be born?"

The scribes answered him straightaway. "In Bethlehem of Judea," they said. "For so the prophet prophesied long ago. We can, if it please Your Majesty, quote the passage?"

"Please do," said His Majesty.

And they did. " 'And you, O Bethlehem, in the land of Judah, are by no means least among the rulers of Judah; for from you shall come a ruler who will govern my people Israel.' "

"Fine. Thank you. Leave!" said Herod to the scribes. And to the messenger he said, "Bring me these wise men. Be fast, little man, and be secret. Go!"

Herod paced while he waited, yanking at his beard and muttering, "If there is no Christ, they will fail in their fool's mission, and I will be satisfied. But if there is a Christ, I will not fail. No, Herod will not ever fail to preserve his throne—"

When the wise men were ushered into his presence, Herod bowed, smiled, and welcomed them right graciously.

"The King of the Jews, is it?" he asked, nodding.

They said, "Yes."

"And by a star you learned of his birth, was it?" he asked, nodding.

They said, "Yes."

"Fine, fine," said the old, dying king. "When, sirs," he continued, "did you first see this star?"

They told him, and he nodded again, as though this were an excellent piece of wisdom. "Then he is nought but a child yet, is

The wondrous star of the East led the wise men to the infant Jesus. Kneeling, they worshiped him. They gave to him treasures of the East—gold and frankincense and myrrh.

he? Good, good. Well, dear sirs!" The king stood up and clapped a hand to the nearest shoulder. "You ask me where this King was born. I will tell you that, and then, perhaps, you will do me one small favor in return. Bethlehem. There is your answer. Search diligently for the child in Bethlehem. And when you have found him, if you will kindly bring me word of his location, I will be forever grateful—since I would like to go and worship him as well."

The king stood at his window while the wise men departed Jerusalem to the south. He was not smiling. Nor was he nodding. He was stroking his beard as though it were a cat, curled and waiting at his breast.

On the way to Bethlehem, the wise men encountered a pure blessing from God. The same star which they had seen in the East reappeared, burning bright and low in the Judean sky and moving before them by gentle degrees until it came to rest over the place where the child was.

With what joy they beheld that star!

With what high dignity these foreigners entered the house of the King. Mary his mother received them; but to Jesus himself went their worship and their gifts. They knelt before him, and they opened unto him their treasures, gold and frankincense and myrrh.

Then the same God who blessed them with a star blessed them again with knowledge by a dream. They were warned not to return to Herod—ever. So they returned to their own land by another route.

Joseph, too, was given warning—to leave Bethlehem and Judea at once, to take both Mary and Jesus as far away as Egypt, and to dwell there. Joseph obeyed, and the little family fled by night.

Daily King Herod stood at his window, watching for the wise men and wondering whether they had failed or succeeded in finding the Christ.

Daily he sent his messenger into the streets to ask for news.

Daily there was nothing. No news, nor any wise men. What then? Was there a Christ or not?

Herod plotted to destroy Jesus. Joseph gathered his little family together and fled into Egypt.

Rage and fear—which together make madness—began slowly to burn behind the old king's eyes.

"You, little man!" he hissed to his messenger. "You and your news began this vexation for me!"

"Well, sir," mumbled the messenger, "that may be true—"

"Get! Get! Get out of here!" cried the king. "Get you to Bethlehem fast as you can! Go look for your wise, wise men!"

Instantly the messenger was gone. Boldly he questioned people in Bethlehem. But with true terror and a failing heart he returned.

"They were there," he reported, "for one night—and then they left—one week ago—avoiding Jerusalem—"

"By God!" the king exploded. "By God! I've been tricked by these foreigners! But I will not be denied! And I will not fail despite their sneaking ways. If I cannot find the Christ, yet my sword shall!" He ripped at his beard so that it flew like fury around his face. *"I command it that every male child in Bethlehem, two years old and younger, shall be put to an immediate death!* For I will be king," he said. "I shall continue king of this place—"

This stark command was carried out. The innocent children died. And then was fulfilled the sad saying of the prophet Jeremiah:

"A voice was heard in Ramah, weeping and bitter lamentation, Rachel wailing for her children, Rachel, who would not be comforted, for they were no more."

Herod himself did not live much longer than these children. The disease that wormed in the old man's vitals took his crown and his rage and his life, all three, and laid them away forever.

Then Joseph felt free to bring his family back to the land of Israel. But because Herod's son began to rule in Judea, they never returned to Bethlehem. They went all the way home again to Nazareth in Galilee, and there they raised the child.

Searching for the boy Jesus, Mary and Joseph found him in the Temple, seated among the teachers.

"My Father's House"

Jesus grew, over the years, into a fine, strong boy, wiser than mortals are wise, and full of the favor of God.

Sometimes even his parents were astonished by his understanding. Once, when he was twelve years old, his parents took him to Jerusalem to celebrate the Passover. Seven days they spent among the multitudes, worshiping and keeping the feast. And then, at the end of it, Mary and Joseph

began the long journey home, walking with their friends from Nazareth and supposing that Jesus was with others, walking in the same direction.

That night they looked for him—but found him nowhere in the group.

"Did you see him?" they asked his friends. But no one had seen him.

"Didn't he come at all?" they wondered. And with fear they realized that no, he had not come. They had left him behind!

Immediately the two turned around and walked alone all the way back to Jerusalem. For three days they searched and worried and blamed themselves for not taking better care of their son.

They found him, finally, in the Temple, sitting quite happily among the teachers, listening and asking questions and talking with such wisdom that everyone was astonished.

But Mary ignored the scholarly conversation. "Son!" she scolded him. "How could you do this to us? Don't you know that your father and I have been worried, looking everywhere for you?"

"Why were you looking for me?" Jesus asked her. "Did you not know that I must be in my Father's house?"

Neither of his parents understood these words. But Mary, when they had returned to Nazareth—Mary would sometimes close her eyes of an evening and remember in silence all the words and the deeds that concerned her son. Thus did she treasure these things in her heart.

And he grew. Jesus grew in wisdom, in stature, and in favor with God and all of the people.

The Years of His Ministry

THE BEGINNING OF THE MINISTRY

THEN CAME JESUS to Israel, preaching the good news of the kingdom of God beginning from Galilee after the baptism which John administered.

God anointed Jesus of Nazareth with the Holy Spirit and with power. Then Jesus went about doing good and healing all who were oppressed by the devil, for God was with him.

And this ministry to his own people began when he was young—but thirty years old.

John the Baptizer

It was in the fifteenth year of the reign of the Roman emperor Tiberius, when Pontius Pilate was the governor of Judea, that God spoke to John, the son of Zechariah. Then John, who had been waiting in the wilderness, began like the storm of God to preach.

"Repent!" he cried.

His voice went up in the wilderness, then echoed through the towns and villages and cities of Judea. And the people heard. And the multitudes went out to him.

They found a bold and eloquent, compelling man. A prophet! He dressed in camel's hair. He wore a leathern girdle about his waist. He ate locusts and wild honey. But it was what the man *said* that drew the people to him, and what he did for them.

"Repent!" he cried. "For the kingdom of heaven is not far away. No, the kingdom of God is at hand!" In drilling, transfiguring language he preached the baptism of repentance for the forgiveness of sins. And then, in the Jordan River, he did baptize a grateful people.

And as they confessed their sins in baptism, so he was preparing them for the coming of the Lord.

"Act your repentance!" he said to the people. "Bear fruits that befit the sorrow in you for your sins. Even now the ax is biting the root of the trees, and every tree which does not bear good fruit shall be cut down and cast in the fire!"

"Fruits?" said the people. "Then what must we do?"

John answered, "Let him who has two coats give one to the man who has none."

Tax collectors said, "Teacher, what should we do?"

John said, "Collect no more than your due from the people."

Soldiers said, "And what about us? What should we do?"

"Rob no one," said John. "Hurt no one. Be content with your pay."

And so he preached. And so he baptized. And so he taught the people. And his reputation swept like a searing wind across the countryside, so that many even in Jerusalem looked at one another and wondered, *Who is this man?*

They thought of several answers to this question but could be sure of none of them until they faced the man directly. So they sent some of their number into the wilderness to speak with him. These found John at Bethany on the east side of the Jordan, where the water was shallow and a person could wade unto baptism.

John stood in the water and looked at them. They stood surrounded by the multitude, their toes on the whispering shore, and called, "We are a delegation from Jerusalem, come to ask you a few questions."

"So," said John. "Ask."

"Here?" They had hiked up their robes away from the mud.

"Here is synagogue enough for all of us," said John. "Ask."

"Well," they called. "Well, who are you?"

John answered immediately, "I am not the Christ."

"Oh! Well, then," said the delegation. "Are you the prophet Elijah?"

"No," said John.

"Perhaps you are the prophet that we have been waiting for?"

"No," said John, and that was all he said. He stood in the water and waited.

"Well, but we must have an answer for those who sent us," they called. "Who are you? What do you say of yourself?"

John began to walk toward the shore. The delegation blinked, but they stood their ground.

"In the words of Isaiah," replied John, " 'I am the voice of one crying in the wilderness, *Make straight the way of the Lord!*' "

"That is no answer," said the delegation, backing away from the approaching figure. "If you are neither the Christ nor Elijah nor the prophet, then where do you get the right to baptize?"

John kept walking toward them, his loincloth dripping water.

"You blind camels! You are asking the wrong man altogether," said John. "I baptize with water. But there stands among you one whom you do not know, one so much mightier than I that I am not worthy to untie his sandals. Ask him who he is. Ask *him* about *his* right to baptize—for he will baptize you with the Holy Spirit and with fire! Behold, he will clear his threshing floor and gather the wheat into bins; but the chaff he will burn with unquenchable fire!"

At this point the delegation thought it wise to depart, thinking they had answer enough, though they did not understand a word of the answer.

They might have stayed. If they had, they would have seen a young man, quiet and intense, now step from the multitude and walk up to John and place a hand on his shoulder.

The Baptism of Jesus

"John," said Jesus of Nazareth, "baptize me."

John turned around. "Do you—" He was about to say *repent,* but the word died on his lips. "You!" he breathed. "No. No, I should be baptized by you." He stared at the slender figure before him. "I may rumble like the thunder, but you are the lightning, the wind, and the rain, all three. I am the voice; but you—you are the spoken word. No. I will not baptize you—"

But even while John spoke, Jesus removed his seamless tunic and walked into the Jordan—water to his knees, water to his waist.

"Come baptize me, John," he said. "It is necessary now that we do every act of righteousness. Come."

And so it was. John followed Jesus into the river where the one leaned down and the other baptized him.

Instantly, when Jesus came up from the water, he saw the heavens splitting open and the Spirit of God descending upon him in the form of a dove; and he heard a voice from the heavens declaring, *"You are my beloved Son. In you am I well pleased!"*

The Temptation of Jesus

Still wet, Jesus draped the tunic over his shoulders, hugged John in gratitude, pressing the other man's forehead into his own

One day Jesus stepped into the Jordan and John baptized him. Looking up, Jesus saw a dove descending and knew it to be the Spirit of God.

neck, then walked eastward without a word. He was under pressure of the Spirit to be gone; he was driven to be utterly alone, just now, and vulnerable in the dry, dead land, the wilderness.

Forty days and nights he wandered, never eating—and the wind was a sigh in old bones. He grew hungry. His stomach shriveled, hardened, and twisted into odd shapes. And then, at the end of that time, the devil came to him.

"If you are the Son of God," said the tempter, the honey-tongued, "then it should be no great thing for you to satisfy your hunger. Son of God, command these stones to turn to bread—and eat."

But Jesus never broke his stride. Walking, walking, his garments billowing, he said, "It is written: 'Man shall not live by bread alone, but by every word that proceeds from the mouth of God.' " Walking, walking, until the tempter snatched him up, swept him to the holy city of Jerusalem, and set him on the highest pinnacle of the Temple.

"Now walk!" said the devil. "Nay, thou Son of God—jump! And I will give you Scripture for Scripture to urge you on. For it is written: 'He will give his angels charge over you. They will bear you in their hands lest you strike your foot against a stone.' Jump, if you are the Son of God. Land lightly and whole in one healthy piece."

But Jesus, at that whistling height, said, "It is also written: 'You shall not tempt the Lord your God.' "

Then the devil whirled round Jesus, transporting him to the top of a lofty mountain. Round and round he went, until he had shown him all the kingdoms of the world and the glory of all nations.

"These will I give to you," he said, and his voice dripped sweetness, "all these, if only you will bow your head and worship me."

Then Jesus faced him squarely and threw his hands in the air. "Satan!" he cried. "Satan, get out of my sight! It is written: 'You shall worship the Lord your God, and him only shall you serve!' "

Suddenly less than a breeze, no more than a skittering leaf, the devil departed, leaving Jesus alone.

And behold, the angels came and gave him comfort, for he was hungry and terribly tired.

John Makes Jesus Known

To see the truth and to speak it right out loud; to love the truth and to proclaim it in the hearing of all the people, whether it be good and beautiful or bad and ugly—this is a special gift of God.

In the world it is a dangerous gift, for the world hates the truth and is willing to punish the truth speaker.

But in the kingdom of God this gift is called the gift of prophecy.

John the Baptizer had this gift. He was a prophet and a truth speaker. The truth that he saw was the same truth that he cried out, and only the deaf could miss the sweetness and the sting of it.

So when John saw Jesus once again on the east side of the Jordan, he raised a finger, pointed, and cried the truth to the multitudes, "Behold! Look! Do you see that man?"

There stood a quiet, intense young man gazing straight into John's own eyes, thin for the ordeal that he had just endured, but in perfect control of himself and of all the ground around him.

"He," cried John, "is the Lamb of God

Jesus fasted in the wilderness for forty days and nights. The devil tempted him sorely, but Jesus ordered him away. Angels came to comfort Jesus when his trial was done.

who takes away the sin of the world! His ministry begins after mine, but he himself was ever before me. I saw the Spirit of God descend upon him as a dove from heaven. I have seen, and I bear you witness that this is the Son of God!"

Jesus then turned and went his way, but this time he did not go alone. Two of John's own disciples, hearing the truth, went after him to join themselves to him. And these two brought two more.

John Is Imprisoned

The truth that John saw was the truth that John cried out, whether good and beautiful or bad and ugly.

Herod Antipas, the son of the Herod who had murdered the children of Bethlehem, also sinned a shameless sin. Although he was already married, he fell in love with Herodias, the wife of his own brother. And though she was his sister-in-law, she returned his love. They began to live together.

When John heard of this deed, he began to cry aloud the truth of it, that it was ugly, sinful, unlawful, and an offense before God.

But truth is despised by a world that loves the darkness. So when John's words reached Herod's ears, Herod arrested the Baptizer and shut him in a dismal prison. There John sat until the end.

The news of John's punishment spread abroad. When Jesus heard it, he quietly withdrew from the south and from Herod Antipas, and with a handful of followers traveled north into Galilee. There he would begin his ministry.

John saw the truth. Good or evil, he spoke the truth. He cried out against the sin of the king. And so Herod commanded that he be shut up in prison, and there John lived out his days.

The Wedding in Cana of Galilee

Quietly Jesus walked into Galilee. With no great acclaim he returned to the towns of his youth—for very few people understood who he was or what he was about to do.

They nodded kindly when they saw him. "Peace be with you," they would say, and then they would stop. "You're from Nazareth, aren't you? Yes, yes, I know you. You are Joseph's son, the carpenter's boy. My, how you have changed! Well, peace to you—forgive me, but what is your name?"

"Jesus."

"Of course. Peace to you, Jesus."

And the intense young man would say, with infinite sense in his words and in his eyes, "Peace be with you, too."

One of his old acquaintances took welcome a step further. "Listen," said a man from Cana, "my son's wedding day is tomorrow. I have already invited your mother to the feast, and I would be delighted to have you there, too, you and your friends. Will you come?"

Jesus smiled and said, "I will."

A wedding feast. A common affair. A happy and joyful occasion. Late in the evening of the following day, Jesus watched the proud bridegroom march through the streets of Cana to the house of his bride. When they both returned through the same streets to the groom's house, Jesus quietly joined the procession. The bride was veiled. The groom was crowned with garlands. Both smelled of wonderful spices. And behind them their friends danced and sang and laughed to a thousand jokes.

At the groom's house a feast was found ready for the eating, and the guests began to eat, to drink, to tell riddles, to applaud the entertainment, to enjoy themselves. A wedding feast. A common and good celebration—

But something happened here in Cana to make it both uncommon and miraculous.

Partway through the feast a rumor began to spread among the guests.

"Is it true? Can it be? Didn't the bridegroom prepare his feast wisely enough?"

"Yes. It is true. They have run out of wine."

When Mary, Jesus' mother, also heard this rumor, she went straightway to her son, sitting quietly in the courtyard.

"There is a problem," she said to Jesus. "They have no more wine."

Jesus gazed at his mother for a moment. "Ah, woman, what does that have to do with me?" he asked.

She laid her finger by her cheek, as if to say, *But I know you. I know.*

Jesus said, "My time has not yet come."

Mary said nothing more to him. Instead, she went to the servants and made them look toward Jesus.

"Whatever that man asks you to do," she said, "please do."

There were six stone jars standing in the courtyard, each large enough to hold twenty gallons. Jesus arose and looked at these and found them empty. Then to the servants he said, "Fill these jars with water."

They did. They filled them to the brim.

When that was done, Jesus said to one of the servants, "Now, take a cupful to the master of ceremonies and ask him to taste of it."

A cup was dipped into one stone jar and carried to the man in charge of the feast. He tasted it and was astonished to find that the cup held an excellent wine.

"Why did you do this?" he said to the groom. "Everyone else serves the good wine first and, after the people have finished that, *then* the poor wine. But you have saved the best till now!"

But Jesus' disciples knew that the groom had nothing to do with it. They knew, rather, that this was a miracle—the first that Jesus performed—and they believed in him.

A great thing occurred at a wedding feast in Cana. The wine failed—there was no more. But Jesus commanded that the empty wine jars be filled with water and the water became finest wine. This was the first of his miracles.

The Galilean Ministry Begins

Then it was that Jesus ceased to be quiet. He went out into the towns and villages of Galilee. He opened up his mouth, and with a sudden, blazing authority he began to preach.

"The time is fulfilled!" he cried in the markets, he cried in the synagogues, preached in the streets and the houses. "It is ready to happen! The kingdom of God is at hand. People! Repent and believe in the good news!"

The people came out and listened to him, for his preaching was a bright, glorious thing, and it seemed to them like a light shining through the deep gloom of their lives. They had been sighing in darkness; but here, standing before this Jesus, they were waking to the morning!

So the word spread about Jesus.

"He preaches with power," they said. And they said, "What authority in his words!"

It was not surprising, then, that the people in his own hometown heard about his preaching even before he returned to Nazareth. They were proud to have him come into their synagogue. They smiled upon one another when he—a son of the congregation—stood up to read from the Scriptures. And then they settled down with their hands on their stomachs, expecting to be the prouder when they heard the young fellow actually preach.

But Jesus stunned them with his words.

First, in gentle tones, he read this prophecy from Isaiah:

" 'The Spirit of the Lord is upon me. He has anointed me to preach good news to the poor. He has sent me to proclaim release to the captives, sight to the blind, freedom for those who are oppressed, and to announce the acceptable year of the Lord.' "

Then he closed the book and handed it back to the attendant. He sat down—all eyes proudly upon him—and he spoke the shocking words:

"Today has this prophecy been fulfilled in your hearing. The Spirit of God is upon *me*. The Lord has anointed *me* to preach good news. *I* am come to heal the brokenhearted—"

A buzzing began in the synagogue, a muttering among the people. Some still smiled at his gracious words. But others heard the profound meaning of those words, and they were offended.

"He makes himself too close to God,"

Then Jesus went into the countryside to preach. At Capernaum, he taught the crowds from a boat that belonged to a fisherman, Simon by name.

they whispered. "Where does he get the right to do such a thing? This is Jesus—Joseph the carpenter's son! We've known his family all our lives! His mother is Mary. His brothers are James and Joseph and Simon and Judas, and his sisters all live in this town. You!" they shouted at Jesus. "Who do you think you are? We know better! We know you too well to be fooled by your words!"

Jesus stopped preaching. The people were angry and would hear nothing else that he might tell them.

"Even so it goes," he said. "A prophet is not without honor—except in his own country and among his own kin and in his own house." So he left them. He left the people who knew him so well. He left Nazareth and went through other parts of Galilee, preaching with an extraordinary might.

And the people came out to hear him. Everywhere, the hungry people came to feed on his words, to stand in his love, and to receive the blessing of his hands. Wherever he went, the crowds appeared—for his ministry was not only in words but also in deeds.

Jesus touched the people. He healed their diseases. He loosened the bones of the paralyzed, straightened the legs of the lame, and cast out demons.

Though he walked gently, this lean young man, and with a perfect self-control, yet there burned a splendid energy behind his eyes, and he struck the land like lightning.

And so it was that in a very short time the desperate crowds did swell. The ministry had begun.

Jesus Calls Four Fishermen

Soon he came to the city of Capernaum, which is on the Sea of Galilee—and the crowds followed him. He preached on the shores of that sea—and the crowds were there in such numbers that he could not be heard.

But he saw two fishing boats beached nearby, and the fishers themselves were cleaning their nets after fishing the long night through.

Jesus spoke to one of them, a muscular, thickset man whose gestures were both skillful and impatient. "Simon," he said.

"What?" Simon whirled around, ready to argue with anyone. He was in a foul mood, having caught no fish last night. But Jesus had kind, level eyes, and the fight went out of Simon. "What is it?" he said.

"Would you row me away from the shore? I have something to say to the people."

Simon looked at the waiting crowds and then at the lean man in front of him, whom the crowds had come to hear. The fisherman shrugged. "Why not?"

So the people sat down on the banks of the sea, which rose from the water like a natural theater, and Jesus preached from Simon's boat, and Simon himself had little choice but to listen, too.

When the preaching was done, Simon took the oars, preparing to row his passenger back to land.

"No," said Jesus. "I would rather that you row out to deeper water."

"What? Why?" said Simon. "What's out there for you?"

"Not for me, but for you," said Jesus as mildly as the breeze. "Let down your nets and you will find fish."

"Look, sir," said Simon, "I am the fisherman in this boat, and I am the fisherman *of* this boat, and I don't mean to offend you, but I know that the day is no time for fishing, and this day in particular, because we took absolutely nothing last night. Now, if I have done enough for you—"

"Simon!" said Jesus.

"What!" said Simon.

"Do it."

An unbelieving Simon let down his nets. An awestricken Simon raised them, heavy with fish.

And, in spite of his conviction that this was all a ridiculous waste of time, Simon did.

But then it was Simon, the fisherman of the boat, who was mortified. For his nets enclosed so huge a catch of fish that they began to break.

"John! John!" he roared. "James! Andrew, help me!"

A second boat rushed out to help with the fish, but even two were too few, and they began to sink under the heavy load.

The burly fisherman looked at Jesus with new eyes. He was frightened to discover who truly sat in his boat with him, and he knelt at Jesus' feet. "O Lord, get away from me," he pleaded. "I am a sinful man!"

But Jesus, as gentle as the wind, touched him on his head and said, "No, Simon, do not be afraid. From this time forward you will be catching people and not fish. Follow me."

The Twelve Disciples of Jesus

And so it was that when they brought their boats to land, Simon and his brother Andrew, James and his brother John, left everything that they owned to follow Jesus.

"You, Simon," said Jesus to the vigorous fisherman, "I will call you Peter." *Peter:* the "rock"!

Thus Jesus began to choose certain individuals to follow him more closely than the common crowds. These walked with him, ate and slept with him, learned of him, and so they were called his disciples. And they believed in him.

Besides the four fishermen, there was Philip, who also brought Bartholomew to Jesus. There was Matthew, who had been a tax collector before Jesus called him from his tables. There were Thomas, and James the son of Alphaeus, and Simon who was called the Zealot, and Judas the son of James. And there was Judas Iscariot, who would one day betray Jesus.

Twelve.

The time had come, the ministry begun.

HEALING AND TEACHING IN GALILEE

"Behold my servant, whom I uphold—my chosen, in whom I delight! I have poured my Spirit upon him, and he will bring forth justice to the nations. He will not scream nor scold nor bellow in the streets. He will not break the bended reed, nor quench the smoldering candlewick. He will not fail nor be discouraged till he has established justice on the earth!"

Thus spoke the Lord God through the prophet Isaiah—and then it was Jesus who came as that servant, and Jesus who did these things.

"The eyes of the blind will be opened, the ears of the deaf unstopped. The lame will leap like a deer, and the tongue of the dumb will sing!"

So prophesied Isaiah—and then it was Jesus who did these things.

Wherever they learned of his presence, the people would come in their distresses, beseeching him, "Master! O Master, please help us!" Then the taut young man would turn a penetrating eye upon them—and help them far beyond their poor imaginings.

An Unclean Spirit

Always Jesus went into the synagogues, the buildings wherein the Jews gathered to worship, and he taught. This was for him a delightful labor, and for them enlightening. On the Sabbath day in particular he would sit down in front of the people and speak new things of the old law of Moses.

But one Sabbath—in the dead middle of a sentence—he suddenly fell silent and gazed over the heads of the people toward the door at the back of the room. People twisted their necks to see what he saw, and shuddered.

For there in the doorway crouched a man whose hair stood up like feathers, whose eyes and lips were loose with a sort of madness. He was staring around himself, trying to find something in the dim light of the synagogue.

Jesus merely waited. The people trembled.

All at once the man sprang upright and shrieked, "You!" He turned and beat on the wall to show an uncontrollable rage. As if that were not enough, he beat his own forehead. "You!" he screamed, and with both hands he pointed at Jesus. It was Jesus he was looking for. "What have you to do with us, Jesus of Nazareth?" he screamed. He began to slouch through the room, and the people shrank away from him.

"Jesus, leave him alone!" they called. "This man has an unclean spirit!"

But Jesus sat and waited.

By idiot steps the man approached him, stabbing his fingers at Jesus as though they were knives and could cut. "Have you come to destroy us?" he screamed, his voice vile, his eyes bright with hatred. "I know who you are, you! You are the Holy One of God!"

"Enough," said Jesus. He stood up and took one step toward the man, then spoke not to the man himself but to the demon inside of him.

"Be silent!" It was an even, quiet command, but it transfixed the man where he stood, his muscles tense and quivering. "And come out of him!"

The man's mouth parted, his eyes on Jesus, and there issued from his throat a long, meaningless scream.

But the scream soon passed away. The man swallowed, rubbed his face, grinned at Jesus with foolish apology, then slumped into the nearest seat, enormously tired and perfectly sane.

"What is this? What is this?" the people murmured among themselves. "Look what he can do! He commands the unclean spirits, and they obey him!"

A Fever

After that singular event there could be no more teaching on that day. So Jesus left the synagogue and walked to the house of Simon Peter.

When he entered there, he found everything hushed. All was whispers and darkness and walking on tiptoe. Peter himself came out of a side room with a care unnatural in one so big. When he saw Jesus, he shook his head.

"My mother-in-law," he whispered. "She is suffering from a violent fever."

Jesus nodded in understanding, then went into the room that Peter had left. He found the woman in bed, dry and hot and breathing with rapid gasps, but he did not grieve. He took her hand and lifted her up, and at his touch alone the fever broke and left her, and the woman was well.

So then the house was filled with happier sounds, laughter and chatter. And the woman herself came out to serve them dinner.

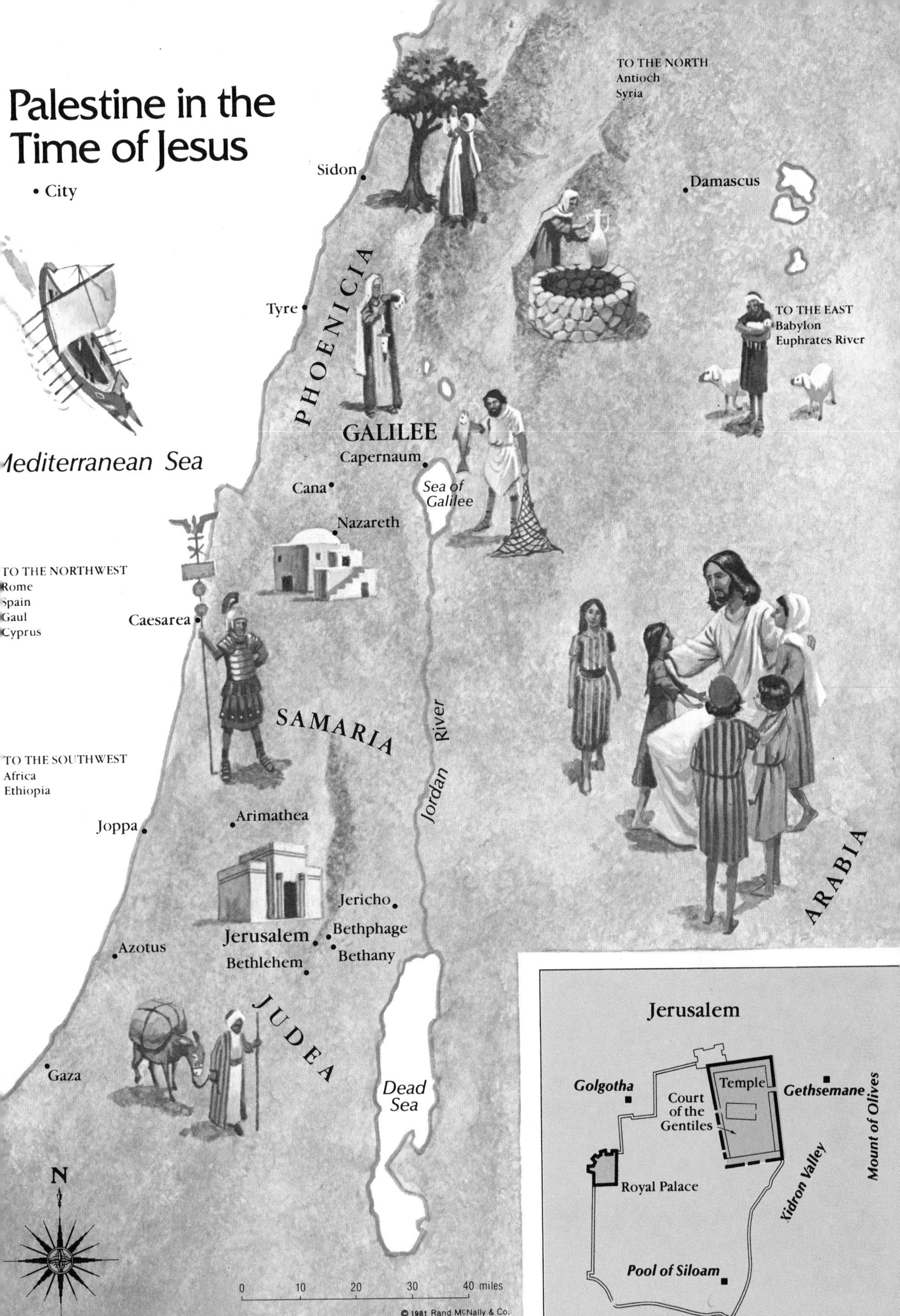

Palestine in the Time of Jesus
• City
TO THE NORTH
Antioch
Syria
Sidon
Damascus
PHOENICIA
Tyre
TO THE EAST
Babylon
Euphrates River
Mediterranean Sea
GALILEE
Capernaum
Cana
Sea of Galilee
Nazareth
TO THE NORTHWEST
Rome
Spain
Gaul
Cyprus
Caesarea
SAMARIA
Jordan River
TO THE SOUTHWEST
Africa
Ethiopia
Joppa
Arimathea
ARABIA
Jericho
Bethphage
Jerusalem
Bethany
Azotus
Bethlehem
JUDEA
Gaza
Dead Sea
N
0 10 20 30 40 miles
© 1981 Rand McNally & Co.
Jerusalem
Golgotha
Temple
Gethsemane
Court of the Gentiles
Mount of Olives
Royal Palace
Kidron Valley
Pool of Siloam
© 1981 Rand McNally & Co.

Leprosy

For a while Jesus stayed and worked his wonders in Capernaum, the city by the sea, so that his lean, restrained figure, his drilling eye, and his compassion became familiar even to those who lived outside the city, separated from its citizens.

People knew him on sight.

"Sir!" cried a man from the top of a hill as Jesus was walking in the country. "Sir, wait! Master, wait a minute!" The man scrambled down the hill and rushed to where Jesus stood waiting.

As the man came closer, Jesus felt his heart go out to him. With pity he saw that half the man's face was swollen; the swellings were a shining, deathly white, and white was the hair that grew on them. The man was a leper, condemned by his leprosy to live and to die alone.

"If you want to," the man puffed, breathless with running and excitement, "you can make me clean."

Then Jesus did what healthy people did not do. He laid his hand upon the man's afflicted face, saying, "I want to. Be clean."

Immediately the skin of the leper tightened and glowed with ruddy health, and he was clean.

"Look! Look! Look at me!" he cried as though this healing should be a grand surprise for Jesus as well. He began to laugh and to run toward the city.

But Jesus called him back. "Listen to me," he said. "Do not speak a word of this to anyone, but go to the priest and offer sacrifice for the cleansing."

The man laughed and nodded and instantly forgot what Jesus said. He told the miracle to everyone he met, then sat up long hours into the night describing in detail what changes Jesus had wrought in his life.

So the crowds that pressed upon Jesus turned into multitudes, and the diseased and the shattered and the twisted and the hurt cried out all the louder before him.

A Paralytic

So when he was preaching, some days later, in a house in Capernaum, the room around him was jammed with humanity. In fact, all of the rooms were tight with people standing shoulder to shoulder; the doorways were blocked, and even outside crowds strained to hear the words of this remarkable teacher.

Behind the crowd, in the middle of the street, stood four men feeling very helpless. They had brought a fifth man to see Jesus, a man so paralyzed that he had to be carried on a pallet. But how could they get to Jesus when all they saw were the people's backs and Jesus was somewhere deep inside?

"I know!" said one of the men. "I know what to do! Let us take him to the roof."

There were stairs that went up the outside of this house, and the roof itself was flat, made of branches and clay that had hardened in the sun.

"Right here," said the man when they stood on the roof. "Crack the clay and lift out a section—make it a sizable hole."

The pounding above silenced the preaching below; and when the hole was large enough, they tied ropes to their friend's pallet and let him down into the darkness, right in front of Jesus' feet.

Jesus was moved, altogether impressed by the faith of the four friends, whose heads he saw bobbing above. He knelt by the paralytic. "My son," he said, "your sins are forgiven you."

Now, there were scribes in that house who had come not to learn of Jesus but rather to judge for themselves this man with such a far-reaching reputation.

When they heard him say, "Your sins are

A gravely ill man was let down through a hole in a roof that he might see Jesus. Jesus healed him. And this was another miracle.

forgiven," they shuffled and grunted and thought, *Blasphemy! Who can forgive sins but God alone?*

But Jesus knew precisely what they were thinking. Without standing up, holding the sick man's head on his lap, he looked at the scribes and said, "Which do you suppose is easier—to say, 'Your sins are forgiven,' or to say, 'Get up and walk' ?"

No one answered him. It would surely be harder to forgive sins, but even if they were forgiven, who could tell? On the other hand, everyone could see whether or not a paralyzed man could walk.

Earnestly, quietly, Jesus said to the

Jesus healed a man's withered hand. But some there were who were distrustful of Jesus who not only healed, but healed on the Sabbath.

scribes, "Watch. I will show you that the Son of Man has power on earth to forgive sins."

He laid the man's head down and stood back. "I say to you," he said in a clear voice, "rise, take up your pallet, and go home."

And then it was as if the paralytic had simply wakened from a sleep. He stood up, and carrying his pallet, he went out before them all.

Happy cheers came from the roof. As for the crowds below, they were ever and ever astonished, saying, "We have never seen anything like this!"

A Withered Hand and Enemies

But the crowds that surrounded Jesus after that were not all kindly, not all needy, not all faithful people seeking to believe in him.

Some suspicious faces appeared among the others. These were the scribes, the scholars of the law; and these were the Pharisees, who made a practice of keeping not only the written laws of Moses but *all* of the laws handed down from the teachers of previous generations. "If you strive to keep the little laws," they said, "then you will never break the big ones."

But they came to catch this teacher in the breach of *any* law, little or big.

And when Jesus looked out and saw these faces among the sick and the sorrowing, he was grieved by the hardness of their hearts, for they looked like stones in a plowed field.

On a certain Sabbath day Jesus noticed a man whose hand was withered, and beside him a Pharisee, both in the multitude that always followed after him.

He said to the man with the gnarled hand, "Come here."

While that man came forward, the eyes of the Pharisee grew narrow with thought. *If Jesus heals the man,* he thought, *then he works on the Sabbath. And if he works, then he breaks the law of the Sabbath which says that he shall not work. And if he breaks the law, ha! Then we can bring charges against him.*

But again, Jesus knew what the Pharisee was thinking.

"Let me ask you something," he said to the Pharisee.

"Me?" The Pharisee was startled.

"You." Jesus took the withered hand into his own. "Is it lawful on the Sabbath to do good, or to do harm?"

No answer from the Pharisee. He seemed to be deep in thought.

"Or if you have a sheep which falls into a ditch on the Sabbath day," said Jesus in a sharper voice, "will you not rescue that sheep—*on the Sabbath day?*"

No answer from the Pharisee.

Jesus held high the poor, withered hand. "But a man," he said in a voice clearly angry, "a man is more valuable than a sheep! Have you never learned that the Sabbath was made for man—for man!—and not man for the Sabbath? And the Son of Man is Lord even of the Sabbath day!"

No answer from the Pharisee, though a turmoil of thought now writhed in his mind.

Jesus turned back to the cripple beside him and spoke words suddenly gentle and controlled. "Stretch out your hand," he said.

The man withdrew his hand from Jesus and held it out in front of him and moved it easily. The hand was healed.

In the commotion that followed, the Pharisee slipped away with others who began immediately to consider how they might discredit Jesus.

Jesus Teaches: The Sermon on the Mount

Out of the city Jesus went with his disciples—not only with the Twelve but with all those who dearly sought the kingdom of God. He led them away through the countryside and up a mountain. And when the disciples had gathered near unto him, he sat down.

For a moment he gazed away into the great blue bell of the sky, now empty, now shot with the free flight of a sparrow. He glanced at the bright scarlet and purple lilies that nodded in the soil around him. And then he turned his eyes upon the disciples, and his heart did love them.

There were no hard faces in this congregation, no stones in this field to break his plowshare. Well might he plow them, then, and plant. Well might he teach.

So he opened his mouth, and this is what he said:

"Blessed are the poor in spirit, for theirs is the kingdom of heaven.

"Blessed are those who mourn, for they shall be comforted.

"Blessed are the meek, for they shall inherit the earth.

"Blessed are those who hunger and thirst for righteousness, for they shall be filled.

"Blessed are the merciful, for they shall obtain mercy.

"Blessed are the pure in heart, for they shall see God.

"Blessed are the peacemakers, for they shall be called the children of God.

"Blessed are those who are persecuted for the sake of righteousness, for theirs is the kingdom of heaven.

"And blessed are you when the world shall mock you, hurt you, and speak every evil against you falsely because of me. Rejoice, my disciples, and be glad when that happens, for your reward is great in heaven. In the same way they mocked the prophets who went before you.

"You," Jesus said unto them, and he found their eyes when he said it. He gazed into their eyes, one disciple after the other. "You are the salt of the earth. But if the salt has lost its savor, how can it ever be salty again? No, then it is good for nothing but to

Away from the city, from the faces suspicious and mean, Jesus led the faithful. Seated among them on a mountainside, he spoke to them about who they were and of how they must live their lives.

be thrown on the ground and trodden underfoot.

"You," he said as though it were the given name of every one of them. "You are the light of the world. But a candle kept under a bushel brightens nothing, while a candle on a stand gives light to all the house. Let your light so shine before men that they may see your good works and give glory to your Father who is in heaven.

"And what of the law?" Jesus shook his head a moment. "I am condemned of ignoring the law," he said sadly, "but it is not true. Listen. I have not come to put an end to the law. I have come to fulfill the law. For this is the truth: Not an iota, not a dot, will pass from the law until everything is accomplished."

Now Jesus leaned forward to his disciples, and with a bold and radical authority he taught them how to understand the law.

"You have heard that it was said to the men of old, 'You shall not kill, and he who kills may be judged and condemned and punished.' But I say to you," said Jesus, "that he who is angry with his brother may be judged as well. He who insults his brother may also be condemned. And he who says 'You fool!' may be punished in the hell of fire.

"And you have heard that it was said, 'You shall not commit adultery.' But I say to you," said Jesus, "that he who gazes at a woman lustfully has already committed adultery with her in his heart.

"And you have heard that it was said, 'An eye for an eye, a tooth for a tooth; let the punishment equal the sin.' But I say," said Jesus, "that an evil done to you gives you no right to do that evil in return! If someone strikes you on the right cheek, show him your left. If someone sues you for your shirt, give him your coat as well. If someone forces you to go a mile, go two. To the man who begs from you, give; and do not refuse the man who wants to borrow.

"And you have heard that it was said, 'Love your neighbor, hate your enemy.' But I say love your *enemies,* and pray for those who hurt you, that you may be children of your Heavenly Father. For his sun shines on the evil and the good; his rain rains on the unjust and the just. But if you love the one who loves you, and him alone, what is special about you then? And if you greet your brother, and him alone, what is special about you then?

"You, my disciples, salt of the earth and light of the world—you must be perfect, as your Father who is in heaven is perfect."

Then Jesus fell silent and closed his eyes

awhile. It was a gesture he had learned from his mother, who used it to store and remember the past. But Jesus used it because he could, as it were, remember the future; and sometimes the memory of what was to come weighed so heavily upon his soul that he simply closed his eyes.

"Lord?" One of his disciples—John—called him out of his darkness. Jesus opened his eyes. "Lord," said John, "were you praying just now?"

Jesus smiled and said, "Yes. Yes, John, in fact I was."

"Will you teach us how to pray?" asked John.

"Come here, little one," the slender Jesus said to the man whose muscles were made on the sea. "Sit beside me." And when John was seated at his knees, Jesus spoke loud enough for all to hear.

"When you pray," he said, "do not babble as the heathen do, who think they will be heard for their hundred hollow words. Rather, know that your Father knows what you need even before you ask it, and when you pray, pray this way:

"Our Father who art in heaven,
Hallowed be thy name.
Thy kingdom come.
Thy will be done,
  On earth as it is in heaven.
Give us this day our daily bread;
And forgive us our debts
  As we forgive our debtors;
And lead us not into temptation,
  But deliver us from evil.
For thine is the kingdom and the power
  and the glory, forever. Amen.

"Ask, and it will surely be given you," Jesus said to them. "Seek, and you will find. Knock, and it will be opened unto you. For

In the healing silence of that mountain meadow, Jesus taught the men, the women, the children how to pray. He taught all who would listen.

askers receive. Seekers do find. And to those who knock, it is opened. Or which of you, when your son asks for bread, gives him a stone instead? Or if your daughter asks for fish, who gives her a snake? Now, if you who are evil give good gifts to your children, how much more will your Heavenly Father give to those who ask him!"

Jesus looked at the disciples sitting around him. They were rapt and peaceful now, but he saw the troubles and sorrows of their tomorrows, and he wanted them, for their own sakes, to learn trust.

"Therefore I tell you," he said, "do not worry about your lives, nervously wondering 'What will I eat? What will I drink? What will I wear on the morrow?' Look at the birds of the air! They sow no seeds, reap no harvest, store no goods in barns—yet your Heavenly Father feeds them. Are you not more valuable than they are?

"And why do you worry about your clothes? Look at the lilies of the field, who neither spin thread nor weave cloth nor sew it together to wear. Yet I tell you that even the resplendent King Solomon was never dressed like one of these. If God so clothes the grass for a day, which tomorrow is burned away, will he not clothe you the more, O you of little faith? Do not worry. No, do not worry. Your Father knows you need these things. Seek first his kingdom and his righteousness, and all these things will be added unto you."

A western sun still touched the top of the mountain and Jesus with amber light, though the rest of the world had sunk into darkness. Night was coming, filling first the lowest places with its gloom. Jesus stood up. A wind pulled at his tunic and his hair, and altogether he seemed to be a soft fire burning.

Suddenly he cried out, "Everyone who hears these words of mine and does them

Last of all Jesus spoke of trust in God. For as God cares for the wild things of the earth, and its flowers, so he cares for his children.

will be like a wise man who built his house upon the rock. The rain fell, the floods came, the winds blew and beat upon that house, but it did not fall because it was founded on the rock."

Then he cried yet louder, that even the spaces below might hear him. "Everyone who hears my words and does not do them," he called, "will be like a foolish man who built his house upon the sand. The rain fell, the floods came, the winds blew and beat against that house—and it fell. And great was the fall of it!"

Jesus did not sit down again. He had finished teaching for the day, and it was a long way back to Capernaum. He passed through the crowd and descended the mountain into lower darkness, while the disciples followed with wonder. "The scribes appeal to Moses for the truth of their words. But this man!" they said. "This man teaches by his *own* authority!"

The Great Faith of a Centurion

The hour was late when Jesus returned to Capernaum. The Teacher was tired and would gladly have rested. But diseases keep no schedule—except that they seem to be worst in the night. And so it was that when a certain man heard the noises of the crowds outside his house and when he was told that Jesus was there, he ran into the streets to look for him.

This man was a Gentile, a Roman, a commander in the Roman Army with the rank of centurion because he had a hundred soldiers under him.

"Lord," he said with great apology in his manner, "my servant is lying at home, paralyzed. My dear servant is suffering terribly."

Immediately Jesus was willing to postpone his rest. "Then I will come and heal him," he said.

"No," said the centurion. "No, I am not asking you to come. Sir, I am unworthy to have you under my roof. Just say the word from here, and he will be healed. I know the reaching goodness of your word, even as in my word there is some little authority. I say to a soldier, 'Go!' and he goes; I say, 'Come!' and he comes."

When Jesus heard the centurion, he raised his eyebrows in wonder, then turned to those who followed him.

"Do you hear this man?" he asked. "I tell you, not anywhere in Israel have I found such a faith! Many people are going to come from nations east and west of here to sit in the kingdom of heaven with Abraham, Isaac, and Jacob; but the faithless heirs of the kingdom themselves will be cast into alien darkness, weeping and gnashing their teeth."

To the centurion he said, "Go home. It is done for you according to your faith."

Within minutes people were running from the centurion's house, crying "Sir! Sir!" and raising such a clatter of happiness that the rest of the city began to waken, though it was the middle of the night.

"Sir, the servant is healed! Look! Here he comes walking to you!"

Indeed, a young boy came surrounded by torches and beaming as though it were his birthday.

Torches flared everywhere up and down the streets, and the multitude swelled.

"What happened? What happened?" Bare feet, tangled hair, eager faces.

"The lad was paralyzed—"

"—healed in an instant—"

Returning to Capernaum, Jesus was met by a man of rank and power, a centurion. Humbly, this man asked that his servant be healed. Such was the centurion's faith—so deep, so strong—that his servant was made whole that very instant.

"—a miracle—"

"Jesus! He is the one who did it!"

"Jesus? Where is he? I need to ask him—"

"Well, he was right here—"

But Jesus and the twelve disciples had slipped away into the night.

Little Faith and a Storm at Sea

Jesus had whispered to his closest disciples, "We need to go," his voice husky with weariness. "Come quickly. We will cross the sea to the other side."

And now they were on the beaches, sliding Simon's boat into water by the weak light of the stars.

"Teacher?" This was a strange voice from a strange figure. Someone had seen them go down to the sea.

Jesus, ready to step in the boat, paused and sighed. "Yes?" he said.

"Teacher, may I go, too? I will follow you wherever you go."

Jesus glanced at his bed for the night, a low boat on the vacant water, and saw in it all of his nights and all of his life in the world. "Foxes have holes," he said to the man, "and the birds of the air have their nests. But the Son of Man has no home where to lay his head."

So the boat was shoved from the shore containing the disciples only, and they pulled for the wide water of the sea. Jesus sat in the stern and, finally, fell asleep.

He slept deeply. He did not count the hours that passed, nor see the stars wink out. He did not feel the sea breeze change into a hard, commanding wind. He did not feel the waves that bunched at the hull of the boat. By wind and waves, a storm! The disciples, dragging their oars, began to panic. And still the Master slept.

The waves swelled to tremendous heights, and the wind ripped spray from the tops of them. The boat was swept down into watery valleys, only to swim up again at a violent angle, and the disciples were terrified, and still the Master slept.

Seeking rest from the pressing crowds, Jesus and his disciples set out across the sea. Weary, Jesus slept. A storm arose and wild winds tossed the little boat. And still Jesus slept.

"Lord!" they shrieked in their terror. "Lord!" and they shook him awake. "Don't you care if we die? We are dying! Save us, Lord!"

There was no hurry in his waking up, nor did he hurry to stand in the boat, nor did he lose his balance standing.

Jesus spread forth his arms and cried to

the winds, "Be silent!" and to the waves, "Be still!"

At once the hard wind ceased, and great calm was everywhere, and the boat sailed lightly on a peaceful water.

But Jesus did not at once sit down. Even in the darkness the disciples felt his eyes upon them. "Why should you be afraid?" It was the same voice as the one that had bound the weather. "O you men, you men of little faith," Jesus said.

And when he sat, they whispered, "What kind of man is this, that even the wind and the waves obey him?"

The Man with Many Devils

On the following morning several sleepy herdsmen stood among two thousand swine and watched while thirteen strangers beached a boat. They stood on a ridge above the sea, so they watched from a distance.

"Who do you suppose they are?" the herdsmen said.

"Well, we will soon know. Here they come."

The strangers had found a winding path that ascended to the top of the same ridge. They were climbing it now in single file, one lean figure ahead of the other twelve, one who found his footing with no difficulty, though the way was steep.

When he had gained the height, that one looked toward the herdsmen as if he knew them, but they looked away because they did not know him.

Suddenly a piercing scream cut through the morning. The swine shuffled and grunted, protesting. The swineherds swung round to stare at a stony cliff where the dead of their city were buried. "Oh, save us!" they muttered. "Here comes the madman again!"

Out of the tombs leaped a man absolutely naked. There were scars on his chest where he beat himself, scars on his wrists and his ankles where the herdsmen and others had bound him with ropes and chains. But he had always broken free of their restraints, for his strength was demonic. He was filled with devils.

The herdsmen grabbed sticks to protect themselves and their swine, but this time they did not have to use them. Like a horse the yowling madman galloped straight for the lean stranger.

"Watch out!" called the herdsmen. "He is danger to people and pigs alike!"

Twelve of the strangers thought this an excellent piece of advice; they retired forthwith down the ridge and back to the boat. But the first one never moved.

"What do you, what do you," screamed the madman. "What do you—want from me—Jesus you—Son of the—Most High God?"

The stranger said, "Spirit, come out of the man!"

Immediately the madman stopped running and began to whirl in circles. The stranger stood as still as a column, and the herdsmen were astonished.

"Don't! Don't do this thing!" screamed the madman. "By God, do not torment me!"

The stranger said, "What is your name?"

"My name," cried the madman, shrinking away, "is Legion, for we are many." Then he hunched and put his hands in front of his face, like a dog begging, and started to cry. "Please, do not send us out of the country," he wept. "There are swine over there—"

The herdsmen were suddenly full of attention. They dropped their sticks and threw up their hands. "Wait! Wait!"

"Send us to the swine," whimpered the madman. "Let us enter the swine."

"No! Wait!"

But the stranger nodded calmly, and the

man fell backward, as though someone had dropped him.

Then the whole herd of swine, like a carpet come alive, began to sway and to squeal, to stamp and to bump one another, as from a terrible itch. And just as the herdsmen jumped free, all two thousand of the swine turned and charged toward the ridge. Over they went and down the high embankment, thumping and rolling until they landed every one of them in the sea, where they drowned.

At first the herdsmen were stunned, so silent had the place become—their animals floating like barrels in the waves. But then they grew frightened—not of the madman who lay on the ground, but of the calm stranger who knelt beside him.

They backed away. They ran into the city. They chattered this story to all that they met. They gathered together a great crowd of citizens, then returned to the ridge with a single purpose in mind.

"Go away!" they said to the stranger.

It did not matter that the man once full of devils now sat dressed and in his right mind, talking calmly. They were afraid. That was what mattered.

"Leave our country. Leave us alone," they beseeched the man of mysterious powers. And the stranger offered them no argument. Quietly he descended the path to the sea and stepped into the boat again.

"Let me come with you!" cried the one he had healed.

But the stranger said, "No. Go home to your friends and tell them how much the Lord has done for you. Tell them what mercy he has had upon you."

Then the boat pulled out to sea, and the herdsmen became conscious of a vast emptiness in their day.

"The Lord?" they said to one another. "Did he say 'the Lord'?"

Death So Close for a Little Girl

Jesus stepped out of the boat again on the beaches of Capernaum and walked into the city by narrow streets. For ten minutes he and his disciples moved alone between the blank, white walls of the houses, because the afternoon heat had driven the people inside. Baked clay, bright sunlight, and dust: The city seemed deserted.

And perhaps he would have gone to rest as well, if a child had not seen him.

"Mama! Mama!" she squealed—loud for a little girl. "Here he is! Jesus is here!"

Peter kicked a little dust, running to silence the child. Jesus called, "Simon! Let her be!" And the girl darted round a corner, squealing, "Jesus! Jesus! Jesus!"

Heads popped out of doorways. Old men climbed down from their roofs. Beggars slipped out of the alleys. Cripples came leaning on canes. Children appeared on the run, and the men and the women, the healthy, the sick, the rich and the ragged, the hands and the mouths and the eyes all full of a need—the people! The people surrounded him once again. The multitude flocked in the streets, and their cries were like sheep's bleating.

"Master! Master!" One voice was raised above the others. "Master! My daughter!"

"It is Jairus," said the people. "Poor Jairus!" They made a path for a weeping, agitated man, respectful of him because he was one of the heads of the synagogue and because his need was very great.

His hair was mussed, his clothes askew; and though at all other times he carried himself with dignity, now he fell at Jesus' feet and wept. "My daughter is twelve years old, sweet as the daylight—and dying! Come—please come! Come and lay your hands on her that she might live!"

Someone among the crowds had touched Jesus. Who? He looked around. Then a woman knelt at his feet, a pale, sick woman who had simply touched his robe that she might be cured. And she was.

Jesus raised Jairus to his feet and said, "Lead me to her."

Blinded to everyone else by his anguish for his daughter, Jairus rushed away, down the middle of the street.

Jesus followed, but the multitude closed round him and he went slowly. The disciples could not keep the people back.

They had almost come to Jairus's house, when Jesus felt some part of his power flow out of him. He stopped and turned around. "Who touched me?" he asked.

The disciples burst out laughing. "A thousand people in the street," they said, "and you want to know which *one* touched you?"

"Who touched me?" Jesus repeated, and a small voice said, "I did."

Trembling, dropping her eyes, a pale woman stepped forward. "The hem of your garment, Master—I touched it for healing, and I am healed."

The disciples were no longer laughing.

"For twelve years I have been bleeding constantly," the pale woman explained, staring at the ground. "I spent my money on doctors until I was poor and none the better for it. Then I saw you. I thought, *Let me touch his hem, just his hem, and I will be well—*"

Jesus took her face between his slender hands and gazed at her until she was able, peacefully, to return his look and to smile.

"Daughter," he said, "your faith has made you well. Go in peace."

She said, "Thank—"

But suddenly there rose such a high, desolate howl of grief that the woman and all the multitude went cold and still.

"No!" It was like the roaring of a beast. "Merciful God, no!"

Jesus turned and saw Jairus, his arms on his stomach and his head thrown back. A handful of friends were patting his shoulders, saying, "No need. No need to bother the Teacher, now that the girl is dead."

Immediately Jesus went to Jairus, put his arm around the man, and said with absolute authority, "You, Jairus, do not be afraid. Only believe." To the friends he said, "Stand back." To Peter, James, and John he said, "Come with us." And he led Jairus into the house.

But what an uproar he found in there! Weepings, wailings, piteous sighings, and helpless sobbings—the relatives mourning the death of a little girl.

Jairus sagged in the Master's arms.

"Why do you make such a noise?" Jesus demanded, and the people were surprised.

"Because she is dead," they said.

"No, she is not dead," said Jesus. "She is sleeping."

Almost at once their sorrow turned to a bitter scorn, and they laughed at Jesus. But he, supporting Jairus in the crook of his arm, pointed toward the door and commanded the others to leave. His word was neither loud nor angry; yet it was delivered with such level power that the house fell silent and the people left—and Jairus found the strength to stand on his own legs.

"Come," said Jesus. Then the parents and the three disciples followed him into the girl's room.

Jairus gasped. Bedded she was on her pallet, frightfully still, her face as pale as marble and as cool. Blue were her lips, and chalk the fingers twined on her breast.

Jesus unwound her loose hands and, keeping one of them, said in his own tongue, *"Talitha, cumi."*

He said, "Little girl, I want you to arise."

She stirred. She sneezed. The color flooded her face and her fingers, and she got up, and she walked.

"Now," said Jesus to a mother and a father lost in wonder, "find her some food and feed her."

Jesus Teaches—in Parables

"I will open my mouth in parables. I will utter what has been hidden since the foundation of the world."

Once, when Jesus was teaching from Simon's boat and the multitude sat on shore—the land and the sea and all the sky

being his schoolroom and everything in them a lesson—the Master stopped short and sat quietly for a while. His boat rocked, and the people wondered at his pausing.

Then he began to talk again, but it did not seem as if he was teaching. Instead, he just told them a story. They felt like little children. They were glad to hear the story, but they were not quite sure why he told it or what it meant.

"Once upon a time," said Jesus, "a farmer went out to sow his seed. He cast the seed everywhere over the field, so some of it fell on the path and the birds came and ate it.

"He cast the seed everywhere over the field, so some of it fell on the rocky ground, where the soil lies thin and warm. Here it sprouted speedily. But the hot sun scorched the tender plants, and because they had no roots, they withered.

"And he cast the seed everywhere over the field, so some of it fell among weeds, and the weeds and the wheat grew together. Then the wild weeds choked the wheat, and the good wheat perished.

"But he cast the seed everywhere over the field, so other seed fell on the good rich ground, and it grew and produced—some a hundredfold, some sixty, and some thirty."

The Teacher sat quietly again, and the boat rocked, and the people blinked. Was that the end of the story?

Yes, that was the end, because now he stood up in the boat and cried out, "He that has ears to hear, let him hear!" Then he signaled Simon to row him back to shore.

People said, "What was he talking about?"

People said, "I don't know."

And the disciples, when they were alone with him, said, "What were you talking about? Why did you tell us a story?"

"That was more than a story," said Jesus. "That was a parable. You may look at it to enjoy it, but you must look *through* it to know the truth. I give you windows, my children, that you might see into the kingdom of God. The farmer, his seed, and the soils—all together are a window."

"What do we see through that window?" asked the disciples. "What does the parable mean?"

Then Jesus showed them the meaning. He said, "The seed is like the word of the kingdom. When someone hears the word

His daughter—dead! Jairus grieved. But Jesus took her hand, and spoke, and the girl arose.

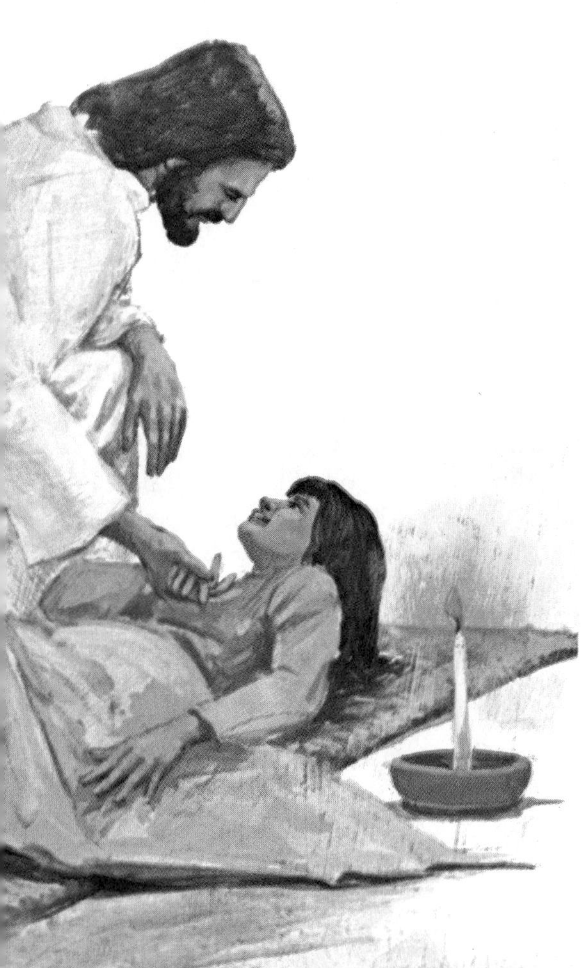

but does not understand it, he is like the hard dirt of the path. The evil one snatches away what was sown in his heart.

"The rocky ground is like the one who receives the word with joy—but it takes no real root in him. So when persecution rises up like the hot sun, when people scorn him for the word, he fails, and the word quickly withers in him.

"The weeds are the worries of this world and the love of its riches. They soon choke the word in some hearts, and it bears nothing.

"But the good rich ground is he who hears the word and understands it. He indeed bears fruit, a hundred times over, or sixty, or thirty.

"Do you see?" said Jesus.

"Now we see," said the disciples.

"Then *keep* seeing," Jesus said. "Everywhere there are windows into the kingdom of heaven—parables! Parables!

"Look at the grain of mustard seed, which is the smallest of all seeds but which, when it is grown, becomes a tree so great that the birds of the air can make their nests in its branches. The mustard seed is like the kingdom of God. I give it to you as a parable.

"Or you—Simon, John—look at the fisherman's net. Men throw it into the sea and gather fish of every kind. When it is full, they draw it ashore, sit down, and sort the bad from the good. The good they keep; the bad they toss away. See the kingdom of heaven in the fisherman's net! For so it will be when this age is over. The angels will sort the evil from the righteous and toss those who are evil into the furnace of fire where they will weep and gnash their teeth.

"Do you see?" Jesus asked them again. "Do you understand?"

"Yes!" said the disciples. "Stories that are more than stories! We do see!"

"Then blessed are your eyes," said Jesus, "for they see what the prophets yearned to see but did not. Blessed are your ears, for they hear."

Who Can This Be?

Thus Jesus of Nazareth ministered throughout Galilee, preaching the word of the kingdom with power, healing the hurt, setting at liberty people oppressed by the devil.

The multitudes called him Master and Teacher. The disciples called him Lord. And everyone carried the name of Jesus through all that land with such wonder and amazement that this man—no longer young, for all his labor, but ever intense, watchful, and compassionate—that this lean man was known even in Judea and Jerusalem, by the common folk, by the priests and the rulers, and by Herod himself. They had all heard of him.

"Who can this man be?" they asked over and over.

Some said, "He is Elijah, come back again."

Others answered, "He is a prophet, just like the prophets of old."

But Herod had another idea, which caused him to be afraid. "He is John," groaned Herod. "John the Baptizer, whom I killed. John has come back from the dead, and the powers are working in him!"

Herod had, indeed, beheaded John the Baptizer. So his fears, though unfounded, were not unnatural.

"I did not *want* to kill him," he said, and he spoke the truth, for it had been the woman Herodias who hated John and wanted him dead. Nevertheless, it had been Herod who gave the command.

The Execution of John the Baptizer

On his birthday Herod had given a banquet for his officers and for all the people of his court.

Such banquets demanded entertainment; so, while Herod's nose grew red and his tongue unloosed from drinking wine, the dancers passed before the tables and the guests applauded—no one louder than Herod himself.

Finally, the daughter of Herodias came in to dance. So sweet was her step, so lilting the music, so charming each turn that she made that the hall was still until her last gesture, and then Herod exploded with praise.

"Ask me whatever you wish," he roared, "and I will give it you!"

"Anything?" said the girl.

Herod stood up and spread his arms in a vast circle. "Anything!" he vowed. He was feeling very good. "Anything up to half my kingdom!"

The girl slipped out to talk with her mother. She was back in a twinkling.

"Please, sir." She curtsied sweetly. Herod

Salome—lovely, young, able to dance like a will-o'-the-wisp—this Salome asked of King Herod a fearful thing: the head of John the Baptizer.

beamed enormously. "I ask that you give me the head of John the Baptizer. On a platter. Now."

Slowly Herod sat down, suddenly sober and feeling very ill. But the girl stood her ground, and her face, despite the horrible sentence spoken, remained bright and innocent. Herod had vowed to give her her wish, and he had made that vow before his officers and all the people of his court. He could not refuse.

"Let it be," he mumbled to a soldier of the guard.

The soldier stepped forward. "Excuse me, sir," he said. "I could not hear you."

"*Let it be done*," Herod bellowed so loud that the command echoed through the building—and it was done.

The head of John was brought into a gloomy banquet hall. A young girl received it on a platter and took it to her mother.

It had been done.

"What did you go to the desert to see?" said Jesus, speaking of John the Baptizer. "A reed shaking in the wind? Or why did you go? To see a man dressed in rich robes? Rich robes are on the backs of those who sit in kings' houses. So why did you go? To see a prophet? Yes! And more than a prophet! John was a messenger—of whom it is written, 'Behold, I send my messenger before your face to prepare the way for you.'

"I tell you truly that never has there arisen one greater than John the Baptizer! Yet the least in the kingdom of heaven is greater than he.

"Until John, the prophets and the law did prophesy. Since John till now, the kingdom of heaven has suffered violence at the hands of the hateful, trying to take it. And who is John, who is this man that stands *between* the times? A messenger, yes, but more: He is *the* messenger. If you are willing to accept it, he is Elijah who is to come!"

Those words also echoed, but not in a building. They echoed up and down the land. They echoed back and forth across the ages. For the times which had been prophesied were coming true.

"Behold!" said the Lord of hosts. "I will send you Elijah the prophet before the great and terrible day of the Lord comes.

"The day that comes shall burn the wicked, so that it will leave them neither root nor branch. But for you who fear my name the sun of righteousness shall rise, with healing in his wings!"

Now John was dead. The kingdom of heaven was at hand.

THE TRAINING OF THE TWELVE

How great was the heart of the Master for the multitudes! How deep and abiding his love for them! But as long as they clung to him, cried after him, and pressed him wherever he went, he could not give particular attention to his twelve disciples.

Yet Jesus had to prepare the Twelve for the great and terrible things to come. He had to teach them glory in disaster—no easy lesson for anyone to learn—and wisdom in folly and strength in weakness and triumph in defeat and life in death. They had no notion of such holy riddles, so there was much, much to teach them.

And he had to instruct them in the duties they would take up when he had gone away from them.

Therefore, Jesus had good reasons to

avoid the crowds, to go away, himself and the Twelve alone.

Jesus Feeds Five Thousand

Early in the morning, just after the rooster's crow, when a mist still sat on a very still sea, Jesus woke his disciples, saying, "Little ones, come. Simon, your boat. Let us find a place of solitude for ourselves alone."

Except that the oars bumped, the boat was nearly soundless in quiet water; and the mist hid them, so they rowed along the shoreline thinking that they went in secret.

But when the sun burned the mist away, they looked landward and saw a curious sight: people! And all of the people were hurrying in the same direction as the boat. Sometimes, when a thick brush stood at the shore, the people disappeared; but as soon as it was open beach again, there were the people, hurrying, hurrying.

"Where do you suppose they are going?" Simon asked. He waved. They waved. Jesus sighed and shook his head.

Sometimes the boat went by villages crouched by the sea. But the people never stopped for any of these. Instead, more people poured out of the houses to join the others running through the village, and the crowds continued to swell. People!

Morning moved to noon. Fewer and fewer villages were passed, and the land went to stone, for they were coming to a poor, lonely area. But still the people kept running along the shore. Mostly men, they were—*many* men, about five thousand men!—but women and children too were in the multitude that spread out almost as far as the eye could see.

Suddenly Simon struck his forehead and cried, "Lord! They're not going anywhere! They're following us!"

Jesus nodded. Not since the mist had lifted hours ago had he taken his eyes from the people. The people! And the water was in his own eyes, now. He had pity for them, because they looked like sheep without a shepherd.

"Beach the boat," he said quietly. "We cannot leave them like this."

"*Jeeeee-sus*!" the people cried in delight as Jesus stepped out of the boat. They sang his name again and again, until he had climbed a small hill and sat down. Then they gathered around him as close as they could, and he opened his mouth and taught them many things.

The disciples sat by their boat through the afternoon. They, too, had compassion for the people, but they did not think of sheep. They thought of physical exhaustion, for the morning's run along the shore had been a long one. They thought of sun sickness, for the afternoon sun was hot. They thought of swoons of hunger, for the evening was nigh and no one had eaten.

Finally, Philip and Andrew went to Jesus and whispered in his ear, "Lord, send the people away. This is a lonely place. For their own sakes, send them back to the villages where they can buy something to eat."

But Jesus spoke aloud. "Philip, how do you propose *we* should feed them?"

The people heard that. Philip was embarrassed. "We?" he whispered. "Lord, we cannot! Wages for two hundred days' work is not enough to buy that much bread!"

"Then how much bread do we have already?" Jesus asked loudly.

"Lord, please keep your voice down," whispered Philip in an anguish. "We should not raise their expectations."

"Why not?" asked Jesus.

"Because," Andrew whispered, "there is a boy here with five barley loaves and two small fish—and that is all the food we have."

"But *I* am here," said Jesus, "and I know

precisely what I am going to do, my poor, polite disciples! Make the people sit down."

Obediently, then, Philip carried this word to the other disciples, and soon five thousand were seated in groups of fifty and a hundred.

Then Jesus took the bread; and looking up to heaven, he blessed it, broke it, and gave it to his disciples to distribute. In the same way he divided the fish. The food went out to everyone, and everyone ate, and everyone was filled. Five thousand were satisfied at the hand of the Lord by five small loaves of bread.

"Philip!" Jesus called, and then he whispered in that disciple's ear. "Gather up the fragments, that nothing be lost."

"Why are you whispering?" Philip asked.

"No reason at all," said Jesus.

When the people saw the baskets full of crumbs, the wonder of their supper struck them. Each disciple took a basket to the boat. Twelve! Twelve baskets full of what they could not eat!

Now Jesus would have gone down to the boat as well, for it was fast becoming night, but the people would not let him.

"No, Master!" they roared. "We want

you to stay with us! We want you to be our king!"

Jesus gazed at them. Though it was dusk, he could see them very well. "Not because you understand this sign," he said, "but because it is only a miracle for you, just because you ate your fill of loaves, you want me as your king. O people! Do not desire the food which passes away, but rather the food which lasts to eternal life, which the Son of Man will give to you."

"We do! We do desire that wonderful food," they cried. "Where is it?"

"The bread of God is that which comes

Five small loaves, two fish—and more than five thousand people to feed. Jesus blessed the food and broke it. And none went away hungry.

down from heaven," said Jesus, "and gives life to the world."

The multitude was moving, now, like a single blind animal. "Give us this bread!" they cried.

Jesus called out, "I AM the bread of life! He who comes to me shall not hunger. He who believes in me shall never thirst!"

They were, in fact, coming toward him,

but not to believe in him. They did not understand his words. Bread alone they understood, chewing it, swallowing it, eating it, satisfaction!

"Jeeeee-sus! King Jeeeee-sus!" they roared.

For the second time in a day Jesus felt enormous sadness for the people—but now they were deadly, a mass of deadly flesh; so this time he turned and slipped into darkness and left them alone.

The multitude stumbled awhile for loss of their king, but soon they remembered the fragments, the disciples, and they surged toward the boat.

"Row!" cried Simon. "Let us go!"

"But where is the Lord?" said others.

"He takes care of himself!" cried Simon, straining at the prow. "Go! Go!"

With great guilt, but afraid of the masses ashore, the disciples pulled for the open sea and safety.

Jesus on the Water

"We should never have left him," said John.

They were six hours at sea, lapped in utter darkness. The noise of the multitude had died away, but the noise of the wind and the waves had arisen, and that was a lonely, frightening howl.

"It was wrong, Simon," said John. "If we love him, we should stand by him."

"I love him as much as you do," Simon puffed. They were rowing into a head wind. The big man's strength was bending his oar. "But I also believe in his power. He met the devil. He met a thousand devils. He can handle a handful of fools!"

John said, "I feel terrible."

James said, "We may be punished for our weakness."

"Take an oar!" shouted Simon. "Take an oar for your guilt and help me row."

But James whispered, "No!"

"What?" cried Simon.

Again, in a terrified voice, James whispered, "O God, no! *Look!*"

They all looked. Rowing stopped. The boat swung loose and rolled.

A dim, wispy light seemed to be floating on the water not too far from them.

"What is that?"

"I don't know. I don't know."

"Look! It's coming closer!"

"Brighter!"

"A ghost!" cried James. "It is a ghost!"

The boat tossed. The disciples gripped the sides. The light took the form of a man—and when it spoke to them, their hearts nearly failed them.

But it said, "Do not be afraid," and the voice was familiar! Then Jesus himself, walking toward them on the water, called, "It is I."

Immediately Simon stood up in the boat and burst with laughter. "What did I tell you?" he roared, thumping John's back. "What did I tell you! Lord, if it is you, let me come to you on the water!"

Jesus said, "Come."

Simon stepped over the side and onto the water, big and bold and walking!

But then—halfway between the boat and the Lord—it was as if he suddenly realized what he was doing. He stopped. He put out his arms for balance. And very cautiously he spoke one reasonable word. "Maybe—"

In that instant he sank into the sea.

"Lord!" he spluttered; he coughed. "Save me!"

Jesus reached down and caught him. "O Simon of so little faith!" he said as he

Wind drove the waves, and the disciples in their small boat were afraid. Suddenly, a soft light appeared in the darkness, hovering over the sea. It was Jesus, walking across the waters, to comfort them.

brought the fisherman back to his boat.

Then the wind ceased, and Simon did small rowing after that.

The disciples worshiped Jesus. And John, with tears in his eyes, said, "Truly, you are the Son of God."

A Lesson: Regarding Certain Pharisees

"We have been watching you!"

This angry declaration was flung at Jesus by certain Pharisees, who were determined to keep all of the laws strictly. After the declaration came a series of cutting accusations.

"You break the Sabbath laws," they announced. "You permit your disciples to crack grain on the Sabbath, which cracking is work, which work is prohibited by Sabbath laws. You yourself, as we have noted, heal on the Sabbath: again, work, and the breaking of laws. Your disciples persist in ignoring the traditions of the elders. They eat with their hands unwashed. Now, tell us, Teacher: How can you righteously allow such loose, unrighteous living?"

"You," said Jesus, his eyes flashing, "you hypocrites! *You* forget the commandments of God, all to chase after the traditions of men! You tithe the little bits, mint and dill and cumin; but *you* have neglected the weightier measures of the law, justice and mercy and faith! You blind guides, straining out a gnat but swallowing a camel!"

"Well!" said the Pharisees around him. Jesus fought hard and suddenly. But they would return the fight with a test to him.

"Well, Teacher," they said, "if you are free to ignore the laws of our ancestors, then prove it. Give us some sign from heaven, and we will know that you have the right to do what you do."

Jesus sighed deeply at their mocking request; and their hard, unseeing hearts did grieve him.

"An evil and adulterous generation looks for a sign," he said. "But there will be no sign except for the sign of Jonah. For as Jonah was three days and three nights in the belly of the whale, so will the Son of Man be three days and three nights in the heart of the earth. Behold! something greater than Jonah is here!"

Some way, some way, thought these people as they left him, *we will mute that man!*

But now Jesus led his disciples away from them and away from the multitudes for a while, away from Capernaum, away from Galilee, off into northern, foreign lands, and they went alone.

It was a distance that they traveled, and it happened that they had only one loaf of bread among them. This caused considerable worry for the disciples, who said louder and louder, until Jesus could hear them, "We have no bread!"

Then Jesus stopped and gazed at them. A young man! He was not much older than when he had begun his preaching. But his face was aging.

"Are your hearts as hardened as the hearts of some of the Pharisees?" he asked. "Do your eyes not see? Do your ears not hear? Oh, beware this creeping yeast of faithlessness in your hearts!"

"But we only spoke about the food," said Simon.

"Why?" Jesus asked him. "Why do you say, 'We have no bread,' though I am right here with you? Behold, man! Behold the *truth!*"

Simon blinked at Jesus.

Jesus said, "When I broke five loaves among five thousand men, how many baskets of crumbs did you pick up?"

Simon said, "Twelve."

Jesus took Simon by his shoulders, so that they stood face to face and very close, and he said, "Do you not yet understand?"

Near Tyre and Sidon, a Canaanite woman beseeched Jesus for her daughter's sake. So great was the woman's faith that her daughter was healed.

A Lesson: In God's Generosity

Now they walked among foreigners and not among Jews, among Gentiles and not the children of Abraham. They had come to the territory around the cities of Tyre and Sidon.

Here a Gentile woman began to follow Jesus, crying, "O Lord, thou Son of David, have mercy on me. My daughter is full of a demon, a violent devil!"

Jesus kept walking, as though he did not hear her, but she only cried the louder and would not stop.

The disciples muttered to Jesus, "Lord, send the foreigner away. Her screeching is an irritation to us."

So Jesus turned to the woman. "I was sent only to the lost sheep of Israel," he said.

Neither did that stop her. She ran up and knelt before his knees, pleading, "Help me, Lord."

"It is not fair," said Jesus in a chilly voice, "to take bread from the children and throw it to the dogs." He shot a glance at Simon.

Neither did that stop her. "Yes, Lord," she agreed, "but even the dogs eat the crumbs that fall from the master's table."

Then Jesus, to the wonder of the disciples, lifted her up, hugged her, and smiled. "Woman, great is your faith!" he proclaimed. "It is done for you as you have asked."

And in that same moment, her daughter was healed.

A Graceful Lesson: Who Jesus Is

In a small garden apart from anyone else, Jesus sat with his disciples, his back to the grizzled roots of an olive tree.

A mighty man was Simon Peter, a man of rock-ribbed faith. Jesus called him blessed. He called him Peter his rock and said that on this rock he would build his church.

Almost casually he asked, "What do you hear? Who do the people say the Son of Man is?"

The disciples smiled at the things they had heard.

"Some say you are John the Baptizer."

"Elijah. I have heard you called Elijah."

"Or Jeremiah."

"They think you are one of the prophets come back again."

Jesus leaned forward and fixed them with his eyes. "But who do *you* say I am?"

Simon answered immediately, almost shouting the words. "You are the Christ," he said, "the Son of the living God!"

Quiet followed that confession, in which Jesus arose, walked to Simon, and took him once again by his shoulders. "Blessed are you, Simon son of Jonah!" he said, gazing into the big man's eyes. "Flesh and blood did not show you this thing, but my Father who is in heaven. And for this reason you are Peter the rock, upon which rock I will build my church, and the powers of death itself shall never destroy it. I will give you the keys of the kingdom of heaven. Whatever you bind on earth shall be bound in heaven, and whatever you loose on earth shall be loosed in heaven."

A Hard Lesson: What He Has to Do

Now he turned toward all of the disciples. The breeze caught his robe and wrapped it close to his body so that he seemed more lean than ever, and age was in his face—an infinity of ages.

"I must go, soon," he said. "Understand what I am about to say to you. I must soon go to Jerusalem, and when I am come in that city, it will seem no victory to anyone who is of this world. I must go to suffer many things at the hands of the authorities in Jerusalem—"

"No!" said Simon Peter.

"So it must be," said Jesus without hesitation, keeping his back to that disciple. "And then, in that place, I will be killed—"

"No!" shouted Simon, standing up.

"So it must be!" Jesus repeated. "And then, on the third day, I will be raised from the dead—"

"God forbid it!" roared Simon Peter, and he grabbed Jesus. "Lord, this shall never happen to you!" He tried to turn the Teacher.

But Jesus stood as hard as a stone and would not turn. His back to Simon Peter, he uttered stinging words—"Satan, get out of my sight!"—which cut Simon like a whiplash. The thick man stumbled backward and sat with a thump, like a bundle of straw. "Your cares are human cares. Your thoughts do not belong to God," said Jesus, "and you do hinder me!"

Silence had followed Peter's confession; silence now followed his folly. Jesus walked back to the olive tree while every disciple

---

Yet Simon Peter refused to hear the hard truth, refused to accept his Lord's bitter fate. And so Jesus called him Satan, and Simon was stunned.

concentrated on holding very still.

"Disciples," said Jesus, facing the tree. "Is that what you are? *My* disciples. Is that what you would be?" He turned, and the ancient tree became his frame, its gnarled roots writhing at his feet, its trunk the sides of him, its leaves his crown and canopy. "You have heard the way that I must go," he said. "Now hear the path laid down for my disciples. If anyone would come after me, let him deny himself, let him take up his cross, and let him follow me. For whoever seeks to save his life, he will lose it. But whoever loses his life for my sake, that man will find it. O my little children! What will you have if you should gain the whole world—but lose your life? As for my disciples and the finding of their lives, listen: When the Son of Man returns with his angels in the glory of the Father, then will he reward each one for what each one has done. My disciples now," said Jesus, "then you will be mine forever."

A Glorious Lesson: The Transfiguration

Simon Peter was a subdued and gloomy figure after that. It seemed to him that he did everything wrong; so he determined to do nothing at all.

But what was worse: He did vigorously and deeply love his Lord and wanted to stay with him forever. But the Lord had predicted terrible things for the future, and that grieved poor Peter, so he put his face down for sadness. And when he had tried to express his sadness, Jesus had called him Satan! It was all very wrong. It was all very confusing. Great Peter became great gloom among the disciples, and for five days he sat alone and brooded.

Then, on the sixth day, Jesus touched him and said, "Come with us."

Peter looked around. James and John were there. "Where?" he asked.

Jesus said, "Come with us," and walked away. He led them up into a mountain, grassy on the top of it. There he raised his arms in the manner of prayer and began in a low voice to pray.

Peter thought that perhaps he too should pray, and he began to raise his own arms—but suddenly that face of the Lord began to change. It grew brighter and brighter until it shined like the sun. And his clothes did glisten. And the brilliance flooded Peter's head, so that he squinted and felt dizzy at the sight.

Jesus was caught up into a great light and spoke with Moses and Elijah. His disciples saw this.

Then, behold! He saw two men standing in the midst of the glory of the Lord, Moses and Elijah, and he heard them talking. They were talking about the departure which Jesus was to accomplish in Jerusalem!

Peter wanted to laugh or to weep, so full was he with the glory of the moment. And when he saw that Moses and Elijah were leaving, he cried out, "Master! It is good for us to be here! Let us make three booths, for you, for Moses, for Elijah—!"

But then a rolling, mighty cloud came down upon them, and the words died on his lips for the fear that he felt. And a voice thundered from the cloud, saying, "*This is my Son, my Chosen One. Listen to him!*"

Peter collapsed and lay trembling with awe. Both James and John fell down on either side of him, and they might have lain there for days—but Jesus came and touched them.

"Rise," he said in familiar voice, "and do not be afraid."

Peter lifted up his eyes, looked around, and saw no one but Jesus. And with what new eyes he looked upon his Lord! His dark gloom was gone, and ever afterward he remembered this bright event with joy.

"We were eyewitnesses of his majesty!" he said of the Lord. "We were with him on the holy mountain! We heard the voice of God the Father giving him honor and glory and saying, 'This is my beloved Son, with whom I am well pleased.' "

The Hard Lesson: Repeated

Jesus and his disciples returned to Galilee, but he was very careful not to let anyone know of his presence, for he was still teaching those closest to him.

"The Son of Man will be delivered into the hands of enemies," he said, "and they will kill him, and when he is killed, after three days, he will rise."

The disciples still did not understand this saying, but this time no one said anything. They were afraid to ask him.

A Lesson: The Greatest in the Kingdom

The disciples were discussing a difficult question, and since they could not come to an answer, they put it to Jesus.

"Lord," they said, "who is the greatest in the kingdom of heaven?"

But Jesus did not give them an immediate reply. Leaving them standing alone, he walked down the street till he came to a small child. He squatted and offered his hand. The child took it. He said a word, and the child placed a cheek against that hand, smiling. Then they walked back together, and Jesus sat and placed the child on his knee.

"This child is," he said. "For this is the truth: Unless you turn and become like children, you will never enter the kingdom of heaven. Whoever humbles himself like this little one, he is the greatest in the kingdom of heaven. And whoever receives such a child as this receives me; but whoever causes one of these little ones who believe in me to sin, woe unto him! It were better for him if a great millstone were tied round his neck and he were drowned in the deeps of the sea!"

Jesus knelt before a child, and the child loved him. Jesus looked up at his disciples—great, tall men—and told them to become like that child.

A Lesson: On Forgiveness

It was Peter who came to Jesus with another question.

"Lord," he said, "how often should I forgive my brother? If he keeps sinning against me, should I forgive him seven times?"

Jesus said, "I do not say seven times, but seventy times seven. Peter, my rock, this is the way that it is in the kingdom of heaven—" Then Jesus told this parable.

"Once upon a time," he said, "a king decreed that everyone who owed him money should pay it at once. But one of his servants owed him ten thousand talents, an enormous sum, an impossible debt.

" 'Pay me!' said the king.

" 'O sir!' said the servant, 'I cannot pay you.'

"The king frowned. 'Very well,' he said, 'then I shall have to sell you and your wife and your children into slavery!'

"When the servant heard that, he began to cry. He sank to his knees and folded his hands and wailed, 'Wait! Wait! I will work for it, sir! Have patience with me, and I will work and pay every penny I owe.'

" 'Let me see,' said the king, and he fell to figuring. He added, and he multiplied, and he discovered that it would take this servant one hundred and fifty thousand years to pay back the debt if he worked for it.

"That made the king feel very sorry for his servant. 'No,' he said, 'do not try to work that long. Instead, I forgive you the whole debt.' He struck a line through his account books and said, 'You owe me nothing any more. Go in peace.'

"That servant bowed very often, being very happy, and left the palace.

"But as soon as he was outside, he saw another servant who owed *him* a hundred denarii. He grabbed the poor man by the throat and said, 'Pay me!'

" 'O sir!' said the fellow servant, 'I cannot pay you.'

" 'Ha!' he said. 'And I suppose you expect me to wait while you work for it?'

" 'Have patience, sir, and I will pay you,' said the fellow servant.

" 'Patience?' he said. 'I have figured it out. You would have to work a hundred days in order to pay me back. No, I cannot have that much patience!' And he had his fellow servant thrown into prison.

"When the king heard what his servant had done, he stood up and roared, 'Get him!'

"So then the servant was standing once again in front of the king.

" 'You wicked servant!' said the king. 'I forgave you your debt because you asked me. Why could you not have mercy on your fellow servant, even as I had mercy on you? *Take this man away!'*

"The king gave the servant to the jailers. The jailers put him in prison. And there he sat until the whole ten thousand talents should be paid.

"Even so," said Jesus, "will my Heavenly Father do to you if you do not forgive your brother from your heart."

Jesus spoke of forgiveness. A king forgave his servant's debt, but the servant did not forgive a debt owed to him. He was cast into prison.

A Lesson: On Receiving Children

A father and a mother and four small children were standing by the road, smiling, when Jesus passed with his disciples. Peter saw them and said nothing.

A little later, there they were again, standing by the road and smiling. This time there were six children and another mother. Peter said nothing.

Still later, Peter saw the same family and eight other children and many parents, all smiling. "What do you want?" Peter asked.

"Only that the Lord would lay his hands on our children and pray," said a father.

Everywhere, the children came to Jesus—more and more children, laughing and chattering. Jesus welcomed them, every one. He blessed them and said that theirs was the kingdom of heaven.

"I am sorry. He is busy," said Peter, and he went to join Jesus again.

Later on, there they were again: twenty-five children and nine parents by the side of the road, smiling.

"Look!" Peter said to them. "He has no time for minor concerns. You will simply have to go—" But a hand descended on Peter's shoulder, and he turned to see Jesus.

"Let the little children come unto me," said Jesus, "and do not forbid them, for to such belongs the kingdom of heaven."

And before he went farther, he laid his lean and tender hands on each of the heads of twenty-five children, and he and they were smiling together.

His Life a Ransom for Many

There came a morning, finally, when the disciples found Jesus already awake and on the road before them. But he was not walking. He stood silently facing the south and gazing with great, dark eyes in the direction of Jerusalem, and Galilee was behind him.

His lips were thin. His cheeks had gone hollow with the years, and his brow bore the scars of human souls. But his eyes were steady, as clear as ever, and serene.

"It is nearly time," he said when all twelve of the disciples had gathered. "We are going to Jerusalem."

Then he began straightway to walk, and the disciples followed, amazed and afraid.

As they traveled in that day, Jesus spoke again what he had said before, and sometimes he closed his eyes over the words as his mother used to do over memories.

"In Jerusalem," he said, "the Son of Man will be delivered to the chief priests, and they will condemn him to death and bind him over to the Gentiles. The Gentiles will mock him, spit upon him, scourge him, and kill him. And on the third day he will rise."

Perhaps it was the sense that great things were about to occur. Or perhaps the sense of urgency drove them, as though they had to ask it now or lose the chance forever. Whatever the reason, James and John came forward and said to Jesus, "Lord, would you do something in particular for us?"

Jesus paused, for they were very serious, and said, "What is it?"

"Give us places of privilege," they said. "When you come into your glory, let us sit on your left and on your right."

Jesus sighed and closed his eyes. "You do not know what you are asking," he said. "Can you drink the bitter cup that I must drink?"

"Yes! Yes, of course we can," they said.

"Well, you will drink that cup," said Jesus, "but it is not for me to distribute seats of honor."

"Listen to them!" the other disciples began to mutter. "Why should they get honor and glory above us? We deserve some recognition, too!"

"Stop it!" Jesus commanded them all. "You know what the Gentiles do, how those who should be ruling strut like roosters and squash the little people with their power. Well, it shall not be so among you! Among you the one who would be great must be your servant. And the one who would be first among you must be the slave of all. And why? Because you are mine! And the Son of Man came not to be served but to serve and to give his life as a ransom for many. Come," said Jesus to the Twelve. "Let us go."

Thus he turned southward and steadfastly set his face toward Jerusalem.

"He is a good man."

"No! He is leading the people astray!"

But those who believed in him said, "When the Christ appears, will he do more signs than this man has done?"

"Signs! Why this man has a demon and performs his signs by the power of the devil!"

"No." Some nodded with utter conviction. "This man is the Christ."

"How can you say that? The Scriptures say that the Christ is to come from David and from Bethlehem. But this man—he comes from Galilee!"

So went the talk all up and down the land. There was a division among the people. Some loved him completely, believed in him, and devoted themselves to him. Some hated him, feared him, and sought howsoever they might to arrest him.

And as Jesus traveled slowly to Jerusalem, the feelings intensified: Love grew the warmer and hate the hotter. . . .

Mary and Martha

"O my Lord! Sit and cool yourself and rest. Rest." A woman of tidy hair and tidy habits threw her arms around Jesus, then drew him into her house. She showed him a place of honor where he could sit, then began at once to bustle about, preparing a lunch, humming for joy that he should have come to her house.

This was Martha, who loved him dearly. So did her sister Mary love him, but in another way.

Mary sat at Jesus' feet, listening, learning.
But busy Martha thought only of her housework.

When Mary saw the Lord, she smiled. She kissed him softly, then gathered her skirts and sank down at his feet. Her eyes said, *Speak to me*—and he did. Soon the two of them were closed in a tight conversation, Jesus teaching, Mary listening as though his words were water and she were drinking them. Out of his heart flowed rivers of living water.

Now this may have been all very well for Mary—but it irritated Martha to distraction! They had stopped noticing her when she came into the room. So she began to set dishes down with a great clatter. A number of times she said, "Oh, bother!" quite distinctly. But nothing raised their faces from the talk.

Finally she decided to abandon good manners altogether, and with her hands on her hips she took up a position right between her sister and the Lord.

Jesus looked up.

"Lord, don't you care that Mary has left me to serve alone?" she complained. "Tell her to get up and help me."

"Martha, Martha, you worry your head over many things," said Jesus, taking one of her hands from her hip. "But there is only one thing needful, and Mary has chosen that one good thing. What she has chosen will never be taken away from her."

"Neither Do I Condemn You"

And in the afternoon Jesus was standing in the village marketplace, speaking to the crowd, when a band of self-righteous men—Pharisees, their eyebrows pinched, their lips drawn small, their chins raised up on high—marched down the street and through the crowd.

They ushered a woman into his presence and commanded her, "Stand there!" She did, with her face in her hands.

"Master!" they announced. "This woman was caught in the act of adultery. In the very act, mind you! Now, we are well aware of the law, that Moses commands us to stone such a sinner. But we thought that we would ask you. What do *you* say we should do to her?"

Men brought a sinful woman to Jesus, wishing him to condemn her. But Jesus stooped and wrote: Let he who is without sin cast the first stone.

For all their solemnity, this was no serious question—except that they meant to trap him in his words. Would he say, *Stone her to death?* Why, then he was a murderer, and love had no place in his heart. Would he say, *Let her live?* Ah, then he was a lawbreaker. Condemn him!

Jesus, however, said nothing.

He glanced at the poor, hunched woman, then stooped and with his finger began to draw in the dust.

Time passed. The silence grew unbearable. The accusers felt silly. "Well? Well? Well?" they demanded.

Finally Jesus raised his face and said, "Let the man among you who is without sin cast the first stone." Then he returned to writing on the ground. They had only his back to look at.

The old, the white-haired men, shook their heads and left. They had little stomach for such casting of stones and condemnations. The middle-aged, conscious of too many sins upon their own heads, next turned away. And then the young firebrands, being left alone, abruptly snapped their fingers and stalked away.

Jesus stood up and looked around. No one was there but the woman, her face still buried in her hands.

"Woman, where are your accusers?" he asked. When she did not answer, he quietly took her wrists and lowered her hands that her face might come out of hiding and into the light. Then he could see her, and she could see him.

"Did no one condemn you?" he asked.

"No one, Lord," she said.

And he said, "Neither do I condemn you. Go, now, and see that you sin no more."

And what light was it that shined on her face and that shined in her face thereafter? Why, it was Jesus himself. For he said before all of the people, "I AM the light of the world! He who follows me will not walk in darkness, but will have the light of life!"

The Light Shines in the Darkness

"Let it be known and commonly understood," went the decree of the leaders of the synagogue, "that anyone who confesses this Jesus of Nazareth to be the Christ shall certainly be put outside the synagogue, losing the right to worship there, losing a place among us!"

From a life of darkness, the blind beggar emerged into the light. His joy overflowed. And this was another of Jesus' miracles.

That was a dire decree, for its punishment was painful, and thus Jesus became a danger to his friends. But friends still turned to him, and people still came to believe in him.

On a certain Sabbath day—and despite the Sabbath laws—Jesus healed a man who had been blind from birth.

He spat on the ground, made a mud of spittle and dust, and said, "As long as I am in the world, I AM the light of the world." Then with the mud, he anointed the eyes that had seen only darkness, and he said, "Go. Wash in the pool of Siloam."

The man obeyed, and as soon as the rinsing was done, he could see. Now he did not tap his way nor did he lean on anyone. He ran back to his neighborhood, laughing all the way, and the people were astonished.

"That is not the blind beggar!" they said, pointing as though he were still blind.

"But it looks like him," they said.

And he, bursting with joy, cried, "Yes! I am the blind beggar—seeing!"

"But how?" they asked.

"A man named Jesus put clay on my eyes and told me to wash in Siloam. I did, and I see!"

This was too weighty a matter for the poor neighbors to handle, so they took the beggar to the leaders in the synagogue.

"What," said the leaders, "on the Sabbath? Well, then this man is not of God because he scorns the Sabbath laws. Beggar, what say you to that?"

"I say," said the beggar, merely happy for the change in him, "that he is a prophet."

"Prophet!" The leaders drew back as though their noses had been pinched. "Well, you," they said, "are probably a liar. Probably you never were blind. Call his parents! We will get to the truth of this."

But the parents came in, clinging to each other, terrified that even to speak of Jesus would cause their punishment and they would be put out of the synagogue. "Yes, he is our son," they chattered. "Yes, he was born blind. But that is all we know. Who healed him? We do not know that. Ask him. He can speak for himself." And then they were gone.

With vast, official dignity the leaders of the synagogue turned to the beggar again. "The whole truth and nothing but the truth," they solemnly intoned. "This Jesus is a sinner, isn't he?"

"Sinner? He may be, for all I know," said the beggar cheerfully. "But if you want the truth, this is the truth, that I was blind and now I see."

"How, man? How? What did he do?"

"I told you already," said the beggar. Then suddenly he beamed with bright recognition. "Now I understand," he said. "You want to hear it again because you wish to be his disciples!"

"Beggar!" roared the leaders standing up. "Insolent beggar! *You* are his disciple! We are disciples of Moses, who spoke for God. As for this man, we do not know where he comes from."

Such wrath should have withered the man who had done no more in his life than beg, but it did not. Instead, he scratched his chin and said, "Why, here is a wonder. He opened my eyes, yet you do not know where he comes from. But we know," he spoke precisely like a teacher, "that God listens not to sinners but to those who do his will. If this man were *not* from God, he could do nothing."

"You! You!" the leaders stuttered in their rage. "You were born in utter sin! Fool, how dare you teach *us!"* And they put him out of the synagogue.

When Jesus heard of the beggar's new circumstances, he went looking for him; and when he found him, he said, "Do you believe in the Son of Man?"

The beggar said, "Who is he, that I may believe in him?"

Jesus touched the man's eyes and said, "Blind man, you have seen him, and it is he who speaks to you."

Immediately the beggar, full of joy, confessed, "Lord, I believe!" And there, on the streets, he bowed down and worshiped Jesus.

"Behold the judgment I bring into the world!" cried Jesus. "Those who did not see do see, and those who thought they saw are blind."

Jesus Teaches: Parables

—The Good Samaritan

A scribe, a student of the laws of Moses, pretended one afternoon to be a student of Jesus. "Teacher," he said, "what should I do to receive eternal life?"

"You are a scribe?" asked Jesus.

The scribe said, "Yes."

"And you know the Torah?" he asked.

The scribe said, "Of course!"

"Good," said Jesus. "What is written there about eternal life?"

The scribe quoted, " 'Love the Lord your God with all your heart, and with all your soul, and with all your strength, and with all your mind. And love your neighbor as yourself.' "

"It is a good answer," said Jesus. "Do this and you will certainly live."

"Yes," the man persisted, "but who exactly *is* my neighbor?"

This question Jesus answered in his own way. He said, "Once upon a time a man was traveling from Jerusalem to Jericho, when robbers seized him, beat him, stripped him of his clothing and his goods, and then left him lying on the side of the road, half-dead.

"Now a priest came along that road. But when he saw the poor man and heard his groans, he passed him by on the other side.

"Later came a Levite, a worker in the Temple of the Lord. But when he saw the man and heard his groans, he also passed by on the other side.

"But then there came a Samaritan, one of those whom most people despise. Yet when he saw this man and heard his groans, he had pity on him. He dressed the man's wounds with oil and wine. He lifted the man onto his own donkey. He took him to an inn, where he spent a full night nursing him. And in the morning he gave two days' wages to the innkeeper, saying, 'Take care of this poor

Only a Samaritan, a man of lowly status but kindly purpose, helped the injured traveler.

man; and if you spend more than this, I will pay you the rest when I return.'

"Now," said Jesus to the scribe, "you answer: Which of these three turned out to be neighbor to the man in misery?"

"Well," said the scribe, "the one who had mercy on him."

"You are a good student," Jesus said. "Go and do likewise."

—The Lost Sheep

One evening certain scribes and Pharisees were standing near the house of a tax collector, a man whom the people hated quite openly because he worked for the Romans and because he had purchased this same house with the people's money, money he took for himself from the taxes.

While they watched, a woman of sinful reputation came and knocked on the door and was admitted inside.

They all nodded knowingly, saying "Yes" and "To be sure" and "I'm not surprised" and "The world is in a sorry state."

But even while they were delivering these opinions upon the matter, Jesus came. He, too, knocked on the tax collector's door. And it was opened to him as well. And before their eyes Jesus greeted *both* the tax collector *and* the woman with a kiss, then went inside, and the door was shut.

The street exploded with more opinions from the watchers. "Did you see that?" "I did! I did! That man debases himself!" "Right into the house!" "Not only does he receive sinners, he actually sits and eats with them!" "Why, I would never—"

Suddenly the door opened again, and there stood Jesus, looking directly at them.

He walked over to them, turned, and faced the house—exactly as they were doing—folded his arms, and stood silently for a while. Everyone stood silently.

And then, as though it were simply a question in conversation, he asked, "Does any one of you have sheep?" He was gazing toward the tax collector's house.

One man mumbled, "I do."

"How many sheep?" asked Jesus.

"A hundred," said the man.

"What would you do," asked Jesus, "if just one of your one hundred sheep were lost? You would leave the ninety-nine, would you not? And because you are a good man, you would go after the lost one, searching the hills and the slopes until you found it. And when you had found the sheep, you would lay it on your shoulders and, rejoicing, carry it home again. And then you would call to your friends and neighbors, saying, 'Rejoice with me! I have found the sheep which was lost!'

"Even so," said Jesus, still gazing toward the house, "there will be more joy in heaven over one sinner who repents than over ninety-nine righteous who need not repent."

Now he did look at those around him, and he smiled. "You will not mind," he asked, "if I tell you a story? Good."

—The Prodigal Son and the Self-Righteous Brother

"Once upon a time," said Jesus, "there was a father who had two sons. The younger son said to his father, 'Father, give me my part of the family property.' Then the father divided his goods and gave to the younger all that he wanted.

"Soon the younger son converted the goods into money, left home with a fat purse, and traveled to a far country.

"Now, this part of the story will not surprise you. There he lived like a wastrel, spending his money without a thought or a care until the last penny had vanished. Then a famine struck the land, and the young man poor became a young man hungry. He was forced to find work, but the only job he found was to feed some other man's pigs, and he grew so hungry that he would gladly have eaten the pods which the pigs ate—but no one gave him anything.

"Finally he came to himself, and he said, 'My father's servants have bread enough and to spare, but I am dying here with hunger! I know what I will do. I will go back to my father and confess that I have sinned against heaven and against him. I am not worthy to be your son, I will say. Treat me simply as a servant.'

"So the young man left the pigpen, his head hanging low, his body and his soul together very weak, and walked home.

"Even while he was some distance away, his father saw him and had compassion and ran to meet him, hugged him and kissed him.

"But the son put up his hands, saying, 'Father, no. I have sinned against heaven and before you. I am not worthy—'

" 'Hush, child!' said his father. Then he called to the servants, 'Bring the best robe and put it on my son! Put a ring on his finger and shoes on his feet. And butcher a calf for a feast. For this my son was dead, and he is alive. My son was lost, and he is found!'

"But while they were celebrating in the house, the elder son came home from the fields. He heard the music, but he did not understand it, since no one had told him about a party.

" 'What is going on in there?' he asked a servant. Then, as the servant told him, his face soured and his jaw clenched. 'You tell my father,' he said bitterly, 'that I will have nothing to do with a party for that sinful son of his!'

"When the father came outside to urge his elder son to join them, the son pushed out his lip and said, 'No! All these years I have worked for you, never disobeying you; yet did you ever, even once, give *me* a party? But the moment this spendthrift comes home, the calf is killed and the feasting begins. No. I will not join his party.'

Jesus told of a younger son who took his portion and left his father's house. He lived wantonly. Only when his money was gone did he return to his father. The old man received him joyously.

Zacchaeus perched in a sycamore tree, to see over the crowds, to see Jesus. Jesus spied him and asked the little man of large faith to come down.

" 'My son, you are always with me,' said the father, 'and all that I have is always yours. But your brother was dead! He was lost. Surely it is right to rejoice at his resurrection!' "

By this time the evening had become the night. Jesus had seated himself among those standing outside the tax collector's house.

Now he invited them, too, to sit down with the words, "Surely, you have time for one more story?"

They sat, frowning at the lights now burning in the house, and lent uncertain ears unto the Lord, who smiled and spoke.

—The Pharisee and the Tax Collector

"Two men," said Jesus, "went into the Temple to pray, the one a Pharisee of proud degree and the other a tax collector.

"The Pharisee stood alone and prayed thus: 'God, I thank thee that I am not like other men, fraudulent, unjust, adulterous—or even like that tax collector there. I fast two times a week. I give a tenth of all that I get—'

"But the tax collector, standing far away from the altar, would not so much as lift his eyes unto heaven. He beat his breast and said, 'God, be merciful to me, a sinner.'

"I tell you the truth," said Jesus. "It was the latter who went home justified, and not the former. For everyone who exalts himself will be humbled, but he who humbles himself will be exalted."

This was, of course, the last story which his audience stayed to hear that night.

"I Am the Good Shepherd"

And so it was that Jesus moved slowly toward Jerusalem, teaching, preaching, and healing on the way; and the word went out from every place where he paused, the word of his marvelous deeds.

—How between Samaria and Galilee he healed ten men afflicted with leprosy, one of whom was moved to give him thanks, and that man a Samaritan.

—How he gave sight to blind Bartimaeus outside the city Jericho.

—How he moved Zacchaeus, tax collector of Jericho, to believe in him, first calling him down from a sycamore tree where the little man had climbed in order to see Jesus over the crowds.

The word went out. The people heard that word. And again—the crowds swelled around Jesus wherever he went. This time people were tight with excitement, because it seemed to them that something great was soon to happen, something catastrophic, something they should witness.

Jesus spoke to them about that something, but he did so in the gentlest terms.

"I AM the good shepherd," he said. "The good shepherd lays down his life for the sheep.

"Hirelings care nothing for the sheep, because they do not own the sheep. Therefore, when the wolf comes they flee away, and the wolf is free to snatch the sheep and to scatter them.

"But I AM the good shepherd. I know my own and they know me—just as the Father knows me and I know the Father—and I lay down my life for the sheep. This is why the Father loves me, because by my own choosing I die for the sheep.

"My sheep hear my voice and follow me, and I give them eternal life. They shall never perish! No one shall snatch them out of my hand! My Father, who has given them to me, is greater than all; no one can snatch them from the Father's hand. And I and the Father are one."

So spoke the Lord, and a few began to understand that all his miracles were merely signs to point their hearts to him. These believed in him. But others followed because they looked for a leader to lead them in revolt against the Romans who oppressed them. Others purely hated him and were drawn perversely to the object of their hatred. The crowd was a tense, restless body in those final days.

"I Am the Resurrection and the Life"

His last pause and his last visitation and his last miracle before Jerusalem happened in this way.

Jesus was abiding east of the Jordan when a messenger, haggard from a hard run, found him and told him that Lazarus was sick unto death. Jesus thanked him for the information, sent him on his way, and did nothing. For two more days he did nothing about the illness, and only when he knew in his heart that Lazarus had died did he mention to his disciples that they must now go to Bethany.

This idleness was remarkable, for Lazarus was the brother of Mary and Martha, who had sent the messenger, and all three were loved by the Lord. Why should he wait until the man was *dead* before he went to him? "That glory might shine in the Son of God," he said. But who could understand such words?

"Why go to Bethany now?" the disciples asked. "That is too close to Jerusalem. You know people there are planning to kill you."

"Because our brother Lazarus has fallen asleep, and I go to waken him," said Jesus.

"Asleep? Is that all?" The disciples did not understand these words either. "Let the man sleep! It is good for him."

Then Jesus told them plainly. "Lazarus is dead. We must go for his sake—and for yours as well that you may believe in me."

Lean, quiet, both young and old at once by the look in his eyes, Jesus began immediately to walk westward—like a lion's the strength of his tread, but the sweet humility in his face was like that of a lamb.

Thomas, looking at his back, said to the other disciples. "We should go too. It is right, if we must, that we die with the Lord." And they followed him.

"Lord!" cried Martha, running down the road to meet him. "Lord!" she shouted, careless who heard her. She ran with the loose gait of someone altogether broken by grief, and she was crying. "Four days ago," she wailed. She fell on his shoulders. He held her up, and his heart ached.

Then her words were muffled at his breast. "Why didn't you come before? If you had been here, my brother would not have died, died, four days ago. Even now God will give whatever you ask—"

"Martha," said Jesus, his chin brushing her head, "your brother will rise again."

"I know that," she said, but she continued to cry. "He will rise on the last day. But what good is that on *this* day?"

Now Jesus held her away from him and gazed into her eyes. "Martha, listen to me," he said. "Martha, I AM the Resurrection and the Life! He who believes in me, though he die, yet shall he live. And whoever lives and believes in me shall never die! Do you believe this?"

Martha's tears had ceased. She was returning his gaze with a suddenly quiet wonder. "Yes, Lord," she whispered. "I believe that you are the Christ, the Son of God."

Jesus said, "Please bring Mary to me."

This time Martha's running was easy and peaceful. With a glance at the Lord she disappeared round a corner toward her house.

It was no more than several minutes before a great lamentation arose in the town; then came Mary, and behind her all the people who had been sitting with her, comforting her. They raised their voices in mourning, for they thought that she was going to weep at the tomb.

But as lightly as dew on the rose she wept before the Lord instead, and she said, "If only you had been here—"

Jesus closed his eyes and touched his temple, for Mary's tears had made him very sad. "Where did you lay him?" he asked.

And when she said so gently, "Come and see," he, too, began to cry.

"Look how he loved the man!" the people whispered to one another. "Look."

They all followed a rising path which ended at a cliff. Holes had been carved in the cliff's face, tombs in which the dead were laid; and when such a tomb contained a body, a rock was rolled in front of it to keep out the scavenging animals.

"Lord, that one." Martha pointed at a tomb closed by a rock.

Jesus said, "Remove the rock from its entrance."

"Oh, Lord, the body is four days in the tomb," said Martha. "It will smell."

"I told you," said Jesus, "that if you believe, you will see the glory of God. Remove the rock."

When the tomb yawned dark and open, Jesus raised his eyes to heaven and said aloud, "Father, I thank you that you have heard me!" Then, more quietly, "Always, you do hear me, but I say this for the people that they may believe you sent me."

Next, Jesus leveled his bright look at the tomb and cried in a loud voice, "Lazarus! Come out!"

With not so much as a sigh, the dead man appeared in the entrance, his hands and feet wrapped in bandages, his face covered with a cloth—and he came out.

"Loose him," said Jesus, "and let him go."

Jesus cried out to Lazarus in a commanding voice, and Lazarus emerged from the tomb.

Caiaphas spoke out in the council. If the crowds that followed Jesus were not controlled, the Romans might destroy the Temple and the people.

Counsel Death

Many people believed in Jesus for what he did and cried their acclaim of him; but others rushed straightway with bitter report to the leaders of the people.

So the chief leaders called the council together to discuss this dangerous Jesus.

"He works wonders," they said. "He is rousing the people so that they mass around him."

"And the Romans will not look kindly on such activity. When they see mobs, they see rebellion!"

"So they slaughter the mobs."

"The mobs, to be sure—but not the mobs only. They slaughter the people, and they destroy every sign of strength."

"Including the Temple! Including our whole nation!"

"And where will that leave us?"

"Powerless! We will be less than puppets. We will be nothing."

"So what are we going to do? In God's name, what will we do about this Jesus?"

Then Caiaphas, the high priest, rose and spoke to the council. "Don't you understand?" he said. "It is better that one man should die for the people than that the whole nation should perish."

From that day forward they made serious plans to put Jesus to death.

Gesture Love

While such talk was going on, Jesus himself was sitting at dinner in the house of people who did dearly love him.

Martha's house. She served the meat.

Lazarus's house. He reclined by the Lord and ate.

Mary's house, and lo! it was Mary who did the memorable thing.

Near the end of the dinner she entered the room, carrying a precious, expensive

In Bethany, at supper in the home of Lazarus, Mary anointed Jesus' feet with nard, a costly salve. Though Judas chided her for expensive waste, her act of love would be forever remembered.

ointment, a pound of pure nard. She went to Jesus, poured the spice over his feet, then wiped his feet with her hair.

Judas Iscariot sniffed. The house was filled with the fragrance of the ointment, and Judas sniffed. Then his eyebrows knotted over his nose when he saw what Mary had done, and he grumbled, "What a waste! It would take me three hundred days to earn the money to buy that much nard! What a mindless waste. At the very least she could have sold it and given the money to the poor."

"Let her alone," said Jesus, for he had felt the nard and smelled it; he had felt her hair across his feet. "The poor will always be with you, but I will not. Mary has prepared my body for burial. And I promise you that wherever the gospel is preached in all the world, her gesture shall be told in memory of her."

But Judas sniffed. Of him a far different gesture would be remembered, and it, too, would be told wherever the gospel was preached; but his would be told in contempt.

The Glory! – Death and Resurrection

JESUS IN JERUSALEM—HIS LAST WEEK

TRULY, GOD IS GOOD to Israel, even to such as are of a clean heart. But as for me, my feet were almost gone, my steps had well-nigh slipped, for I was grieved at the ungodly.

Is it nothing to you, all ye that pass by? Behold and see if there be any sorrow like unto my sorrow, which is done unto me, wherewith the Lord hath afflicted me in the day of his fierce anger!

Now all the things of Jesus' life became one thing, and all the roads he traveled, one road. It is in this thing that the loving Father gave his only begotten Son unto the world, believing in whom we shall not perish but have eternal life.

Jesus died. Jesus rose again to life.

And it is this singular deed—done among the people—this hard, holy, and glorious thing which now we watch.

Hard—for he himself cried out in anguish, "Now is my soul troubled! And what shall I say? 'Father, save me from this hour'?"

Holy—for he answered his own question by saying, "No! For this very reason have I come to this hour. Father, glorify your name!"

Glorious—for next a voice came from heaven saying, "I have glorified it, and I will glorify it again!"

Glorious, the suffering and the death of Jesus Christ. Glorious, the Resurrection which followed.

Sunday: Jesus Enters the City

It came to pass that Jesus stood outside the village of Bethphage, gazing at Jerusalem in the distance. It was time, now, that he should enter that city, death being but six days away....

"Go into the village," he said to two disciples. "You will find a donkey which has never been ridden. Untie it and bring it to me. And if anyone questions you, simply say, 'The Lord has need of it.' "

The disciples departed.

The crowd forever at his back—the seekers, the believers, the zealots, and the watchers—they saw the disciples go. They searched the face of Jesus for something signaling what this meant but only saw that he was gazing at Jerusalem.

Then the disciples returned with a donkey, and the crowd began to buzz. "Jerusalem!" they said. "He is going to Jerusalem."

When the disciples threw their garments over the back of the beast, the buzzing swelled to a low roar. Groups of runners broke from the crowd, dashing toward the city, crying, "He is coming! The Christ is coming!"

And when Jesus himself mounted the beast and began to ride, a thousand throats opened up in jubilation and in song. "Hosanna! Hosanna!"

People tossed their garments down in front of Jesus, pleased to have his beast walk on them. People cut branches and spread them in his path. People raised their hands on high in victory, running beside him, running behind him. And in a mighty thunder roll they roared, "Blessed is the King who comes in the name of the Lord! Hosanna in the highest!"

Down from the Mount of Olives he rode and into Jerusalem, where another multitude was surging forth to meet him, among whom the children, too, were crying, "Hosanna to the Son of David!"

The chief priests knifed their way through the crowd, utterly confounded by this display and terrified by what the Romans would make of it. They snatched at Jesus' clothing and shouted, "Silence them! Silence them! They are calling you all of the names of Messiah! Silence them!"

But Jesus answered, "If these were silent, the very stones themselves would cry out loud."

And then—but who could see it for all of the people and who could hear it for all of the noise?—and then, while he rode and looked at the stones of the city, Jesus began to weep.

"If only you knew," he said. "If only you knew *right now* the things that bring peace! Ah, but you are so blind. The days are coming when your enemies will surround you and cut you down with such destruction that not one stone will be left standing on another. If only you knew that now is the time of your visitation!"

Far, far away seemed the voices of those who were hailing him *King*. Distant seemed the refrains of their praises—though they were right next to him. His thoughts had traveled far beyond them, now.

He rode to the Temple and looked with enormous sorrow upon the things that took place there. "If only you knew," he sighed, and he left.

But he would return tomorrow.

Monday: The Cleansing of the Temple

Great billows of smoke went up from the altar of burnt offering in front of the Temple. The fat hissed on the fire, the priests bespoke an excellent sacrifice, and the air was full of the smell of roast meat. This, the ceremonious activity, took place in the Inner Court of the Temple grounds.

The Outer Court, the Court of the Gentiles, looked like a marketplace. Here the meat was alive, still mooing, cooing, bellowing, bleating, caged and tethered and roped. Here the animals of sacrifice were for sale. Here money was changed from Roman coin to Temple currency. Here tables were set up and business was transacted. And much of this was necessary for the proper keeping of the ritual—but profit was not.

To the Court of the Gentiles, like a devouring fire that will not be turned aside, came Jesus on the following day.

He stood in the open and cried "My Father's house! My Father's house!" with such conviction and with such sharp accusation that the buyers, the sellers, and the moneychangers fell silent and stared at the lean individual.

"It is written," said Jesus, pacing among them, " 'My house shall be called a house of prayer for all nations.' But you!" he cried, and suddenly he threw over a table that had been holding money. The coins spun a thousand ways. "You!" he shouted, breaking cages, setting free the birds, tossing tables, driving back the people. "You have made it a den of thieves!"

He made a whip of cords and scourged the merchants, with their sheep and oxen, out of the court.

The chief priests stood by, trembling in their wrath. They did nothing then, for they feared the people who still followed Jesus and listened to him. But in their minds they sought mightily some way to silence him.

Entering the Temple, Jesus came upon merchants and moneychangers. His anger overflowed and he drove them from the Outer Court.

Tuesday: Jesus Teaches: The Coming of the Kingdom

On the following day Jesus was back in the Temple, teaching; and though many of his followers sat listening with rapt expressions, it was to the chief priests that he spoke, and there was an iron edge to his voice.

"You will not mind if I tell you a story?" he asked.

Watch out for his stories! they thought, but they did not answer either way, since they were outnumbered by the multitudes.

"Good," he said. "Listen carefully. Once upon a time there was a landowner who planted a vineyard, hedged it, dug a winepress, erected a tower—in short, did everything necessary for its good production. Then he let it out to renters and left for a far country.

"When the grapes began to ripen, he sent servants to the renters to receive his rightful portion of the produce. But the renters seized his servants—beat one, killed another, and stoned the third.

"Again, the landowner sent other servants, more than the first time. Again, the renters hurt and abused them.

"But the landowner was a man long suffering, willing to give the renters every opportunity to obey the right and to acknowledge his authority. So he decided to send his own son to them. *Surely*, he thought, *they will respect my son.*

"But they did not.

"When they saw him coming, the renters muttered, 'Here comes the son and heir. Listen! Let us kill him. If we do away with him, then we will get the whole inheritance!'

"So they seized him and dragged him out of the vineyard and killed him."

Jesus paused as though this were the end of his story, but it was not. He laid his hand on the shoulder of a priest and said, "Finish the story for me. What did the landowner do when he came himself to the renters?"

"Well, I suppose he put the wretches to death," said the priest, "then rented his vineyard to those who would pay him his due. That seems likely."

"Most likely," said Jesus, not removing his hand, but squeezing with invisible, frightening power. "Most accurate. Most true! For just as you have rejected the one whom God has sent to you, so God will take from you his kingdom and give it to a nation who will produce the fruits of it."

I knew it! I knew it! thought the chief priest. *His stories are scorpions! They sting with their tails.* But he said nothing aloud.

He sat with a blank look on his face when Jesus released his shoulder, leaving an ache behind. With a blank look he endured another story, this one about a marriage feast for a king's son, to which none of the invited came, since each was busy about his worldly affairs; so the hall was filled with the outcasts of society.

With a determined, fierce, and willfully blank look he watched Jesus rise to leave the Temple precincts, and he heard his parting words. "O Jerusalem, Jerusalem, killing the prophets and stoning those who are sent to you! How often would I have gathered your children together as a hen gathers her chicks under her wings—and you would not! Behold, your house is forsaken. You will not see me again until the day you say, 'Blessed is he who comes in the name of the Lord.' "

Thus spoke Jesus. Then he left with his disciples—and suddenly that blank look of the chief priest shattered like a mask.

He ran to his friends, almost weeping in anger and hissing, "Something! Something! We must do something with Jesus!"

Some there were who were enraged by Jesus' actions. They were fearful of the crowds that followed him and they vowed to silence him.

"But not among the multitudes!" they said. "And the crowds are growing because of the Passover feast this week."

"Then do it in quiet. Do it in some private place. But *do it!*"

"We will," they said, and their plan began to take its shape. They would discover some quiet, private place to which Jesus often went alone, and there arrest him.

So they whispered the word through the streets: "Does anyone know the habits of Jesus? Does anyone know where he goes in private? Does anyone know his moments alone? Does anyone know him that well? Anyone? Anyone? Anyone?"

—Signs of the End of the World

When Jesus left the Temple, it was toward the Mount of Olives that he led his disciples. And as they walked, the disciples were discussing the Temple building itself—what an excellent piece of work it was, how noble the stones of it, and how admirable their joining together!

But Jesus shook his head in warning. "The days are coming," he said, "when it will be destroyed so completely that not one stone will be left standing on another."

This thought itched in the minds of the disciples, so that when they had seated themselves on the Mount of Olives, they asked, "When, Lord? When will this happen? And what will be the signs of the end?"

Slowly, carefully, Jesus answered. "Be watchful that no one leads you astray," he said, "for many are coming in my name who will say, 'I am the Christ,' and foolish people will believe them. You will hear of wars and rumors of wars; even then do not be alarmed; the end is not yet. Nation will rise up against nation, and there will be famines and earthquakes—but all this is just the beginning of the birth pains.

"Then people will persecute you and put you to death. You will be despised by all the nations for the sake of my name, so that many will fall away from me, betraying and hating one another. In the spreading wickedness, love will grow cold. But he who endures to the end shall be saved!

"The good news of the kingdom of God will be preached throughout the whole world first—and then the end will come.

"The end. The sun will be darkened, the moon wink out, the stars fall down from the sky, and the powers of the heavens will be shaken. Then all the tribes on earth will see the Son of Man coming on the clouds of heaven with power and blazing glory. He will send out his angels by the blast of a trumpet, and they will gather his elect from the four winds, from one end of heaven to the other. And then, and then it is the end.

Jesus told of the wise and foolish maidens. Only the prepared entered the wedding feast.

"But listen to me," Jesus said with an intensity that none of them forgot. "No one can tell you when this will happen. Of that day and that hour, no one knows, not the angels in heaven, not even the Son. The Father alone—he knows. Therefore, watch! Be ready! Always and always be ready—"

He paused in the midst of this warning, his dark eyes dancing with the force of it, and he thought for a moment. Then he told them this story.

—The Wise and Foolish Maidens

"Not in the time which was, but rather in the time which is to come," he said, "the dawning of the kingdom of heaven will be like ten maidens who took oil lamps and went to meet the bridegroom. But five were wise and five were foolish, for five brought with them extra flasks of oil, and five did not.

"Now the bridegroom was long in coming. He did not come at the expected hour. Night fell upon the maidens, and they nodded and slept.

"Suddenly, at midnight, the cry went up through the streets, 'The bridegroom! The bridegroom! Come out and meet him!'

"The maidens awoke and trimmed their lamps—but the lamps of the foolish flickered and went out. 'Please,' they pleaded with the others, 'give us some of your oil.' And the wise maidens said, 'In fact, there is not enough for all of us together. Go and buy your own.'

"While the foolish were buying their oil, the bridegroom came, and those who were ready went into the feast with him. The halls were bright with cheer, but the doors were shut, and dark was the night outside.

" 'Lord! Lord! Let us in!' cried the foolish maidens when they had returned.

"But the bridegroom said, 'I do not know you.'

"Watch!" said Jesus to his disciples. "Be ready. Always and always be ready. For you know neither the day nor the hour."

—The Last Judgment

"When that hour comes, when the Son of Man descends in all his glory," said Jesus, "then he will sit on his glorious throne, and the angels will blaze all around him. Before him shall be gathered the nations of the world, whom he shall separate as a shepherd separates the sheep from the goats, the sheep on the right hand, the goats to the left of him.

"Then the King will say to those upon his right hand, 'Come, O blessed of my Father! Come, inherit the kingdom prepared for you from the foundation of the world. For I was hungry and you gave me food; I was thirsty and you gave me drink; I was a stranger and you welcomed me, naked and you clothed me, sick and you came, in prison and you visited me.'

"The righteous will say to him, 'Lord, when did we see you hungry and feed you, or thirsty and give you drink? When did we welcome you as a stranger, or clothe you, or visit you?'

"And the King will answer them, 'Truly, when you did it to one of the least of the people on earth, you did it to me.'

"Next he will say to those on his left, 'Away from me, you cursed! Away to the fires eternal, burning for Satan and all of his servants! For I was hungry, but you gave me no food, thirsty, but you gave me no drink. I was a stranger who found no welcome from you, naked and given no clothing by you, sick and no visit, imprisoned, no visit from you!'

" 'When, Lord?' the wicked will say, shocked at the sentence and gravely ignorant of their crime. 'When did we see you in need and do none of these things for you?'

Judas went to the chief priests and offered to deliver Jesus into their hands. For this, they paid him thirty pieces of silver.

" 'Truly, when you denied kindness to the least of these,' the King will announce, 'you denied kindness to me.'

"Then the wicked will be brought unto eternal punishment—but to life everlasting the righteous."

When Jesus had finished all of his teaching, he rose and returned to Bethany, to Mary and Martha and Lazarus. He had need of a rest. Friday was not far away.

Wednesday: Judas Plots Betrayal

Because Judas Iscariot carried the money for the disciples, it was not unusual for him to go off alone in order to purchase bread or some other necessity.

Therefore, when he left them on the following morning, frowning so thoughtfully that his black eyebrows did cover his eyes, no one said, "Where are you going?" Everyone supposed that he knew where Judas Iscariot was going.

Does anyone know the habits of Jesus? Does anyone know him that well?

Judas had heard those words yesterday, and he had thought, *Who knows Jesus better than I?* He was going to the Temple, to the chief priests, to bargain and not to buy bread.

Judas was shrewd in business, cunning at the trading table, convinced that he accomplished his own will in every exchange—or why else did he hold the one purse for the

Twelve? Now his eyebrows beetled, and he began to bargain.

"How much will you give me," he said to the chief priests, "to deliver unto you Jesus of Nazareth?"

The chief priests, hearing his Galilean accent, were interested.

"Do you know Jesus?" they asked.

"Very well," he said.

"Do you know his habits?"

"As well as any man."

"Do you know some private place to which he retires, some place where the crowds do not follow him?"

"Yes," said Judas. His eyebrows lifted a bit. He knew such a place.

"Understand that we cannot arrest him openly," said the chief priests, "or the people may riot and the whole purpose of this important labor may be lost. Time and place are critical; make them late and lonely if you can."

Judas, shrewd bargainer, giving so little to get so much, said, "I can do that."

"Then you are a friend to us, Judas Iscariot," said the chief priests. "And this is what we give to you." They weighed thirty pieces of silver into his hand, which hand dropped them not into the common purse but into his own, and Judas left, content. A little knowledge for a lot of money! It had been a successful conversation.

Thursday: Preparation for the Passover

Peter would cheer his Lord if he could; but he sincerely did not understand the sorrow that thickened in Jesus' throat or the sigh expelled by his every motion. He could only be quick to obey and hope that his own active love would gladden the Lord.

He did not know, on Thursday morning, that Jesus had slept his final sleep.

"Peter," said Jesus.

Straightway the strong disciple was at his side, bursting with obedience. "Yes, Lord? Here I am."

"Go with John into the city," said Jesus, "and prepare the Passover feast for us. We will eat it together tonight."

"Certainly, Lord. John, come here! Lord, where shall we prepare it?" said Peter.

"When you have entered the city, you will meet a man carrying a pitcher of water," said Jesus. "Peter, control yourself then, and do not speak to him. Just follow him until he goes into a house. Then to the householder, say, 'The Teacher says that his time is at hand. He asks to use your guest room, where he will eat the Passover feast with his disciples.' The householder will show you a large upper room already furnished. In that place prepare the Passover feast."

"Please don't worry, Lord," Peter almost pleaded with Jesus. "There is nothing to worry about. We will do as you say, and you will be happy."

Then he and John did everything exactly as Jesus had said it.

Jesus Washes the Feet of the Twelve

There was a strange moment at the beginning of the feast when everyone was at table, yet no one spoke and no one ate. In profound silence, with love and almost groaning for his own pain, Jesus gazed one by one at each of the disciples.

He knew that the time was here for him to depart for the Father. He knew, too, from whom the betrayal would come.

Judas rolled a wine cup between his hands, frowning.

Simon Peter looked directly back at Jesus and smiled. Jesus did not.

John, reclining next to Jesus, let his head rest on the Master's breast.

James and Philip and Thomas, Matthew, Bartholomew, Andrew, and James of Alphaeus, the other Simon, and the other Judas all reclined around the table in various attitudes of expectation or uncertainty: *What is coming? What is he thinking?* Their legs and feet extended from the table; they leaned on their elbows.

Suddenly Jesus arose, laid his robe aside, and wrapped a towel round his waist. He poured water into a pitcher, then bent down and washed the feet of the nearest disciple, John, who turned and watched the ministration, almost weeping that his Lord's hands should be so cool upon his feet.

Jesus dried John's feet with the towel, then went to the next disciple and did the same—and so on, until he came to Peter.

Peter drew back his feet and sat on them. "Are *you* going to wash *my* feet?" he said.

Jesus, kneeling face to face with him, said, "You do not now understand what I am doing, but you will understand in the future."

"No!" said Peter, shaking his head. "No, Lord. You will never wash my feet!"

Jesus began to stand up, saying, "Peter, if I do not wash you, you have no part in me."

Immediately Peter changed his mind. He stuck out not only his feet but his hands, arms, shoulders, head. "O Lord! My feet and my hands and my head—"

"Ah, Simon my rock," said Jesus, laying slender hands on Peter's hard feet, "the one who has bathed has no need to wash; he is clean all over. And you, my disciples, you are all clean—but one."

Judas rolled his wine cup between his palms, staring at the red inside of it.

When Jesus had robed and reclined again, he said, "Do you understand what I have done for you? You call me Lord. It is well. You call me Master, and so you should, for so I am. But if I, your Lord and your Master, do wash your feet, then certainly you should do the same for one another. Learn of me, remember my example," said the Lord, "and serve."

Judas, Judas, You Will Do This Thing

The roasted lamb went round the table, the disciples cutting portions for themselves, the disciples eating; but the Lord ate none of it. An immeasurable sorrow rose in his eyes. Unleavened bread was also handed each to each, the disciples breaking pieces for themselves, the disciples dipping it in sauce and eating; but the Lord ate none of it. An inexpressible grief pulled at the corners of his lips. He breathed deeply and sighed.

"Truly," he said softly, "truly I say to you—one of you will betray me."

At once the eating stopped.

The disciples stared at one another. Someone dropped a knife. The clatter broke their shock, and they began to chatter nervously, grievously. "Lord, is it I? Is it I?"

Without moving, without raising his voice, as though he had not heard their question, Jesus said, "The Son of Man shall now go step for step as it was written he would go. But woe to him by whom he is betrayed! It were better for that man if he had never been born!"

Peter signaled to John that he should ask Jesus who this was. John leaned his head onto Jesus' breast and whispered, "Who, Lord? Who is the man?"

Jesus said, "I am going to dip a morsel of food in the dish. The man to whom I hand the morsel—he is the one."

The morsel just touched a vinegar sauce before it was laid on the plate of Judas Iscariot.

Judas did not so much as raise his face. His eyebrows trembled like the wings of a stunned insect. "Me? Teacher?" he muttered, staring at the morsel and twisting his lips into the shape of a grin. "You mean me?"

"What you have to do, do quickly," Jesus said. Then Judas arose and silently passed into the night.

And Peter, You Will Deny Me

"It is now about to happen," Jesus said into the silence of the disciples, "and the Son of Man is nearly glorified. Little children, I am leaving you—"

Peter stiffened to hear these words. But he struggled not to talk. He should not talk!

"—and though you will seek me, where I am going, you cannot come."

You cannot come! The words struck Peter like a rod, but he ground his teeth and fought the impulse to talk. He talked too much. He should not talk!

"So I am giving you a new commandment," said Jesus, "both for yourselves and for a witness to all the world, that the world may know me through you. Love one another. Even as I love you, love one another. By this will all men know that you are my disciples, if you love one another—"

Peter exploded. "Why, Lord? Why can't I follow you, Lord?" His tone was almost brutal; it came from an aggressive love.

Jesus regarded the strong man with gentle understanding and said, "You will, Peter. You will certainly follow the path that I am going to take—but hereafter and not now."

"Why not?" Peter demanded. "Why can't I follow you right now?"

"Ah, Peter—the things you do not understand," said Jesus. "Because, my rock-disciple, you are not able." Peter was visibly stung by that. Jesus continued, "This very night each one of you will stumble, fall, and scatter from me like sheep when their shepherd is attacked—"

"Not me!" Peter struck his chest. "They might. Andrew might. James and John might fall away from you—but not me! Lord, I will follow you even to prison, even to death!"

"Peter!" Jesus spoke sharply, and he closed his eyes—a gesture that always disabled the rash disciple. It stole his Lord from him and into mystery. It judged him. And it forced him to wait upon the next words. "Peter." Jesus spoke with his eyes still closed. "Before the cock crows an end to this night, you will deny me three times!"

Peter was reduced to mumbling. "No, I will not," he mumbled. "They can threaten me with death and still I will not deny you."

My Body, My Blood

This meal had become like no other meal the disciples had ever eaten. The next thing that Jesus did fixed it in their minds forever.

He took the unleavened bread and spoke a blessing over it. Then he broke it and gave it to his disciples with the words: "Take it. Eat it. This is my body."

Slowly they chewed the bread and swallowed it, watching Jesus. His body!

Next he took the cup of wine, gave thanks to God, and gave the cup to them with the words: "Drink this, all of you. It is my blood of the covenant, my blood shed for many people for the forgiveness of sins."

They handed the cup around, and drank. His blood!

"I tell you the truth," said Jesus. "I will not again drink wine until the day when I drink it in my Father's kingdom, when it will be new wine, my friends, shared with you."

Good-Bye, My Friends

Miserably bewildered, the disciples stared at their plates, neither eating nor speaking.

Jesus took John's head upon his breast and kissed the young man's forehead. "Ah, children, do not be so troubled," he said.

As was the custom, Jesus and his disciples partook of the Passover feast. Jesus spoke to them words of love and comfort and wisdom. Then he took bread, blessed it, broke it, and gave it to them, saying, "This is my body."

After the Passover feast, Jesus and his disciples went out of the city, beyond its walls, to a garden called Gethsemane.

"You believe in God. Believe also in me. In my Father's house are many, many rooms. I am going to prepare a place for you, and then I will return to take you to myself, that where I am you may also be. And you know the way where I am going."

Thomas fairly shouted, "No, Lord! We do not know where you are going! How can we know the way?"

"The way," said Jesus, gazing deep into Thomas's eyes. "Thomas, look at me. I AM the way and the truth and the life. No one comes to the Father but through me. If you knew me, you would see the Father. But from now on you do know him; you have seen him.

"Children, children!" Jesus called them with a yearning, heartbreaking love, and silently John began to cry. "I am not going to leave you here like orphans," Jesus said. "When I am gone, I will send you another from the Father. I will send the Counselor, the Holy Spirit, the Spirit of Truth. He will be my witness, teaching you everything and reminding you of all that I have said to you. Peace I leave with you. My peace I give unto you. Not as the world gives do I give unto you. Do not be troubled." He touched the tears from John's cheek. "Never be afraid."

Then he stood up and walked to the door and opened it. It was black night outside.

"I will not say much to you any more," he said, "because the ruler of this world is coming now. Understand that he has no power over me to take my life. I myself do lay it down. I lay it down because I love you, my friends, and because I obey the will of the Father.

"Come, now. Come with me. We will find a private place for ourselves."

A Quiet, Private Place Apart

So Jesus, lean in the night wind, and eleven disciples walked the streets of Jerusalem.

He prayed aloud to the Father as they went, beseeching God to keep all who believed in him—to keep them holy, to keep them joyful, to keep them in the truth, to keep them one.

In this wise did they cross the Kidron Valley, and they came to the Mount of Olives, wherein there was a little place called Gethsemane, quiet, private, and apart.

"Who has believed what we have heard? Who has seen the arm of the Lord at work? For he grew up like a root out of dry ground—not comely that we should look at him; not beautiful that we should desire him.

"He was despised. He was rejected by men, a man of sorrows and acquainted with grief.

"But he bore our griefs and carried our sorrows. He was wounded for our sins, bruised for our transgressions. Upon him was the punishment that made us whole. And by his stripes—we are healed!"

Thus had Isaiah prophesied. And thus was it coming to pass.

Gethsemane

In darkness Jesus threaded his way through the trees of the Mount of Olives. In darkness his shoulders were invisible, and none saw how they sagged. But even in darkness his voice carried the low note of agony, and the disciples gasped to hear it.

"Peter, James, John, come with me," said Jesus. "The rest of you, please wait here."

As they entered the Garden of Gethsemane, Jesus murmured, "My soul is heavy with sorrow, even unto death."

These words burned in Simon Peter. But he had nothing whatever to say.

"Wait here," said Jesus. "Watch with me." Then he himself went on, cloaked in darkness. He might have stumbled on the bunched roots of an olive tree and, lacking the strength or the will to catch himself, fallen. Or his legs might have for very grief failed him. "O my Father!" Jesus wailed, collapsing to the ground, a horrified cry in the night. "Father, Father," he repeated with his cheek against the earth, "Father,"

There, Jesus asked the disciples to wait and watch with him. Going beyond, he fell to the earth and prayed. And his sorrow was an agony.

But the disciples slept. They could not watch even one hour with Jesus.

he prayed, "if it is possible, remove this cup from me." Sweat broke on his forehead and ran down in heavy drops, and the soil received it as though it were blood.

Long, long the Lord lay curled upon the earth and praying. And this is what he prayed, and this is how he ended it: He said, "Yet not my will—thine be done."

Softly he returned to the three disciples.

"Peter? John? James?"

There was no answer.

He put his hands to their faces and found them sleeping. "Ah, could you not watch with me but one bare hour?" he whispered.

The night was utterly black. A light wind wept in the trees and touched all things with a deadly chill. The disciples were leaning together for warmth, sleeping. And Jesus stood alone.

He shook Peter's shoulder. "Watch. Watch," he whispered, waking him. "Pray that you enter not into temptation, my rock-disciple. Your spirit indeed is willing, but your flesh is weak."

Peter, greatly ashamed, groaned and struggled to stand up.

Jesus shook John, saying, "It is time, now. The Son of Man is betrayed into the hands of sinners." Likewise, he woke James. "Arise. The betrayer is at hand."

The three disciples were confused and guilty and foggy from their sleeping. They did not know what to say—

Chink, chink! Chink, chink!

A distant sound, like an alarm, brought them suddenly, coldly awake.

Chink, chink! CHINK, CHINK!

Metal on metal! They stared toward Jerusalem and perceived a line of torches winking through the trees. Soldiers!

Peter's hand stole toward a short sword. If he could not speak an apology, he could act one. But something made him wait before he drew the weapon. The dim figure at the head of the procession—he looked familiar.

A torch flared orange, and Peter recognized the dour set of eyebrows.

"Judas!" he whispered. He tried to see Jesus in order to understand what was happening here; but the face of the Lord was lost in darkness.

Now torches were passed before each one of the disciples, and when all had been seen, Judas, smiling in the torchlight, stepped toward Jesus.

"Hail, Master," he said, and he kissed him.

"Ah, Judas," Jesus whispered, "do you betray the Son of Man with a kiss?"

Betray?

In the darkness, Judas came to Gethsemane. He kissed Jesus, and by this sign he betrayed him.

Suddenly things began to happen. The soldiers stepped forward to take hold of Jesus. But Peter was laying about him with his short sword and roaring in a great rage. The soldiers fell back, beginning to draw their own weapons. They were not afraid of the fisherman—just cautious. But one fool, a servant of the high priest, thought to engage the man himself and had his ear sliced off for the trouble.

It was Jesus who muffled Peter. He threw his arm around the disciple's neck with the sharp command, "Put that sword away!" Astonishing strength in a slender arm! The sword flew out of Peter's hand, and he was quiet.

"Those who take the sword," said Jesus, easily healing the servant's ear, "will certainly perish by the sword." Now he turned to the soldiers with the words, "The Scriptures are being fulfilled."

They did not understand that. They understood only their orders and that all obstacles had been removed for their arresting him. So they bound his hands and began to lead him away.

"This is your hour," said Jesus, "and the power of darkness."

And the disciples, like frightened sheep, fled.

The Trial Before Caiaphas

"Testimony!" said the high priest from his place of honor, rapping a table and glaring about the room. "Testimony!" He was hunched. His robes had been cast on in a hurry, for it was the small hours of the morning—no regular time for court to be held—and so they were furiously wrinkled. "Testimony!"

The walls were thick with chief priests and others with reason to see Jesus condemned—while Jesus himself stood solitary in the center of the room, the folds of his robe falling in purely straight lines from his shoulders to the floor.

"Testimony!" This hasty trial was taking place in the house of the high priest. His own people filled the courtyard outside the door; no friends for Jesus waited there—save Simon Peter, who had slipped into the yard and was warming himself by a fire.

"Testimony!" demanded Caiaphas, the high priest. "Bring me witnesses against this man, and tell me the crime that shall put him to death! Testimony!"

Timidly or else too loudly, one witness after another brought accusations against Jesus, who gazed silently into their eyes. But their stories were lies born of hatred, fear, and bribery and soon broke down because they could not agree.

"Testimony!" Caiaphas struck his table and leaned forward. "This is no good, you know, unless two witnesses agree. Bring me two who agree!"

Only Jesus did not flinch at the high priest's rebuke.

A man peeled himself from the wall and stepped forward. "I heard—"

"Speak up!" Caiaphas commanded.

The man shouted in a ridiculously high voice, "I heard Jesus say he would destroy the Temple, the Temple of God, and build it up again in three days."

"I agree!" another man cried immediately. "I agree! Those were his words, his very words!" Neither man looked at Jesus, for it was a false witness.

Caiaphas showed his satisfaction by a pinkness around his ears. "Well, Jesus of Nazareth?" he said. "You have heard the testimony, accusations of a very damning sort. How do you answer them?"

The chief priests wet their lips, for they would counter by studied arguments whatever Jesus said. The others folded their arms, for they would hate whatever Jesus said. The servants set their teeth, for they would hiss whatever Jesus said—

But Jesus said nothing.

"Answer the charges!" Caiaphas demanded.

But Jesus stood, a slender column, and held his peace.

"I adjure you by the living God!" The high priest planted his knuckles on the table and lowered his head, so that his high elbows looked like the legs of a spider. "Answer! Tell us whether you are the Christ, the Son of God!"

Now Jesus spoke. He said, "I am." Not a priest said a word to such an astounding claim, and hissing froze on the servants' lips. "And I tell you," Jesus continued, "that you shall see the Son of Man sitting at the right hand of power and coming on the clouds of heaven."

"Blasphemy!" The high priest rose up like a mountain erupting and began to rip his robes. "Blasphemy!" He swept his arms around the room. "You have all heard his blasphemy. There is no need for another witness. Then what," he cried of the council, "is your verdict?"

"Death!" People began to close in on Jesus. "We find him guilty, deserving death!"

Jesus was taken before the high priest. There, Jesus declared that he was the Messiah, the Son of God. And it was agreed: Jesus must die.

"Death!" The high priest hit the table with finality. "So be it."

Suddenly the people were like dogs who had snapped their leashes. Jesus bowed his head before their snarling rush. Some of the people spat on him. And some of the people beat him. And some, with their lips slung low in a leer, tied a blindfold round his eyes, then slapped him, crying, "Prophesy, you Christ! You Christ! Who hit you?"

He was pushed from one to another until he was caught by the officers, and the officers led him to the door.

Peter's Denial

In the meantime Peter had been staring at the fire in the courtyard, lost in morbid thinking. He had not noticed that one of the women present continued to study his face.

Finally she touched his shoulder, and he jumped.

"Forgive me," she said, "but weren't you with Jesus the Galilean, the man inside?"

Peter looked nervously around to see whether anyone else had heard her words. "No," he said. "Someone else. I have no idea what you are talking about. No." He hunched over the fire as though that were the only thing in his life right now, and the sweat on his forehead glistened orange. But the night was chilly.

"I know I'm right," mumbled the woman as she left the courtyard.

In a little while Peter saw her return with three men. He did not look up. Yet he was keenly aware that she was pointing at him, and suddenly the courtyard seemed crowded with enemies.

He leaped up, shouting, "Woman! I am not with that man!"

Heads everywhere turned to look at him. An ashy dawn light dusted every face. People were pale and all too visible.

"Your accent, sir, is Galilean," said one man. "You must be his disciple." And another: "I saw you in Gethsemane! You cut my cousin's ear, and you were with Jesus!"

Peter denied knowing Jesus—three times he denied him. And then the cock crowed. Peter wept.

Peter, his eyes rolling like a beast's at bay, began to curse and to swear, "I was not! I am not! I swear it by God: I do not know the man!"

In that same instant, the cock crowed. The door swung open, and the officers brought Jesus through the courtyard. He stumbled. His face was swelling. He seemed frightfully thin—and he looked at Peter.

Peter heard the cock's crow, and Peter received his Lord's long look like a silent dagger in his heart. *Deny me three times.* He ran from the courtyard into an alley and leaned his head against a wall and wept bitterly.

Friday: The End of Judas Iscariot

With the dirty light of the dawn, the word went out into the streets: "Jesus will be condemned to death! Jesus will die, will die."

"No!" The voice of desolation, the voice of Judas Iscariot. "No! No!" he wailed at the news. "That was not in the bargain! No! No! No!"

Holding his stomach against a murderous pain, Judas hastened to the Temple, to the same room in which, two days ago, he had struck his bargain with the chief priests.

He burst into that room, and the chief priests turned to him with annoyance.

"I have sinned!" he wailed, the shock of it still swelling under his eyebrows. "This has gone too far! You said nothing of an execution!"

"You played your part, we played ours," said the chief priests, "and now the thing is out of our hands. The man is on his way to Pilate—"

"Oh, God!" groaned Judas.

"—whose Roman will, you know, we must obey. But a criminal life deserves a criminal death."

Judas wailed, "I have betrayed innocent blood!"

With contempt the chief priests turned their backs to him. "Go away," they said.

Judas began to claw in his purse, his hand scooping inside the leather. Weeping, he flung all thirty pieces of the silver onto the Temple floor, and he left.

It irritated the chief priests that they themselves had to bend down to pick up the money—blood money, they called it—and that they could not return it to the Temple treasury, because it *was* blood money.

Among their other, more important decisions that morning, they decided to purchase a potter's field with it, in which to bury the bodies of strangers. To this day that field is called the Field of Blood.

As for Judas, no word went out into the streets to say that he had died. No word was whispered that he had gone and hanged himself. But he had.

The Trial Before Pontius Pilate

Pilate considered the band of religious leaders who gathered before his palace—so sinfully early in the morning!—to be important enough to merit his attention; but he also thought that their problem would be a minor one, briefly resolved. Therefore he stepped out to meet them at a brisk pace.

"Well, let's see to it," he said, rubbing his arms against the morning chill. "What is your charge against this man?"

"Sir, he is an evildoer," announced one of the chief priests.

"Oh, well! An evildoer," said Pilate. "There are thousands of those. You take this one and judge him according to your own laws." He bowed and turned to go in.

"Wait!" The chief priests moved forward with stern dignity. "Sir, you know as well as we do that we cannot put a man to death."

"Death?" Pilate paused. "This is a matter of death?"

"We think so," said the chief priests.

Now Pontius Pilate considered the prisoner, a lean man with arresting eyes, and he was startled to see that the prisoner was at the same time considering *him*. No fear, no guilt nor bitterness in that face, but sorrow and, could Pilate admit it, an authority so dominating that it seemed to ask obedience of him—of Pilate!

"Who is this man?" said Pilate.

"Jesus of Nazareth," said the chief priests, and they took advantage of the moment to murmur again the incriminating information into Pilate's ears.

"Curious," Pilate said. "Curious." The chief priests thought he was reacting to their report, but he was not. He meant his own feelings concerning this Jesus, who must be either innocent or a fool to stand in chains and to act so lordly both at once. He felt drawn to this mystery, yet strangely threatened by it. Do you save such a man alive, or kill him?

Abruptly, Pilate commanded, "Send him in," and he entered his palace.

Pilate sat facing Jesus. Jesus stood, his face askew from swelling, but his eyes were starkly clear.

Suddenly Pilate raised his chin and said, "Are you the King of the Jews?"

Jesus responded immediately, with not a motion. "Do you speak of what you know, or did others tell you this of me?"

"What *I* know! Come, come, man! Am I a Jew?" Pilate was uncomfortable. He had come not to *be* asked but to ask. "Your own people, your own chief priests, found it desirable to hand you over to me, and to my sole disposition your life. Do you understand that? Now you tell me what you did to deserve such treatment."

Jesus said, "My kingship is not of this world. If it were, my own servants would fight to keep me from these people, and I would be handed over to no one."

"Ah!" said Pilate. Here was something treasonable. "So you are a King?"

"As you say," said Jesus, "I am a King."

Pilate shivered at these words, because here, also, was something calmly mighty. Almost, almost, he said, *And am I a citizen?* But he did not. That were a treacherous question, however he might ask it.

Jesus continued, "It was for this reason that I was born into the world, to bear witness to the truth. Everyone who is of the truth hears my voice."

In spite of himself, Pilate now asked a question like the one he had denied. Cynically, as if to say, *It does not matter;* yet yearningly, as if to say, *Can I be of the truth? Can I know it, too?*—Pilate asked, "What is truth?"

Jesus did not answer. He had spoken once, and Pilate could have heard him. He did not speak again. He stood motionless directly in front of the governor.

Finally, *No,* thought Pilate. *One should not kill such a man.*

He arose and directed that the prisoner be taken outside with him. There he raised his own voice before the people and said, "I, Pilate, the sixth Roman governor of Judea, find no fault in this man."

But in his absence, the little band of reli-

gious leaders had grown into a multitude. The whole court in front of his palace was packed with people, and they did not accept Pilate's decision. They curled their lips and hurled new accusations at Jesus.

Pilate was surprised. Jesus said not a word.

The chief priests interpreted. Pointing at the mob they had gathered, they cried, "Do you see? Do you recognize the danger of this man? Pilate, he riles the people. He makes them restless wherever he teaches. He has created an explosive situation—you might even say a political situation."

Pilate turned to Jesus, who stood in perfect silence within the storm. "Man, have you nothing to say for yourself?" he asked. "Do you not hear the crimes they charge you with?"

Jesus said nothing, and Pilate was perplexed. Would this prisoner not offer even a shred of defense for himself?

Abruptly, Pilate broke off the meeting and strode into his palace.

Jesus was bound and led to Pontius Pilate, the Roman governor, that he might be found guilty and put to death.

Barabbas

"Guards!" he roared. "How long to bring Barabbas out of his cell and here to me?"

"Barabbas?" This was a strange request.

"Barabbas! I want him here at once!"

Pilate paced his room in a thoughtful fury. Barabbas was a foul creature, to be sure, and a murderer. But that was precisely why he wanted Barabbas out—for just a moment.

It was the custom that every Passover the governor should release one prisoner unto the people. Pilate would now, he schemed, let the crowd have its choice—between one horrid and one gentle. Surely, surely, they would choose the gentle man, and Barabbas could be returned to his cell in short order.

Then the thought crept into his soul: Why was he doing this for Jesus of Nazareth, unremarkable in his body? But his claims! But his eyes . . .

So there were brought onto the porch of the palace two men. Barabbas, his eyes snapping about like a jackal's. And Jesus, his eyes ever steady upon the people.

The multitude hushed at this new development, and Pilate spoke with sweet civility.

"Custom commands me," he cried, "to grant you a Passover kindness. I will release one prisoner. And you—you shall choose which one." He lifted his left arm. "This man? Barabbas, condemned for murder? Or this man"— he lifted his right arm—"Jesus, the King of the Jews."

In a twinkling the priests were off the porch and among the people, buzzing sharp words into their ears, buzzing, buzzing.

Soon it was not the priests' voices, but the vast breath of the multitude that went up before Pilate. "Barabbas!" was the cry. "Barabbas!" was their choice. "Release unto us Barabbas!"

Pontius Pilate was astounded. He cried out, "Then what shall I do with Jesus?"

"Crucify him!" thundered the multitude. "Crucify him!"

"Why?" Pilate demanded. "What evil has he done?"

But they only thundered the louder, "Crucify him!"

"No!" Pilate snatched at his own authority. He shook his head. And though no one could hear the order for the roar, he shouted in a guard's ear, "Have him scourged."

Scourging

Soldiers removed Jesus from the porch. They led him to separate quarters, and there they stripped him of his clothing. His body naked was not lean but thin and vulnerable. His ribs were visible, might even be counted.

They bound his arms around a post, and then they whipped him. The skin was laid apart. He bled.

" 'King' did he say?" said the Roman soldiers. "None is a king except the public make him one. So it is up to us! *We* can make and unmake kings. We will make him one!"

In mockery, they threw a purple robe around his shoulders. The blood of his back soaked into it. They wove an idiot's crown from thorny branches and pressed this down upon his head. Then they bowed and jeered him as king. "Hail, King of the Jews!" they said.

Jesus, pale for the loss of blood; Jesus, wincing for the ribboned flesh of his back; Jesus, crowned with weeds and robed in bloody purple—Jesus was a most pitiable figure.

And that was just what Pilate wanted. He wanted to move the people to pity. Therefore, Jesus, in exactly this condition, was once more led before the multitude, and Pilate cried, "Look! I find no fault in him; but your findings have been satisfied. *Behold the man!*"

Instantly, the cry went up again, "Crucify him!"

Pilate spat back at them. "Crucify him yourselves!"

At this loss of his self-control, the chief priests knew they were succeeding. Coolly they told him, "We have a law, and by our law he ought to die because he made himself the Son of God. But we cannot execute him. Governor, *you* must."

Pilate whirled on Jesus. "Where," he hissed, "where do you come from?"

Jesus did not answer him. His eyes were closed.

"Answer me! I have the power to release you and the power to execute you. *Answer me!*"

Jesus spoke without opening his eyes. "You have no power over me," he said, "except what has been given from above."

"Pontius Pilate," the chief priests said.

Pilate whirled again. "What!"

"If you release this man," they said, "you are no friend to Caesar. Everyone who calls himself a king is Caesar's enemy."

Pilate sneered. "Shall I crucify your King?"

Pilate ordered that Jesus be scourged. This the soldiers did. Then they clothed him in a purple robe and put a crown of thorns on his head. They mocked him, calling him King of the Jews.

The chief priests answered, "We have no king but Caesar."

Then, since the crowd was so close to a riot, Pontius Pilate chose to obey the rulers of the world, himself a citizen of the pitiless.

Touching the tips of his fingers to water in a basin and never again looking at Jesus of Nazareth, he announced, "I am innocent of this man's blood. Do as you please with him."

Then the governor released Barabbas to the people and handed Jesus into the soldiers' custody, to be crucified.

The Way of Sorrows

"How thin!" the women said. "How thin he has become!" They wept to see the change in him.

Jesus was being led once more through the streets of Jerusalem. But this time there was a cross in the processional, that which would lift him, his body and his life, into the air. Simon, a visitor from Cyrene, was compelled to carry that cross.

And this time women followed, weeping.

Jesus heard and turned his soiled face to them. He paused, and the whole procession stopped.

"Hush, sweet daughters of Jerusalem," said Jesus, his voice oddly strong. "Weep not for me but for yourselves and for your children. The days are near when you will hurt to see your children hurt, and motherhood itself will be a sorrow. Hush."

But the women and the rest of the crowd followed—out of Jerusalem, past the city walls, unto a place called the place of a skull, in Aramaic, *Golgotha.*

On the Cross

There, at nine in the morning, they crucified him.

To the left of him they hung a thief. To the right of him they hung a thief. And Jesus, the spikes through his hands and his feet, hung between.

Between heaven and earth the Son of Man was stretched, and the women were right: He looked terribly thin and sere. His bones, straining through the skin, seemed out of joint. The strength of his muscles was drained. And his tongue cleaved to his jaws.

"Father," he whispered. Spittle crackled round that word. He swallowed. "Father," he said, "forgive them. They know not what they do."

At his feet: a fast and serious dice game among four soldiers. They had ripped his garments into four even pieces and shared them as spoils; but his robe was seamless, woven all of a piece from top to bottom, and there was no good way to divide it except that they cast lots for it.

Then the soldiers rose up. One of them rolled the robe around his arm. Another leaned a ladder against the cross; climbed the ladder, carrying a shingle; then hung that notice above the head of Jesus. It read: *"Jesus of Nazareth, the King of the Jews."*

Thereafter, all who passed by could behold and see and read it—everyone, for it was written in Hebrew, Greek, and Latin.

The chief priests, who until this moment had been satisfied with the proceedings, suddenly took offense at that sign. Two of them went straightway to Pilate to complain about his cynical sense of humor.

"Why do you insist on calling that man our king?" they demanded. "Are you taunting us after all? Change that sign. Do not write 'King of the Jews,' but *'He said* I am the King of the Jews'!"

Pilate, however, was at this point a most humorless man and altogether weary of their endless demands. He was done with the whole affair. "What I have written," he said, "I have written." And so it stayed.

On Golgotha the crowd was swelling, the deathwatchers, the contemptuous, those who take their victories from others' defeats, those who know their own lives only by the contemplation of another's death. This was a far different multitude from those that followed Jesus in the days of his miracles. These people spoke of miracles only in scorn.

"So you will destroy the Temple and build it again in three days? Wonderworker, save yourself!"

"Son of God! Come down from the cross!"

"He saved others, this Christ. Himself he cannot save."

"Come down, thou Christ, that we might all see and believe!"

Even the thief at his left, twisting around, joined the mockery. "The Christ?" he growled. "So the Christ is sharing my sentence! Save yourself, Christ—and save us, too!"

But the thief at his right rolled his head sideways and said, "Man, you are up against death, and you don't fear God? We are dying for the evil of our deeds, and it is just. But this man has done nothing wrong. Jesus," the thief gasped, "remember me when

---

At a place called Golgotha, they crucified Jesus. Lifting his head, he cried out, "Father, forgive them. They know not what they do."

you come into your kingdom."

And Jesus answered him with gentleness, "Truly I say unto you, today you will be with me in paradise."

Not all in this multitude scorned him. Jesus' eyes, moving so painfully—for even to look caused thought and to think made him aware of the ripping spikes and his own dead weight—Jesus' eyes found his mother there, weeping, and her sister Salome and Mary Magdalene and Mary the wife of Clopas: the women. The women had come to be with him.

Then he saw the face of young John, the disciple whom he loved.

"Woman," Jesus whispered to his mother. Perhaps no one else heard him, but Mary did. "Woman," he said, glancing at John, "behold your son." And to John he said, "Behold your mother."

Then John embraced Mary and led her away, and Jesus saw that they were both weeping. The other women stayed and watched, and wept and watched. The women were his witnesses.

The Death of Jesus

At noon the weather and all creation went into mourning. Darkness descended like a pall upon the land, and only the form of the Lord Christ could be discerned in violent slump upon the cross. He did not twist. He did not groan against his pain—nay, did not so much as open up his mouth but, like a lamb at the slaughter, was dumb. From twelve until three the sunlight failed, and in mortal isolation Jesus suffered toward his death.

Then at three in the afternoon, he threw his body outward from the cross, raised his face, and cried to the pitchy heavens, *"Eli! Eli! Lama sabachthani?"*

"My God! My God! Why have you forsaken me?"

The few straggling people who had waited even in the darkness whispered, "Listen! He is calling for Elijah! Do you think Elijah will come to save him?"

Then they were shocked to hear him speaking straight to them out of the gloom. "I am," he groaned above them in a hoarse, hollow voice, "I am thirsty."

A soldier took a sponge and jammed it on a reed. He dipped it in vinegar, then held it up to Jesus, and Jesus sucked the vinegar.

Once more he lifted his head. His gaunt chest pumped vigorously. And once more he uttered such a loud, reechoing cry that the soldier leaped backward.

In the ninth hour, Jesus gave up his spirit. The earth shook and rocks split apart.

But the soldier crept forward again, for he heard the Crucified whisper, "It is finished. Father, into your hands I commend my Spirit."

Jesus' head leaned sideways; but finding no pillow even upon his own shoulder, his head dropped forward on his chest, and he breathed his last, and he died.

Truly, the Son of God

Straightway, the curtain in the Temple was ripped in two from the top of it to the bottom. The earth trembled, the rocks rolled loose, the tombs tumbled open, and many of the saints who had died were raised.

And the Roman soldier, a centurion, murmured at the foot of the body, "Truly, this was the Son of God."

And though some of the people now departed, beating their breasts for all they had seen, the women stayed and watched. The women wept and watched.

Burial

It was a filthy light that saw two soldiers come unto the Crucified late that afternoon.

IESUS NAZARENUS REX IUDAEORUM
ΙΗΣΟΥΣ Ω ΝΑΖΟΡΑΙΟΣ
Ο ΒΑΣΙΛΗΥΣ ΤΩΝ ΙΟΥΔΑΙΩΝ

Joseph of Arimathea and the women lowered Jesus' body from the cross. Sorrowing, they wrapped it in clean linen and laid it in a rocky tomb. Then they rolled a great stone before the door.

They did not acknowledge the women standing by; indeed, they intended to say nothing at all, for theirs was a dolorous task.

They were to break the legs of the criminals in order to speed their dying so that none should be left hanging on a cross after dusk. Such was the law.

And so they did. They broke the legs first of one thief and then of the other. But when they came to Jesus, they were astonished to find him hanging too low and too pale; and they spoke.

"Is he dead? Already?"

One of the soldiers pierced the side of the Lord with a spear, and there flowed out both blood and water, mingled.

"Dead," he breathed in wonder.

Now, he who saw this declares that it is true. He saw it. It truly happened! And he cries the fact aloud, that you, too, might believe.

Soon came a good man to the cross, a respected member of the Jewish council of elders and a seeker after the kingdom of God. Joseph of Arimathea, having obtained permission from the governor to take the body of the Lord, strung cords from the cross and lovingly lowered Jesus' corpse.

"How light he has become," breathed the women who watched him bear the body away. They were surprised that it took so little strength to carry him.

They followed Joseph to his own tomb, newly hewn in solid rock. They watched as the thin, unresisting body was wrapped in a clean linen cloth. They saw the ledge within the tomb, where he was laid. And they heard the crunch of the great stone rolled in front of the entrance.

Only now did they turn away. Only now did they leave the Lord; but even now they went to prepare spices and ointments to anoint him. They would return on Sunday, and then they would mourn.

RESURRECTION!

"God has exalted him," wrote the Apostle Paul of Jesus Christ. "God has lifted him up, and has given to Jesus a name over all other names! At the name of Jesus, the knees bow down, in heaven, on earth, and under the ground! And the tongues confess that *Jesus is Lord,* to the glory of God the Father!"

Sunday: The Empty Tomb

The earth trembled at the dawn of Sunday, the first day of the week. But the three women walking to the tombs outside Jerusalem hardly noticed that.

Mary Magdalene, Mary the mother of James, and Salome carried their spices in delicate grief and sighed. They were going to anoint the body of the Lord before its last corruption.

"Sisters," whispered Mary Magdalene, "who will roll the stone away for us?"

Neither of the others spoke. Neither had an answer. But the answer lay ahead of them.

When they came in view of the tomb, they saw that the stone had already been rolled back. The entrance stood open, dark and yawning and—so it seemed to Mary Magdalene—empty.

"Why do you look for the living among the dead?" Suddenly two men in blinding robes stood by the women, talking to them; and the women were terrified. "Come, see the place where they laid him. See that he is not there. He is risen, just as he told you."

But Mary Magdalene did not go and see. She dropped her spices, grabbed her skirts, and ran back into the city without another word. She thought she knew what had happened.

"Peter!" she cried as she burst into his room. The huge disciple grabbed her and hugged her because she seemed so grieved. But Mary would not be still. "Peter, they have stolen the Lord, and we do not know where they put him!"

Before she could turn around, Peter was gone from the room, racing toward the tombs, and John was running with him.

Mary arrived behind them, in time to see John go in. She saw their forms; both were crouching in the tomb. But she stayed at a distance, wringing her hands and trying desperately not to cry. Now and again she stamped her foot. "Gone!" she whispered. "Why would they have taken him? What for?"

Then Peter and John emerged from the tomb, blinking in the morning light and walking toward her. She ran to them with her hands on her cheeks.

"What did you see?" she whispered.

"Gone," said Peter. And immediately Mary burst into tears.

"I knew it! I knew it!" She wept.

"It's strange," Peter continued. "The burial linen is disarranged, but the napkin for his head is in the corner, neatly rolled. Strange." Then he went with John back to the city, lost in the strangeness of it all.

But Mary had finally begun to cry, and now she could not quit. The tears streamed down her cheeks and dropped from the end of her nose.

She stumbled toward the tomb, leaned against the cold rock face, then stooped and looked in.

At the head and at the foot of the place where Jesus had lain were two angels. But Mary did not see them as angels. Tears and desolation blurred all the world around her.

"Woman," they said, "why are you weeping?"

"Because," she sobbed, "they have stolen my Lord, and I do not know where they put him."

She turned away from the darkness of the tomb and at once saw Jesus standing in the sunlight. But she did not recognize him. He was no more to her misty eyes than another man—the gardener.

"Woman," he said, "why are you weeping? What are you looking for?"

"Sir, please, please," she wept, "if you have carried him anywhere, only just tell me and I will take him properly away."

Then in a single word, all Life and Light and Truth came clear to her. The word was a common one, but yet that word could measure an infinity of love. It was her own name.

Jesus called her by name. He said, "Mary." At once she heard the voice that her heart knew. Her tears danced in gladness, and she laughed while she cried.

"Master, my Master!" She stretched her arms to him.

But he cautioned her. "Mary, do not clutch me yet," said Jesus, lean and wistful and alive. "I have not yet ascended to my Father. But go back to my disciples and tell

On Sunday, carrying spices to anoint Jesus' body, the women went to the tomb. The heavy stone was rolled back, and two men in shining garments stood at the door, saying, "He is risen."

them that I am ascending to my Father and your Father, to my God and your God."

With what lightness Mary ran the distance back to the disciples' room! With what indestructible joy she told them the message that the living Lord had given unto her. So glad was she that even their disbelief did not destroy the spirit in her, and she ran to tell the other women. These hugged her and laughed with a sky-born faith—for the women: The women were his first witnesses.

His Disciples Become His Apostles

The disciples, on the other hand—great Peter, gentle John, imperious James, and the others—spent most of that Sunday behind locked doors in a single, stuffy room, fearful that the people who had killed Jesus meant also to seek and destroy them. The afternoon passed in gloom; and only when the darkness fell did one of them, Thomas, sneak away to find food.

It was then, in the absence of Thomas, that Jesus quietly and suddenly stood among them.

He said, "Peace be unto you."

They said nothing. They shrank away from him and stared, though the face and the form were the Lord's, and the voice was very familiar. But no one had rattled the bolt at the door; no one had made the hinges squeak; no one had let him in!

Slowly Jesus extended his hands to them, palms up, and they saw there the wounds from the spikes—

"Jesus?"

Next he gathered back his clothing, and there, in the flesh of his side, was the long, serious wound from the spear.

"Lord? Master? *Jesus?*"

Peter let out one bark of laughter. John sank to his knees before the Lord, tears in his wide-open eyes. Disciples clutched their hands together, rubbed their eyes, and

laughed and called his name.

"Lord, it is you!" It was Jesus and none other, Jesus and no spirit, Jesus alive from the grave, and his deep eyes sparkling!

Once again Jesus said, "Peace be unto you," for such he had promised them a lifetime ago. "You have been disciples, students of mine, lo, these three years together. Now," he said, "I make you my *apostles*, messengers of mine, for I send you out into the world even as the Father sent me into the world."

Now Jesus stepped near to each one of his apostles in turn. What he did then moved them so much that they lowered their heads and trembled in silence. He breathed on them, and the breath went into them, and they wept.

"Receive the Holy Spirit," he said.

Jesus, not dead! Jesus, risen! He stood among the disciples, and their joy was boundless.

"When you forgive sins, they are forgiven indeed. When you retain sins, they are retained."

Thomas, Be Not Faithless

High, holy delight broke out among the apostles when they were alone again. There was a fine laughter, a telling and retelling of the stories of those who had seen the Lord, and the door was thrown open to the night wind.

Thomas was astonished and not a little nervous to find that door open when he returned. He was not smiling like the others.

"Lock it!" he demanded.

"No!" they shouted, much too loudly. "Everything has changed, Thomas," they howled as though this were the best of all jokes. "We have seen the Lord!"

"Well," said Thomas. He put the food in a corner. His face was suspicious. "That is precisely what Mary Magdalene said this morning, and you did not believe her. Why should I believe you tonight?"

"Because this time we have *all* seen him," Peter cried, "and we are no longer what we were. Isn't that right?"

All the apostles nodded vigorously and affirmed the fact with many wonderful details.

"Well," said Thomas, still fussing with the food, "maybe you did. Maybe you didn't. But it is certain that I did not. Therefore, until I see the print of the nails in his hands and put my finger there and until I put my hand in his side, I will not believe. That is that. Have some bread."

Eight days later the apostles were gathered again in the same room, and this time Thomas was with them.

Even as he did before, Jesus came among them, and again he said, "Peace be unto you." But he was looking at one man alone, at Thomas, whose hand had locked midway between his plate and his mouth. "Jesus?"

The Lord Jesus took the bread from Thomas's hand, laid it aside, and said, "Thomas, touch the wounds in my hands. Thomas, put your hand in my side, and do not be faithless, but believe."

"Oh!" Thomas breathed. "My Lord and my God."

"So you believe," said Jesus. "And have you believed because you see me? Blessed, Thomas, are those innumerable who have not seen yet believe in me."

Jesus, who had begun his teaching ministry by blessing those who were deprived, was now ending his ministry in the same way. Blessed, blessed, blessed are they forever.

Peter, Feed My Sheep

And then they did not see the Lord for a while. They traveled back to Galilee, but Peter found his old home hollow without the presence of his life, his Lord; so he sought to fill the emptiness with a piece of his earlier life. He said to the others, "I'm going fishing."

Thomas had not seen and Thomas scoffed. Then Jesus came to him, that he too might believe.

Suddenly the fishermen knew who had called to them. Now Peter had no time for sails and oars. He leaped into the water and swam to shore.

They found the boat still seaworthy, and the weather and all things else as they had been; so Peter and Thomas, Bartholomew, James and John and two others became fishermen again for a night, casting their nets and, as happened before, catching nothing.

"Yo, children!"

In the dim light of the dawn they saw a man standing on shore. "Have you caught any fish?" he called.

This was a common morning question. Nothing at all had changed since they left this labor to follow Jesus. "No, friend, nothing!" they cried back.

"Then cast your nets," called the man, "from the right side, and you will."

They did that, and suddenly their nets were so full of the squirming fish that they could not pull them in.

This, too, had happened once before—

John grabbed Peter. "Do you know who that is?" he shouted gleefully. "It is the Lord!"

For Peter, the boat was all at once too slow and too far away from shore. He leaped straightway into the sea and swam with all his might to Jesus, then came up on the shore dripping, laughing, and thoroughly happy. Besides Jesus, he saw food and a fire for breakfast.

Jesus said, "Bring some of the fish you caught," and Peter, who had hurried here, turned round immediately and hurried back to help the others drag the nets ashore. He was bursting with the joy of this meeting.

The fish were cooked over the fire, then Jesus called them to eat with him. He took the bread and divided it, gave them fish, and they ate. Peter sat down beside his Lord.

Near the end of the meal, Peter realized that Jesus had been looking at him for some time, and he was flooded with gratitude. But the look on Jesus' face was solemn.

"Simon, son of Jonah," he said slowly, "do you love me more than these?"

Such a formal question and, after all, unnecessary, thought Peter. "Yes, Lord," he said. "You know that I do." But it was good to have the chance to say so. He smiled around his words and nodded.

Jesus said, "Feed my lambs."

But even then the Lord did not remove his eyes from Peter, and it was as if he had not yet answered the question at all.

"Simon, son of Jonah," said Jesus a second time, "do you love me?"

But Peter had just said so! And he felt it with every fiber of his being! Why would Jesus ask him *twice?* "Yes!" said Peter. "Yes, Lord, you know that I love you."

Jesus appeared to the eleven, gathered on a mountainside. He commanded them to go out to all nations, teaching and baptizing.

Jesus said, "Tend my sheep."

The eyes of the Lord, which had so often shed a warm and healing light, now shined so bright a penetrating glare that Peter felt unprotected. It was as though he wore no clothes before this gaze, and every blemish shivered to be seen. Peter cowered in distress.

"Simon, son of Jonah," Jesus said a third time, no louder than before, but the words rang like a judge's in his courtroom, "do you love me?"

"O Lord!" Peter was grieved. "You know everything. You know that I love you."

Jesus said, "Feed my sheep."

And then, when Peter felt most estranged and lonely, Jesus put his arms around the huge, battered man and hugged him—and Peter was a child again.

"Truly, I say to you," said the Lord, "when you were young, you dressed yourself and went wherever you wanted to go. But when you are old, Peter, you will stretch out your hands and someone else will dress you and lead you where you do not want to go." This he said, full of kindness, to show by what death Peter was to die for the glory of the Father.

"Peter?" His cheek was by the rough cheek of his most headlong friend.

"What?" said Peter.

And Jesus said, as once he had so long ago, "Follow me."

All Authority Is Mine

Jesus appeared unto more than five hundred of his followers—and then he met with the eleven whom he had chosen. They gathered in grateful worship before him upon an appointed mountain in Galilee, and he spoke.

"All authority in heaven and on earth has been given unto me," said the Lord. "Therefore I myself commission you: Go out. Make disciples of all the nations. Baptize them in the name of the Father and of the Son and of the Holy Spirit. Teach them to observe everything that I have commanded you. And hear me, my dear ones, my laborers—I am with you always, even to the end of this age."

Now, Jesus did many other signs in the presence of his disciples, which wonders are not recorded here. For if they were written down, the world itself could not contain the books of his deeds. But these are written that you may believe that Jesus is the Christ, the Son of the living God—and that believing, you might have life in his name.

THE CHURCH

JESUS ASCENDS INTO HEAVEN

FINALLY, AFTER the risen Lord Jesus had spent forty days appearing to the people and declaring the kingdom of God, he gathered his apostles into one place. So watchful and still was his manner that they sensed some great thing about to occur.

"Lord," they asked, "is this the time? Will you now restore the kingdom to Israel?"

Jesus said, "It is not for you to know the times and the seasons which the Father has fixed. Rather, you will receive power when the Holy Spirit has come upon you, and then you shall be my witnesses. Speak of me in Jerusalem and all Judea and Samaria. Carry my name to the end of the earth."

Then even while they looked at him, the wonder occurred. He was lifted up, high, high above the dull and lumpish globe, until a cloud swaddled him and took him from their sight.

Gone from view was Jesus. Yet the apostles continued to stare heavenward, gaping—when behold! two men in white robes stood by them and gently drew their longing down again unto the earth.

"Men of Galilee," they said to the apostles, "why do you stand gazing into heaven? This Jesus, who was taken up from you, will return in the same way as you saw him go."

Slowly their eyes descended to this world below, blinking against the round reality of bald hills, gray stone, and one another's faces. Slowly they walked the way to Jerusalem, there to wait for the promise of the Father.

For Jesus had said, ere his departure, "John baptized with water, but before many days you will be baptized with the Holy Spirit."

They returned to the holy city, and they waited.

Jerusalem, Judea, and Samaria

THE CHURCH IN BIRTH AND INFANCY

THOUGH JESUS' PHYSICAL BODY—his lean frame, his scarred hands, and riven side—had been taken up from the earth, yet another body of his still remained active, visible, and alive among the people. This other body was composed of all who believed in Jesus. This body of Christ was called the church!

Thousands of people would make up the church, and all of them different one from another. Yet all of them together were, by their faith in Christ and their love for one another, just one body.

As a body has many parts which serve the whole, so this body of Jesus had many parts. Some of the people were its eyes, and some its ears, and some its nose. Some were feet to carry it, others hands to do.

This body was born in Jerusalem, on the day when the Holy Spirit came down upon the followers of the church to give the body life, on the day called Pentecost. Pentecost: the birthday of the church!

And then, like every other healthy body, it grew—first in Jerusalem and then through Judea and then into the half-foreign territory of Samaria. After that it grew to include the Gentiles, all the nations, Rome, and the end of the earth.

Pentecost

Devout Jews from every nation under heaven felt the need to travel to the holy city of Jerusalem at least one time in their lives, there to celebrate before God at least one of the appointed festivals. One such festival which drew them by the hundreds and the thousands was the Feast of Weeks, also called Pentecost because it came fifty days after the Passover. At this festival leavened loaves of bread, the first two baked from the wheat harvest of that year, were offered to the Lord God.

In the year of the death of the Lord Jesus, Pentecost also fell fifty days after his Resurrection, ten days after he ascended from the sight of the apostles, and on the same day as the coming of the Holy Spirit.

Therefore, when Jesus' followers gathered in a single place on the morning of that remarkable day, Jerusalem was crowded. All the world was represented there, and thousands heard the stirring of the baby church at birth. . . .

Suddenly, without warning, a sound whistled down from heaven, swept through the streets, and whirled into the house where the apostles were sitting. It was an urgent noise, like a high wind screaming, so that the multitude of devout people followed it bewildered and came to the place of the gathered people of Jesus. There they beheld a sight, and they heard a holy wonder.

Resting upon the head of each of the followers was a tongue as of fire; and with their fleshy tongues—but by the power of the Holy Spirit—they were speaking, speaking. They were telling everyone of the mighty works of God. And the wonder was that every foreigner did clearly understand what they were saying, for they were speaking in every language of every nation under heaven! The Spirit gave them the utterance!

"What does this mean?" the astonished people said to one another. "How can this happen?"

But others, seeking some kind of explanation, said, "Drunk! These men are drunk."

"Not drunk!" said Peter to the people. "This is not drunkenness, because it is still the morning, not yet nine o'clock. People of Judea and all who dwell in Jerusalem, listen to me! This is the fulfillment of the prophecy of Joel; these are the things of the latter days. For the Lord God said, 'I will in the last days pour out my Spirit upon all flesh, and your sons and your daughters shall prophesy. Your young men shall see visions, and your old men shall dream dreams. I will show wonders in heaven above and signs on the earth beneath. And it shall be that whoever calls upon the name of the Lord shall be saved.'

"People of Israel," Peter cried, "listen to me! Jesus of Nazareth, who performed by God mighty works and wonders and signs; Jesus of Nazareth, who was delivered up by the plan of God, who was crucified, whom

the world killed by the hands of lawless men; this same Jesus of Nazareth God did raise from the dead! He was not abandoned in the pits of the lifeless. His flesh did not see corruption. God raised him to life, and we are the witnesses. God lifted him to the right hand of the throne of glory, and now he is pouring out his Spirit upon us, and *that* is what you see and hear. Let all the Family Israel know that God has made both Lord and Christ this Jesus whom the world crucified!"

When the people heard these words of Peter, they were cut to their hearts, and

they pleaded with all of the apostles, saying, "Brethren, what shall we do?"

"Repent," said Peter. "Be baptized every one of you in the name of Jesus Christ for the forgiveness of your sins, and you will receive the gift of the Holy Spirit. For the promise is to you and to your children and to all that are far off—to everyone whom the Lord our God calls."

Thus Peter preached. Words, testimony, exhortations, Peter preached: "Save yourselves from this crooked generation!"

And those who received his word, who were baptized, who were added to the church that day, were some three thousand souls.

Life in the Infant Church

From that time forward the apostles taught powerfully of the Lord and of his Resurrection, and the believers devoted themselves joyfully to their *teaching*.

Willingly they shared with one another. No single person went hungry or lacked for anything, because those who had lands or houses sold them, and the proceeds were distributed by the apostles. Goods were divided among those who had need for them, and no one said, "This is mine. I own it." But all belonged to all: *fellowship*.

Daily, generously the believers ate together in their houses, for this was the nourishment of their bodies. But more than that, it was a remembrance of the Lord and communion in his body and his blood. As Jesus had repeatedly performed it, even so they named it: *the breaking of bread*.

And faithfully these children of their fa-

People from every part of the world saw and heard a wonder, that day in Jerusalem. Tongues as of fire rested on the heads of the apostles. All heard and understood in their own languages.

ther Israel attended the Temple together, devoting themselves to the *prayers*.

Power in the Church

Many wonders and signs were done through the apostles.

On a certain morning Peter and John were entering the Temple by an eastern gate, going to pray at the appointed hour, when suddenly a man behind them set up a clamor.

"Alms! Alms!" he cried. "Pennies for the poor are treasures for the giver. Alms!"

Peter turned to see this beggar, who was just being settled into his customary spot by friends and who was straightway beginning his day of begging. His feet and ankles were dreadfully twisted as, in fact, they had been from his birth.

"Alms?" he said.

Peter returned to him and said, "Look at us."

The man did, his eyes searching their robes for some bulge in the shape of a purse.

Peter said, "I have no gold. I have no silver. But what I do have I will give to you. In the name of Jesus Christ of Nazareth—walk." He took the cripple by his right hand and, muscular apostle, lifted him to his feet. Immediately those feet were strengthened and bore the man's full weight. The cripple stood a moment, then walked, then leaped like a child and began to shout praises to God.

When Peter and John entered the Temple, so did this man, clinging close to them and roaring praises to Almighty God. So the people looked, then recognized him as the habitual beggar and were astonished. The word of this miracle flew instantly from mouth to mouth, and a great crowd met Peter and John in Solomon's Portico.

"People of Israel," said Peter, "why do you stare at us as though we by our own power made this man to walk? We did not. The name of Jesus and faith in his name gave strength to feeble feet. Jesus, whom the God of our fathers Abraham, Isaac, and Jacob has glorified. Jesus, whom you denied in the presence of Pilate. Jesus, the holy and the righteous, the Author of life, whom some of you preferred crucified that a murderer might run free—but whom God raised from the dead. It was faith through Jesus which has given this man his perfect health!

"Now turn, every one of you, from your

The church grew, as did the apostles' works. Peter healed a beggar, a gift greater than coins.

wickedness. Repent, that your sins may be blotted out and that God may bless you according to the promises he made to Abraham!"

Enemies of the Young Church

While Peter was yet speaking, the priests, the captain of the Temple, and the Sadducees—who did not believe that there was a resurrection from the dead—surrounded him and led both him and John to jail.

"We cannot have this sort of disturbance," they said, "or this kind of teaching. It is both foolish and dangerous—"

Dangerous indeed. Many of the people who heard Peter believed his word, and the church had grown to about five thousand people.

On the morrow Peter and John were ushered into the place of the high priest. The same Peter who had denied Jesus in a dim morning courtyard now stood face to face with Caiaphas and Annas and the temple authorities. He heard the stern demand, "By what name did you do this thing?" and he did not wither before their eyes.

Rather, tingling with the power of the Holy Spirit, he spoke boldly. "Be it known unto you all and to the people everywhere in Israel that by the name of Jesus Christ of Nazareth—whom people crucified, whom God raised from the dead—a cripple found his feet and stands upright before you. There is salvation in no one else!" Peter proclaimed, his massy head held high, his vast shoulders thrown back. "Nay, there is no other name under heaven given among men whereby we must be saved!"

Here was a marvelous thing! Bold, eloquent words proceeding from the mouth of an uneducated fisherman. And not words only, but deeds, for there beside him stood the cripple uncrippled and healthy! The Temple authorities could not deny the truth and the power of Peter's actions, so they took a lesser route.

"Hereafter," they commanded, "you will neither speak, preach, nor teach in the name of Jesus. Do you understand the decree?"

Peter understood. But he would not bow before it. "Whether it is right before God to listen to you rather than to him, you judge—for right or wrong, we will do the will of God. We have no choice but to speak of the things that we have heard and seen."

Threats the temple authorities then laid on him, but threats were all they could administer. They could not punish Peter, because all the people praised God for the wonder of this healing. The cripple was more than forty years old.

Peter and John were released.

The Sin of Ananias

Among those who sold their property to share the money with the church was a man born in Cyprus, a Levite whom the apostles called Barnabas. He laid the money from the sale at the apostles' feet.

So did another come with money from a sale of land. Ananias deposited a certain amount with Peter and smiled and said that this was the total payment, praise be to God.

But it was not. It was but a part of the payment, since he and his wife, Sapphira, had conspired to keep back some money for themselves alone.

Peter sighed when he saw it. "Ananias," he said, "do you think we are only mortals together, creating some merely human community? God is among us! The Holy Spirit moves among us! Then why did Satan fill your heart to lie to the Holy Spirit? You did not have to sell your land. You did not have to bring us money. And you surely did

Sapphira plotted to keep her wealth from the church. But God knew.

not have to say that a portion was the whole of it. Ananias, not to men have you lied, but to God!"

When Ananias heard these words, he collapsed and died. A shivering fear seized those who saw this, and quietly, with holy dread, the young men rose and wrapped the body and carried it out and buried it.

Three hours later Sapphira came to Peter, sweetly ignorant of her husband's death.

"Tell me," Peter said cautiously—he was walking a sad, blasted path by his question—"is this the amount for which you sold your land?" He showed her the money Ananias had brought.

She smiled and said, "Yes, thanks be to God."

Peter sagged. "Then it was a scheme, a plan," he said. "You agreed together. Oh, lady, how could you tempt the Spirit of the Lord? Listen: Do you hear the footfalls at the door? Those are the men who just buried your husband, and now they will carry you, too."

Immediately Sapphira fell down before Peter and died, and the young men entering found her there. It was a dolorous thing to perform twice the same sad rite; but they carried her out and buried her beside her husband.

Enmity Increases

The power of the apostles caused wonder and faith and a following among the multitudes, not only in Jerusalem but also in the towns around the city. The church grew. Believers were added to the Lord. People carried their sick into the streets, laying them on beds and pallets, so that as Peter passed, the shadow of the apostle might brush them with grace. And unclean spirits were cast out.

This swelling thing did not go unnoticed by the high priest. And since the apostles acted ever in the open, he had no difficulty arresting them a second time, all of them.

Neither did the Lord have difficulty releasing them, for at night the angel of the Lord opened the prison doors, and by the morning light the apostles were in the Temple again, teaching the words of life.

And again, itching with frustration, the

captain and the officers of the Temple gathered them up and brought them before the council.

"We strictly charged you," the high priest said to the apostles, "not to teach in the name of this man!"

"And we clearly answered you," replied Peter, "that we must obey God rather than men! This man, the world killed by hanging on a tree. This man, the God of our fathers raised. This Jesus, God exalted as leader and savior to call repentance from Israel and to give the forgiveness of sins. And we are his witnesses. Oh, we will teach in his name!"

Some members of the council rose up in rage against the apostles, angry enough to execute the lot of them. But they were restrained. Instead, they had the apostles whipped, and they commanded again that they never speak publicly in the name of Jesus.

But the apostles went out rejoicing that they had suffered for Jesus' name. And every day in every place they continued preaching Jesus as the Christ.

The apostles laid their hands upon the heads of seven devout men chosen by the people.

Help for the Apostles

The growing numbers of believers caused certain problems within the church. Some of the widows, whose poverty in those days was severe, were being forgotten in the daily distribution.

"But we," said the apostles to the rest, "cannot watch over everything. We should not neglect preaching in order to serve tables."

And so it happened that a problem became a benefit, and the leadership of the church expanded.

"Brethren," said the apostles, "select from among you seven men of good reputation, in whom are wisdom and the Holy Spirit. We will give them the duty of this service and then attend ourselves to prayer and to the ministry of the word."

Even so the multitude did. They brought forward Stephen, a man full of faith and of the Holy Spirit, and Philip and Prochorus and Nicanor and Timon and Parmenas and Nicolaus. Then the apostles prayed and laid their hands upon these seven.

Duties had been divided.

Stephen's Disputation

What a fine, right choice was Stephen! What a bright, rich voice he lifted on behalf of Jesus! What mighty words when he spoke, and what wisdom! No unbeliever could withstand the Spirit in him. And so there were many who, watching, listening, and feeling defeat before his eloquence, hated him.

These secretly roused certain people against Stephen, whispering accusations. "We heard him speak blasphemies," they said, "against Moses and God." Then it was not long before these people seized him and brought him to the council, bribing witnesses to lie in order to prove him evil. "He speaks against the Temple," they said, "predicting its destruction!"

When the high priest had heard their testimony, he turned to Stephen and said, "Do they speak the truth?"

"Brethren and fathers, hear me," said Stephen. "The God of glory appeared to our father Abraham—" And he began to recount the holy history of the Family Israel. While he spoke, his face was radiant, like that of an angel.

He spoke of Abraham, Isaac, and Jacob. He recalled how the twelve sons of Jacob, the Patriarchs, went with their families into Egypt, where the people multiplied. He remembered Moses, and he dwelt particularly upon the times that Israel refused Moses, disobeyed him, thrust him aside. Then he touched on David and Solomon and the building of the Temple, saying, "Yet the Most High does not dwell in houses made with hands!" And he quoted the prophet to prove it: " 'Heaven is my throne, the earth my footstool. What house will you build for me, says the Lord. Did not my hand make all these things?' "

Finally, with scorching voice, Stephen directed his bold delivery straight at the elders, the accusers surrounding him. "You stiff-necked people, uncircumcised in heart and ears!" he declared. "You always resist the Holy Spirit. As did your ancestors, so do you. Which of the prophets did not your forebears persecute? They killed those who prophesied the coming of the Righteous One, whom you yourselves betrayed, whom you then murdered!"

Stephen—Martyr

When they felt the lash of Stephen's speech, his enemies were enraged and ground their teeth against him. But his voice suddenly softened. He cast bright, innocent eyes heavenward. He opened his mouth, first to sigh and then to speak. "Behold," he whispered in a distant voice, "I see the heavens opened and the Son of Man standing at the right hand of God."

That maddened them the more. They roared at such sweet blasphemy. They stopped their ears. In a body they rushed upon him and cast him outside the city. They ripped off their robes, dumping them at the feet of a man named Saul, and began to hurl stones at Stephen.

"Lord Jesus," Stephen prayed, "receive my spirit!" He went down under the heavy hail, crying, "Lord, hold not this sin against them!"—then passed into his death.

Persecution

In that same day the enmity against the young church changed from merely hard words to hard action.

People—the man named Saul particularly—ravaged the believers. Saul entered their houses and dragged off men and women together and committed them to prison.

So frightening was the uproar in Jerusalem that many believers escaped the city and scattered throughout the regions of Judea and Samaria.

Sad was the motive that moved them out; but the end was excellent, for they took with them the name of Jesus and everywhere preached good news about the kingdom of God and his Christ and everywhere baptized both men and women.

WHAT GOD HAS CLEANSED DO NOT CALL COMMON

Philip the Evangelist

While the apostles remained in Jerusalem, wonders were done in the name of the Lord far away from them.

Philip, anointed with Stephen by the apostles, preached among the Samaritans, casting out unclean spirits, healing the lame, and turning many to Christ. But his success was not restricted to Samaria, for an angel of the Lord soon directed him south, to the road that went from Jerusalem to Gaza. This was a deserted stretch, and the old city of Gaza itself was void of people, eyeless stones unblinking in the sunburnt wilderness. Nevertheless, Philip obeyed and went.

As he traveled, he heard behind him the clop of horses at a walk and the slow grind of chariot wheels. He turned and saw a man who did not see him. Philip was neither hiding nor invisible; but this swart, frowning man had simply given his horses their head and was reading something so intently that he was blind to all the world around him. The insignia that he bore, the wealth of his carriage, and the easy power in his brow announced him a high minister in the court of the Ethiopians. But the frown between his eyebrows suggested some confusion with the text before him.

"Go up," the Spirit said to Philip. "Join this chariot." So Philip ran to the dark man and asked, "Do you understand what you are reading?"

The man lifted his eyes and blinked.

On the road from Jerusalem to Gaza, Philip met an Ethiopian eager to hear the words of Jesus. And Philip baptized this man of goodwill.

"How can I," he said, "if no one guides me?" He invited Philip to come and sit with him and showed him the difficult passage.

It was from the prophet Isaiah and read thus: "As a sheep led to the slaughter, as a lamb that is before its shearer dumb, even so he opens not his mouth. In his humiliation justice was denied him. Oh, who can describe this generation? For his life was taken from the earth."

"Please tell me," said the Ethiopian, "whom does the prophet mean? Himself, or some other man?"

Then Philip began to speak, and now the chariot carried two men hunched in earnest conversation, both of them blind to the scenery. Starting with Isaiah's words, Philip told the dark man all the good news of Jesus, and miles of travel became for him a progress toward salvation. When, finally, the Ethiopian looked up, he saw water and cried out in his joy, "See! Here is water! What is to keep me from being baptized?"

"Stop the chariot!" Philip commanded with wonderful conviction. So they both went into the water, and he baptized him.

When they came out of the water, Philip was caught up by the Spirit of the Lord, and the Ethiopian saw him no more but went his way rejoicing.

Philip appeared in Azotus, near the coast of the Mediterranean Sea, whence he went north preaching the good news in every town until he came to Caesarea.

Saul Is Paul, Apostle to the Gentiles

So widely scattered had the believers become after Stephen's death that they were found as far away as Phoenicia and Cyprus and Antioch. Much closer, but still some distance from Jerusalem, they worshiped and preached and made themselves known also in Damascus.

Now Saul's fiery desire to destroy the church could not be contained by the little city of Jerusalem. He was so fanatically zealous for the old traditions that he would silence the name of Jesus *wherever* it might be found. So he obtained the right to rout believers even from Damascus, to bind them, and to bring them back to Jerusalem.

Letters in hand, then, he took to horse, he and his men, and journeyed northward, nothing hindering the threat and the havoc he intended.

But suddenly, close on the city of Damascus, a mighty light blazed all around him and blasted him to the ground. Then came a voice, saying, "Saul! Saul! Why do you persecute me?"

The poor opposer, the poor little man, was stunned by the bright divinity, and he mumbled, "Who? Who are you, Lord?"

"I am Jesus," said the voice, "whom you are persecuting!"

The men with Saul stood speechless, hearing a voice but seeing no one and understanding nothing.

"Rise!" said the voice. "For by my appearing I appoint you my own servant to preach me among the Gentiles. Open their eyes. Turn them from darkness to light. Turn them from Satan to God that they may receive forgiveness of sins and a place among the faithful."

Saul stood up and straightway stumbled. His companions had to grab him and lead him—for he was stone blind and helpless.

For three days he sat in a Damascan room, in a house on a street called Straight, neither eating nor drinking nor seeing, but praying fervently. Then with hesitation, but under

Zealous Saul persecuted the Christians. On his way to Damascus to destroy the new church there, a blinding light struck him down. He heard the voice of Jesus.

pressure from the Lord, a disciple of the Lord named Ananias came to him.

"Saul?" he said.

"Yes," said the blind man quietly.

"*Brother* Saul?"

"Yes! Yes!" Saul raised his sightless face hopefully. He had been called brother.

"The Lord Jesus, the Just One, has sent me that you may regain your sight and be filled with the Holy Spirit. Thus!" Ananias laid his hands on the trembling head. Immediately something like scales fell from Saul's eyes, and he could see. Then he wasted no time in explanations or in discourse, but he rose and was baptized.

In the next several days Saul appeared among the believers in the synagogues. These had been his destination, but now his purposes had changed. He arrested no one. Rather, he proclaimed that Jesus was the Son of God, and vigorously he entered into arguments with his fellow Jews, confounding them with spirited words and proving that Jesus was the Christ.

Perhaps more than an enemy, people despise the brother who has turned away from them. For soon a few of the Jews were plotting to arrest the transfigured Saul. And when they could not find him, they placed watchmen at all the gates of the city to catch him in flight.

But quickly and deeply do people love the enemy who has turned into a brother. Those believers who knew truly of the change in Saul took him to the city wall and lowered him over the side in a basket, and so he escaped.

Years later, calling himself "Paul an apostle, not through man but through Jesus

In Damascus, the hunter Saul became the hunted. His friends let him down from the walls, and he fled, to become Paul, apostle to the Gentiles.

Christ and God the Father," this believer wrote that he had taken his way from Damascus into Arabia, where he spent three years ever before he met great Peter in Jerusalem.

That Gentiles May Also Believe in the Christ

From the beginning the young church preached Jesus as Christ to those who had long awaited the coming of Christ: to the Jews, for unto the Family Israel had God made his promises of a Messiah.

But what of those who had *not* been the chosen people of God for centuries? Should the Greek, the Roman, the non-Jew—the *Gentile*—have part in the church with the Jews who believed in Jesus? Should the apostles proclaim that Jesus had come to save the Gentile too, and not just the Jew? And if so, should this Gentile be required to keep the laws of Moses and be circumcised, as Jewish believers were required by heritage and by holiness to do? And what about eating? Should Jewish believers actually sit down and eat with the Gentiles, possibly swallowing nonkosher food, although that was forbidden by Moses? One, two, three—three hard matters for the learning church, all three wrapped in one question: What about the Gentile?

Two of the questions—circumcision and the eating together—would have to be answered by the church leaders in close debate. But the first question—did Jesus come to save the Gentile, too?—was answered by Jesus himself. Thus:

At Caesarea, on the coast of the Mediterranean Sea, there was stationed a cohort of Roman soldiers commanded by a man named Cornelius. He, too, was Roman. He was a Gentile. Yet he feared God and gave alms to the people and prayed devoutly, constantly to the Lord God.

A Roman and a Gentile, Cornelius loved God. An angel bade him speak with Simon Peter.

One day while he was praying, he was terrified to see an angel of God enter the room and stand before him.

"Cornelius," said the angel.

Staring, shrinking backward, Cornelius said, "What is it, Lord?"

"Your prayers and alms have ascended to God," the angel said. "Now send messengers to Joppa and bring hither one Simon who is called Peter—"

Stalwart Peter, in a trance, saw all manner of animal. The voice of God commanded that he kill and eat of them. Yet Peter could not. Soon he would learn the meaning of his vision.

Indeed, Simon Peter was then in Joppa with people whom Philip had called unto Christ. And his presence in that town was no secret thing, for he had raised to life a woman most beloved of that town, Tabitha. People knew where to find one so full of the Spirit.

On the day after Cornelius's vision, Peter had betaken himself to a housetop in order to pray when, at noon, he grew sharply hungry. But before the food could be prepared, he fell into a trance.

His eyes rolled upward, and he saw the heaven opened; then down from heaven floated a strange container; something like a great sheet gathered at its four corners descended to the earth. Aground, the sides sank down, and Peter saw therein all kinds of animals, reptiles, birds, and he heard a voice commanding him: "Rise, Peter. Kill and eat."

Peter was shocked at the mistake. "No, Lord!" said Peter the ever abrupt. "Oh, no!" said Peter, compulsive apostle, so sure of himself. "I have never eaten anything judged common or unclean—"

"What God has cleansed," the voice returned, "do not call common!"

Twice more the voice invited Simon Peter eat. Twice more the tough believer hesitated to touch an unclean beast—and then the sheet was snatched back into heaven, and Peter heard a knocking at the door below.

He was perplexed, wondering what this vision could mean, when the Spirit said to him, "Peter, three men are looking for you.

Get up. Go down to them. Then go most willingly away with them—for I have sent them."

Peter did descend to meet these men. "I am the one you are looking for," he said. "What do you want?"

"Well, we are from Cornelius, a centurion in Caesarea," they said, "an upright and God-fearing man—"

A Roman! A Gentile! The common, the unclean! thought Peter.

"He received direction from a holy angel to send for you that he might hear in his own house what you have to say—"

Go with them willingly, the Spirit had said.

"Will you come with us?" they asked.

Sometimes Peter spoke so loudly, something near a bellow for all his certainty. Sometimes Peter spoke most low, when he discovered what a fool he had been to bellow in the first place. Now it was that Peter answered their request with three low, humble words: "I will go."

When Peter came to Caesarea and entered the house of the centurion, Cornelius bowed down at his feet and worshiped him. But Peter lifted him up. "Stand," he said, still in lowly voice. "I am a man as you are."

Humbly, Peter followed the three men to Cornelius. There he learned and taught of God's love.

Then he looked around and saw many people gathered to meet him: Gentiles! Gentiles.

"You know how we Jews hesitated to preach the word of God to Gentiles," he said. "But God has shown me that I should call no one unclean or common. Truly," and now his voice began to rise, for it was of the Lord he meant to speak. "Truly, I perceive that God shows no partiality. He lifts no single people up above the others. But in every nation everyone who fears him and does what is right is acceptable to him!"

Then Peter opened his mouth and spoke the words of Jesus Christ, his life, his death, his Resurrection by the Father. With these words were the hearts of the Gentiles filled, and with more, for the Holy Spirit fell on them. They then did just what the apostles had done on Pentecost. They spoke in tongues, praising God.

If God gives them what he gave us when we believed in Christ, thought Peter in amazement, *then who am I to oppose him?* "Bring water!" he commanded. And the Gentiles were baptized in the name of Jesus Christ!

Persecution

In those days a new King Herod ruled Judea, Galilee, and the surrounding area. This was not the Herod of Jesus' birth but his grandson. Nor was he the Herod of Jesus' death, but his nephew. Yet, exactly like his forebears, he caused anguish for the body of Christ.

Violently he seized some of the visible leaders of the young church and imprisoned them. Among those thrown under his grisly power was James—the brother of John, the fisherman, the disciple who had walked three years with the Lord, the apostle.

This James, Herod murdered by the edge of the sword—and Jewish leaders were happy to hear of it.

Now, Herod was concerned to establish a good reputation among these leaders. Therefore he reasoned that if one murder pleased them, two would surely delight them, and he would have good praise of it. Generously, then, he commanded that the most important apostle of the young church be arrested—and so it was that Simon Peter was seized and held in prison under four squads of soldiers. There he would linger, thought Herod, until the days of the Passover (now being celebrated) were over and he could bring the burly believer to trial.

Hard, serious prayer went up to God from the church in those few days.

And then, the very night before Herod meant to make his prize public, the Almighty God annulled the power and plan of the king.

Peter was sleeping in two chains, between two soldiers, behind doors and sentries guarding more doors—when suddenly an angel of the Lord appeared in his cell, shedding a brilliant light. He struck Peter on the side, arousing him with the words, "Get up, quickly!" In the same instant the chains fell from Peter's hands. "Dress yourself," the angel directed. "Put sandals on your feet. Wrap your mantle round you. Come, follow me." And so Peter did, rising and following the angel past a first and then a second gate, and all was done as in a dream. Indeed, Peter thought that he was dreaming.

The iron gate that led to the city swung open of its own accord. They passed through and walked a city street when suddenly the angel disappeared, and Peter came to himself with a great shaking of his

---

Arrested, bound in chains, guarded by soldiers, Peter was imprisoned behind locked doors. An angel appeared to him. The chains fell away. The doors swung wide. And Peter was free.

head. But for all his blinking, he could not cancel the fact of his freedom. It was no dream. He stood dressed and chilly in the open night, and the stars alone stood watch around him. "Now I am sure," he said, "that the Lord has sent his angel to rescue me from Herod—"

Peter ran—as big men run, with heavy, trouncing steps—straight to the house of Mary, mother of John Mark, where a dim light burned. Even at this hour members of the church were praying. He pounded on the gate. A maid named Rhoda came to answer.

"Who, please?" she called through the gate.

"Me, child," he called back. "I am Peter, freed by the angel of the Lord."

Rhoda squealed in her joy and raced back to the others, forgetting to open the gate.

"Peter!" she cried, clapping her hands and laughing. "Peter's at the gate!"

The others paused in praying long enough to point out the improbability of her announcement. They suggested that she was mad and returned to their praying.

But Rhoda burst into tears, insisting Peter stood outside that very gate. They then granted her, for all her energy, that someone may, perhaps, be standing there—but not Peter. An angel, maybe—but not Peter.

It was thunder at the gate that brought their arguing to an end—a constant, loud, imperious pounding most unlike an angel's rap. So they opened the gate, and they saw him, and they were, as they should have been, amazed.

So were Herod and the sentries amazed when they stood staring at empty chains and open doors, but there was no joy in their faces. Herod was amazed by his mysterious defeat. The sentries were amazed by Herod's orders following this defeat: that all the sentries should be put to death.

To the End of the Earth

PAUL—APOSTLE OF CHRIST

HE WHO HAD BEEN SAUL, who persecuted the church of Christ with such fierce zeal, who met that same Christ on the road to Damascus and who was changed, thereby, into a believer and an apostle; he, the same, yet known throughout the church as Paul—he wrote this of the time that followed his conversion:

"After three years I went to Jerusalem to visit Peter and stayed with him fifteen days. I saw James the Lord's brother but none of the other apostles, then went north and west into the regions of Syria and Cilicia. There I preached the faith which once I sought to destroy—and that labor alone is what they heard of me in Judea, and they glorified God for it."

Christians in the Syrian city of Antioch (*Christians,* for so they were called then and in that place) recognized the goodness and force of Paul's preaching. Under direction of the Holy Spirit, they laid their hands on him and Barnabas and so commissioned them to carry the word westward, to all the peoples.

Thus, Paul, a Jew by birth, of the tribe of Benjamin; Paul, able to claim himself a citizen of Rome and trained a tentmaker (no mean occupation); Paul, by conviction a Pharisee, but by the grace of God a Christian and a preacher of the good news of Christ; Paul, all things to all people that by all means he might save some—Paul went forth with the word in his mouth, to Asia Minor and to Macedonia and to Greece and to the end of the earth.

Cyprus

The island of Cyprus was homeland for Barnabas, familiar to him and a good place for the commissioned ministry to begin. He and Paul landed at Salamis and, proclaiming the word of God in all the synagogues, passed through the whole island unto Paphos on the western shore.

Here the Roman proconsul summoned Barnabas and Paul, to hear the word they preached. But a certain magician, a Jew named Bar-Jesus, who worked for the proconsul, stood up and argued violently with the Christians. He did not want his employer to be persuaded by the new faith.

In the midst of this railing, Paul turned a cutting eye on Bar-Jesus and raised his own voice that he might be heard. "You son of the devil!" he said. "You enemy of righteousness! You bellyful of deceit! When will you stop making crooked the straight paths of the Lord? Behold, the hand of the Lord is upon you. You shall be blind and the sun be black for you!"

Immediately, mist and darkness swirled around the helpless magician, and he went about seeking people to lead him by the hand.

Then the proconsul, astonished at the teaching of the Lord, believed. A Roman, a Gentile, his name was Sergius Paulus.

Galatia

Soon Paul and Barnabas sailed north to the mainland, disembarking at Perga, where they did not stay long. Rather, they struck inland, crossing into the old Roman province of Galatia and arriving at the Pisidian city of Antioch.

Here Paul followed his custom of entering the synagogue on the Sabbath day. Nor was it unusual that he was asked, after the reading of the Scripture, to speak a word for the people.

Paul did speak his word.

"People of Israel, and you who fear God, listen!" he began; then he recounted the history of Israel, leading up to the coming of the Savior, Jesus, as was promised. "To us has been sent this message of salvation!" Sadly he announced that the priests in Jerusalem, blind to the promises, themselves fulfilled these promises by putting Jesus to death. "But God raised him from the dead. Let it be known to you that through this man is the forgiveness of sins proclaimed to you. By the laws of Moses you could not be freed, but by Jesus everyone who believes in him is most certainly freed!"

Now the people, who had heard a little, begged Paul and Barnabas to tell them more. They followed them out of the synagogue with questions and pleaded that they return the next Sabbath to preach.

Paul did return.

And this time nearly the whole city gathered together to hear the word of God. But such numbers and such a massive interest shocked and angered certain of the Jews. So now they argued with Paul, challenged him, contradicted him, and mocked him.

Boldly Paul replied, "It was right that the word of God should be spoken first to you. But since you thrust it away, behold: We turn to the Gentiles!"

This pronouncement pleased the Gentiles, and many of them believed. But it did nothing to cool the anger of these Jews, who incited the leading women and men of the city in order to cause persecution of Paul and Barnabas.

Finally, these two were driven away by the persecution, and thus began a pattern

which would happen again and again. Paul would preach in the synagogue; some, Jews and Gentiles alike, would believe; but certain Jews would react in enmity, stirring people against the apostle. Paul would then remove his preaching from the synagogue to establish a community of believers—a church—apart from it. Paul would, often, suffer from Jewish hostility, and then, in time, he would depart for another city.

So it happened in Iconium, the city to which they went from Antioch.

And so it happened in Lystra. But here the Gentiles also misunderstood the truth of the apostles' presence. For when Paul healed a man who had been crippled from birth, the people were swept with a giddy excitement.

"The gods!" they cried in their native tongue. "The gods have come in the likeness of men!" They pointed at Barnabas and called him Zeus. Paul they called Hermes, because he was the chief speaker.

"The gods!" they shouted up and down the streets, so that even the priest of Zeus hurried down to the apostles with oxen and garlands to offer sacrifice before them.

Then Paul and Barnabas understood what the foreign chatter was all about, and they tore their garments in distress.

"Why are you doing this?" they cried. "We are men, no more than men, men the same as you! Only, we bring you good news, that you should turn from these hollow rituals to the living God who made all things—"

By a rush of preaching, Paul scarcely restrained the pagans from sacrificing to them. But thus the preaching was begun in Lystra, and with it the same sad pattern that dogged him wherever he went. Again, certain Jews grew hostile, hostility increased until he and Barnabas were driven from the city by stoning, and finally Paul was left on a country road as though dead.

When he recovered, the two went on to Derbe.

Finally, Paul and Barnabas turned around and took their way home again, stopping at each of the churches they had started in Galatia, strengthening, teaching, encouraging the disciples in every place, and saying, "Through much tribulation we enter the kingdom of God."

Crisis! Paul's Preaching Criticized

"After fourteen years," wrote the Apostle Paul, "I went again to Jerusalem with Barnabas, and I laid before the leaders of the church that gospel which I preach among the Gentiles."

Paul was having trouble with some of the Christians, his own brethren, who thought that he should not forget the laws of Moses

---

In Lystra, Paul healed a cripple. The people took Paul and Barnabas for gods and, to the apostles' horror, wished to offer sacrifices to them.

and particularly not the ancient rite of circumcision. They had complained of Paul to Jerusalem, and Paul found it necessary in Jerusalem to defend himself.

This is what he had been teaching:

"Until Christ came, we were children who needed watching; we needed restraint against our sinful inclinations. During all those centuries, the law was our watcher, our guardian, trustee, and tutor. But when the time had fully come, God sent forth his Son, born of woman, born under the law to set free those who were under the law, so that we might be adopted as children. Through God we are no longer slaves, but his children!

"So we do *not* become the children of God by doing the works of the law, but through faith in Jesus Christ. No one can become God's child by the works of the law—no one! Those who rely on the law are cursed. On the other hand, *everyone* may, in Christ Jesus, become a child of God through faith. For as many as are baptized into Christ do put on Christ, the first Son of God. This is how children of God are made!"

And that is what Paul had preached all through Galatia.

Most of the Galatians who heard him were Gentiles who had, of course, never been circumcised. Paul told them that there was no need for their circumcision, because that was a part of the old law, and they could only become slaves thereby, not children and heirs. For a while they were happy with that explanation.

But then certain Christians who were Jews first, who *had* been circumcised, went into Galatia after Paul and said, "No! He is wrong! You must be circumcised! For God made his promises to the offspring of Abraham, and how can you be the offspring of Abraham unless you do what he was required to do—circumcise?" That frightened the Galatians, who dearly wanted the promises of God; so they thought they ought to keep this law, this one law.

"No!" thundered Paul, angry at his fickle churches. "If you keep one law, you are bound to keep the whole law! I, Paul, say to you that if you receive circumcision, Christ will be no good for you! You are cut off from Christ, you who would be saved by the law. You have fallen away from grace! And are you worried about being offspring of Abraham? You fools! You are already his offspring. It was his faith that made him righteous before God; it is your faith that makes you his offspring, too, and children of God!"

And so it was that after fourteen years of preaching, Paul hurried to Jerusalem, found James, Peter, and John, and laid his gospel, his message, his preaching before them in order that the whole church be not torn apart by this division. Otherwise all of his preaching would have been utterly wasted.

When these leaders of the church heard what Paul had to say, they recognized the grace that had been given to him. They saw that God had truly entrusted him with the gospel to the Gentiles, just as Peter had been entrusted with the gospel to the Jews. They laid no laws upon him nor added any requirements to the message which he was already preaching. Instead, they offered him the right hand of fellowship, and Paul was satisfied.

The church, so young, had been saved from splitting.

Timothy

"Now," said Paul, resting in Antioch but ever restless to be gone and busy about his ministry,"I think we should go back to the cities where we have already proclaimed the

word of the Lord. I want to see how they are doing."

And soon upon the plan came the departure. Not with Barnabas, now, but with Silas, Paul traveled familiar routes through Syria and Cilicia and Galatia, to Derbe, to Lystra. Here he met a man who would afterwards love him, labor faithfully beside him, and who would receive from Paul his lasting, lively, and divine affection: Timothy. Timothy, whose mother was Jewish, whose father was Greek. Timothy, so tight with Paul that again and again the apostle would refer to this friend in his letters. Timothy traveled westward with Paul from Lystra.

To Macedonia

Northwest they went, directed by the Spirit of Jesus, until they came to Troas on the westward coast, and the water of the Aegean swelled before them.

At night Paul saw a man, no real man, but a vision, standing before him and pleading, "Come over to Macedonia, and help us."

Immediately he was convinced that God had called him to preach the gospel there; and he went. Paul and the word crossed to the Greeks.

Again Paul preached the word. In Philippi, on the riverbank, he taught. The women especially heard him, and one, called Lydia, was greatly touched.

Philippi

From Troas by sea to Samothrace; on the following day to Neapolis; and thence to Philippi, where Paul meant to stay awhile.

In Philippi he sought the place where Jews gathered to pray, and on the Sabbath he went there, outside the city on the banks of a river. He sat down, after the manner of teachers, and he taught.

Paul, intense and eaten with the energy of his faith, touched the women who heard him, and their hearts were opened to the word of the Lord. One in particular—Lydia, a dealer in purple goods, no Jew but a worshiper of God—leaned forward. Lydia frowned with hard listening; slowly, unconsciously, began to nod and then, at the corners of her lips, to smile. The smile spread to her eyes. A pure blush rose to the roots of her hair. She breathed air as though it were sweet and altogether new. She put her hands to her cheeks and whispered, "Yes."

Lydia, never taking her eyes from Paul, believed *Jesus Christ is Lord!* Soon this woman and every member of her household—servants, workers, and relatives alike—were baptized. Then she came to Paul in her joy, saying, "If you have found me faithful to the Lord, come, stay in my house." And Paul, while he continued in Philippi, did.

So he began his preaching in that city with wonderful success and ever after remembered that church as dearest among his children. But the city of Philippi also caused him suffering.

There was a slave girl there who could, by a spirit, divine the future and reveal hidden things, a talent which brought her owners a great deal of money. She followed Paul wherever he went, and she would squeal before all the people, "These men are servants of the Highest God! They tell you the way of salvation!" This was, of course, the truth; but it was also a nagging irritation and an unseemly way of declaring the truth. After many days of noise Paul turned on the girl and spoke to the spirit in her. "I command you in the name of Jesus Christ, come out of her!" It did. So Paul no longer had his noisy chorus behind him; the girl no longer had her talent—but her owners, then, no longer had an income. Paul was relieved; the owners were enraged.

They seized Paul and Silas, dragged them before the city magistrates, identified them as two unruly Jews, and placed formal charges against them.

"They're disturbing the peace," they said, "teaching customs which are clearly against our Roman law and principles!"

It is never difficult, when someone—someone *else*—is in trouble with the law, to raise a mob. People love passion wherever they find it. So it was now. A crowd formed around the accused, and soon others quickly joined in attacking Paul and Silas.

Some in Philippi cast Paul and Silas into prison. But that night an earthquake freed the prisoners.

The magistrates, then, demonstrated a proper distress at the charges and ordered the two Jews to be beaten with rods.

After this punishment had been inflicted, they threw Paul and Silas into prison and commanded the jailer to keep them safely. Since the jailer took his duties seriously, he placed them in an inner cell and fastened their feet in stocks.

It was done. City government had performed its function with a fine dispatch. Everyone went to bed satisfied, for it was most admirably done.

But at midnight, when Paul and Silas were singing loud hymns to God in the hearing of the other prisoners, an earthquake shook the foundations of the prison. The walls broke apart; the doors swung open; and all the fetters fell unfastened to the ground.

The jailer, too, was shaken from his sleep and ran as quickly as he could to the prison. When he saw all the doors open, he believed with a hopeless terror that the prisoners were gone. He drew his sword, preparing to kill himself—but Paul roared from the bowels of that place, "Wait! Do not hurt yourself! We are all here!"

"Lights! Lights!" called the poor, bewildered jailer. And with lanterns he rushed in, bowed before Paul and Silas, then, like a scared servant, brought them out into the night.

"Men, what," he begged, "what, sirs, must I do to be saved?"

However he meant the question, Paul answered it in the truest way. "Believe in the Lord Jesus," he said, "and you will be saved." Then Paul, content in any circumstance and always ready to preach, spoke the word of the Lord not only to the jailer but to his whole house—while servants fed them and dressed their wounds. Before the night was passed, the jailer and his family were baptized and rejoiced that they had come to believe in God.

To a jailer, now a Christian; to a merchant of purple, now a Christian; and to all the saints in Philippi, Paul wrote the following words when he had gone from them:

"Stand firm in the Lord, my beloved, whom I love and long for, my joy and my crown. Rejoice in the Lord always. Again I say, rejoice! Let everyone know your forbearance. The Lord is at hand. Have no anxiety about anything, but in everything by prayer and petitions, with thanksgiving, let your requests be made known to God. And the peace of God, which passes all understanding, will keep your hearts and your minds in Christ Jesus."

Some Christians in Thessalonica died and Paul wrote comforting words to the grieving friends: Those asleep in Jesus would rise.

Thessalonica

Next Paul labored long in Thessalonica to establish a church. With full conviction did he preach the gospel of Christ, but also gently, like a nurse taking care of her children. He said, "Serve the true and living God, and wait for his Son from heaven, whom he raised from the dead, Jesus—who delivers us from the wrath to come." And he labored with his hands as well, making tents to make a living, that no one should have to support him.

But then the sad pattern of Jewish hostility against their teachings rose again, and Paul and Silas were forced to leave by night.

Some time later, several Christians in Thessalonica died. The church was not only saddened by this but frightened as well, for they said, "Will the dead miss seeing Jesus when he returns? Will they not be with us to meet the Lord?" They sent a message to Paul, saying, "We loved them! What will happen to those that died?"

And Paul wrote back, "You need not grieve as others do who have no hope, my beloved. We believe that Jesus died and rose again; even so, through Jesus, God will raise up those who have fallen asleep in Jesus. This we declare to you by the word of the Lord, that we who are alive shall not go ahead of those who are asleep.

"For the Lord himself will descend from heaven with a cry of command, with the archangel's call, and with the sound of the trumpet of God; and the dead in God will rise first! Then we who are alive shall be caught up together with them in the clouds to meet the Lord in the air, and so we shall always be with the Lord. Ah, my children, comfort one another with these words."

Corinth

In Beroea, next, Paul met both with success upon his preaching and with persecution from certain Jews who had followed him out of Thessalonica.

In Athens, though he spoke most nobly in the Areopagus, he was neither very successful nor much harrassed. Indeed, very little happened in that place of Grecian wisdom.

But long, long, with love and anguish and love again, did Paul serve the church which next he established in Corinth.

It began in blessing, for he came to that city weak and trembling and alone. Silas and Timothy were in Macedonia, and there was no one with whom to share the essential failure of Athens. But then there came a gift from God. Paul met a man named Aquila, a tentmaker like himself, a stranger to the city like himself, a Jew and a Christian—like himself! A friend. Soon this friend, with his wife Priscilla, invited Paul to work and to live with them, and he did.

Then, when Silas and Timothy also arrived at Corinth, Paul began in joyful earnest to persuade both Jews and Greeks that Jesus was the Christ.

The usual pattern happened: Certain Jews disowned him and then persecuted him. But here in Corinth two things worked to weaken their power over him.

The first was a vision of the Lord himself, who spoke to Paul, saying, "Do not be afraid, nor be silent; for I am with you. No one shall attack you to harm you!"

And the second was that the Roman proconsul, named Gallio, who knew nothing either of Jesus or of Paul, wished to keep it that way. His willful ignorance saved Paul, for when certain Jews made formal charges against the apostle, Gallio said to them, "This is no vicious crime, but a matter for your own law. I refuse to judge these things. Get out of here."

Paul stayed, then, a year and a half in this place, freely preaching and knitting together a church. By speaking of nothing except Christ crucified, he called together many Gentiles—the poor of the city and only a few of the wealthy; the uneducated, the laborers, slaves; the people of no importance and no ennobled name; the weak, the low, and the despised, the nothings of society. These all came from various backgrounds. Some had been cynics, for whom the only truth was that there was no truth save selfishness alone. Some had worshiped the goddess Aphrodite, whose religion allowed a thousand evils of the flesh. Some had worshiped Isis, some Demeter, while others had bent their knees before the altars of Poseidon, Hermes, Zeus, Apollo, Dionysus, Heracles.

To them all Paul preached: "Christ died for our sins in accordance with the Scriptures and was buried. On the third day he was raised, in accordance with the Scriptures, and he appeared to Peter and to the Twelve. Then he appeared to more than five hundred at one time, most of whom are still alive. Last of all, as to one born late in the family, he appeared to me."

And so, by the one Holy Spirit, many in Corinth formed a single church, each one an individual member of the body of Christ. They confessed in faith, "Jesus is Lord!" And they shared their love by eating together frequently, at which meals they also partook of the table of the Lord, eating bread which he had called his body, drinking the cup which he had called the new covenant in his blood.

When all this was done, Paul smiled and took his leave from Corinth, commending them to the Lord.

It had been a fine, successful ministry.

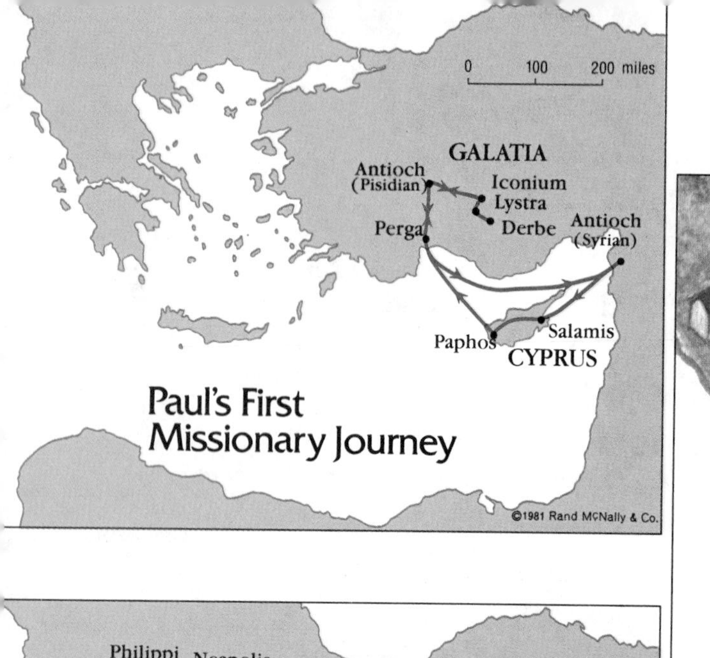
0 100 200 miles
GALATIA
Antioch
(Pisidian)
Iconium
Lystra
Derbe
Perga
Antioch
(Syrian)
Salamis
Paphos
CYPRUS
Paul's First
Missionary Journey
©1981 Rand McNally & Co.

Philippi
Thessalonica
Neapolis
Beroea
SAMOTHRACE (island)
0 100 200 miles
Troas
GALATIA
Athens
Ephesus
Corinth
Lystra
Derbe
CILICIA
Antioch
(Syrian)
SYRIA
Paul's Second
Missionary Journey
Caesarea
©1981 Rand McNally & Co.

Philippi
0 100 200 miles
Troas
MACEDONIA
Ephesus
Corinth
Miletus
Anitoch
(Syrian)
Tyre
Paul's Third
Missionary Journey
Ptolemais
Caesarea
Jerusalem
© 1981 Rand McNally & Co.

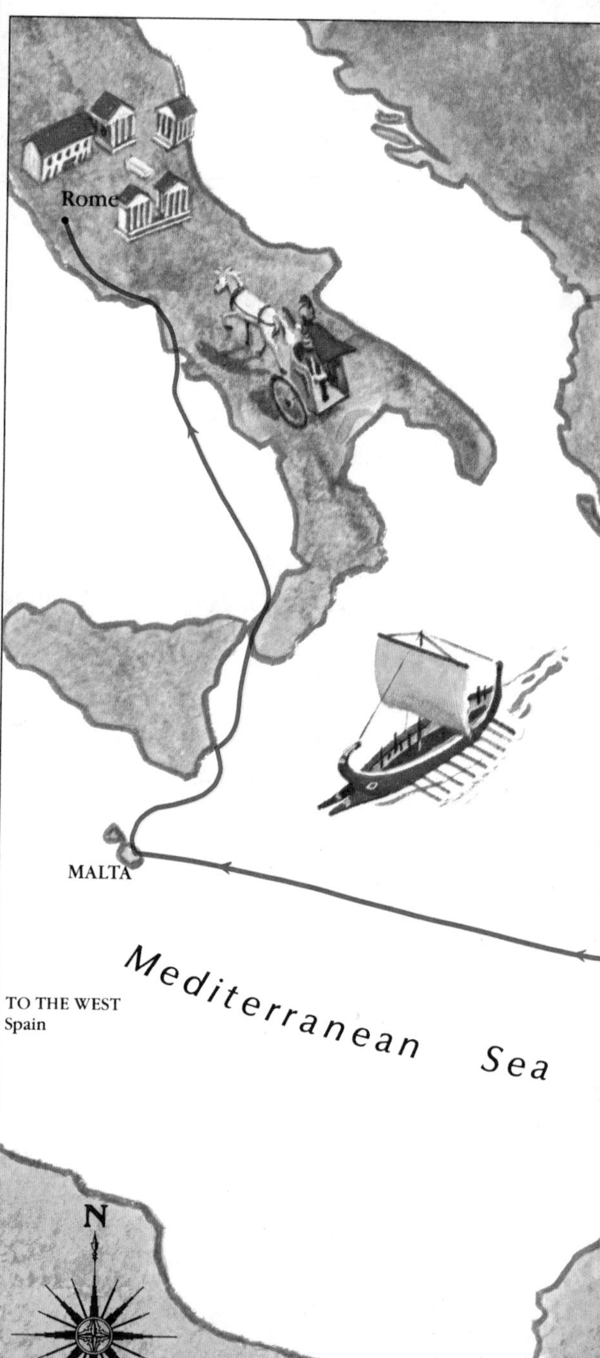
Rome
MALTA
Mediterranean Sea
TO THE WEST
Spain
N
0 50 100 150 200 miles
© 1981 Rand McNally & Co.

Paul's Journeys
Route
Boundary
EDONIA
Philippi
Neapolis
ssalonica
roea
SAMO-
THRACE
Troas
ASIA
GALATIA
Aegean Sea
Athens
orinth
Corinth
GREECE
Ephesus
Miletus
PATMOS
Antioch
PISIDIA
Iconium
Lystra
Derbe
Perga
CILICIA
Antioch
SYRIA
CRETE
Phoenix
Fair Havens
CAUDA
Salamis
Paphos
CYRPUS
PHOENICIA
Damascus
Sidon
Tyre
Ptolemais
GALILEE
Caesarea
Jordan River
Samaria
Joppa
Jerusalem
JUDEA
Gaza
Mediterranean Sea
ene
ARABIA
EGYPT
Red Sea
TO THE SOUTH
Ethiopia

He sailed to Ephesus and thence, with a stop in Jerusalem, to Antioch where he spent the winter.

Finally he returned to Ephesus—and there sad news was brought to him: The church at Corinth was breaking down! All at once Paul's gladness turned to grief.

Other preachers, good men, had spoken of Christ in Corinth since Paul had gone; and though there was little difference in their message, the Corinthians began to follow men more than the Lord. "I belong to Paul," some of them said, while others said, "I belong to Peter," and others, "I belong to that silver-tongued preacher Apollos." The one body was cracking into pieces, and Paul was horrified.

"What is the matter with you?" he wrote from Ephesus. "Do you think that Christ is divided? Or was Paul crucified for you that you should follow *him?* Agree! Agree with one another, please! And be united in the same mind!"

Also, members of the church were slipping back into the old habits of immorality, sinning several ways with their bodies, while the church itself winked and did not seem to mind.

"Oh, you are arrogant!" Paul wrote them. "Mourn for the sin among you! Mourn and remove the sinner. Do you not know that your bodies are members of Christ? Then how can you join the members of Christ to a prostitute? Or do you not know that your bodies are temples of the Holy Spirit, which you have from God? He dwells in you. You are not your own. You were bought with a price. Therefore, glorify God in your bodies!"

Moreover, when the Corinthians came to eat together, there was less and less of fellowship; for the rich ate alone, stretching their bellies with their own foodstuffs, while the poor stayed thin for hunger.

And different members of the church who had different gifts from God made much of their gifts. They put the distance of contempt between themselves and the others who lacked these gifts. Those who could speak in tongues made tongues a matter of pride, and pride a matter for separation—and so the church at Corinth was, for a number of reasons, crumbling.

"Your differences," Paul wrote, "should never divide you but rather bind you the tighter together! For each gift is given to each that the *whole* body might be served, just as the eye sees also for the hands and for the feet and not for itself alone.

"Tongues? Do you think it is something to speak in tongues? I tell you, it is not *what* you can do which is important, but *how* you do it, and *why*. He who speaks in tongues, but *without love*, benefits no one but himself. Nay, it goes deeper than that....

"If I speak in the tongues of men and of angels but have not love, I am a banging gong and a clanging cymbal. Let love be the way. If I have as my gift prophetic powers and understand all mysteries and all knowledge and if I have all faith, so to remove the mountains, but have not love, I am nothing. Then let love be the way! For if I give away all that I have and if I deliver my body to be burned but have not love, I gain nothing. Brothers, let love be the excellent way among you!

"Love is patient and kind, not jealous or boastful, arrogant, rude. Love does not insist on its own way, is not irritable or resentful, does not rejoice at wrong but rejoices in the right. Love bears all things. Love believes all things. Love hopes all things. Love endures all things. And love shall never pass away.

"Every other gift dies, save three alone which have no end. Faith and hope and love

Timothy brought word to Paul that the Corinthians had rejected him. Paul grieved deeply.

go on forever, these three; but the greatest of these is love."

With these and many other words Paul fought to keep his Corinthian church healthy and whole and holy. But he was busy in Ephesus. His words had to go by letter, and his own love for them could only be spoken by his dear friend Timothy, whom he sent to Corinth in his place.

But for all his urging, things did not improve. The church deteriorated the more. And then it was that Paul suffered a humiliating anguish on account of the Corinthians.

Some alien "apostles" (they were not of the Twelve, but they styled themselves apostles) had come attacking Paul directly, convincing the weakened Corinthians that their first preacher was to be dismissed as false and foolish. Timothy returned to Ephesus with the sad news that Corinth no longer accepted Paul's leadership.

Immediately Paul left everything in Ephesus and rushed across the sea to Corinth. He went to see his beloved face to face; but they no longer loved him, and they snubbed him. He went in full authority to his young, straining church; but they no longer believed him, and they scorned his authority. Paul met, in Corinth, nothing less than a rebellion—the more painful for that it was personal—and he found that he could not even stay there. In sorrow he sailed back to Ephesus, whence he wrote them another letter. He wept while he wrote this letter. He was sad.

"Those men who preach among you," he wrote, "who boast of their mission and their miracles, who proudly let you support them—which I did not because I love you—they are false apostles, deceitful workmen merely disguised as apostles of Christ! And no wonder! Just as Satan pretends to be an angel of light, so his servants pretend to be servants of righteousness.

"Do they call me inferior? I should never boast of what I am. But you who believe these superlative apostles, you force me to it. You must see that they are false and that though I am nothing, yet Christ has chosen me! Whatever they dare to boast of—oh, this is idiocy!—so do I.

"Are they Hebrews? So am I. Are they descendants of Abraham? So am I. Are they servants of Christ? I am a better one! I have far greater labors, far more imprisonments than they—and countless beatings and often near death. Five times I received the thirty-nine lashes; three times beaten with rods; once stoned; three times shipwrecked; a day and a night adrift at sea; in danger from rivers, robbers, my own people, the Gentiles, the wilderness, the sea, and from false friends! I have toiled through hardship, hunger, thirst, the cold, and exposure—and all the while I have been in daily anxiety for all my churches. Who is weak but that I am weak with him? Who falls and I am not indignant?

"If I must boast, I will boast of my weakness. The God and Father of the Lord Jesus knows that I do not lie!"

Thus wrote Paul, then he sent this letter of tears with Titus to the Corinthians, and he waited in fever to find out what effect it had on them.

The letter—its judgment and its love—and Titus, too, were powerful among the church in Corinth: The people repented. And Paul, with a shout of joy, forgave them at once, traveling back again through Macedonia to visit them, this time in dear and lovely peace.

He was smiling when he stretched out his arms to them. His eyes stung with glad tears. "Ah, you children! You Corinthians!"

Love, anguish, and then, again, love—even so did Paul labor to build up the body of Christ, till all should attain to the oneness of faith; even so did he train his children up.

In Troas, Paul spoke far into the night. Young Eutychus, dozing at the window, slipped and fell.

Looking to Rome, Paul Turns Back to Jerusalem

While he spent that winter in Corinth, Paul wrote a long and peaceful letter to Christians in a city he had never seen: Rome. He told them in detail the gospel which he preached—and then he ended by declaring himself proud of his work for God, for he felt that he had now finished his mission to Asia, Macedonia, and Greece.

"Now," he wrote, "since I no longer have room for work in these regions, I hope to see you as I travel on to Spain"—to the end of the earth. "But first I will go to Jerusalem with a contribution for the saints there, money offered by the churches in Macedonia and Greece. When I have done that, look for me to pass west through Rome!"

With the spring in his nostrils, then, Paul left Corinth for the last time. He journeyed to Philippi, then crossed the water to the city that had been his European gate, Troas, where he stayed seven days.

On Sunday during that period he gathered with the saints in an upper chamber, third floor. He broke bread with them and then talked; and since he meant to leave them on the following day, he talked long into the night.

A young man named Eutychus, sitting in the window, began to nod. His eyes drooped; and finally, after midnight, he sank altogether into sleep. His body went limp, slipped, and he fell out of the window.

"Eutychus!"

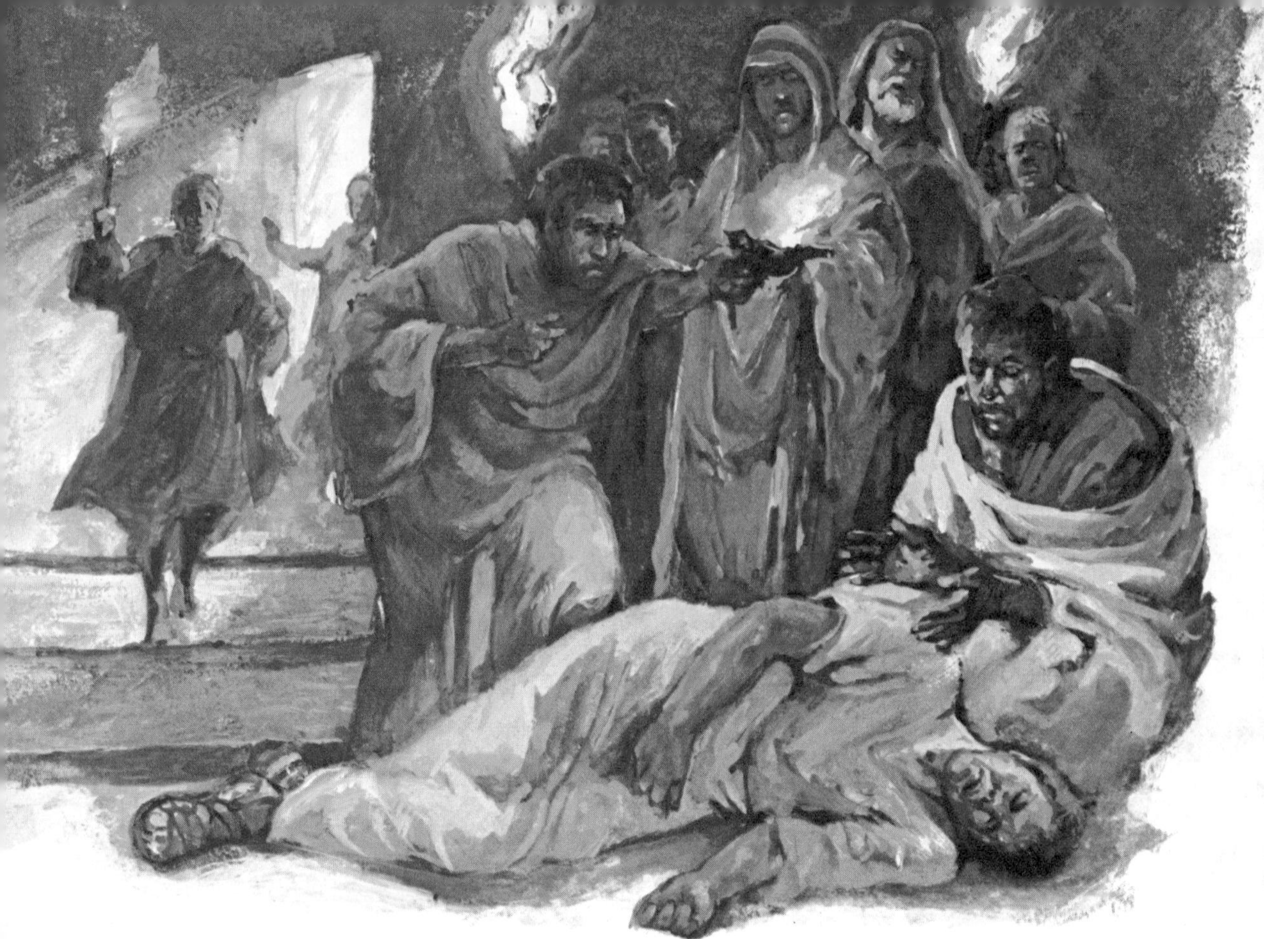

Three stories below lay Eutychus, dreadfully still. Paul leaned down to embrace him.

Some of the people ran to the window; others snatched lanterns and rushed downstairs. Those who saw the stillness of the young man and those who touched him cried, "Eutychus! Eutychus! Don't be dead!"

But Paul went down and bent over him. Kneeling, he embraced the man, then said, "No, do not be alarmed. His life is in him."

Before the night was done, they bore the man away alive; and before the morning was far gone, Paul departed south.

He did not enter Ephesus when he came near that city; but in order to bid the church there farewell, he invited its elders to meet him in Miletus.

"You know how I lived among you," he said to them in a solemn voice, "serving the Lord with all humility, with tears and trials, teaching, testifying of repentance to God and of faith in our Lord Jesus Christ. Behold, now I am going to Jerusalem, not knowing what shall befall me there. One thing I know, that all you whom I have told of the kingdom will see my face no more—"

Some of the elders winced to hear that, and sorrow sank deeply into their eyes. Some began quietly to cry. But Paul continued speaking.

"As for me," he said, "I am innocent of your blood, for I did not shrink from declaring to you the whole counsel of God. As for you, beware! Take heed to yourselves and to the whole flock in your care! For fierce wolves will come among you, and some of your own number will arise speaking perverse things to draw the disciples away!

"Be strong in the Lord. Put on the whole armor of God that you may stand against the wiles of the devil. For we are not contending against flesh and blood, but against the principalities, the powers, the world rulers of this present darkness, the spiritual hosts of wickedness. Stand, therefore! Gird your loins with truth. Put on the breastplate of righteousness. Shoe your feet with the gospel of peace. Above all, take the shield of faith, with which to turn aside the flaming arrows of the evil one; and the helmet of salvation, take it! And in your right hand, the sword of the Spirit, which is the word of God.

"And so do I commend you, my beloved, to God. The grace of the Lord Jesus Christ and the love of God and the fellowship of the Holy Spirit be with you all—forever."

When Paul had finished these words, he knelt down and prayed with them, and they wept and embraced him and kissed him, grieving most that they should never see him again. Then they brought him to the ship. The sails were hoisted. The soft wind and the swelling sea took him, and he was gone.

The people bid him a tearful farewell at Miletus and Paul set his course for Jerusalem.

PAUL—AMBASSADOR IN CHAINS

Warnings

The ship anchored at Tyre in order to unload cargo, and Paul took the opportunity to stay with Christians in that place. It was a seven-day visitation, happy and peaceful in all respects save one: The people, by the truth of the Spirit, urged Paul not to go on to Jerusalem. But his purpose was firm. He meant definitely to discharge his bounden duty, to bring the money to the saints in that place. And at the end of seven days, he sailed.

By way of Ptolemais he came, next, to Caesarea, where he stayed with Philip the evangelist. Again the warning was raised—but this time in terms more stark.

A prophet named Agabus came from Judea, bearing in memory the angry tension that existed in Jerusalem between the Jewish leaders and the Christians who permitted Gentiles to flout the laws of Moses. There were Jews there who still nursed a particular hatred for Paul, the same Jews who had fought him in the cities of Asia and Macedonia; for he, who once had kept the law as a zealous Pharisee, had too much crossed the law, becoming their foremost enemy.

Agabus found Paul in Philip's house. Quietly he took the apostle's belt and with it tied his own feet and then his hands.

"This is what the Holy Spirit says," said Agabus, " 'So shall the people in Jerusalem bind the man who owns this belt, and they will deliver him into the hands of the Romans.' "

When they heard this, all the people surrounding Paul begged him not to go to Jerusalem.

But Paul said, "Please! Why do you break my heart with your weeping? I am ready for anything—whether it be imprisonment or even death for the name of the Lord Jesus!" And no one could change his mind.

Finally they swallowed their fears and said, "The will of the Lord be done."

Arrest!

It was near the festival of the Pentecost when Paul arrived in Jerusalem; therefore, as at that first enspirited Pentecost, the city was crowded with Jews from every nation under heaven. Yet, despite the press of the people, Paul came in a somewhat lonely man.

Not only had he no communion with the Jews, but he was even suspected by the Christians. He was, it seemed, too loose with their doctrines. So his first job was to assure James and the Christian leaders that he was still one with them.

Paul would rather have done that quietly, by a simple face-to-face meeting, so that his presence in Jerusalem could be kept a secret. But such a meeting was not enough. Neither was it enough to report all that God had done through him. And he had brought delegates from the Gentile churches to meet James—but neither were they enough. In order to prove his unity with the Christians in Jerusalem—and before they would accept the offering that Paul had brought—he was asked to go to the Temple itself, and there to participate in lawful Jewish ceremony. Openly. Before anyone who cared to look.

Paul agreed.

The first time that he entered the Temple, he felt quite naked. But nothing happened. No one recognized him, and he left safely. Yet this was a seven-day ceremony. Again he had to return to the Temple, and again, and again—

Jerusalem's crowded streets held danger for Paul, yet he returned despite his friends' warnings.

By the seventh day Paul's heart was racing. Tomorrow, if all went well! Tomorrow he would depart, tomorrow make for Rome and the end of the earth! But such a tomorrow never came. The seventh day held danger for the man who did not leave on the eighth.

For while he stood in the Temple, some Jews from Asia recognized Paul.

Then they did not whisper nor politely tug at his cloak. They raised hands of horror. They threw back their heads and screamed, and the Temple rang with their violent accusation.

"Help! Help! Men of Israel, help! Here he stands! This is the man who everywhere preaches against us, against the Torah, against this holy place! This is the one who defiled the Temple itself with Gentiles—and here he stands! Help us! In the name of God, help us!"

Their screaming stunned and then fired the people. From the Inner and the Outer courts, from the city surrounding the Temple, first scores and then hundreds of people ran together, also screaming in mob madness, converging on Paul. They dragged him into the open air, and those that were nearest beat him with the demented intent to kill him.

Within minutes news was brought to the Roman tribune that Jerusalem was rioting. He commanded centurions and soldiers to follow, then ran to the scene. At his arrival the beating stopped, but the fury of the crowd was nothing the less.

"Who is this man?" he cried, motioning soldiers to arrest Paul. "What has he done?"

While the soldiers bound Paul in chains, the crowds roared a thousand accusations against him and, spurred by their own voices, made ready to grab him again.

"Get him out of here!" the tribune ordered. "We can learn nothing in this place. Take him to the barracks!"

When they came to the steps of the barracks, the pressure and rage of the crowd was so great that the soldiers had to pick Paul up and carry him.

"Away! Away with him!" the mob was screaming.

The doors slammed against the people's roaring, and the tribune, breathless, stared at Paul. "It must be something dreadful this man has done, he said. "Scourge him to make him confess the truth."

Straightway, soldiers began to tie him with thongs to a post, preparing him for the lash. But Paul said to a centurion, "Is it lawful to scourge a Roman citizen uncondemned?"

It was not, and the centurion was shaken to hear these words. He went to the tribune.

"Do you know what you are doing?" he said. "Do you know that this man is a Roman citizen?"

The tribune caught his breath. "Is this true?" he called to Paul. "Are you a citizen of Rome?"

Paul said, "Yes."

The tribune said, "I bought my citizenship for a great sum of money."

Paul said, "I was born to mine."

Then the tribune was frightened, for it was a grievous thing to punish a Roman without a trial. Yet he did not release Paul, for the Jewish leaders now laid charges against him that had to be tried in court.

And so it was that the seventh day saw the end of the apostle's freedom—forever.

Defense

On the following day the tribune arranged that Paul should be brought before the chief priests, the leaders of the Sadducees, and of the Pharisees, and the council.

"I will learn the real reason that they accuse him," he said. But he did not learn much, for there was little peace in the proceedings.

"Speak," the high priest Ananias said to Paul.

Paul took a silent moment to mark each member of the council with his eyes, fearlessly gazing into theirs. He was, as much as he might, making the time his own.

Betrayed, captured, lashed to a post, Paul—a Roman citizen—demanded Roman justice from his captors.

Then he began. "Brethren," he said full reasonably, "I have lived in all good conscience before God even up until this day—"

The high priest interrupted. "Strike his mouth!"

"God will strike you," Paul shot back, "you whitewashed wall!" His eyes were blazing. "Do you, according to the law, sit in judgment of me and yet against the law command that I be struck?"

Those near to him cried, "Silence! This is God's high priest whom you revile!"

"Oh, pardon me!" Paul raised a supercilious brow. "I did not know that such a man would be the high, high priest of all the Jewish nation! Well, then I will watch my tongue, for it is written, 'You shall not speak evil of a ruler of your people.' "

This was not a good beginning. Anger flashed from the first words spoken, and little arguments crackled throughout the room. But Paul controlled himself, listened to the whispering, and perceived that the council was divided between some who were Sadducees (who did not believe in resurrection nor in angels nor in souls) and some who were Pharisees (who believed in all of these). The two parties were in conflict with each other, and Paul thought to turn this conflict to his own advantage.

"Brethren!" he cried for attention. "I am a Pharisee! I am a son of Pharisees! And you ought to know that for my hope in the resurrection of the dead am I on trial!"

"Well!" said the Pharisees, glaring at the Sadducees. "This is a piece of important news. The man is suffering for the truth of his beliefs."

"Well!" said the Sadducees, glaring at the Pharisees. "Important news indeed! The fool has chosen to believe in nonsense. Foolish in one thing, foolish in all!"

The Pharisees grabbed Paul's right arm.

Paul's eyes flashed anger. Fearlessly he faced his accusers, matching them argument for argument.

"We find nothing wrong in him," they announced.

The Sadducees grabbed Paul's left arm. "The greater fools you!" they said. "Donkeys deserve a drubbing!"

"And what if an angel spoke to him?" The Pharisees yanked Paul's arm.

"Then he is more than a fool. He is mad and ought to be muzzled!" The Sadducees yanked his other arm.

Eye to eye, jaw to jaw, and yank for yank, the argument went from words to violence, and soon the tribune feared that Paul would be torn to pieces between them. He commanded his soldiers to remove him from the discussion by force and bring him back to the barracks.

Still the tribune did not know good reasons for the charges brought against this man. This was fast becoming a frustrating case.

Assassins

If they could not be rid of Paul by one means, then those who hated him would try another, for they would be rid of him!

More than forty of them met in secret and bound themselves by a solemn oath neither to eat nor drink until they had killed the apostle themselves. Then, having sworn, they went to the chief priests and the elders with a plot.

"Request of the tribune the chance to question Paul further," they said. "Ask that he be brought to you again. We will hide on the route of his coming and ambush him and kill him before he comes near."

So the chief priests agreed to do; but Paul's nephew heard of the plan and hurried to Paul with the information.

"Exactly as you told it to me, tell the tribune," said Paul; and he sent the boy by way of a centurion to the tribune.

The tribune, in his turn, believed what he was told; and now he took the opportunity to free himself of this confusing case.

Paul was a Roman citizen? Then Paul would be sent to the Roman governor of the province. No more would he stand before the Jewish Sanhedrin, although his crimes fell only under Jewish law, if crimes they were.

The tribune called his centurions and ordered them to carry Paul to Felix the governor in Caesarea. "Protect the prisoner," he said. "Take him by night."

And so it was done. Paul was spirited away, never again to see the holy city Jerusalem.

Awaiting Trial

For a long time nothing of consequence happened for Paul in Caesarea, save that he stayed a prisoner.

In a brief hearing, Felix the governor listened to the accusations against Paul (they called him a pestilent fellow, a political agitator—serious charges) and then listened to Paul's defense. But he made no judgment on the case. "We will wait," he said, "until the tribune can come from Jerusalem with further information." The tribune never came.

Later Felix brought his wife Drusilla, a Jewess, to Paul in order to hear him speak of faith in Christ Jesus. But Paul chose also to speak of justice and of moral self-control and of the coming Judgment. That kind of talk alarmed Felix (a governor and a husband none too moral himself), and so the conversation came to a speedy conclusion—and nothing was accomplished.

Felix also hoped that Paul would give him money to purchase freedom. But Paul gave him nothing, and Felix did not set him free. Nothing buys nothing. For two years nothing happened.

Then, finally, Felix's rule over that province came to an end, and he was ordered away. But when he had gone, Paul was still in prison—as a favor from Felix to the Jews.

Appeal to Caesar

It was the coming of the new governor, Porcius Festus, which broke the long pause in Paul's life; and then Paul himself made a demand that took him halfway round the world.

In Jerusalem this new governor listened

to the priestly leaders who argued that Paul should stand trial again.

A trial in Jerusalem? That was a dangerous suggestion for several reasons. They would try to ambush Paul on the way to the city. Failing that, they would certainly find him guilty—and then Festus himself, when he came to judge Paul on political grounds, would do the same. Hopeless! There was no hope for Paul down the road to Jerusalem.

Therefore, when Festus met Paul and asked, "Do you wish to go to Jerusalem, there to stand trial?"—Paul said, "No!" He said, "Certainly not!" And then came the request that would alter the rest of his life.

"If I have done anything for which I should die, I do not seek to escape death," he said. "But if there is nothing in these charges against me, that will be found only in the proper court. To Jerusalem? No! I wish to go to Rome. I appeal to Caesar."

Paul, the Roman citizen, had the right to make such a request. Festus, the Roman governor, also had the authority to deny it, but he did not. After conferring with his council, he announced to Paul, "You appealed to Caesar; to Caesar you shall go."

At Sea

Even under good conditions it would have been a long voyage from Caesarea to Rome. But the group of prisoners that embarked in the late summer of that year met with foul weather and foolish decisions. Endless seemed this passage and, more than hazardous, deadly!

The northwester was never friendly to ships that wished to sail west; they had to depend on sea currents instead, or tack directly into it, or else make much of the inconstant winds that sometimes blew down from the east. But for Paul and the prisoners and the centurion who guarded them, it seemed that all the winds had together sworn an oath of enmity, to tease, to play with, and to hate whatever ship they sailed in.

From the beginning they found the northwester hard against them, like a great, restraining hand; so for a while they put the island of Cyprus between them and it, and then they sailed close to the southern coast of Asia. With the greatest difficulty they came to the southeastern tip of Asia. But then the open sea was in front of them, and the northwester absolutely forbade them to go on. They turned south, toward the island of Crete. Here they struggled into a port called Fair Havens and anchored.

Now they had lost much time, and it was close to the vicious season of the winter. A dispute arose among the people.

"If we go on," Paul argued, "we risk injury and loss, not only of our cargo but also of our lives!"

But Fair Havens was a miserable port to winter in. Some of the people suggested a quick, desperate course toward Italy, while the captain and the owner of the ship were persuaded they should sail forty miles farther west to Phoenix, an excellent port for wintering. The centurion agreed with them, and so it was decided.

Soon a gentle south wind blew. It lifted the spirits of the sailors, who raised the anchor, and they set sail west.

But the south wind was deceitful, sweetly luring them out to sea, where they were helpless before the attack of a harder, more violent wind—

For suddenly the tempestuous northeaster tore down across the island, slammed into their little ship, and never drew back but beat and beat them with a hateful fury. They could not face so fierce an enemy. They gave way to it and were driven.

At one point they found tiny refuge behind a small island called Cauda. There they

To Rome Paul would go for justice. But the voyage seemed doomed as violent winds tore at the ship.

About to abandon ship, the sailors found their escape boat cut away. Paul had so ordered. For if the sailors left the ship, none would survive.

began to undergird the ship; but the northeaster threatened to pitch them toward quicksand, so they lowered the gear and were driven again.

The ship groaned, thrown high and low by the muscular, sheeting waves. Sailors began to dump cargo overboard. By the third day they were casting out the tackle of the ship. And when more than a week was gone and neither the sun nor the stars had shown through the smoking, rolling rage of the wind, they despaired. They abandoned every hope of being saved.

For fear, for labor, and for illness, they had eaten nothing, so they were the more weakened. Paul looked into their wet, exhausted faces, and suffered for them. "Take heart! People, take heart!" he called above the roaring wind. "We shall lose the ship, but not a single life with it! For I have received promise from the God whom I worship that I must stand before Caesar and that all your lives shall be saved. Take heart, for so it shall be! But we shall have to run on some island—"

At midnight of the fourteenth day, the sailors heard a deeper thunder, like breakers on a beach, and suspected that they were nearing land. None could see through the deep gloom, so they measured the depth of the waters and found it twenty fathoms. Shortly they measured again: fifteen fathoms! They were driving toward some shore! Immediately they dropped four anchors astern to hold them back from rocks, and they prayed for the day to come.

But in the unholy darkness the sailors did one other thing to save their lives: They began to lower a boat in which to escape.

Paul saw the sin. "Unless they stay with us," he shouted to the centurion, "we cannot be saved!" So the soldiers cut the ropes to the boat. It fell and spun away, an empty chip in the night.

Just before dawn Paul raised a loaf of bread before them all and called, "Eat now for your strength! Fourteen days you have not eaten. Now you need the food. Eat!" He gave thanks to God, broke the bread, and began himself to eat. So did the others.

Then came the day and the light, and they

could see a small bay in the land; they decided to make for that. So they cut the anchors away, loosened the rudders, hoisted sail before the wind, and the ship leaped forward. But soon—still at distance from shore—it struck a shoal, and the bow caught tight. The everlasting waves beat against the stern and began to break it up. The soldiers rushed for their prisoners, intending to kill them so that they would not escape; but the centurion wanted Paul alive.

"There will be no murders here!" he cried. "Swimmers—go! Dive in the water and make for the shore on your own!" There followed a rain of humanity into the sea, and then the waves bore heads and thrashing arms. "Those of you who cannot swim—cling to pieces of ship!Go! *Go!*"

Rolling their eyes in terror, the rest fell into the sea. Gasping, coughing, hugging wood and howling, two hundred and seventy-six bodies swirled forward through the surf until they had been cast, every one of them, ashore, where they lay in a long line like the junk of a tide.

The northeaster had been cheated. Not a soul had died.

Malta

Not long after this strange landing, the natives of that place appeared and offered the poor survivors remarkable kindness.

The day was dreary and cold, and as if their sea-soaked clothing were not wet enough, rain began to pelt them. So the natives kindled a fire. Paul helped by gathering wood. As he brought a bundle of sticks to the blaze, a viper slid out and struck his hand.

The natives saw it hanging there, its teeth in Paul's flesh. "Well, this man must be a murderer," they said. "He survived the sea, but justice will kill him with a snake."

Paul shook off the viper over the fire, and the natives watched, waiting for him to swell up or drop dead.

But he did neither. So they decided he was not a murderer, but a god.

Saved from the sea, ashore at last, Paul was bitten by a viper. He neither sickened nor died.

For three months Paul and the others stayed on Malta—the name of this island—receiving the praise and the good care of its people. And in the end they left with all necessary provisions and gifts besides.

Fair weather sped them the rest of their voyage, and so it was that Paul arrived in Rome.

Dear Child, My Timothy

Although he was kept under continued Roman arrest, Paul was allowed to stay by himself under guard of a single soldier. For two whole years he welcomed all who came to him, he preached the kingdom of God, and he taught about the Lord Jesus Christ.

But for Paul the end was not far away. Nor was he afraid to speak of his death. When, ever, had Paul been afraid? Angry, to be sure, as with the Galatians; grief stricken, as with the Corinthians; saddened, as at his many leave-takings—but never had he been afraid. Rather, he had learned in any state to be content.

Therefore, it was that with a peaceful soul that the apostle wrote his friend of the piteous things to come. Thus:

"Paul, an apostle of Christ Jesus by the will of God according to the promise of the life which is in Christ Jesus, to Timothy, my beloved child. Grace, mercy, and peace from God the Father and Christ Jesus our Lord!

"I charge you in the presence of God and of Christ Jesus, preach the word. Be urgent in season and out of season. Convince, rebuke, and exhort. Be unfailing in patience and in teaching.

"For the time is coming when people will not endure sound teaching but with itching ears will gather teachers who meet their own likings, and they will turn away from listening to the truth and wander into myths. But you, my Timothy, always be steady. Endure suffering and the persecutions that are to come. Do the work of an evangelist. Fulfill your ministry.

"For I am already on the point of being sacrificed; the time of my departure has come.

"I have fought the good fight; I have finished the race; I have kept the faith. Henceforth there is laid up for me the crown of righteousness, which the Lord, the Righteous Judge, will award to me on that Day, and not only to me but also to all who have loved his appearing."

Even in Rome, under the watchful eye of a guard, Paul preached to all who came to hear him.

PERSECUTION

When, in the course of time, it became dangerous for someone to proclaim faith in Jesus Christ—dangerous because such witness threatened not only freedom in the Roman world but life as well—then the leaders of the church encouraged the disciples with strong words uttered in holy conviction.

Many who heard these words did die most wretched deaths beneath the persecution. But the faith for which they died did not; and the words which made death, even death, a joyful opportunity to serve the Lord—these words continue still.

From Peter

"Beloved, do not be surprised at the fiery ordeal which comes upon you to prove you. But rejoice in this: You share Christ's sufferings and so will rejoice when his glory is revealed!

"Let none of you suffer as a murderer, or a thief, or a wrongdoer, or a mischief-maker. But if someone suffers as a Christian, let him not be ashamed, but under that name let him glorify God.

"Humble yourselves beneath the hand of God, that he may in due time exalt you. Cast all your cares on him, for he cares for you. Be sober. Be vigilant! Your adversary the devil prowls around like a roaring lion, seeking someone to devour. Resist him, firm in your faith, knowing that the same hard suffering is required of all the faithful throughout the world.

And after you have suffered a little while, the God of all grace, who has called you to his eternal glory in Christ, will himself restore, establish you and strengthen you! To him be dominion forever and ever. Amen."

The Writer to the Hebrews

"You are not alone in the struggle. You are surrounded by a great cloud of witnesses who by their faith did not shrink back but rather performed the tasks to which God did call them. Remember them.

"Remember Abel, his sacrifice acceptable to God; and Enoch, taken up to heaven so that he should not see death; and Noah, who by faith heard God and built an ark.

"Remember Abraham, called out to a foreign land; and Sarah, able in her old age to conceive a son; and Isaac, who was that son; and his son Jacob, and Jacob's son Joseph. All of these were given a promise by God but died before the promise was fulfilled. By their faith the promise was real unto them. By faith they lived between the giving and the keeping of the promise.

"Remember Moses and Israel, who by faith did cross the Red Sea as if on dry ground. Remember Gideon and Samson, Samuel and David and the prophets!

"Remember those who were mighty in war, and those, too, who were tortured, suffered mocking, scourging, chains.

"Remember—and know that you are not alone! These faithful surround you, *for you have received the promise they were looking for!* Therefore, lay every weight aside and every sin which clings so closely, and run with perseverance the race set down before you.

"Most of all, most of all remember Jesus, the pioneer and perfecter of our faith; Jesus, who is the promise perfectly fulfilled; Jesus, who for the joy ahead of him endured the cross and is seated at the right hand of the throne of God. Remember him, you who would grow weary. Remember Jesus."

THE REVELATION TO JOHN

I JOHN, YOUR BROTHER, *share with you in Jesus the persecution and the kingdom and the patient endurance, for I was exiled to the tiny island called Patmos on account of my testimony of Jesus. In that place I was given to see and to hear the things that are to come.*

I was in the Spirit on the Lord's day, when I heard a loud voice behind me, like the blaring of a trumpet. "Write what you see in a book," it said, "and send it to the seven churches of Asia."

I turned to see who was speaking to me and saw seven golden lampstands and, in the midst of them, one like a son of man. He was clothed with a long robe and a golden belt around his breast. His head and his hair were white as wool, as white as the snow. His eyes were like bright flames of fire, his feet like burnished bronze refined in a furnace, his voice like the roar of a waterfall. In his right hand he held seven stars; from his mouth there issued a sharp, two-edged sword; and his face blazed like the sun at noonday.

I fell down at his feet as though dead, but he laid his right hand upon me and said, "Do not be afraid. I am the First and the Last and the Living One. I died, and behold! I am alive forevermore, and I have the keys to

Death and to the Halls of the Dead."

After this I looked, and lo! in heaven was an open door! And the trumpet-voiced said, "Come up and I will show you what must take place."

At once I was in the Spirit, and I saw a throne and one seated upon the throne, one finer and more brilliant than jasper and carnelian. Twenty-four elders, crowned and clad in white garments, surrounded the throne, and on four sides, four living creatures: the first like a lion, the second like an ox, the third with the face of a man, and the fourth a flying eagle. These creatures, never ceasing to sing, sang: Holy, holy, holy is the Lord God Almighty, who was and is and is to come! *And the twenty-four elders fell down before him who sat upon the throne and worshiped him who lives forevermore.*

In his right hand he held a scroll sealed with seven seals. An angel cried, "Who is worthy to break the seals and open the scroll?"

But not in heaven, nor in earth, nor under the earth was anyone found worthy; and I wept much that there was no one worthy to open the scroll or to look inside.

But an elder said, "Weep not. One is worthy."

Then I saw a Lamb that looked as though it had been slain, yet was standing! The Lamb took the scroll from him on the throne, and the elders and the creatures sang a new song, singing: Worthy art thou to take the scroll, for thou wast slain and by thy blood didst ransom men for God from every tribe and tongue and nation, and hast made them priests to God, and they shall reign on earth!

Then when the Lamb opened one of the seals, I heard one of the creatures with a voice of thunder call,

"Come!" And behold, I saw a white horse, and its rider had a bow. He was given a crown, and he rode forth conquering and to conquer.

When he opened the second seal, the second creature cried, "Come!" Then there came stamping another horse, bright red, whose rider had permission to snatch peace from all the earth that men should slay each other. And he rode forth with a great sword.

He opened the third seal. The third creature cried, "Come!" A black horse passed, its rider holding in his hand a balance—for the bloodred horse brought war, and war brings famine, and famine makes the price of food so dear that it must be weighed in a balance that a few might eat a little.

Then the fourth seal, and the fourth creature lifted up his voice and called, "Come!" Behold! Behold! There came a pale horse, and its rider's name was Death. Over

a quarter of all of the earth he had power to kill—by sword and by famine to kill; by plague, by the teeth and the talons of untamed beasts to kill, to kill.

The breaking of the fifth seal showed me those who had been slain for the word of God and for the witness they had borne. "O Lord!" they cried. "How long before you will avenge our blood on those who dwell on earth?"

"Rest, rest a little longer," they were told, "till all the martyrs shall be killed as you have been."

After this I looked, and behold! a great multitude which no man could number, people from every nation, tribe and tongue standing before the throne and the Lamb, crying aloud: "Salvation belongs to our God, who sits upon the throne, and to the Lamb!"

An elder said to me, "Who are these, clothed in white robes, and whence have they come?"

I said, "Sir, you know."

And he said to me, "These are the people who have come out of the great tribulation. They have washed their robes and made them white in the blood of the Lamb. Therefore they are before the throne of God, serving him day and night within his Temple. And he who sits upon the throne will cover them with his presence. They shall nevermore hunger, nor thirst any more; the sun shall not strike them nor any scorching heat. For the Lamb will be their shepherd, to guide them to springs of living water; and God, even God himself, will wipe away every tear from their eyes."

Then when all was done and wars had ceased and God had taken to himself his victory—for Satan was

made helpless in the lake of fire and Death with him—then I saw a new heaven and a new earth, for the first heaven and the first earth had passed away, and the sea was no more. And I saw the holy city, new Jerusalem, coming down from heaven, prepared as a bride made lovely for her husband. And I heard a great voice from the throne saying: "Behold, the dwelling place of God is now with men. He will dwell with them, and they shall be his people! God himself will wipe the tears from every eye, and death shall be no more. Neither shall there be

mourning nor crying nor pain any more, for the former things have passed away."

And he who sat upon the throne said, "Behold, I make all things new!" Also he said, "Write this, for these words are trustworthy and true. It is done! I AM the Alpha and the Omega, the Beginning and the End. To the thirsty I will give water without price from the fountain of the water of life. To him who conquers I will give this heritage, and I will be his God and he shall be my son."

He who testifies to these things says, "Surely, I am coming soon."

Amen!

Come, Lord Jesus!

BCDEFGHIJK